Contents

Contents

1 Devices and Device Modelling

1.1 The PN Junction Diode

The PN junction is one of the fundamental 'building blocks' of semiconductor devices, and as such it forms a useful starting point for the study of electronics at the higher level. Its operation and important features need to be appreciated if an understanding of other discrete and integrated components is to be achieved. Naturally, some previous study of basic semiconductor theory is assumed.

The basic PN junction diode is created during manufacture by diffusion or ion bombardment, so that two doped regions of semiconductor material result. One of these is doped with acceptor impurity to give an excess of holes (P type), and the other with donor impurity to give an excess of electrons (N type). Doping levels are not high, and are typically in the range of one part in 10^7 or 10^8, which means that careful control during the manufacturing process is essential. A variety of semiconductor materials is used — typically silicon, germanium and gallium arsenide. Of these, silicon is used for the majority of electronic active components, and the following notes refer to devices created using that material.

A representation of the PN junction is shown in Fig. 1.1 where, under zero bias conditions, a thin depletion layer is formed on either side of the junction. This occurs because the initial hole–electron recombination at the junction sets up fixed positive charges on the N side, and fixed negative charges on the P side. These charges result from the atoms on either side losing or gaining an electron. On the N side, if a donor atom loses an electron the atom becomes positively charged, whereas if an acceptor just inside the P region gains an electron, it becomes negatively charged. These fixed charges — ionized atoms within the

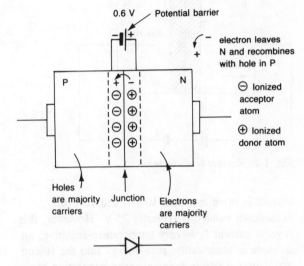

Fig. 1.1 PN junction diode with zero bias

crystal lattice structure — set up a potential barrier at the junction which prevents any further transfer of free carriers across the junction. For silicon, the potential barrier is approximately 600 mV. In this way a thin region — which might be a micrometer or less — empty of charge carriers occupies the space around the junction. This is referred to as the 'depletion layer'.

A reverse voltage, making the P side more negative than the N, further increases the potential barrier: the depletion layer becomes wider and very little reverse current flows. The current that does flow (called I_R) is the result of minority charge carriers (free electrons in the P material and free holes in the N) and hole–electron pair generation within the depletion layer (I_S), plus any general leakage around the outside of the device (Fig. 1.2). I_S, the reverse saturation current, is almost constant with increases in reverse voltage until breakdown is approached. In a small signal diode such as the 1N4148, the total leakage

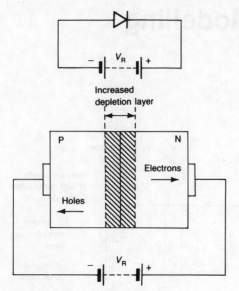

Fig. 1.2   Reverse-bias condition

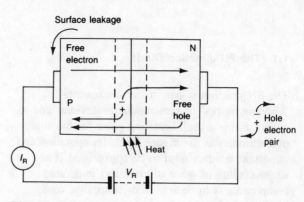

Fig. 1.3   Leakage current with the junction reverse-biased

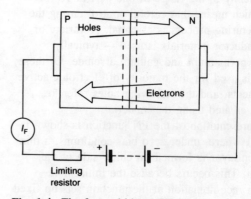

Fig. 1.4   The forward-biased PN junction

current is often less than 10 nA, and reverse breakdown voltage is typically 75 V. However, this reverse current I_S is very temperature-sensitive: an increase in temperature puts energy into the silicon and causes a rise in hole–electron generation at the junction (Fig. 1.3). Typically, *the reverse saturation current doubles for every 10 °C rise*. As we shall see later, this temperature dependence has an implication for all devices that are built up using PN junctions.

When a forward bias is applied (Fig. 1.4), the external voltage reduces the effect of the potential barrier, and carriers (both hole and electronics) can be given sufficient energy to cross the junction. Thus, as the forward bias is increased towards 600 mV the forward current rises rapidly. The generally accepted equation for diode current is

$$I = I_S \left(e^{qV/KT} - 1 \right) \tag{1.1}$$

where

I = diode current
I_S = reverse saturation current
q = charge on the electron 1.6×10^{-19} coulomb
K = Boltzman's constant 1.38×10^{-23}
T = temperature in degrees Kelvin
V = voltage across the diode.

The exponential term in equation (1.1) represents the probability of a charge carrier obtaining enough energy to surmount the potential barrier at the junction.

At room temperature, where $T = 290\ °C$,

equation (1.1) becomes

$$I = I_S (e^{40V} - 1) \qquad (1.2)$$

Suppose a reverse voltage is applied, *i.e.* $V = -1$, then e^{40V} becomes much smaller than unity, and $I = -I_S$. In other words, the diode current is equal to the reverse saturation value.

For a forward voltage of more than 100 mV (V greater than $+0.1$) the exponential term becomes larger than unity, therefore

$$I = I_S\, e^{40V} \qquad (1.3)$$

The current rises exponentially with applied voltage.

This holds fairly well for germanium devices, which have a low junction barrier potential of about 200 mV, but for silicon PN diodes, to account for the 600 mV forward bias necessary to obtain conduction, it has been suggested by some workers that for a voltage of a few tenths of a volt equation (1.3) should be modified to

$$I = I_S\, e^{20V}$$

and that above 500 mV the standard equation, with e raised to the power of $40V$, should apply. However, for dynamic analysis, it is the shape of the characteristic that is important, not the actual cut-in point. For example, suppose we wish to determine the a.c. resistance of the forward-biased diode — and this point is important for the understanding of a basic transistor model — we obtain

$$r_d = \delta Vf/\delta if$$

The conduction ($1/r_d$) can be found by differentiating equation (1.3), which gives the slope of the forward characteristics:

$$dIf/dV = 40I_S\, e^{40V}$$

but since $I_F = I_S\, e^{40V}$

$$dIf/dV = 40I_F$$

If we put I_F in mA, then

$$r_d = dV/dIf = 1000/40I_F\ \Omega \text{ (with } I_F \text{ in mA)}$$

or $r_d = 25/I_F\ \Omega$ (with I_F in mA) $\qquad (1.4)$

This is illustrated in Fig. 1.5, where it can be seen

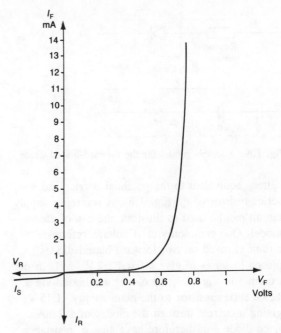

Fig. 1.5 Forward characteristics of a silicon diode

that the diode's a.c. resistance reduces rapidly as the forward current increases. At an I_F of 2 mA, r_d will be 12.5 Ω, whereas when I_F is 10 mA, r_d will fall to 2.5 Ω. Of course this cannot be taken to the extreme point where the resistance becomes almost zero, nor are the figures given above exactly the same for all diodes; there will be differences depending on the size and doping levels of the device. When the forward current in a diode is increased beyond a few hundred milliamps the a.c. resistance will be limited to the bulk resistance of the fully conducting silicon, with the addition of the anode and cathode contact resistances. The forward current then assumes a straight-line characteristic with forward voltage.

In the analysis of circuits it is often useful to have models for any active components connected in the circuit. The model, which may only be valid for a restricted set of conditions, can be helpful in discovering changes in the overall circuit performance, for example, in estimating the input resistance of an amplifier at one particular frequency, or the voltage gain at that frequency. A very simple model of a forward-biased diode, useful for some analytical purposes, consists of a

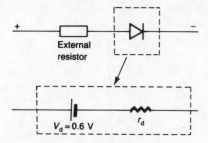

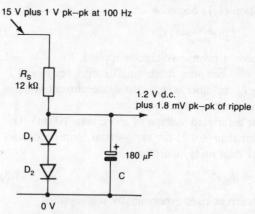

15 V plus 1 V pk–pk at 100 Hz

R_S 12 kΩ

1.2 V d.c.
plus 1.8 mV pk–pk of ripple

D_1

D_2

180 µF

C

0 V

Fig. 1.6 A simple model for the forward-biased diode

Fig. 1.8 Adding a decoupling capacitor to further reduce the ripple

battery equivalent to the potential barrier and a series resistor of r_d (Fig. 1.6). A reference supply circuit can be used to illustrate the use of the model. One commonly used voltage reference circuit is based on two forward-biased diodes placed in series to give a fixed 1.2 V level. In the example in Fig. 1.7, the diodes are biased via a 12 kΩ series resistor to the main supply of 15 V, giving a current through the diodes of 1.2 mA. Each diode will therefore have an a.c. resistance of about 22 Ω. Suppose the 15 V d.c. input has a 1 V pk–pk 100 Hz a.c. ripple superimposed on it — what effect will this have on the reference output?

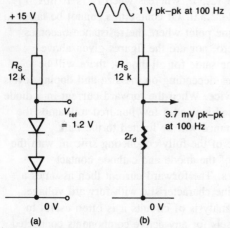

Fig. 1.7   (a) Voltage reference; (b) equivalent for a.c. signals

The a.c. change in diode current is given approximately by

$$i_d = v_{in}/R1 = 83 \ \mu A$$

therefore, $vo = i_d(2r_d) = 3.7$ mV pk–pk at 100 Hz.

In other words, the a.c. ripple on top of the 1.2 V reference voltage will be about 3.7 mV. If we wished to attenuate this ripple still further, a decoupling capacitor would be required in parallel with the diodes, as in Fig. 1.8. If this capacitor has a reactance which is simply the same value as the resistance of the two series diodes ($Xc = 44 \ \Omega$), the ripple on top of the reference will be reduced by only 3 dB. To be really effective in reducing the ripple, the capacitor must have a reactance at 100 Hz of at least one-fifth of the a.c. resistance of the circuit.

Therefore, $Xc = 8.8 \ \Omega$

$$C = 1/(2\pi \ 8.8 \ f) = 180 \ \mu F$$

Returning to the basic diode equation of $I = I_S \ (e^{qV/KT} - 1)$, let us investigate the effect of temperature on the forward characteristics. In the forward direction we have

$$I_F = I_S \ e^{qV/KT}$$

and it can be seen that the current I_F is temperature-dependent, since T appears in the equation, and also — more importantly — because I_S, the reverse saturation current, is very temperature-sensitive. The general rule is that I_S doubles for every 10 °C rise. It is this change in I_S with temperature that has the most marked effect on the forward characteristics. We have seen that when V is greater than +0.1 V, the forward current at room temperature is given by

$$I_F = I_S \ e^{40V}$$

In investigating the effect of I_S it would be useful to make V the subject of this formula, as follows:

$$I_F/I_S = e^{40V}$$

Taking logs of both sides gives

$$40V = \ln (I_F/I_S)$$
$$V = (1/40) \ln (I_F/I_S)$$

Suppose we keep I_F constant at, say, 1 mA, and find the effect on the forward voltage of a small increase in I_S: using the general rule of thumb that I_S doubles for every 10 °C rise, and assuming that I_S is 0.5 nA at 20 °C, it will therefore increase to 0.55 nA at 21 °C.

At 20 °C $V_F = (1/40) \ln (1 \times 10^{-3}/0.5 \times 10^{-9})$
$= 0.3627$ V
and at 21 °C $V_F = (1/40) \ln (1 \times 10^{-3}/0.55 \times 10^{-9})$
$= 0.3603$ V

The change in V_F is -2.4 mV per °C.

Although some simplifying assumptions have been made to obtain this result, the value is about typical for all PN junctions. In other words, for a constant value of I_F the forward voltage of a diode will fall by 2.4 mV per degree Celsius rise in temperature (the figure is often taken to be in the range of -2 mV to -2.5 mV per °C).

The effect of temperature on the forward characteristics for a typical small signal diode is shown in Fig. 1.9.

The ratings and parameters of most importance in the diode specification are:

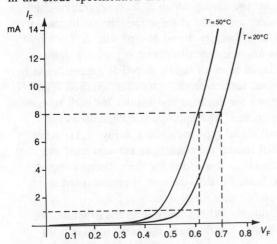

Fig. 1.9 Effects of temperature on the forward characteristics of a silicon diode

V_{RRM} = repetitive reverse maximum voltage
I_{FRM} = repetitive forward maximum current
I_{AV} = maximum average forward current
V_F = forward voltage (quoted at a given value of forward current)
I_R = reverse leakage current
P_{tot} = maximum power rating
t_{rr} = reverse recovery time.

For a commonly used small signal general purpose diode such as the 1N4148, the short-form data are:

Diode	V_{RRM}	I_{FRM}	I_{AV}	V_F	I_R	t_{rr}
1N4148	75 V	225 mA	75 mA	1 V at 10 mA	25 nA	4 ns

The parameter t_{rr} might need further clarification:

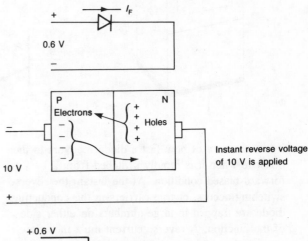

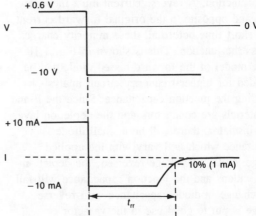

Fig. 1.10 Illustration of recovery time in a diode

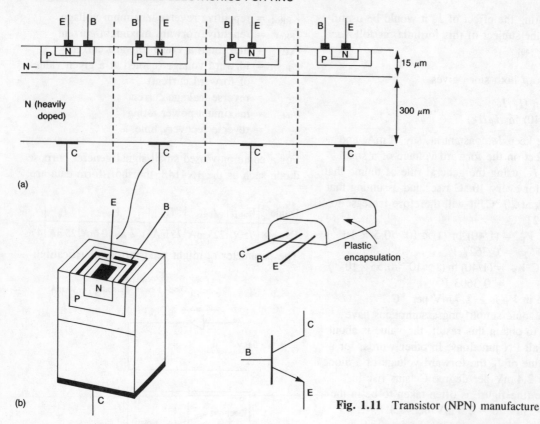

Fig. 1.11 Transistor (NPN) manufacture

it is a measure of how fast a diode recovers to the off state when it is rapidly switched from a forward-biased condition. At the instant the reverse switching occurs, charge carriers in the conducting diode are trapped in large numbers on either side of the junction. A reverse current must then flow, equal and opposite to the original forward current, for a short time before all these minority charges recross the junction. This is shown in Fig. 1.10.

The model of the forward-biased diode can be extended for higher-frequency circuit analysis by including the junction capacitance. Since the P and N materials are conductors and the depletion layer is an insulator, there will be a small diode capacitance which will vary with the applied voltage. With the voltage reversed, the depletion layer widens and the junction capacitance will fall. This change in diode capacitance with reverse voltage is put to good use in the varactor or varicap diode, which is used as an automatic tuning element in VHF and UHF circuits.

1.2 The Bipolar Junction Transistor (BJT)

The typical fabrication process for a silicon planar transistor, during which at least several hundred devices are made at the same time, is begun with a wafer of heavily doped N-type silicon. On top of this low-resistance substrate is grown a thin epitaxial layer of lightly doped N material, and by several further process steps the required P and N regions for the base and emitter for each transistor are created. The approximate dimensions for a small signal type are shown in Fig. 1.11. After initial testing the transistors are separated and connections are added for the collector, emitter and base. Finally, the unit is encapsulated in plastic or in a metal case.

Using the NPN transistor as the example, we shall now briefly study the basic operation for normal bias conditions (Fig. 1.12). The collector base PN junction is reverse-biased, causing a relatively large depletion region to be set up at this

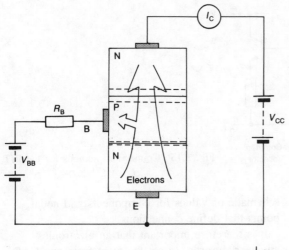

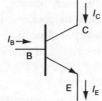

Fig. 1.12 Normal bias for a BJT

$$I_E = I_C + I_B \tag{1.5}$$
$$h_{FE} = I_C/I_B \tag{1.6}$$

(h_{FE} is therefore the current gain between base and collector)

and

$$h_{FB} = I_C/I_E \tag{1.7}$$

(h_{FB} is the current gain between emitter and collector).

From equation (1.6),

$$h_{FE} = \frac{I_C/I_E}{I_B/I_E}$$

$$= \frac{I_C/I_E}{(I_E - I_C)/I_E} = \frac{h_{FB}}{1 - h_{FB}} \tag{1.8}$$

Since h_{FB} is a value that is close to unity (i.e. 0.99–0.999) and depends entirely on the relative doping levels of the base and emitter regions, it can be seen that only a small percentage change in h_{FB} will result in a very large change in h_{FE}. For example:

with $\quad h_{FB} = 0.99 \quad h_{FE} = 100$
but with $h_{FB} = 0.995 \quad h_{FE} = 200$

a half percentage change in h_{FE} results in a 100 per cent in h_{FE}. This means that, although h_{FE} is a key parameter that is quoted for a transistor on its data sheet, there is often little point in using it for precise calculations, since it simply gives a guide to the probable gain performance of the device.

Consider now the BJT used as a simple amplifier. The three possible configurations — which refer to the way the transistor is connected — are common emitter, common base and common collector, as shown in Fig. 1.13. It is the CE connection that provides the highest gain and is the most often used, so this is the connection that we shall analyse. A simple circuit is shown in Fig. 1.14, where forward bias to the base is provided via R1 to set up the d.c. operating point to give, ideally, a d.c. voltage of 1/2 Vcc at the collector. Small a.c. signal levels applied via C_1 will then modulate the base current, which in turn will produce a larger change in collector current ($i_c = h_{fe} \, i_b$) so that an a.c. voltage signal is developed across R_3. It is useful to analyse the circuit to discover the likely voltage gain, input resistance and output resistance at a signal

junction, while the base emitter junction is forward-biased with the necessary 600 mV. The controlled doping levels during manufacture ensure that the emitter is more heavily doped than the base. Thus, when a small forward bias is applied between base and emitter, electrons from the emitter move into the base region. Here, these electrons meet few holes and so only a small amount of recombination takes place. This recombination or exchange of charge carriers makes up the base current I_B. Most of the electrons move across the base region by diffusion — a process that is analogous to the spreading of a drop of dye after it has been introduced into a liquid — and when the electrons reach the collector base depletion layer they are swept up by the positive collector field and pass into the collector. It could be said that, for every 100 electrons emitted from the emitter and crossing into the base, 1 recombines with a hole in the base and the remaining 99 are finally swept up by the collector. Thus, neglecting any leakage, we have the basic transistor equations of

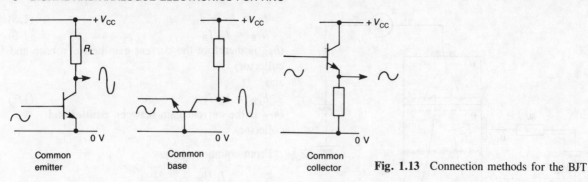

Common emitter

Common base

Common collector

Fig. 1.13 Connection methods for the BJT

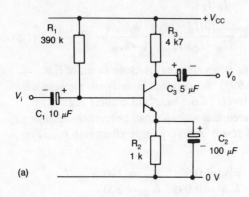

(a)

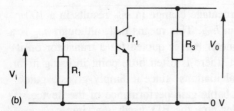

(b)

Fig. 1.14 (a) Simple common emitter amplifier; (b) first stage a.c. equivalent circuit

frequency of 1 kHz. There are two main methods for achieving this:

(1) Create a 'model' or equivalent circuit that is valid for the frequency being considered.
(2) Use a CAD software tool such as PSPICE, ANALYSER or MICRO-CAP, run on an IBM PC or compatible machine.

What the CAD tool does is to use an equivalent model for the circuit within the software and then compute, from user data and input requests, the values of gain, input and output resistance, and the bandwidth. But the model is hidden from the user and all he or she has to do is to enter either the

schematic or values for components and nodal points that define connections.

It is therefore important that an electronics engineer, in order to get the most from any CAD analysis package, has an understanding of the analysis process. At this stage we are only interested in developing useful models for the BJT; the full use of a CAD tool is discussed in later chapters.

For any a.c. equivalent circuit to be valid, the following conditions usually have to be met:

(1) The active device (BJT in this case) is biased in class A as a linear amplifier.
(2) Only small signal levels are considered.
(3) The frequency is such that device capacitance and coupling/decoupling capacitors can be ignored. This frequency is normally taken to be 1 KHz.

The first stage in producing a useful a.c. equivalent is to replace any coupling and decoupling capacitors with short circuits. At a frequency of 1 KHz the reactance of C_1, C_2 and C_3 will be very small and can therefore be replaced by short circuits. Also note that the power rail will have a very low impedance to 0 V. Therefore, for any a.c. equivalent V_{cc} is the same node point as 0 V. If you find this concept difficult, try to visualize the power supply itself and recall that, back in the power supply, there will be a large smoothing capacitor connected directly across power rails.

In this way, the a.c. equivalent for Fig. 1.14(a) is as shown in Fig. 1.14(b). Here the input is applied directly across R1 and between the base and emitter. The output signal appears across R3.

The next step is to replace the BJT itself with a suitable model, one that is valid for small signals at a signal frequency of 1 kHz. There are several models that could be used; for example, the transistor can be represented by a set of impedances:

An input impedance Z_{ie}
A forward transfer impedance Z_{fe}
An output impedance Z_{oe}
A reverse transfer impedance Z_{re}

But such a model would present problems for the analysis procedure because the output circuit of the model would have to consist of a voltage generator ($Z_{fe} \cdot i_b$) not a current generator. What is required is a model that can more closely represent the action of the transistor. Two such models are in common use: the h-parameter model, and the hybrid-pi model.

Consider the h-parameter model first; the parameters are called h for hybrid, since they include a mix of impedance, admittance and dimensionless parameters. In common emitter mode the four parameters are

h_{ie} the input impedance (Ω)
h_{re} the reverse voltage ratio (dimensionless)
h_{fe} the forward current transfer ratio
      (dimensionless)
h_{oe} the output admittance (Siemen) (Fig. 1.15).

Note that the lower case suffixes have been used to indicate small signal values.

The two equations that describe the transistor's action are:

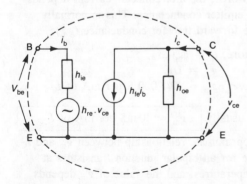

Fig. 1.15 h-parameter model for the BJT in common emitter

on the input side:
$$v_{be} = h_{ie}\, i_b + h_{re}\, v_{ce} \qquad (1.9)$$
on the output side:
$$i_c = h_{fe}\, i_b + h_{oe}\, v_{ce} \qquad (1.10)$$
If i_b is held constant ($i_b = 0$), from equation (1.9) we obtain

$$h_{re} = v_{be}/v_{ce}|i_b = 0 \quad \text{[typical value } 1 \times 10^{-4}]$$

and from (1.10)

$$h_{oe} = i_c/v_{ce}|i_b = 0 \quad \text{[typical value 20 }\mu\text{S]}$$

Also, when v_{ce} is held constant, from (1.9) we obtain

$$h_{ie} = v_{be}/i_b|v_{ce} = 0 \quad \text{[typical value 1 k}\Omega \text{ to 20 k}\Omega\text{]}$$

and from (1.10)

$$h_{fe} = i_c/i_b|v_{ce} = 0 \quad \text{[typical value 50–750]}$$

For most practical purposes h_{re} is very small, indicating that there is very little voltage feedback within the transistor at low frequencies. Thus its effect can usually be ignored. Also, in cases where the external load resistance is about one-tenth the value of $1/h_{oe}$, the effect of h_{oe} can be neglected. Thus the example amplifier can be represented by the equivalent shown in Fig. 1.16.

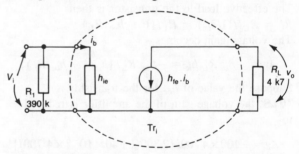

Fig. 1.16 a.c. equivalent for the common emitter amplifier using a simplified model to replace the BJT

If we want to find the voltage gain:

$$Av = vo/vi$$

but $vo = i_c R_L = h_{fe}\, i_b R_L$ (here $R_L = R_3$)
and $vi = v_{be} = i_b h_{ie}$
Therefore $Av = -h_{fe}\, i_b R_L/i_b h_{ie}$
$$Av = -h_{fe}\, R_L/h_{ie} \qquad (1.11)$$

(The minus sign in the above equation simply indicates a phase reversal between the collector and base signals.) To do any practical analysis and obtain a value for voltage gain we would need to know the values of h_{fe} and h_{ie}. Suppose these are given in the data sheet for the transistor as $h_{fe} = 100$ and $h_{ie} = 2\,300$, the voltage gain is then

$$Av = -h_{fe}\,R3/h_{ie} = -100 \times 4\,700/2\,300$$
$$= -204$$

Now let us consider the effect of h_{oe} on voltage gain. If h_{oe} is to be included, it appears as an admittance in parallel with R_L (Fig. 1.17).

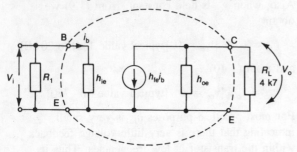

Fig. 1.17 Including h_{oe} in the equivalent circuit

First convert h_{oe} to an equivalent impedance:

$$Z_{oe} = 1/h_{oe}$$

The effective load to the transistor is then
$$R'_L = R_L//(1/h_{oe}) = R_L/(1 + h_{oe}.R_L)$$
The voltage gain becomes

$$Av = -h_{fe}\,R'_L/h_{ie} = -h_{fe}.R_L/\{h_{ie}(1 + h_{oe}.R_L)\}$$

Suppose the value of h_{oe} for the transistor is $40\,\mu S$, the voltage gain of the amplifier is reduced to

$$Av = -100 \times 4\,700/\{2\,300(1+40 \times 10^{-6} \times 4\,700)\}$$
$$= -172$$

An understanding and appreciation of the h-parameter equivalent is valuable, but there is often little point in expecting accurate results from its use in analysis, because all the h-parameters vary from transistor to transistor, and also with the operating conditions for a particular transistor. Only by careful measurement of all the parameters of the transistor at the operating values of I_C, V_{CE} and I_B in the circuit, can an accurate assessment of amplifier performance be obtained. A more useful model is one which can closely resemble the

physical operation of the transistor. One such model is called the hybrid−pi equivalent. Before we look at this in detail let us simply consider the operation of the transistor when it is correctly biased. The forward bias on the base−emitter junction sets up a d.c. emitter current which, since h_{FE} is large, is almost the same as the collector current, therefore

$$I_C = I_E$$

The PN junction diode formed by the base emitter will therefore have a resistance of

$$r_e = 1\,000/40(I_C)$$

where I_C is in mA (see Fig. 1.18).

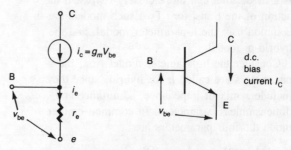

Fig. 1.18 Simple model for a transistor

Any a.c. signal voltage applied between base and emitter will set up a small a.c. current i.e.:

$$i_e = v_{be}/r_e$$

but $i_c = i_e$ and $r_e = 1\,000/40(I_C)$

Therefore $i_c = \dfrac{40v_{be}}{1\,000}\,(I_C)$

In other words, the a.c. collector current depends upon the emitter conductance. This is normally called the forward transfer conductance (g_m).

Therefore, $i_c = g_m v_{be}$
where $g_m = 1/r_e$
therefore $g_m = 40/1\,000$ S per mA of I_C

Or more usually $\boxed{g_m = 40\,mS \text{ per mA of } I_C}$

This approximate relationship between g_m and I_C holds true for all bipolar junction transistors at room temperatures, and the value of g_m depends entirely on the d.c. bias current flowing through the transistor.

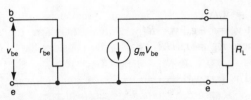

Fig. 1.19 Simple model for a transistor using gm

For example, at $I_C = 6\,\text{mA}$, g_m is about $240\,\text{mS}$, and with $I_C = 40\,\text{mA}$, g_m becomes about $1.6\,\text{S}$.

A very simple model for a transistor common emitter amplifier is therefore as indicated in Fig. 1.19, and consists of an input resistance r_{be} and an output circuit consisting of a current generator $g_m \cdot v_{be}$ driving the a.c. current through the collector load R_L.

Voltage gain $Av = v_o/v_i$

$$= -\frac{g_m\,v_{be}\,R_L}{v_{be}}$$

$$= -g_m\,R_L \qquad (1.12)$$

Previously, using h-parameters, we found

$$Av = -\frac{h_{fe}\,R_L}{h_{ie}} \qquad (1.13)$$

We can therefore say that g_m must be equivalent to h_{fe}/h_{ie}. Another proof of this is as follows:

$$g_m = i_c/v_{be}$$

$$g_m = \frac{i_c/i_b}{v_{be}/i_b} = \frac{h_{fe}}{h_{ie}} \qquad (1.14)$$

Using the 'rule of thumb' that, at or near room temperatures, g_m is about $40\,\text{mS}$ per mA of I_C, it can be seen that, if h_{fe} remains almost constant with changes in I_C, then h_{ie} falls as the bias current is increased. This is what we would expect, since the forward-biased base emitter junction's a.c. resistance will decrease with increasing d.c. current.

Therefore, $r_{be} \approx h_{fe}\,r_e \qquad (1.15)$

Example

A transistor with collector load of 2k2 is operated with a d.c. collector bias of $3.4\,\text{mA}$. The h_{fe} of the transistor is a minimum of 150. Determine:

(1) The approximate voltage gain of the circuit at a signal frequency of 1 kHz.
(2) The minimum input resistance of the transistor at 1 kHz.

Since I_C is $3.4\,\text{mA}$, $g_m = 136\,\text{mS}$
$$Av = -g_m\,R_L = -300$$

$$r_e = \frac{1\,000}{40(I_C)} = \frac{25}{3.4} = 7.35\,\Omega$$

Input resistance $r_{be} = h_{fe}\,r_e = 1\,100\,\Omega$

The hybrid—pi equivalent builds on this basic model to include features that enable the prediction of high-frequency circuit performance (Fig. 1.20). For this reason this model is more often used within CAD software packages.

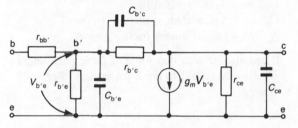

Fig. 1.20 Full hybrid-pi model

In the hybrid—pi model, to account for the fact that the real base of the transistor exists only between the emitter and the collector regions, a resistance $r_{bb'}$, called the base spreading resistance, is included. The real transistor base is given the node letter b', and the outside base connection is b. The base spreading resistance is the total resistance of the relatively low-conductive base material that connects to the real base, plus the ohmic contact of the base lead. A typical value for $r_{bb'}$ is between 50 and $150\,\Omega$. It has the effect of reducing the input signal that reaches the transistor, and a more profound effect on high-frequency performance. The components in the model are:

$r_{bb'}$ = base spreading resistance
$r_{b'e}$ = resistance of the actual base emitter junction
$r_{b'c}$ = the very high resistance of the reverse-biased base collector junction

r_{ce} = the output resistance

$g_m\,v_{b'e}$ = the current generator in the collector

$C_{b'e}$ = the capacitance of the conducting base emitter junction

$C_{b'c}$ = the feedback capacitance from the collector to the base due to the reverse-biased collector base junction

C_{ce} = the small capacitance between the collector and emitter.

Typical values for a small signal transistor operating at a d.c. current of 1 mA are:

$r_{bb'}$ = 75 ohms (Ω)

$r_{b'e}$ = 2 000 ohms (Ω)

$r_{b'c}$ = 1.5 megohms $(M\Omega)$

r_{ce} = 40 kilohms $(k\Omega)$

$C_{b'e}$ = 20 picofarads (pF)

$C_{b'c}$ = 1.5 picofarads (pF)

C_{ce} = 0.5 picofarads (pF)

g_m = 40 milliSiemens (mS)

It can also be seen that some of these parameters are directly related to the h-parameters. For example:

h_{ie} = $r_{bb'} + r_{b'e}$

h_{re} = $r_{b'e}/r_{b'c}$

h_{fe} = $g_m(r_{bb'} + r_{b'e})$

h_{oe} = $1/r_{ce}$

At low frequencies (less than about 50 kHz) the effect of the capacitances in the model can be neglected, and since $r_{b'c}$ is usually large compared to $r_{b'e}$, it can also be ignored (this is similar to ignoring the effect of h_{re} in the h-parameter model). Therefore, the low-frequency equivalent using the hybrid−pi is as shown in Fig. 1.21. The similarity to the h-parameter circuit is immediately apparent.

To find the voltage gain:

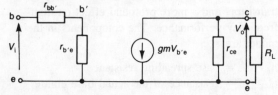

Fig. 1.21 Simplified low-frequency model for a transistor from the hybrid-pi

$A_v = v_o/v_i$

but $v_o = -g_m\,v_{b'e}\,R_L'$

where $R_L' = r_{ce}//R_L$

and $v_{b'e} = v_i \cdot \dfrac{r_{b'e}}{r_{bb'} + r_{b'e}}$

$v_i = v_{b'e} \dfrac{(r_{bb'} + r_{b'e})}{r_{b'e}}$

$$A_v = -g_m\,R_L' \frac{r_{b'e}}{r_{bb'} + r_{b'e}} \qquad (1.16)$$

When R_L is much less than r_{ce}, and where $r_{b'e}$ is much greater than $r_{bb'}$, we get

$A_v = -g_m\,R_L$ (as before).

The two models will be used in Chapter 2 for the analysis of small signal amplifiers. Before we leave the BJT, the method by which the frequency limitation of the device is stated will be examined. As the operating frequency of the input signal to a transistor is raised, a frequency will be reached when the current gain value begins to fall. This is due to the time taken for the carriers to diffuse across the base, which is a relatively slow process.

The three cut-off frequencies used to specify BJT performance are:

$f_{h_{fb}}$ the frequency at which the magnitude of common base current gain has fallen 3 dB from its low-frequency value.

$f_{h_{fe}}$ the frequency at which the magnitude of common emitter current gain has fallen 3 dB from its low-frequency value.

f_T the transition frequency, or gain bandwidth product, the frequency at which the magnitude of common emitter current gain has fallen to unity (Fig. 1.22).

From the above definitions we get:

$$h_{fb} = \frac{h_{fbo}}{1 + jf/f_{h_{fb}}} \qquad (1.17)$$

where h_{fbo} is the low-frequency value of h_{fb}, and f is the signal frequency. The magnitude of h_{fb} is given by:

$$|h_{fb}| = \frac{h_{fbo}}{[1 + (f/f_{h_{fb}})^2]^{1/2}} \qquad (1.18)$$

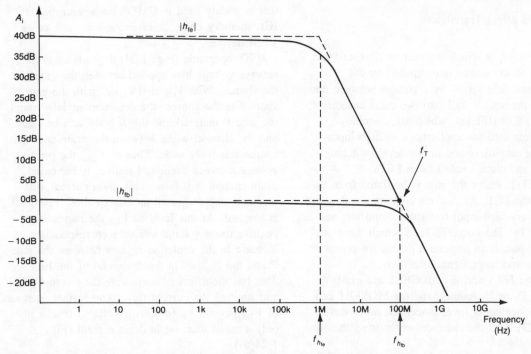

Fig. 1.22 Illustration of the relationship of transistor current gain with frequency

Thus at $f_{h_{fb}}$ $|h_{fb}| = h_{fbo}/\sqrt{2}$ and the phase angle is $-45°$.

Since $h_{fe} = h_{fb}/(1 - h_{fb})$, by using equation (1.17) we can write

$$h_{fe} = \frac{\dfrac{h_{fbo}}{1 + jf/f_{h_{fb}}}}{1 - \dfrac{h_{fbo}}{1 + jf/f_{h_{fb}}}}$$

Therefore,

$$h_{fe} = \frac{h_{fbo}}{1 - h_{fbo} + jf/f_{h_{fb}}}$$

By dividing by $(1 - h_{fbo})$ we then get

$$h_{fe} = \frac{\dfrac{h_{fbo}}{1 - h_{fbo}}}{\dfrac{1 - h_{fbo} + jf/f_{h_{fb}}}{1 - h_{fbo}}} = \frac{h_{feo}}{1 + jf/f_{h_{fb}}(1 - h_{fbo})}$$

Thus $h_{fe} = \dfrac{h_{feo}}{1 + jf/f_{h_{fe}}}$ \hfill (1.19)

where h_{feo} is the low-frequency value of h_{fe}, and $f_{h_{fe}}$ is the frequency at which the magnitude of h_{fe} is 3 dB down.

Here, $f_{h_{fe}} = f_{h_{fb}}(1 - h_{fbo})$ \hfill (1.20)

At one particular frequency, called f_T, the magnitude of h_{fe} will have fallen to unity.

$$f_T = f_{h_{fe}} h_{feo} \hfill (1.21)$$

It therefore follows that, for frequencies above $f_{h_{fe}}$ when f_T is known, then $|h_{fe}|$ can be determined.

Example

A 2N3571 transistor has an f_T of 1.2 GHz. Determine
(a) Its current gain magnitude at 300 MHz.
(b) The value of $f_{h_{fe}}$ if at low frequencies h_{fe} is 65.

Solutions (a) $|h_{fe}| = f_T/f = 1200/300 = 4$
(b) $f_{h_{fe}} = f_T/h_{feo} = 4.62$ MHz

1.3 Field-Effect Transistors

These devices, in which the current flowing from the drain to the source is controlled by the electrostatic field set up by a voltage between the gate and the source, fall into two main categories: junction FETs (JFETs), which are discrete components used for applications in high-input-resistance amplifiers and in low-level switching circuits, and metal oxide silicon FETs (MOSFETs), where the gate is insulated from the body of the FET. As discrete components they are used in very-high-input-resistance amplifiers and as PowerFETs. The PowerFET, of which there are several types, is an important device for power switching and large signal amplifiers.

Both the JFET and the MOSFET are available as either P- or N-channel, and the MOSFET can also be a depletion- or enhancement-mode device (Fig. 1.23). It is the enhancement-mode structure

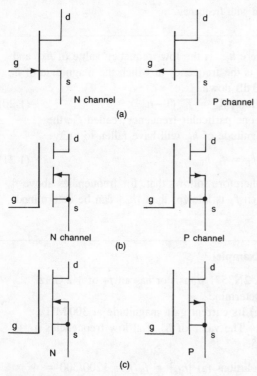

Fig. 1.23 FET symbols. (a) Junction FETs; (b) Enhancement-mode MOSFETs; (c) Depletion-mode MOSFETs

that is widely used in CMOS linear and digital ICs, memory chips, microprocessors, and other VLSI devices.

JFET operation (Fig. 1.24) depends upon the reverse voltage bias applied between the gate and the source. With V_{GS} at 0 V, i.e. with the gate shorted to the source, the depletion regions round the gate P material and the N body will be small, and the channel width between the drain and source relatively wide. Thus as V_{DS}, the positive voltage between drain and source, is increased, drain current will flow. This drain current will increase with V_{DS} until an effect called 'pinch-off' is reached. At this level of V_{DS} the increasing positive drain voltage sets up a corresponding increase in the depletion regions between the gate P and the N body at the drain end of the FET. This has the effect of narrowing the channel width and limiting the current flow. Any further increase of V_{DS} beyond V_P (pinch-off voltage) results in only a small increase in drain current (Fig. 1.24(b)).

Thus with $V_{GS} = 0$ V and $V_{DS} > V_P$ we get $I_D = I_{DSS}$ (drain current with gate shorted to source). Control of I_D is achieved by varying the reverse bias applied to the gate with respect to the source. The depletion regions increase and the drain current for a given V_{DS} falls. Thus one of the key parameters for the FET is the forward-transfer conductance.

$$g_m = i_d/v_{gs} \mid \text{holding } v_{ds} \text{ constant}$$

A typical value of g_m for a small signal JFET is from 2 mS up to 5 mS.

The simplest model for a JFET consists of an open circuit between gate and source, to represent the very-high-input resistance of the reverse-biased gates, and a current generator on the output side with a parallel output resistance r_{ds} (Fig. 1.24(a)).

For a common source amplifier as shown in Fig. 1.25, the equivalent circuit for small signals can be drawn as in Fig. 1.25(b).
Voltage gain $= v_o/v_i$
but $v_i = v_{gs}$
Therefore $v_o = -g_m v_{gs} R'_L$,

where R'_L is r_{ds} in parallel with R_L,

therefore $A_v = -g_m R'_L$ (1.22)

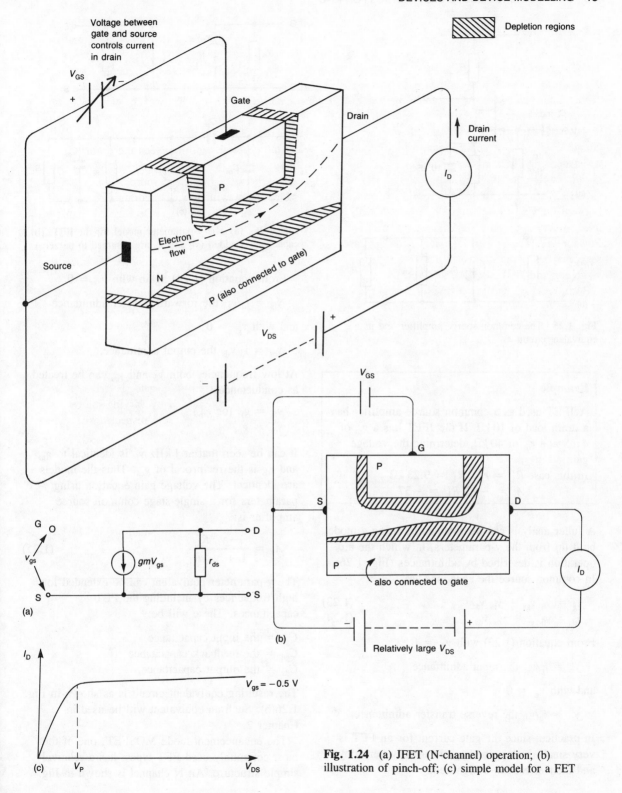

Fig. 1.24 (a) JFET (N-channel) operation; (b) illustration of pinch-off; (c) simple model for a FET

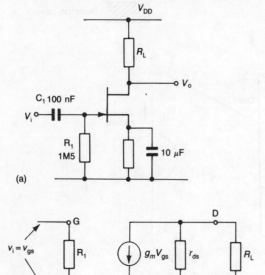

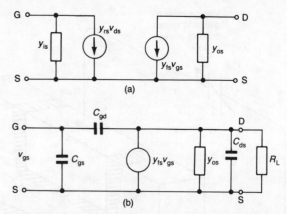

Fig. 1.25   The common source amplifier and its a.c. equivalent circuit

Fig. 1.26   (a) The y-parameter model for the FET; (b) capacitances added (y_{is} and y_{rs} are assumed to be zero)

Example

A JFET used as a common source amplifier has a drain load of $10\,k\Omega$. If the JFET has a g_m of $4\,mS$ and r_{ds} of $40\,k\Omega$, determine the voltage gain.

In this case $R'_L = r_{ds}//R_L = 9.23\,k\Omega$

$$A_v = -g_m.R'_L = -37$$

A fuller analysis can be obtained by using a model built up from the y-parameters, in which the a.c. operation is described by admittances (Fig. 1.26). In common source the equations are:

$$i_g = y_{is}\,v_{gs} + y_{rs}\,v_{ds} \quad (1.23)$$
$$i_d = y_{fs}v_{gs} + y_{os}\,v_{ds} \quad (1.24)$$

From equation (1.23) with $v_{ds} = 0$

$y_{is} = i_g/v_{gs}$ the input admittance

and with $v_{gs} = 0$

$y_{rs} = i_g/v_{ds}$ the reverse transfer admittance.

In practice, since the gate current for an FET is very small, both y_{rs} and y_{is} are usually very tiny and their effect can be ignored.

From equation (1.24) again with $v_{ds} = 0$

$y_{fs} = i_d/v_{gs}$ the forward transfer admittance

and with $v_{gs} = 0$

$y_{os} = i_d/v_{ds}$ the output admittance.

At low frequencies both y_{fs} and y_{os} can be treated as conductances:

$$y_{fs} = g_{fs}\ (\text{or}\ g_m)$$
$$y_{os} = g_{os}$$

It can be seen that at $1\,kHz$ y_{fs} is identical to g_m and r_{ds} is the reciprocal of g_{os}. Thus the models are identical. The voltage gain equation using y-parameters for a single-stage common source amplifier is:

$$A_v = \frac{-y_{fs}\,R_L}{1 + y_{os}\,R_L} \quad (1.25)$$

The y-parameter equivalent can be extended for high frequences by including the FET capacitances. These will be:

C_{gs} = the input capacitance
C_{gd} = the feedback capacitance
C_{ds} = the output capacitance.

The resulting equivalent circuit is as shown in Fig. 1.26(b). Such an equivalent will be used in Chapter 2.

The enhancement-mode MOSFET, one of the most commonly used FET types, has a relatively simple structure. An N channel is shown in Fig.

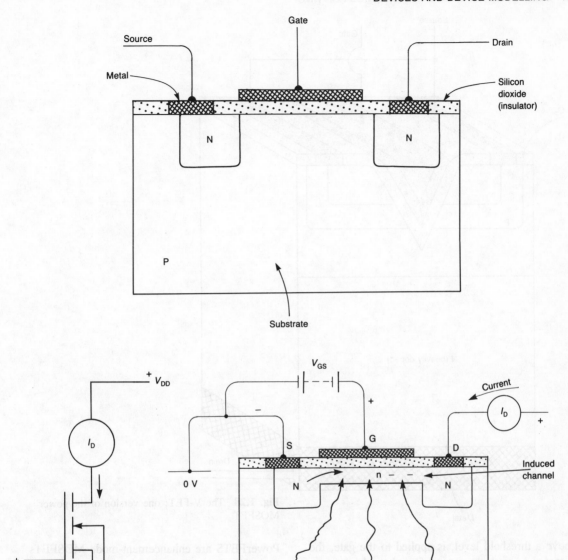

Fig. 1.27 MOSFET operation

1.27 in cross-section. It consists of a P substrate and two heavily doped N regions for the source and drain. The gate is insulated from the substrate by a thin layer of silicon dioxide. The connection to the source also makes electrical contact to the P body, so that when a voltage is applied between

gate and source the electric field operates across the body of the FET. With V_{GS} set to 0 V, when the gate is shorted to the source, and with the drain positive with respect to the source, P material separates the two N regions and the drain current is zero. When a sufficient positive voltage,

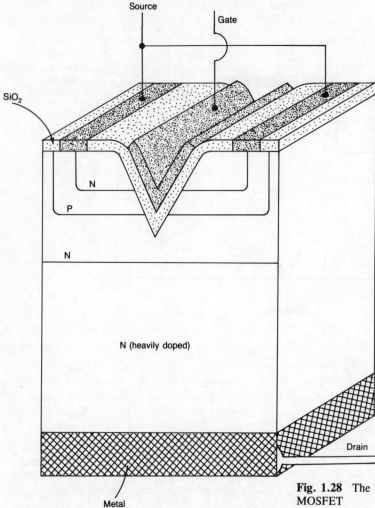

Fig. 1.28   The V-FET: one version of the power MOSFET

above a threshold level, is applied to the gate, the P region beneath the gate is forced to change to N, as any free electrons are attracted to the gate region. In this way a conducting channel between the source and the drain is created, and drain current will flow. The greater the positive field at the gate, the deeper the N channel becomes and the larger the drain current. Key parameters of an enhancement-mode MOSFET are:

$V_{GS(th)}$ the gate-to-source threshold voltage at which a measurable drain current (typically 0.1 mA) begins to flow. This voltage is usually between 2 V and 4 V.
and G_{fs} the forward transfer conductance.

PowerFETS are enhancement-mode MOSFETs designed to pass large drain currents. Several constructional methods exist, with the object of achieving a short thick channel which will have a low resistance when the FET is turned on. The VFET, produced by Siliconix, was one of the first available types. The construction is shown in cross-section in Fig. 1.28. In this vertical FET, a V-shaped groove is etched through the NPN diffusions on top of a heavily doped N substrate. Silicon dioxide — the insulator — is deposited on either side of the groove, and the gate metal on top of the insulation. The resulting structure has a very short channel — 1 μm — between the top N regions (the source) and the bottom N region (the drain). The low-resistance N substrate forms the drain connection, which can be directly attached to the case of the FET to dissipate heat. Operation is exactly the same as previously described for the enhancement-mode MOSFET, except that powerFETs have very large values of forward-transfer conductance, a typical value for this being between $0.5\,S–2.5\,S$. The gate-to-source threshold voltage $V_{gs(th)}$ is normally about $2–4\,V$. Other powerFET structures, not using the V-groove technique, depend upon many parallel cells, connected at the process manufacturing stage and therefore allowing the drain current to be shared by several channels.

1.4 The BJT and FET used as switches

Most of the applications of transistors are not as linear amplifiers, but as switches in digital circuits where the device is either off (non-conducting) or on (saturated or fully conducting). This area of study is obviously of great importance. Consider the ideal switch, which will have the following important properties, in addition to low cost and unlimited operation time:

Zero on resistance (no voltage drop in the on state)
Infinite off resistance (zero leakage in the off state)
Instantaneous switching action
Almost zero input operating power.

Keeping this ideal in mind we can now look at the operation of the BJT and FET in turn.

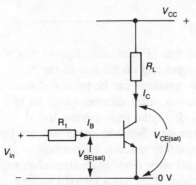

Fig. 1.29 The BJT as a common emitter switch (on state)

The common emitter switch, which is the most efficient of the three possible configurations, requires an input voltage in excess of $0.6\,V$ to ensure that it conducts fully. In the conducting state the transistor saturates — in other words, the base becomes full of electrons that have been injected into it by the forward-biased emitter (Fig. 1.29). In practice, to ensure full switching, an I_C to I_B ratio of $10:1$ is assumed in the design of the switch. Thus in the on state we have:

$V_{CE(sat)}$ = the saturated value of the collector to emitter voltage;
$V_{BE(sat)}$ = the saturated value of the base to emitter voltage.

where $I_C = \dfrac{V_{CC} - V_{CE(sat)}}{R_L}$ (1.26)

and $I_B = \dfrac{V_{in} - V_{BE(sat)}}{R_1}$ (1.27)

The value of $V_{CE(sat)}$ depends to a large extent on the size of the collector current flowing in the transistor. For a small signal transistor operated at a low current of about $2\,mA$, $V_{CE(sat)}$ would probably be less than $100\,mV$, but for a power-switching transistor with an I_C of $1A$, $V_{CE(sat)}$ could be as high as $1\,V$. However, it is fair to say that as a switch in the on state, the BJT performs well. For example, supppse we have a V_{CC} of $50\,V$ and a load of $50\,\Omega$ used with a transistor that has a $V_{CE(sat)}$ at $1\,A$ of $0.75\,V$. The power in the load and the transistor when the switch is on are:

$P_L \approx V_{CC}\,I_C = 50\,W$

and $P_C \approx V_{CE(sat)}\,I_C = 0.75\,W$

Clearly, very little power is being wasted in the transistor and most of the power taken from the supply is reaching the load.

One problem with the BJT is that a relatively high input power is required to switch it on and to keep it on. Take the example where $I_B = 0.1$ and $I_C = 100\,mA$, since $V_{BE(sat)}$ will be about $700\,mV$, the base dissipation is approximately $70\,mW$.

If the input voltage is $5\,V$, a base-limiting resistor of $43\,\Omega$ is indicated, and this resistor dissipation is $430\,mW$. Thus the total input power to operate the switch is $700\,mW$. The power gain of the circuit, for this example, is only 100.

Let us turn now to study the BJT common emitter switch in the off state. The input voltage is now zero and the transistor turns off. The output voltage rises to $+V_{CC}$ and only a small leakage current flows through the transistor. For a transistor, the leakage currents are defined as:

I_{CBO} = the leakage current through the reverse-biased collector base junction with the emitter open circuit.

I_{CEO} = leakage current through the collector emitter junction with the base open circuit.

I_{CER} = leakage current through the collector emitter with the base connected to the emitter with a specified value of resistance.

I_{CES} = leakage current through the collector emitter with the base shorted to the emitter.

I_{CEX} = leakage current through the collector emitter with the base emitter reverse-biased.

In the common emitter connection, I_{CBO} is amplified by the transistor and appears as a much larger current in the collector (Fig. 1.30).

Here, $I_{CEO} = I_{CBO} + h_{FE} \cdot I_{CBO}$
$$= I_{CBO}(1+h_{FE}) \qquad (1.28)$$

Since this is the worst-case leakage condition, for when a resistor or a short is between the base and emitter some of the collector base leakage is removed, I_{CEO} is the parameter normally quoted on the transistor's data sheet. This will be at a specified value of V_{CE}. A study of a transistor will

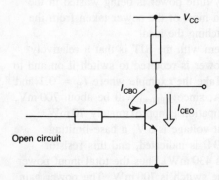

Open circuit

Fig. 1.30 BJT switch in the off state (base-open circuit)

show that leakage current for a modern silicon transistor is very small; for a medium-power device I_{CEO} will often be less than 100 nA, a value that shows a transistor being an excellent switching device in the off state.

The switching condition from off to on and vice versa is called the transition state. Consider the transistor off and a step input voltage of V_i applied. There will be a short delay before collector current starts to flow, since the emitter has to inject carriers into the base and these carriers then have to diffuse across the base region before being swept up by the collector (Fig. 1.31). Thus the total turn-on time is

$$t_{on} = t_d + t_r$$

This turn-on time depends upon the type of transistor and the value of I_C, and can vary from a few nanoseconds for a small signal transistor, to several microseconds for a large-area power transistor.

Once collector current is established, the collector emitter voltage falls to a very low value ($V_{CE(sat)}$) which means that the field to attract electrons (positive in the case of an NPN transistor) is very weak. This is why a 10 : 1 ratio between I_C and I_B is required. In turn, this means that the base is saturated with electrons — minority carriers in the base — and thus, when the transistor is turned off by V_i returning to zero, all the stored electrons must be swept up by the collector before the collector current can fall. This effect, called minority charge storage, is the limiting factor in the switching speed of the BJT (Fig. 1.31):

$$t_{off} = t_s + t_f$$

t_s can vary from tens of nanoseconds up to tens of microseconds, depending on the size of the transistor. If the transistor can be prevented from going into saturation, the switching speed can be much improved. In digital logic circuits this is achieved by diffusing a Schottky diode between the base and the collector, to create a Schottky transistor. The Schottky diode is an aluminium to silicon PN junction which has a forward voltage drop of typically only 300 mV, and which is extremely fast in operation. When the transistor is

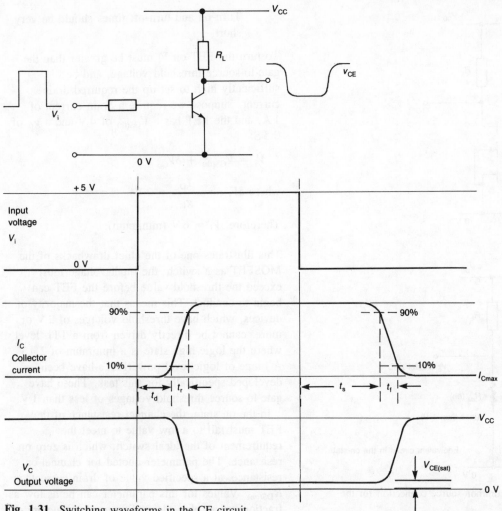

Fig. 1.31 Switching waveforms in the CE circuit

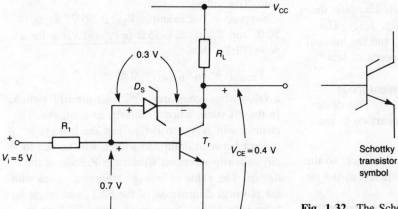

Fig. 1.32 The Schottky transistor, which is non-saturating

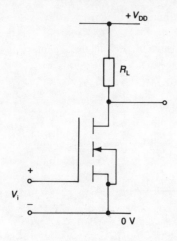

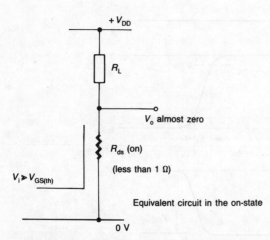

Fig. 1.33 The common-source connection for the MOSFET switch

forward-biased the base voltage will rise to 0.7 V and the Schottky diode will conduct, clamping the collector voltage to about 0.4 V (Fig. 1.32). The Schottky transistor cannot saturate, and the turn-off delay time is reduced. Switching speeds of less than 10 ns are then possible.

Now let us consider the enhancement-mode MOSFET (N) as a switch (Fig. 1.33). This device has two obvious advantages in comparison to the BJT:

(1) It is a voltage controlled at the input, so the input power necessary to switch it to the on state is very small.
(2) Since it is a unipolar device it cannot suffer from a minority charge storage effect.

Turn-on and turn-off times should be very short.

To turn the FET on V_i must be greater than the gate-to-source threshold voltage, and be sufficiently high to set up the required drain current. Suppose we require a drain current of 1 A, and the FET has a $V_{GS(th)}$ of 4 V and a g_{fs} of 0.5 S:

$$V_i = V_{GS(th)} + \delta V_{GS}$$

where $\delta V_{GS} = \dfrac{I_D}{g_{fs}} = 2\,\text{V}$

Therefore, $V_i = 6\,\text{V}$ (minimum).

This illustrates one of the chief drawbacks of the MOSFET as a switch: the input voltage must exceed the threshold value before the FET can begin to conduct. This means that the majority of devices, which have threshold voltages of 2 V or more, cannot be directly driven from a TTL level where the logic high state is a minimum of 2.4 V. A range of logic-level powerFETs have been developed specifically for this task. These have gate-to-source threshold voltages of less than 1 V.

In the on state, the channel resistance of the FET must fall to a low value to meet the requirement of the ideal switch, which is zero on resistance. The parameter quoted for channel-on resistance, at a specified value of drain current, is $R_{DS(on)}$. Values for this parameter can be as low as fractions of an ohm, depending on the structure of the FET, the drain current, and the amount of gate-drive voltage.

Suppose in our example V_{DD} is 50 V, R_L is 50 Ω, and $R_{DS(on)}$ is 0.35 Ω (a typical value for a powerFET); then

$$V_{DS(on)} \approx I_D R_{DS(on)} = 0.35\,\text{V},$$

a value which compares well with the BJT switch. In the off state, when V_i returns to zero, the channel will revert to P type and the leakage current between drain and source will be due to any minority electrons within the P body of the device. The value of leakage therefore varies with the physical dimensions of the FET, and might be from only 100 nA for a small signal FET up to 1 mA for a large-area powerFET. As with any semiconductor, leakage will increase with temperature.

In the transition state the turn-on and turn-off times are almost identical, and can be as low as a few nanoseconds.

From the previous paragraphs it can be seen that the enhancement-mode MOSFET makes an excellent switching device. Another advantage is that $R_{DS(on)}$ has a positive temperature coefficient. This can prevent thermal runaway in situations where the supply voltage is relatively low — say 10 V or less — and also allows several powerFETs to be easily paralleled to pass higher currents. If one device gets too hot, its $R_{DS(on)}$ resistance rises and more current flows through other parallel FETs.

A summary of device-switching characteristics is given in Table 1.1. In this, the small signal MOSFET is included for comparison and to cover the structures used in CMOS logic and other LSI and VLSI chips. In these integrated circuits the on-state channel resistance can be several hundred ohms, and this can restrict the switching speed of the more basic CMOS to less than TTL (transistor–transistor logic). Improved versions of CMOS use several parallelled MOSFETs to obtain

lower on resistance and corresponding faster operation. These are the 74AC/ACT and the 74HC/HCT types discussed later in the Chapter.

1.5 The operational amplifier

The op-amp — so called because it was originally developed for use in analogue computers to carry out mathematical operations — is a key component in linear design. In this section the op-amp will be treated as a discrete component; applications will be discussed in later chapters. Basically, the op-amp is a very high-gain directly coupled differential amplifier. Its output voltage is a magnified copy of the difference between the voltages on its two input pins. If we ignore for the moment the effects of offset voltage, from Fig. 1.34 we obtain:

$$V_o = A_{vol}(V_1 - V_2) \tag{1.29}$$

Since A_{vol}, the open-loop differential voltage gain, is often in excess of 100 dB, it only requires the difference between V_1 and V_2 to be fractions of a millivolt for a large-output voltage to result. As an

Table 1.1 Summary of device switching characteristics

Device type	'On state'	'Off state'	Switching speed	Input requirement	General comments
Small signal BJT ($I_C \approx 100$ mA)	Low 'on' state voltage $V_{CE(sat)} \approx 100$ mV	Very low leakage current $I_{CEO} < 100$ nA	Good 10 ns typ	Current drive $I_B \approx 1/10\ I_C$	Easy to use. Relatively fast. Speed improved by Schottky mod
Large signal BJT ($I_C > 1$ A)	Higher 'on' state voltage $V_{CE(sat)}$ up to 1 V	Relatively low leakage current $I_{CEO} < 10\ \mu$A	Fair 10 μs typ	Current drive $I_B \approx 1/10\ I_C$	Rugged and proven devices. Darlington versions have higher gain
Small signal MOSFET ($I_D \approx 10$ mA)	Relatively high channel resistance typ 200 Ω	Very low leakage	Fair/good 20 ns	Voltage drive Therefore high input resistance	Used in CMOS ICs LSI and VLSI.
PowerFET ($I_D > 1$ A)	Very low on resistance $R_{DS(on)} < 0.4\ \Omega$ or less	Low leakage I_{DSS} typ 50 μA or less	Excellent Can be as low as 5 ns	Voltage drive. But a V_{GS} threshold value must be exceeded	Rugged and easy to parallel. Simple to interface.

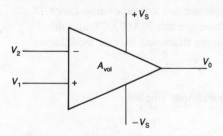

Fig. 1.34 The op-amp

example, suppose an op-amp has an A_{vol} of 104 dB, V_1 of +0.31 V, and V_2 of +0.29 V; to find the possible output voltage we must first convert A_{vol} from decibels to a ratio:

$$A_{vol} = \text{antilog } (104/20) = 158\,000$$

Therefore,

$$V_o = 158 \times 10^3 (0.31 \times 10^{-3} - 0.29 \times 10^{-3})$$
$$= 3.16 \text{ V}$$

For an effective input of only 20 μV the output is above 3 V.

If the difference input becomes negative — which would occur with, say, V_1 at +0.31 V and V_2 at +0.32 V — then the output also becomes negative, for this reason, most op-amp circuits require a positive and a negative power supply. With V_s set to ± 10 V and still assuming that any input offset is zero, the op-amp transfer characteristics are as shown in Fig. 1.35. Saturation levels are typically about 1 V away from the power rail value.

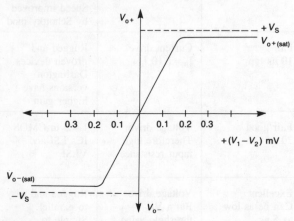

Fig. 1.35 Ideal op-amp transfer characteristics when offset is considered as negligible

The important op-amp parameters are:

A_{vol}	=	open-loop voltage gain
R_{in}	=	input resistance (open loop)
R_o	=	output resistance
V_{io}	=	input offset voltage
dV_{io}/dT	=	temperature coefficient of input offset voltage
I_b	=	input bias current (the average of I_b^+ and I_b^-)
I_{io}	=	input offset current
dI_{io}/dT	=	temperature coefficient of the input offset current
CMRR	=	common mode rejection ratio — the ratio of differential to common mode voltage gain
PSRR	=	power supply rejection ratio — the ratio of the change in V_{io} to power supply voltage changes
Slew rate SR	=	The average time rate of change of the output signal for a step input under closed-loop unity-gain conditions
GBP	=	gain bandwidth product — the frequency at which the small signal open-loop differential gain has fallen to unity
I_{os}	=	the maximum output current that the op-amp can deliver into a short circuit
V_{opp}	=	the maximum peak-to-peak output voltage swing that the op-amp can deliver to a defined load without saturation or clipping occurring (typically 5% Total Harmonic Distortion — THD)
PBW	=	full power bandwidth i.e. the frequency at which the voltage gain is 3 dB down while the op-amp is delivering V_{opp} into a stated load.

The input circuitry of any op-amp will consist of some form of differential amplifier. This important linear circuit, which forms the basis of many amplifiers and other electronic circuits, will be more fully analysed in Chapter 2, but a grasp of its important features is essential if the op-amp is to be fully appreciated.

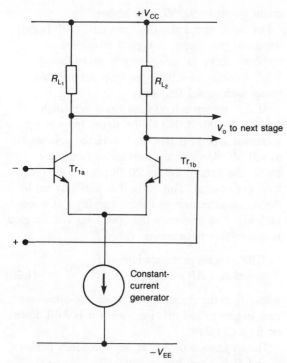

Fig. 1.36 Basic input stage of a bipolar op-amp

In the bipolar version of the circuit, two transistors will be wired as shown in Fig. 1.36. The actual circuit arrangement in an op-amp will be more complex than this, but the structure will be the same. The two transistors with both bases tied to 0 V will be balanced so that the current supplied from the constant current generator will divide equally between them. If one input is made slightly more positive than the other, the transistor associated with the more positive voltage will conduct more than the other, and an out-of-balance signal will be generated between the two collectors. In an op-amp this signal is further amplified, level-shifted and finally delivered to the output pin via a push–pull output stage.

The balanced nature of the differential circuit means that any drifts in input bias voltages (typically -2.5 mV per °C for a BJT) tend to cancel out because both inputs will be moving in the same direction. This feature, which means that any signals common to both inputs are cancelled, is essential for any d.c. amplifier circuit. In the op-amp the two transistors are diffused in the same

piece of silicon, and will thus be well matched, giving good common-mode rejection. However, the match cannot be perfect and the input bias currents and voltages required to set up balanced conditions will not be exactly identical. As an example, imagine that, when both inputs are tied to 0 V, one transistor requires an input bias current of 185 nA and a bias voltage of 558 mV, while the other needs a current of 165 nA and 556 mV. The offsets are therefore

$$I_{io} = I_{b^+} - I_{b^-} = 10 \text{ nA}$$
$$V_{io} = V_{be1} - V_{be2} = 2 \text{ mV}.$$

In precision op-amps offset values are made extremely small (see the specification figures for the OP-07), but general-purpose op-amps have the sort of values given above.

The effects of fixed offsets can usually be nulled by some external components or by a voltage source of opposite polarity, but it is the drifts of these offsets with temperature that can often mask a small d.c. voltage being amplified by an op-amp circuit. These small drifts are again due to slight differences between the two input transistors. If one has a V_{be} temperature coefficient of -2.4 mV/°C, while the other has one of -2.35 mV/°C, the input offset drift will be $+0.5$ mV/°C.

At d.c. and low frequencies a simplified equivalent of the op-amp is as shown in Fig. 1.37. This can be useful in analysing designs for offset and offset drift effects. The circuit has two input bias current generators, I_{b^+} and I_{b^-}, and the offset voltage V_{io} is shown as a voltage generator in series with the input. The amplifier's input resistance is across the input terminals and the output resistance is in series with the output.

At higher frequencies, parameters such as slew rate and gain bandwidth product (GBP) become important. Slew rate is the large signal response or rate of change of the output under unity gain conditions, usually measured in the inverting mode with two equal medium-value resistors, and with the op-amp's output driven from one saturation level to the other (Fig. 1.38). Slew rate is then measured in volts per microsecond. General-purpose op-amps have slew rate values of a few volts per microsecond, while really fast types

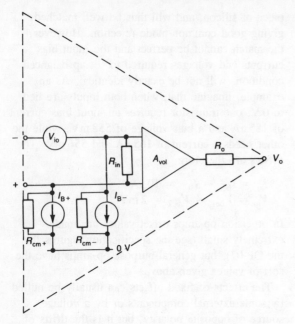

Fig. 1.37 Simplified equivalent circuit for an op-amp

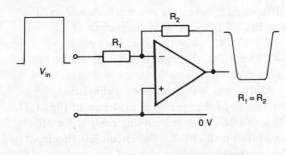

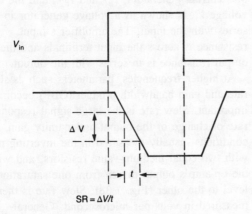

Fig. 1.38 Slew rate measurement

might go up to 500 V/μs or higher.

For small signal amplifier circuits, GBP is the important parameter. A typical frequency–response curve for an op-amp is given in Fig. 1.39, showing how the open-loop voltage gain varies with signal frequency.

At d.c. the open-loop gain has a very high value, say 100 dB, but as the signal frequency is increased a point is reached where the gain starts to roll off. Any further increase in frequency causes the gain to fall by 20 dB per decade (or 6 dB per octave). This roll-off is normally set by the IC manufacturer to ensure stability. At some high value of frequency the open-loop voltage gain is unity. This frequency is called f_T.

$$GBP = \text{gain} \times \text{bandwidth} = f_T$$
$$\text{therefore } GBP = A_{vol} f_h \qquad (1.30)$$

where f_h is the frequency at which the open-loop gain begins to roll off, i.e., when it is 3 dB down on its d.c. value.

The magnitude of A_{vol} at any frequency between f_h and f_T is given by

$$|A_{vol}| \approx GBP/f$$

where f is the signal frequency.

Suppose an op-amp has a GBP of 3 MHz and an A_{vol} value at d.c. of 100 dB, then $f_h = 300$ Hz.

What is $|A_{vol}|$ at 50 kHz?

$$|A_{vol}| = GBP/f = \frac{3 \times 10^6}{50 \times 10^3} = 60$$

1.6 Logic families

In order to implement digital logic designs it is essential to have a clear understanding of the operating principles, parameters and special functions of each of the major logic families. These basic logic types are:

TTL   = transistor transistor logic
CMOS = complementary MOS logic
ECL   = emitter coupled logic

Within each family there are several variants, and also types that are termed 'common logic', where for example some CMOS ICs are designed to be

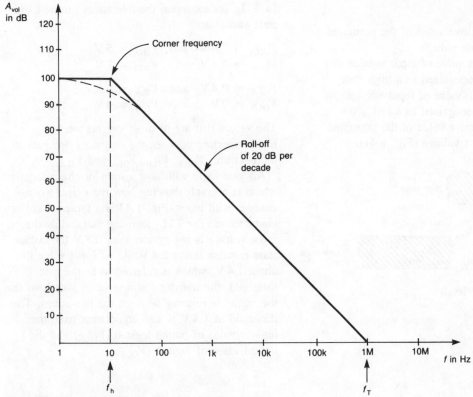

Fig. 1.39 Open-loop frequency response of an op-amp

pin and logic-level compatible with some versions of TTL.

The use of BJTs and FETs as individual switches has already been discussed, and what follows builds on this knowledge so that a more complete grasp of gate logic function can be achieved.

The general parameters for any logic family, which allow designers to distinguish between logic types, are:

- Logic level
- Noise margin
- Fan-out
- Propagation delay time
- Power consumption.

Logic level refers to the range of values that, for one particular type of logic, can be accepted as a true high state and true low state at both the output and inputs of gates within the family. At the output these guaranteed values are specified as:

V_{OHA} The maximum value of the high-state output voltage

V_{OHB} The minimum value of the high-state output voltage

V_{OLA} The maximum value of the low-state output voltage

V_{OLB} The minimum value of the low-state output voltage

(see BS 6493: Section 2.2 and IEC 748-2) (Fig. 1.40).

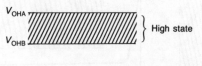

Fig. 1.40 Output logic levels

and at the input as:

V_{IHA} The most positive value of the permitted input high-state voltage

V_{IHB} The minimum value of input voltage that will still be recognized as a high state

V_{ILA} The maximum value of input voltage that will still be recognized as a low state

V_{ILB} The least positive value of the permitted low-state input voltage (Fig. 1.41).

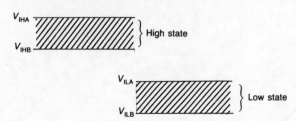

Fig. 1.41 Input logic levels

In TTL, for example, the tolerances on the logic-state values are

$$V_{OHA} = 3.9\,V \quad \text{and} \quad V_{IHA} = 5\,V$$
$$V_{OHB} = 2.4\,V \qquad\qquad V_{IHB} = 2\,V$$

$$V_{OLA} = 0.4\,V \quad \text{and} \quad V_{ILA} = 0.8\,V$$
$$V_{OLB} = 0\,V \qquad\qquad\; V_{ILB} = 0\,V$$

The values that are of most interest when interconnecting between the output of one gate to the next are: V_{OHB}, V_{ILB}, V_{OLA} and V_{ILA}.

All gate logic will have a transfer characteristic, which is a graph showing how the output voltage changes with input. Fig. 1.42 is a typical transfer characteristic for TTL, showing that, while the input voltage is not greater than 0.8 V the output state remains above 2.4 V. At an input value of about 1.4 V, which is referred to as the gate threshold, the transfer characteristics switch so that the output is midway between the two states. This threshold of 1.4 V is also equidistant from the highest value of output logic 0 (V_{OLA}) and the lowest value of logic 1 (V_{OLB}).

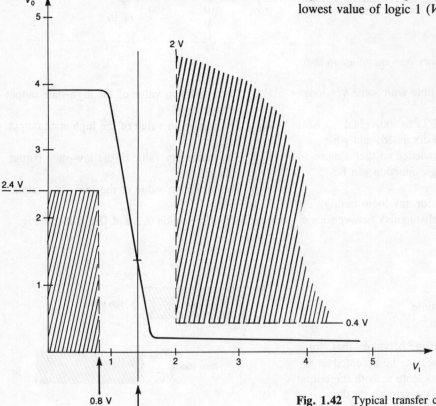

Fig. 1.42 Typical transfer characteristics for a TTL gate

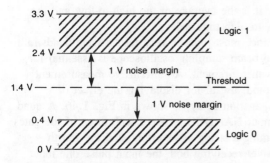

Fig. 1.43 Threshold noise margin in TTL

This leads on to a consideration of noise in digital systems. Unwanted signals will always be present, but if the amplitude of any noise superimposed on a logic level is not allowed to cause the total signal level to be greater than the threshold voltage, then no false output should arise (Fig. 1.43).

In TTL, this suggests that the noise margin or noise immunity is 1 V, which is a value often quoted for TTL noise immunity. However, at the gate input there will be a spread or tolerance on the threshold level which gives rise to the two values V_{ILB} and V_{ILA} (for TTL these are 2 V and 0.8 V, respectively). Thus the worst-case noise margin will always be the difference between:

(a) For the high state V_{OLB} and V_{IHB}
$$2.4 - 2 = 400\,\text{mV for TTL,}$$
and (b) in the low state V_{ILA} and V_{OLA}
$$0.8 - 0.4 = 400\,\text{mV for TTL.}$$

It is these values that are specified in BS6493 (Fig. 1.44). It is worth noting that as long as the noise picked up or injected on to a TTL gate input is less than 400 mV, it cannot be amplified and propagated around the system. As we shall see later, the noise margins of CMOS and ECL, using the worst-case definitions, are different from TTL.

Fan-out is a term used to describe gate-loading effects, and is defined as 'the number of gate inputs that can be driven by a standard gate output without the output state being forced out of specification'. This can vary, depending on the type of gate and whether the output is acting in source or sink mode. Normally for any logic family the fan-out is designed to be identical for both output states.

Suppose a gate can sink, in the logic 0 output state a current of 24 mA and each input requires a current of 2 mA. The fan-out is calculated as follows:

$$\text{Fan-out} = I_{OL}/I_{IL} = 24/2 = 12$$

The other two major parameters of logic are

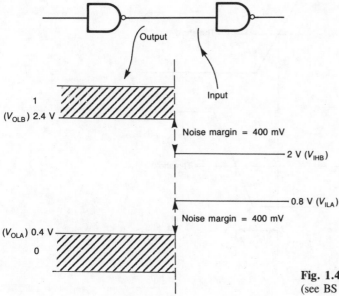

Fig. 1.44 Noise margin as normally specified (see BS 6493)

propagation delay time and power consumption. Usually the values of these two parameters are mutually incompatible, meaning that if a logic gate is designed for fast operation it usually consumes more power. For this reason, logic is often compared by the speed/power product measured in picojoules. For example, a gate with a switching speed of 10 ns and a power dissipation of 3 mW will have a speed/power product of 30 pJ.

The propagation delay time of a gate is the time delay taken for the output to respond to a logic change of state at the input. This delay time is caused by the switching transition times of active devices (BJT or MOS), and the time taken for stray and load capacitors to be charged and discharged. To minimize these delay effects, load resistors and currents within the IC must be relatively large, hence the increase in power consumed as the design speed is increased. The specification for propagation delay time, given in BS6493, is shown in Fig. 1.45, in this case for an inverting output. The time delays (t_{PHL} and t_{PLH}) are measured from the gate input threshold point to the gate output threshold level. Here,

$$\text{Threshold} = (V_{IHB} + V_{ILA})/2$$

Thus propagation delay time = 0.5 ($t_{PHL} + t_{PLH}$),

i.e. it is the average of the high-to-low and the low-to-high time delays.

Since most logic is very fast, a wide-bandwidth dual-beam sampling oscilloscope is essential for this measurement. An alternative measurement method, useful for displaying the effect of propagation delay, is shown in Fig. 1.46. A quad 2 input NAND IC is wired with three of the gates forming a string of inverters, and the fourth NAND receiving both the input pulse one input and its delayed complement on the other. The resulting output of the gate will be a pulse with a width equal to three propagation delay times. With standard TTL this pulse will only be about 40 ns, so a wide-bandwidth oscilloscope connected to the gate output via a low-capacitance probe is required. If a 4 000 CMOS IC is checked in the same way, the pulse at the gate output can be clearly observed using a general-purpose 20 MHz bandwidth oscilloscope.

In the static state and at low-frequency operation, the power consumption for most types of logic will be at a minimum. With TTL this is usually about 10 mW per gate, while for CMOS the power taken from the supply is almost negligible at 10 nW per gate. However, most logic is required to carry out functions at high speed,

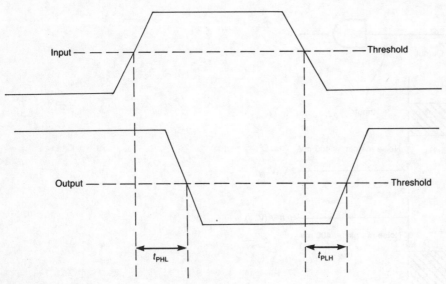

Fig. 1.45 Definition of propagation delay time in a gate

switching at relatively high frequencies. This means that the dynamic power consumption figure is often much more meaningful for comparison of logic types. Every time a gate switches, some current is drawn from the supply and, as switching frequency rises, so does power consumption. This is more apparent in some types of logic than others, CMOS being a good example of the effect. At a frequency of 1 MHz a CMOS gate running from a +5 V supply consumes approximately 1 mW. This effect is illustrated in Fig. 1.47.

A table showing comparisons of speed, power consumption, noise margin and other parameters is

given later in this section. Before that, let us look briefly at logic gate function for the main families.

TTL operation

The circuit of one of the two gates inside the 7420 is shown in Fig. 1.48. To ease the understanding of the circuit operation it can be split into three sections:

Tr_1: A multi-emitter transistor, performing the AND function on inputs A, B, C, D.

Tr_2 a phase splitter.

Tr_3 and Tr_4: an output stage having a low

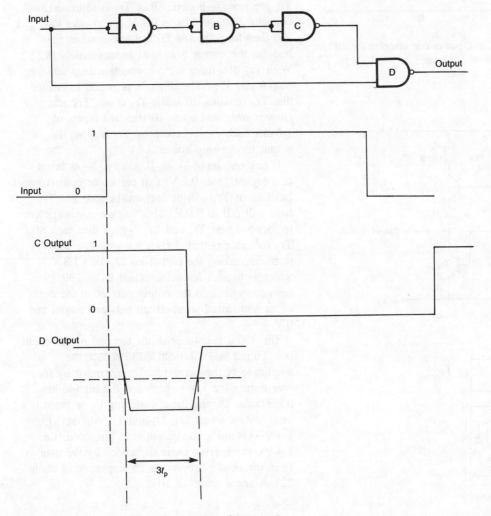

Fig. 1.46 One method for measurement of propagation delay time

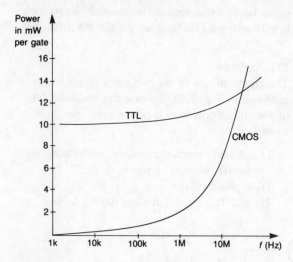

Fig. 1.47 Comparison of power consumption for TTL and CMOS

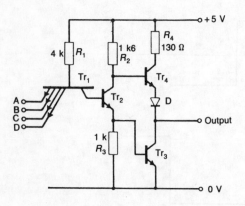

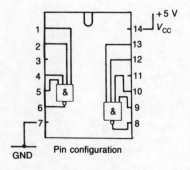

Fig. 1.48 TTL NAND gate ($\frac{1}{2}$ 7420)

output impedance in both logic states (known as the totem pole stage).

Assume that all inputs A,B,C and D are high. Because the base of Tr_1 is connected to $+V_{CC}$ via R_1, all the emitter/base junctions will be reverse-biased. The base/collector junction of Tr_1 will be forward-biased and current will flow via R_1 into Tr_2 and Tr_3, turning them both on. The output of the gate will be at logic 0. Under these conditions, the voltage on Tr_1 base will be approximately 2.1 V (i.e. $V_{BE3} + V_{BE2} + V_{BC1}$). therefore, as long as the input levels on A, B, C and D are all greater than 2 V, all the emitter/base junctions of Tr_1 are reverse-biased. Since Tr_2 is saturated, its collector voltage falls to 0.8 V (i.e. $V_{BE3} + V_{CE(sat)2}$) and therefore Tr_4 and D_1 are non-conducting because the output is only at approximately 0.2 V. With Tr_4 off, there is no connection between the output and V_{CC}. The diode is provided to ensure that Tr_4 remains off while Tr_3 is on. Tr_3 acts as a *current sink*, and up to 10 standard inputs of 1.6 mA each can be taken by Tr_3 without the output level rising above 0.4 V.

If any one input — A, B, C or D — is taken to a logic 0, i.e. 0.2 V, that particular emitter/base junction of Tr_1 will be forward-biased, and Tr_1 base will fall to 0.9 V. This voltage is insufficient to forward-bias Tr_2 and Tr_3, which then turn off. Tr_2 collector potential rises towards V_{CC} and Tr_4 turns on, taking the output via D_1 to +3.3 V, which is logic 1 level. Note that R_4, a 130 Ω resistor, will limit the output current in the event of an accidental short-circuit between output and 0 V.

The 130 Ω resistance in the top end of the totem pole output stage is included to reduce the amplitude of the current spike demanded by the gate during the low-to-high and the high-to-low transitions. During these switching times there is a brief instant when Tr_3, D_1 and Tr_4 conduct (Fig. 1.49). Assuming the output is at threshold (i.e. 1.4 V), the current pulse demanded by the gate from the power supply has an amplitude of about 22 mA and a width of 10 ns.

$$I_p \approx \frac{V_{cc} - [V_{th} + V_d + V_{ce(sat)}]}{130} \approx 22 \text{ mA}$$

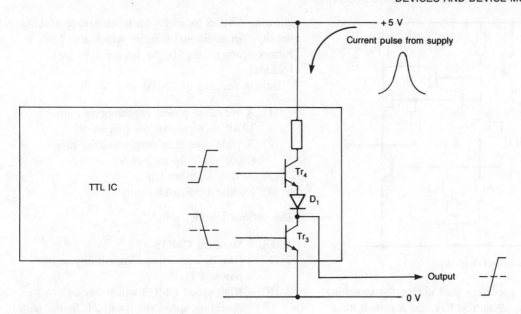

Fig. 1.49 Current spike caused by switching of the TTL output

For this reason, TTL ICs must be provided with ceramic decoupling capacitors so that excessive power supply noise is not generated. A typical rule of thumb is to use 10 nF decoupling capacitors for every two to three gate-type ICs, and one 10 nF for each MSI chip.

Standard TTL, a design which first appeared in the early 1960s, is based on saturating transistors which limit the operating speed and result in a propagation delay time that can vary from 10 ns up to 25 ns, depending on the gate function. The design of the totem pole output stage means that the output can charge and discharge load capacitance rapidly, but an improvement in design, using Schottky transistors which are non-saturating, enables switching speeds to be further increased. The various TTL Schottky types are:

74S Schottky TTL
74LS Low-power Schottky
74AS Advanced Schottky
74ALS Advanced low-power Schottky
74F FAST TTL (Fairchild advanced Schottky technology)

A typical Schottky TTL NAND gate circuit is shown in Fig. 1.50. The basic circuit of the

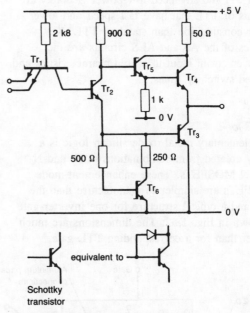

Fig. 1.50 Schottky TTL NAND gate

standard TTL gate is preserved, with improvements such as the Darlington drive (Tr_5 and Tr_4) for the high-state output, and the active load Tr_6, which improves the turn-off time of Tr_3. Tr_6 is termed an 'active turn-off' element and it

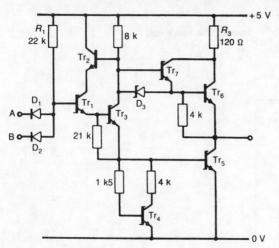

Fig. 1.51 Low-power Schottky

operates as a non-linear load during the switching of Tr_2 and Tr_3. Schottky TTL has a propagation delay time of 3 ns, but a power dissipation of 20 mW per gate. Low-power Schottky (circuit in Fig. 1.51) and advanced low-power Schottky are variants of TTL that have fast speed and lower power consumption than standard TTL. Key features of the AS and ALS circuits are the improvement in input threshold characteristics and reduced switching times.

CMOS logic
Complementary metal oxide silicon logic is a family created from combinations of P- and N-channel MOSFETs. These enhancement-mode MOSFETs are simpler to manufacture than the BJT, and a typical structure for one inverter gate is shown in Fig. 1.52. The dimensions are much smaller than for a corresponding TTL gate,

allowing CMOS to achieve a much higher packing density. An additional feature, which also leads to further space-saving, is that no resistors are required.

Unique features of CMOS are:

(1) A very low power consumption (only 10 nW per gate at low frequency)
(2) A wide operating supply voltage range (from +3 V up to +18 V)
(3) A very high fan-out
(4) Excellent noise immunity.

The various families are:

4000B: Standard CMOS
74C: CMOS with some compatibility to low-power TTL
74HC: High-speed CMOS which has an operating speed similar to 74LS, but with lower power consumption and better noise immunity. It can drive 10 LSTTL inputs. 74HC therefore has speed, function and pin compatibility with 74LS, but its input levels are not TTL-compatible.
74HCT: High-speed CMOS that can directly replace 74LS TTL. 74HCT has TTL-compatible inputs.
74AC: Advanced high-speed CMOS with 74 TTL pin compatibility. It almost matches 74F in speed, and has a much lower power consumption. Maximum propagation delay time is about 8.5 ns, and outputs can sink or source 24 mA.
74ACT: Advanced high-speed CMOS with TTL pin compatibility. These are selected 74AC types that have input circuits designed to accept TTL logic levels. They

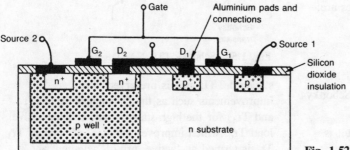

Fig. 1.52 Typical CMOS structure (inverter)

can be used as direct drop-in replacements for TTL.

The 74HCT and 74ACT types show the merging that has taken place in logic types in recent years, so that now there is much commonality between TTL and these versions of CMOS. This means that all the advantages of CMOS are available as a replacement for TTL.

In order to appreciate the unique features of CMOS we return to the simple inverter structure, shown in Fig. 1.53. This is shown with a simplified version of the essential protection components for clarity. When a logic 0 is applied, T_2, the N channel, will be off since the input voltage will be well below the required threshold value. However, the P channel FET, T_1, will be forward-biased since it will have a gate to source a voltage of nearly $-V_{DD}$. T_1 is therefore on, and presents a low resistance to the positive power rail V_{DD}. The output is in the logic-high state.

If the input is now taken to $+V_{DD}$, the P channel MOSFET T_1 is turned off, effectively disconnecting the output from $+V_{DD}$, and at the same time the N-channel device T_2 turns *on*, connecting the output to 0 V via its conducting channel. The equivalent circuits for these two possible input states are shown in Fig. 1.54.

For CMOS gates logic 0 = 0 V to $0.3\,V_{DD}$
logic 1 = $+V_{DD}$ to $0.7\,V_{DD}$

From the description of operation it can be seen that

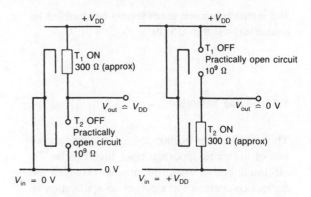

Fig. 1.54 Equivalent circuits for two input conditions

(1) Since the gates of the MOSFETs are insulated from the substrate, the input impedance is extremely high ($10^{12}\,\Omega$ or greater). It is this high input impedance that gives CMOS such a high fan-out capability.

(2) In the static state, one device is on while the other is off. Thus the power taken from the supply is almost negligible.

(3) The operation of the circuit is independent of the value of the supply voltage.

(4) The output swings from $+V_{DD}$ to 0 V.

(5) The input threshold is one-half of the supply, giving a noise margin that it typically 45 per cent of V_{DD}.

A closer look at the circuit will show that, when the input is changing state, there must be a brief instant when both devices conduct. A small current pulse will be taken from the supply. Therefore, power dissipation of CMOS increases with operating frequency and is typically 1 mW/MHz per gate. It is also important that inputs are not left open-circuit, otherwise the small gate capacitance will slowly charge up and put the devices into their active regions. When this happens all devices in the package conduct and a very large current may be taken from the supply, causing the IC to overheat, and possibly burn out. All unused inputs, including those of unused gates in an IC, *must be connected somewhere*. As a general rule, spare inputs to gates should be connected to another driven input, or to an appropriate voltage level ($+V_{DD}$ for a NAND),

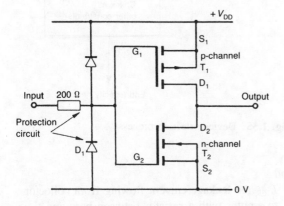

Fig. 1.53 CMOS inverter circuit

and inputs to unused gates should be disabled by connecting them to 0 V or $+V_{DD}$.

1.7 Device Selection

This short section is intended as an introduction to one of the more important tasks involved in electronic design work: the process in which the correct component for a particular application is chosen. Naturally, a good understanding of device parameters is going to be essential to this process, but here it is the principles of selection which are being covered. In other words, the text deals with the way in which any design engineer should approach the task of choosing the best-fit components. The transistor switch — the example that follows — is used simply as a vehicle for the understanding of this process.

In order to create a working electronic circuit or system, the various components that go to make up the system must be specified both in terms of the parameters of concern in the design, and the values of these key parameters. Only in this way can the components which best fit the requirement be selected. The process, outlined in Fig. 1.55, involves a number of defined steps, and the simple d.c. relay switch circuit of Fig. 1.56 will be used as an illustration.

In this circuit, a Darlington transistor is used as a common emitter switch to amplify a TTL logic 1 state (2.4 V at 0.5 mA) and to operate a 24 V 500 Ω relay coil. When the TTL level is high, R_1 sets the base current of Tr_1 to about 0.5 mA, and the transistor is switched into saturation. A coil current of 50 mA flows to operate the relay. With a Darlington switch the I_c to I_b ratio is normally set to 100 : 1 to ensure saturation.

Let us consider the selection process for the Darlington switch. First, those parameters and ratings that are important in this application must be identified. In the off state, these are:

V_{CER} the maximum voltage across the collector emitter junction with a resistor between base and emitter

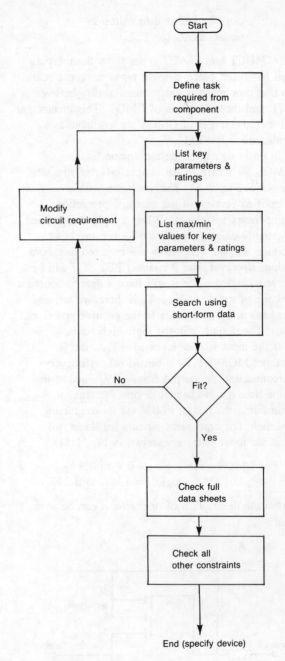

Fig. 1.55 Device selection process

and

I_{CER} the leakage current flowing from collector to emitter with a resistor between base and emitter.

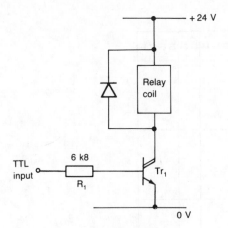

Fig. 1.56 Relay switch circuit

In the on state they are

$V_{CE(sat)}$ the saturation voltage

$I_{C(max)}$ the maximum collector current
and

h_{FE} the static value of the forward current transfer ratio.

Since transistors are relatively fast devices compared to relays, the turn-on and turn-off delay times of the Darlington need not be considered. Other parameters such as output admittance (h_{oe}), feedback capacitance (C_{bc}) and noise figure are also not of interest in this switching circuit. The actual values of the ratings and parameters can then be determined from a study of the circuit conditions. This will give the absolute maximum or minimum values that are allowed. In this case these are:

V_{CER} : 25 V (including a small voltage drop across the protection diode)
I_{CER} : 250 μA
I_C : 50 mA
$V_{CE(sat)}$: not greater than 2 V
P_{tot} : about 100 mW.

Since no component should ever be operated at or close to its rated limits of voltage, current or power, a derating factor of at least 50 per cent should be added to the above values. Derating is a standard design technique to improve the overall reliability of a circuit by operating components well below their maximum rating; for example,

specifying a diode with a 75 V reverse voltage rating when the circuit voltage is known not to exceed 40 V.

The general data obtained from the circuit with derating applied mean that a small signal NPN switching Darlington must be selected from devices that broadly meet the following specification:

V_{CEO} : at least 35 V
I_C : not less than 100 mA
$V_{CE(sat)}$: not greater than 2 V
I_{CEO} : 1 mA maximum
h_{FE} : better than 500 at IC = 50 mA
P_{tot} : at least 250 mW

In short-form data, and often in the full data sheet, it is the breakdown voltage between collector and emitter with the base open circuit (V_{CEO}) that is normally quoted rather than V_{CER}, since the former is the worst-case condition. Similarly, I_{CEO} is the leakage current flowing in the collector with the base-open circuit. This is typically 1.5−2 times greater than I_{CER}.

Before we study the short-form list in Fig. 1.57 it must also be noted that other considerations apart from technical merit will play a part in the selection process. These will be factors such as availability, sources of supply (a back-up or secondary source is often necessary), pin layout, mechanical fixing and any standardization requirement within the organization. These factors, which must be allowed for, may well force the designer to select a device that may not be his first choice. In our case, some suitable Darlingtons are listed in Fig. 1.57. The search through short-form data, where only the main features and characteristics of a device are given, allows the selection process to be narrowed to a few competing devices. However, the final choice should never be made using these short-form data alone. A check on the characteristics, ratings and parameters given in the full data sheet is essential. The shortened data may well conceal some change in a parameter or rating that would disqualify the use of the selected component in the intended application. From the list, devices such as the 2N5308, BCX38A, BSR50 or even the TIPP110 would appear to be suitable.

Darlington Transistor Selection

IC(AV) max Amps	Ptot watts @25°C	hfe min	@ IC A	NPN PNP	Package and Pin Connection	VCEO (V) 20—45	60	80	100	120—150	160—500	Mftr
0.3	0.4	7000	0.002	NPN	TO-92 (a)	2N5308 (40V)						NSC
	0.625	10000	0.01	NPN	TO-92 (b)	MPSA13-NSC (30V)						ZET
	0.75	20000	0.01	NPN	TO-92 (e)	MPSA12 (20V)						ZET
	0.75	10000	0.1	NPN	TO-92 (e)	MPSA13 (30V)						ZET
	0.75	20000	0.1	NPN	TO-92 (e)	MPSA14 (30V)						ZET
0.8	1	1000	0.5	NPN	TO-92 (e)		BCX38A					ZET
	1	4000	0.5	NPN	TO-92 (e)		BCX38B					ZET
	1	10000	0.5	NPN	TO-92 (e)		BCX38C					ZET
	1	10000	0.5	PNP	TO-92 (e)		ZTX712 NEW					PC
1	0.8	2000	0.5	NPN	TO-92 (h)	BSR50 (40V)						PC
	0.8	2000	0.5	NPN	TO-92 (h)	BSR60 (45V)						PC
	0.8	2000	0.5	NPN	TO-39	BSS50 (45V)	BSS51	BSS52				PC
	0.8	2000	0.5	PNP	TO-39	BSS60 (45V)						PC
	1	2000	1	NPN	TO-92 (e)			ZTX603				ZET
	1	2000	0.5	NPN	TO-92 (e)				ZTX704	ZTX605 (120V)	ZTX601 (160V)	ZET
	1	10000	0.5	PNP	TO-92 (e)					ZTX600 (140V)		ZET
	1	3000	1	NPN	TO-92 (e)					ZTX600B (140V)	ZTX601B (160V)	ZET
	5	2000	0.5	PNP	TO-126	BDX42 (45V)		BDX44				PC
2	0.8	1000	1	NPN	TO-92 (a)		TIPP110	TIPP111	TIPP112			TI
	0.8	1000	1	PNP	TO-92 (a)		TIPP115	TIPP116	TIPP117			TI
	50	1000	1	NPN	TO-220		TIP110	TIP111	TIP112			ST
	50	1000	1	PNP	TO-220		TIP115		TIP117			TI
	50	1000	1	NPN	TO-220		TIP110-TI, TIP115-TI					TI
4	40	750	1.5	NPN	TO-126	BD675 (45V)	BD677	BD679	BD681			ST
	40	750	1.5	PNP	TO-126	BD676 (45V)	BD678	BD680	BD682			ST
5	65	1000	3	NPN	TO-220		TIP120	TIP121	TIP122			ST
	65	1000	3	PNP	TO-220		TIP125	TIP126	TIP127			ST
	65	1000	3	NPN	TO-220		TIP120-TI	TIP121-TI	TIP122-TI			TI
	65	1000	3	PNP	TO-220		TIP125-TI	TIP126-TI				TI

Fig. 1.57

BCX38A
BCX38B
BCX38C

NPN Silicon planar Darlington transistors

DESCRIPTION

The BCX38 series of silicon planar Darlington transistors is designed for medium power applications requiring very high current gain and high input impedance. The monolithic construction has the inherent advantages of fast switching times, low saturation voltages and low leakage currents. Application areas include: driver and output stages of audio amplifiers; direct interfacing with integrated circuits; lamp, relay and hammer driving.

The E-line package is formed by injection moulding a SILICONE plastic specially selected to provide a rugged one-piece encapsulation resistant to severe environments and allow the high junction temperature operation normally associated with metal can devices.

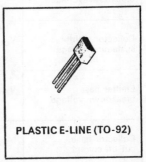

PLASTIC E-LINE (TO-92)

E-line encapsulated devices are approved for use in military, industrial and professional equipments.

Alternative lead configurations are available as plug-in replacements of TO-5/39 and TO-18 metal can types, and for flat mounting.

ABSOLUTE MAXIMUM RATINGS

Parameter	Symbol	Value	Unit
Collector-Base Voltage	V_{CBO}	80	Volts
Collector-Emitter Voltage	V_{CEO}	60	Volts
Emitter-Base Voltage	V_{EBO}	10	Volts
Continuous Collector Current	I_C	800	mA
Power Dissipation ($T_{amb} = 25°C$)	P_{tot}	1	Watts
Operating and Storage Temperature Range		−55 to +200	°C

THERMAL CHARACTERISTICS

Parameter	Symbol	Max.	Unit
Thermal Resistance : Junction to ambient	$R_{th(j-amb)}$	175.0	°C/W
Junction to case	$R_{th(j-case)}$	87.5	°C/W

Ferranti Electronic Components Division

Fig. 1.58

BCX38 series

ELECTRICAL CHARACTERISTICS (at 25°C ambient temperature unless otherwise stated).

Parameter	Symbol	Min.	Max.	Unit	Conditions
Collector-base breakdown voltage	$V_{(BR)CBO}$	80	—	V	$I_C = 10 \mu A$, $I_E = 0$
Collector-emitter sustaining voltage	$V_{CEO(sus)}$	60	—	V	$I_C = 10$ mA, $I_B = 0$
Emitter-base breakdown voltage	$V_{(BR)EBO}$	10	—	V	$I_E = 10 \mu A$, $I_C = 0$
Collector-base cut-off current	I_{CBO}	—	100	nA	$V_{CB} = 60V$, $I_E = 0$
Emitter-base cut-off current	I_{EBO}	—	100	nA	$V_{EB} = 8V$, $I_C = 0$
Static forward current transfer ratio h_{FE} *BCX38A*		500 1,000	— —		$\left.\begin{array}{l} I_C = 100 \text{ mA} \\ I_C = 500 \text{ mA} \end{array}\right\} V_{CE} = 5V*$
BCX38B		2,000 4,000	— —		$\left.\begin{array}{l} I_C = 100 \text{ mA} \\ I_C = 500 \text{ mA} \end{array}\right\} V_{CE} = 5V*$
BCX38C		5,000 10,000	— —		$\left.\begin{array}{l} I_C = 100 \text{ mA} \\ I_C = 500 \text{ mA} \end{array}\right\} V_{CE} = 5V*$
Collector-emitter saturation voltage	$V_{CE(sat)}$	—	1.25	V	$I_C = 800$ mA, $I_B = 8$ mA
Base-emitter on voltage	$V_{BE(on)}$	—	1.8	V	$I_C = 800$ mA, $V_{CE} = 5V*$

* Measured under pulsed conditions. Pulse width = 300 μs. Duty cycle ⩽ 2%.

BCX38 series

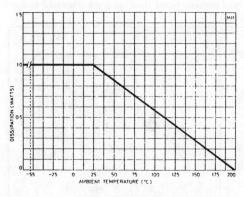

DERATING CURVE

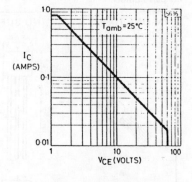

SAFE OPERATING AREA

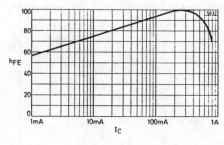

h_{FE}/I_C

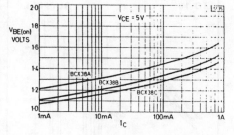

$V_{BE(on)}/I_C$

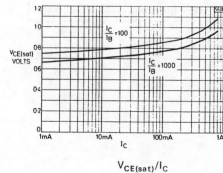

$V_{CE(sat)}/I_C$

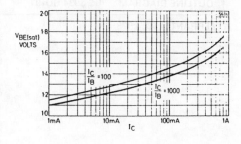

$V_{BE(sat)}/I_C$

BCX38 series

LEAD CONFIGURATIONS

Devices can be ordered with the following lead configurations by adding the indicated suffix to the part number.

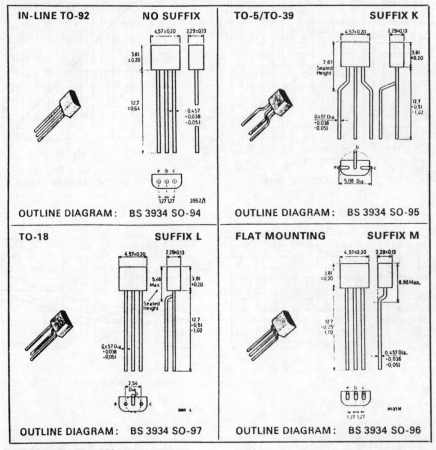

© FERRANTI LTD. 1978

A choice now has to be made, and of the listed devices the BCX38A, a plastic device which has the full data given in Fig. 1.58, is considered one of the most suitable. It has a maximum value of $V_{CE(sat)}$ of 1.25 V at a collector current of 800 mA (I_c to I_b ratio of 100 : 1). A further study of the device characteristics reveals, from the graph of $V_{CE(sat)}$ against I_c, that $V_{CE(sat)}$ at 50 mA is typically only 0.85 V. This low value of $V_{CE(sat)}$ means that the power dissipation of the switch when on and driving the relay, will be only 43 mW. The derating curve indicates that the transistor would be safe from overheating, even at ambient temperatures in excess of 50 °C.

1.8 Problems

(1) A small signal silicon diode is forward-biased with a current of 3.5 mA. The value of V_F is measured as 0.635 V. Determine the diode's static and dynamic resistance.

(2) A BJT has an emitter current of 65 mA and a collector current of 64.8 mA. Determine the value of h_{FE} and I_B. Neglect any leakage current.

(3) A BJT in common-emitter connection has a load resistance of 1.8 kΩ and a d.c. collector current of 4.2 mA. If the h_{fe} of the transistor is quoted as 75 minimum to 325 maximum, determine, at a frequency of 1 kHz:
   (a) The probable voltage gain.
   (b) The maximum and minimum values of h_{ie}.

(4) A transistor has a d.c. value of h_{fe} of 420 and an f_T of 750 MHz. At what frequency will h_{fe} be 3 dB down on its low-frequency value? At what frequency will the magnitude of h_{fe} be 50?

(5) A JFET is operated as a CS amplifier with a drain load of 22 kΩ. The FET has y_{fs} equal to 3.5 mS and the voltage gain of the circuit is measured as 40. Determine the value of y_{os}.

(6) A powerFET (N-channel) is used as a switch to interface CMOS logic running from a +5 V supply to a resistive load of 2 A in a 24 V d.c. supply. The powerFET has:

$$g_{fs} = 1.5 \, S$$
$$V_{GS(th)} = 2.4 \, V$$
$$R_{DS(on)} = 0.25 \, \Omega$$

   (a) Sketch the circuit.
   (b) State whether the V_{GS} drive voltage is sufficient.
   (c) Determine the value of $V_{DS(on)}$.
   (d) Calculate the drain dissipation.

(7) An op-amp has an open-loop voltage gain of 104 dB and a GBP of 10 Mhz. At what frequency will the open-loop gain be 3 dB down?

1.9 Suggested research and assignment work

(1) Describe the operation, detailing all key parameters, of a medium-power thyristor. Show two typical applications for such a device.

(2) An op-amp is required as a buffer between the hold capacitor (220 pF) and an ADC. What special features will be required from the op-amp? Explain how a sample-and-hold circuit operates and show how such a circuit is specified.

(3) A lamp-failure indicator is shown in Fig. 1.59, where the LED current, when it is on, is set to 20 mA.

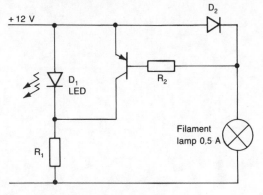

Fig. 1.59 Lamp-failure indicator

(a) Explain the operation of the circuit.
(b) Calculate the nearest preferred values for R_1 and R_2.
(c) Select a suitable transistor for Tr_1 position. State all steps in your selection process. The LED can be assumed to have a V_F of 1.5 V and D_2 has a V_F of 1 V.

(4) Most logic families have some ICs within the range which have open-collector or open-drain outputs.
(a) Find the circuit diagram for such a gate in TTL or Schottky TTL.
(b) Explain the purpose of such a gate by showing one simple application.

2 Linear Circuit Analysis

2.1 Linear classifications

The term 'linear electronics' is used to describe obvious circuits such as amplifiers, active filters, oscillators and power supplies, and also the less obvious such as comparators, ADCs and DACs. In fact, any circuit or device that operates on or processes analogue-type signals can be considered as belonging to the linear classification. The increasing use of digital components has meant that linears (i.e. analogue) are left with only a modest share of the total market in electronic parts and systems, digital circuits and systems making up for more than 80 per cent of sales. However, the real world is analogue, and therefore certain linear functions will always be with us; in addition to this, digital circuits themselves are really a subset of analogue. This is because a digital gate operates as a very high-gain amplifier, switching from one saturated state to the other. Therefore the study and analysis of linear circuits remains an important area. Some aspects of digital circuits, particularly at high frequencies, can only be fully understood by using linear analysis.

A feature of linear analysis as compared to digital is that more parameters and characteristics usually have to be specified. For example, an amplifier would require at least the following points to be included in its specification:

- The intended use: preamplifier, buffer, d.c. amplifier, video or tuned.
- The class of operation: Class A, B, AB, C or D.
- The value of voltage, current or power gain.
- The bandwidth.
- The noise and distortion levels.
- The input and output impedances.
- Maximum undistorted output.

This indicates the variety of analysis tools and techniques that might be required in linear design to predict parameter values. Some of these tools must, of necessity, be very sophisticated.

Above all, any analysis needs to answer the question: 'How will this system respond to the required range of input signals?' Here, range implies both signal amplitude, shape and frequency. This chapter discusses ways of analysing and predicting performance for some of the more typical linear circuits and devices. This general approach can then be adapted for the analysis of other similar circuits and systems.

Before we begin the full analysis of small signal amplifiers, it will be worthwhile for us to briefly revise frequency response and bandwidth definitions. The frequency response of an amplifier is shown in Fig. 2.1 for reference. Such a graph shows how the gain of the amplifier varies with changing input frequency. In this example, where

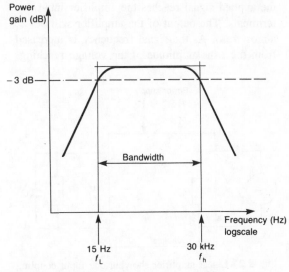

Fig. 2.1 Frequency response of an amplifier

power gain is plotted against frequency, the amplifier is assumed to amplify signals in the audio range from 15 Hz up to 30 kHz. Between these two frequencies the gain of the amplifier is substantially flat. The 15 Hz and 30 kHz are called the lower and upper cut-off frequencies, and represent the frequencies at which the power gain is one-half of mid-band value: in other words, the output is 50 per cent, or 3 dB, down. The bandwidth is the difference between these two frequencies. When voltage or current gain response is being considered, the cut-off frequencies are those where the gain is 0.7071 of the mid-band value; this is also the 3 dB down point.

Consider a linear amplifier system that has just two CR networks — an input coupling capacitor in series with the input resistance R_{in}, and a load of R_L in parallel with C_L. We shall assume that the rest of the system is directly coupled, as shown in Fig. 2.2. The value of $C_1 R_{in}$ is also considered as being much larger than $C_L R_L$. It is the input coupling network that affects the low-frequency response of the system. At very high frequencies the reactance of C_1 ($Xc = {}^1/_{2\pi fC}$) will be very small, and can be considered as almost a short-circuit. In this way, all the input signal will be applied across R_{in}. At the other extreme of the frequency spectrum, at low frequencies, the reactance of C_1 will be almost infinity, and appears as an open circuit so that hardly any of the applied signal reaches the amplifier input terminals. The output of the amplifier will be almost zero. As the signal frequency is increased from d.c., the amplitude of the voltage reaching

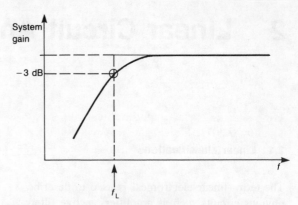

Fig. 2.3 Low-frequency response — loss of input signal due to input coupling capacitor

the amplifier's terminals rises. At one frequency, called f_L — the low-frequency cut-off — the system gain will be 3 dB down on the mid-band value (Fig. 2.3).

The simple C_1 R_{in} series network has the phasor diagram as shown in Fig. 2.4, and at the frequency where Xc_1 is equal to R_{in}, the value of V_s will be equal to $V_i/\sqrt{2}$ and the phase angle 45 °. Thus for the system the low-frequency cut-off is given when

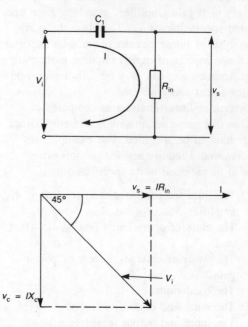

Fig. 2.4 Phasor diagram for input coupling circuit at f_L

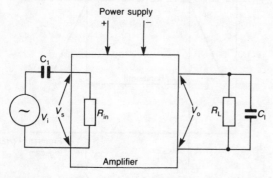

Fig. 2.2 Linear amplifier showing one input coupling network

$$Xc_1 = R_{in}$$

$$\frac{1}{2\pi f_L C_1} = R_{in}$$

$$f_L = \frac{1}{2\pi C_1 R_{in}} \qquad (2.1)$$

At f_L, since the actual input to the amplifier has fallen by 0.7071, the voltage gain will be 70.71 per cent of its mid-band value.

Therefore, at f_L

$$|A_v| = A_{vMB} \ (20 \ \log \ 0.7071 \ dB)$$
$$= A_{vMB} \ (-20 \log 1.414 \ dB)$$
$$= A_{vMB} \ (-3 \ dB)$$

(Fig. 2.5).

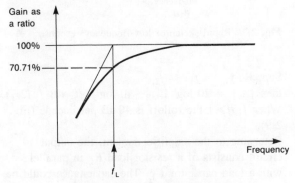

Fig. 2.5 Voltage gain of system at low frequencies

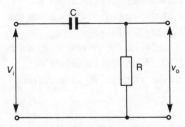

Fig. 2.6 General series CR network

For a CR network (Fig. 2.6)

$$V_o/V_i = \frac{R}{R - j1/WC} = \frac{1}{1 - j1/WCR}$$

therefore

$$V_o/V_i = \frac{1}{1 - j\dfrac{f_L}{f}}$$

where $f_L = \dfrac{1}{2\pi CR}$ as before

This gives an equation that describes the transfer function in terms of f_L, the low-frequency cut-off, and in f the signal frequency. For the amplifier, the low-frequency response of voltage gain is now given by:

$$A_v = \frac{A_{vMB}}{1 - j\dfrac{f_L}{f}} \qquad (2.2)$$

The magnitude of gain is:

$$|A_v| = \frac{A_{vMB}}{\sqrt{1 + \left(\dfrac{f_L}{f}\right)^2}} \qquad (2.3)$$

(see Appendix A for a proof of this result) and when f is equal to f_L we get

$$|A_v| = \frac{A_{vMB}}{\sqrt{2}} \qquad (2.4)$$

In other words, at f_L the gain is 3 dB down on the mid-band gain.

As the signal frequency is decreased from f_L the gain will fall by 20 dB per decade change in f.

Since $|A_v| = \dfrac{A_{vMB}}{\sqrt{1 + \left(\dfrac{f_L}{f}\right)^2}}$

$|A_v|$ in dB $= 20 \log |A_v|$

$$= 20 \log A_{vMB} - 20 \log \sqrt{\left[1 + \left(\dfrac{f_L}{f}\right)^2\right]} \ dB$$

when $f_L \gg 1$ $\quad A_v = 20 \log A_{vMB} - 20 \log \dfrac{f_L}{f} \quad dB \ (2.5)$

Therefore, when f is one-tenth of f_L, the voltage gain is 20 dB down. This allows the predicted frequency response of an a.c. coupled system to be rapidly sketched. For example, if an amplifier has a mid-band voltage gain of 100 (40 dB) and a low-frequency cut-off of 100 Hz, the sketch of the low-frequency response is as given in Fig. 2.7. The magnitude of gain at a signal frequency of 10 Hz is 20 dB, and at a frequency of 1 Hz it is down to 0 dB. However, this result only applies when just one CR network is present in the system, as in our example. Such a system is referred to as a first-order system, since the transfer function contains terms in ω only.

A two-pole transfer characteristic is given by:

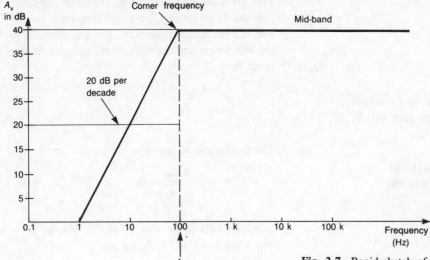

Fig. 2.7 Rapid sketch of low-frequency response

$$A_v = \frac{A_{vMB}}{\left[1 - j\dfrac{f_{L_1}}{f}\right] \cdot \left[1 - j\dfrac{f_{L_2}}{f}\right]} \qquad (2.6)$$

Where f_{L_1} is the first cut-off frequency and f_{L_2} the second. A response like this would imply another CR coupling network within the system (Fig. 2.8).

$$|A_v| = 20 \log A_{vMB} - 20 \log \sqrt{\left[1 + \left(\frac{f_{L_2}}{f}\right)^2\right]}$$

$$- 20 \log \sqrt{\left[1 + \left(\frac{f_{L_1}}{f}\right)^2\right]} \quad dB$$

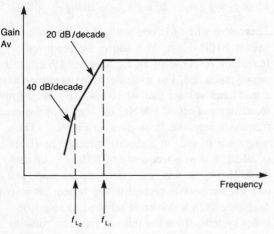

Fig. 2.8 A response with two cut-off frequencies
(second order)

Suppose $f_{L_1} = f_{L_2} = f_L$
then $|A_v| = 20 \log A_{vMB} - 40 \log f_L/f \quad dB \qquad (2.7)$
When $f_L/f \gg 1$ the rolloff is 40 dB per decade (Fig. 2.9).

Returning to the amplifier system, the output circuit consists of a resistor load R_L in parallel with a load capacitor C_L. The capacitance could be caused by a cable plus other stray circuit capacitance. This network affects the high-frequency response of the amplifier and causes the voltage gain to fall at higher frequencies.

For a parallel CR network the phasor diagram is as shown in Fig. 2.10. When the capacitor's reactance is equal to the value of R_L, the current

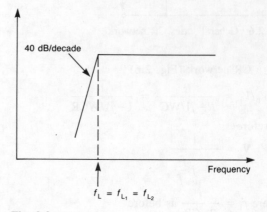

Fig. 2.9

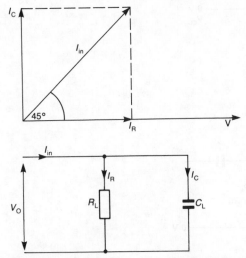

Fig. 2.10 Parallel CR network and phasor diagram at f_h

through the load resistor will be 0.7071 of the input current. Therefore the output voltage will be 3 dB down from its mid-band value. Another way of looking at this is to realize that at a very high frequency, C_L appears as almost a short-circuit and most of the signal current will then be shunted away from the load resistor R_L. The output voltage will then be almost zero. The voltage gain above the mid-band value can be represented by

$$A_v = \frac{A_{vMB}}{1 + jf/f_h}$$

where, in this case, $f_h = \dfrac{1}{2\pi C_L R_L}$

Therefore

$$|A_v| = \frac{A_{vMB}}{\sqrt{[1 + (f/f_h)^2]}}$$

f_h is called the upper cut-off frequency, and is the frequency where the gain is 3 dB down (Fig. 2.11).

As before, where there is only one parallel CR network, the gain rolls off at 20 dB per decade. For second-order systems the roll-off is 40 dB per decade, and a third-order system will roll off at 60 dB per decade change in frequency.

In most designs, particularly when a circuit has negative feedback, it is important to minimize the number of coupling and parallel CR networks so that gain roll-off is not too steep, and stability is maintained.

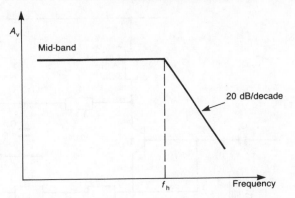

Fig. 2.11 First-order system high-frequency response

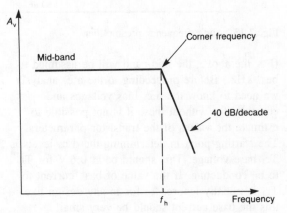

Fig. 2.12 Frequency response for a second-order system

2.2 Analysis using small signal equivalents

In Chapter 1, small signal models for the BJT and the FET were introduced and some simple single-stage amplifiers analysed. This work can now be extended to examine the performance of a two-stage audio-frequency amplifier, as shown in Fig. 2.13. This circuit consists of a common emitter input stage (Tr_1) and an emitter follower (Tr_2) with a d.c. loop to stabilize the operating point. The circuit is designed as an audio preamplifier, so the following features need to be predicted:

- Mid-band voltage gain.
- Input impedance at mid-band.
- Output impedance at mid-band.
- The bandwidth.

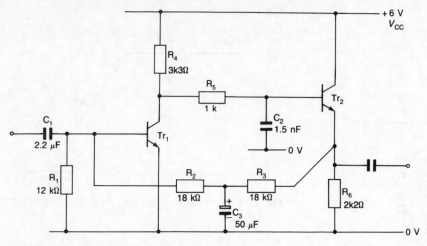

Fig. 2.13   Audio frequency preamplifier

(For the above, the mid-band will be assumed to be 1 kHz.) Before proceeding to the a.c. analysis we need to know the d.c. bias voltages and currents, for without these it is not possible to estimate the values of the transistor parameters. The starting point in determining the d.c. levels is Tr_1 base voltage. This should be at 0.6 V for Tr_1 to be conducting. If the value of base current to Tr_1 is initially ignored — for in any design like this the base current should be very small compared with bias currents — the current through R_3 and R_2 will be equal to that flowing in R_1. The bias current is normally arranged to be much greater than any base current, so that changes in h_{FE} of the transistors do not alter d.c. voltage bias levels.

Therefore $I_{R_2} = V_B/R_1 \approx 50\,\mu\text{A}$

$\therefore\ V_{E_2} = V_{B_1} + I_{R_2}(R_2+R_3)$ (2.8)

$\qquad \approx 2.4\,\text{V}$

$\therefore\ I_{C_2} = V_{E_2}/R_6 \approx 1.1\,\text{mA}$

Also, since $V_{BE_2} = 0.6\,\text{V}$ $V_{B_2} = 0.6+V_{E_2} \simeq 3\,\text{V}$. Any base current to Tr_2 will also be small, so V_{C_1} will be almost the same as V_{B_2}.

Therefore $I_{C_1} = \dfrac{V_{CC}-V_{C_1}}{R_4} = \dfrac{3}{3.3 \times 10^3}$

$\qquad = 0.91\,\text{mA}$

We can now predict the g_m value for the two transistors:

For Tr_1 $g_m \approx 40\times0.91\,\text{mS} = 36.4\,\text{mS}$

For Tr_2 $g_m \approx 40\times1.1\,\text{mS} = 44\,\text{mS}$

The a.c. analysis can now be made to determine the mid-band voltage gain. For this, an a.c. equivalent using either the h-parameter or the hybrid−pi models is used. These are shown in Fig. 2.14. In the h-parameter circuit, any effects of h_{re} and h_{oe} have been ignored.

In the amplifier, the first stage produces the voltage gain and the output stage, being an emitter follower, provides a low-output impedance. Since the output stage presents a small but finite load to the collector of Tr_1, we shall start by analysing the emitter follower. The equivalent circuit for this is shown in Fig. 2.15. Note how the collector is connected to a.c. ground but the emitter has R_6 and R_3 in parallel to ground. The effective emitter resistance, R_E is therefore about 2 kΩ. If we assume that the transistor's h_{fe} is about 200 (a typical value) then h_{ie_2} given by:

$$h_{ie_2} \approx \frac{h_{fe_2}}{g_{m_2}} = \frac{200}{44}\,\text{k}\Omega = 4.5\,\text{k}\Omega$$

The a.c. current flowing through R_E ($R_6//R_3$) is:

$$i_{b_2}+i_{b_2}h_{fe} = i_{b_2}(1+h_{fe})$$

$$\therefore\ A_v = V_{o_2}/V_{i_2} = \frac{i_{b_2}(1+h_{fe})R_E}{i_{b_2}h_{ie_2}+i_{b_2}(1+h_{fe})R_E}$$

$$= \frac{1+h_{fe}R_E}{h_{ie_2}+(1+h_{fe})R_E}$$

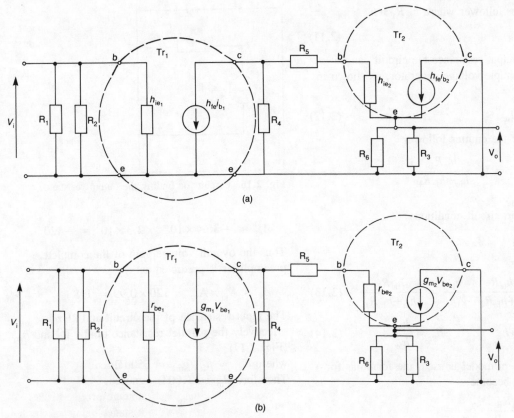

(a)

(b)

Fig. 2.14 A.c. equivalent circuits for the preamplifier.
(a) h-parameter; (b) hybrid−pi

In practical circuits $h_{fe} \gg 1$, therefore for any emitter follower

$$A_v = \frac{h_{fe}R_E}{h_{ie}+h_{fe}R_E} \qquad (2.9)$$

and where $h_{fe}R_E \gg h_{ie}$

$$A_v \approx 1$$

In this case we get, using 2.9

$$A_v = \frac{h_{fe_2}R_E}{h_{ie_2}+h_{fe_2}R_E} \qquad (2.10)$$

$$A_v = \frac{200 \times 2}{4.5+(200 \times 2)} = 0.988$$

The input resistance is given by

$$R_{i_2} = \frac{V_{i_2}}{i_{i_2}} = \frac{i_{b_2}(h_{ie_2}+h_{fe_2}R_E)}{i_{b_2}} = h_{ie_2}+h_{f3}R_E$$

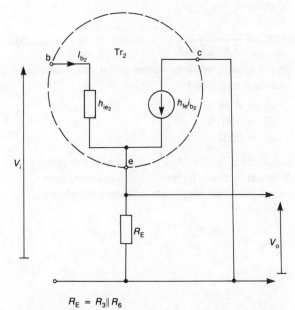

$$R_E = R_3 \| R_6$$

Fig. 2.15 The emitter follower a.c. equivalent circuit

For an emitter follower where $h_{fe}R_E \gg h_{ie}$

$$R_i = h_{fe}R_E \qquad (2.11)$$

To find the output resistance the circuit can be treated as a simple voltage generator, as shown in Fig. 2.16.

$$R_o = V_{oc}/i_{sc} \qquad (2.12)$$

In the case of the emitter follower

$$V_{oc} = A_vV_i = V_i \frac{h_{fe}R_E}{h_{ie}+h_{fe}R_E}$$

and $i_{sc} = i_b h_{fe}$
but under short-circuit conditions

$$i_b = V_i/h_{ie}$$

therefore

$$R_o = \frac{V_i h_{fe}R_E}{h_{ie}+h_{fe}R_E} \frac{h_{ie}}{V_i h_{fe}} = \frac{h_{ie}R_E}{h_{ie}+h_{fe}R_E} \qquad (2.13)$$

When $h_{fe}R_E \gg h_{ie}$ $\qquad R_o \approx \dfrac{h_{ie}}{h_{fe}} \qquad (2.14)$

If the hybrid–pi model is used, the formulas for A_v, R_i and R_o become

$$A_v = \frac{g_m R_E}{1+g_m R_E}$$

$$R_i = r_{be}+g_m r_{be}R_E$$

$$R_o = \frac{R_E}{1+g_m R_E} \qquad (2.15)$$

In the circuit, with the values given, the following results are obtained:

$$A_v = 0.99$$
$$R_i = 400 \text{ k}\Omega$$
$$R_o = 25 \text{ }\Omega$$

Since the effective input resistance of the emitter follower is much larger than the collector load (R_4) of the first stage, the voltage gain of this stage is:

$$A_{v_1} \approx \frac{-h_{fe}R_4}{h_{ie}}$$

or

$$A_{v_1} \approx -g_m R_4$$

therefore

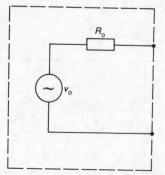

Fig. 2.16   Circuit for finding the output resistance

$$A_{v_1} \approx -36.4 \times 10^{-3} \times 3.3 \times 10^3 = -120$$

Thus the overall voltage gain of the complete preamplifier is predicted as:

$$A_v = A_{v_1} \times A_{v_2} = 120 \times 0.99 = 118$$

The input resistance of the circuit at 1 kHz is effectively the parallel resistance of R_1, R_2 and h_{ie_1} (Fig. 2.17)
where $h_{ie_1} \approx h_{fe_1}/g_{m1} = 5500 \text{ }\Omega$
Therefore $R_{in} \approx 3100 \text{ }\Omega$

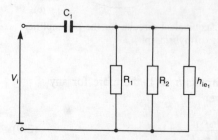

Fig. 2.17   Circuit for input resistance

To determine the low-frequency cut-off (f_L) it is necessary to study the circuit and determine those CR networks that will reduce gain at lower frequencies. These are: C_1 with R_{in}, and C_3 with R_2 in parallel with R_3. In the latter network, C_3 is used to decouple the negative feedback loop so that only d.c. feedback exists over the bandwidth of the amplifier, and since its value is 50 μF the time constant formed by it and the feedback resistors is much larger than that set by C_1 and R_{in}. C_1 and R_{in} are used in this design to set the lower cut-off point. The voltage gain will be 3 dB down when:

$$X_{C_1} = R_{in}$$

$$\therefore f_L = \frac{1}{2\pi C_1 R_{in}}$$

$$\therefore f_L = 23\,Hz$$

The high-frequency cut-off point is set by the shunt capacitor C_2. If the equivalent circuit at Tr_1 output is redrawn as in Fig. 2.18, where the current generator is converted into an equivalent voltage generator, we get a circuit with two resistors (R_4 and R_5) in series with the capacitor C_2. When the reactance of C_2 is equal to the series value (the sum) of R_4 and R_5, the voltage gain will be 3 dB down on its mid-band value.

$$f_h = \frac{1}{2\pi C_2 (R_4 + R_5)} \quad \therefore f_h = 30\,kHz$$

For the whole circuit we get the following predicted values of performance at a frequency of 1 kHz:

$$A_v \approx 41.4\,dB$$
$$f_L \approx 23\,Hz$$
$$f_h \approx 30\,kHz$$
$$B_W \approx 30\,kHz$$
$$R_o \approx 25\,\Omega$$

This completes the analysis of the example circuit;

a useful exercise is for the reader to breadboard the circuit and verify the predicted performance.

An important circuit, widely used in linear systems and therefore of interest in all branches of electronics, is the *differential amplifier*. This circuit will now be analysed using an appropriate model. The differential circuit forms the input stage for op-amps, comparators and line receivers, and is used because its balanced nature means that common-mode signals are rejected. A common-mode signal to a differential circuit is one that is applied in phase equally to both inputs. In the basic circuit shown in Fig. 2.19, a common-mode signal would mean that V_1 is equal to V_2 in all respects.

In the circuit, a small differential signal $(V_1 - V_2)$ is amplified by the two transistors and gives an output signal between the two collectors of the two transistors.

An equivalent circuit, valid at 1 kHz for small signals and using the hybrid−pi model is shown in Fig. 2.20. The current flowing through R_E will be the sum of the two current generators:

$$i_e = g_m (V_{be_1} + V_{be_2})$$
$$V_1 = V_{be_1} + g_m R_E (V_{be_1} + V_{be_2}) \tag{2.16}$$

and

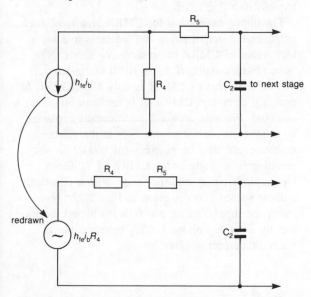

Fig. 2.18 Output circuit at Tr_1 collector

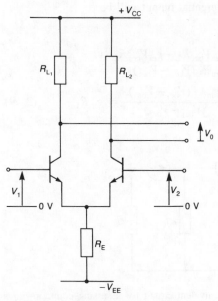

Fig. 2.19 Basic differential amplifier

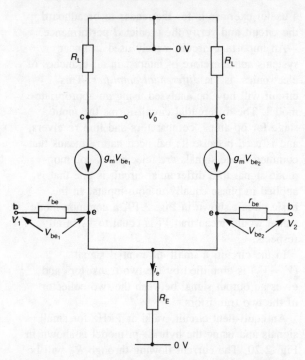

Fig. 2.20 A.c. equivalent for the differential amplifier

$$V_2 = V_{be2} + g_m R_E (V_{be1} + V_{be2}) \quad (2.17)$$

The differential input is $V_D = V_1 - V_2$
therefore $V_D = V_{be1} - V_{be2}$ $\quad (2.18)$
and the differential output will be:

$$
\begin{aligned}
V_{oD} &= V_a - V_b \\
&= g_m V_{be1} R_L - g_m V_{be2} R_L \\
&= g_m R_L (V_{be1} - V_{be2})
\end{aligned}
$$

$$\therefore A_{vD} = \frac{g_m R_L (V_{be1} - V_{be2})}{(V_{be1} - V_{be2})} = g_m R_L \quad (2.19)$$

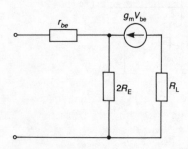

Fig. 2.21 Equivalent circuit for assessing common-mode gain

The output from one collector only, referred to as a single-ended output, will be half that of the differential output.

Single-ended output voltage gain $= \frac{1}{2} g_m R_L$ (2.20)

Since the circuit is symmetrical, the common-mode voltage gain for one output can be assessed by considering one side of the circuit; in this case the emitter resistance must be represented by $2R_E$ (Fig. 2.21).

For common-mode signals $V_1 = V_2 = V$

$$A_{vc} = \frac{V_{o1}}{V_o} = \frac{g_m V_{be} R_L}{V_{be} + g_m V_{be} 2R_E} \quad (2.21)$$

therefore $A_{vc} = R_L / 2R_E$ (2.22)

The ability to reject common-mode signals and amplify tiny differential signals is called common-mode rejection ratio (CMRR), and is the ratio of differential gain to common-mode gain.

$$CMRR = \frac{A_{vd}}{A_{vcm}} \quad (2.23)$$

For single-ended output

$$CMRR = \frac{1}{2} \frac{g_m R_L}{R_L / 2R_E} = g_m R_E \quad (2.24)$$

Since CMRR is normally large, it is usual to express its value in dB.

The above expression for CMRR is derived for single-ended output mode and indicates that for a high value of CMRR the resistor R_E needs to be large. For example, if R_E is 10 kΩ and gm is 40 mS, the value of CMRR is only 400 (52 dB). In practical circuits a CMRR of better than 60 dB is essential. For this reason R_E is normally replaced by a constant current source, where the effective emitter could then be in excess of 100 kΩ, resulting in a single-ended CMRR of 72 dB. A typical differential amplifier stage with a constant current source (Tr_2) is given in Fig. 2.22. A reference supply, using two forward-biased diodes, sets up a stable voltage for Tr_2 base and the collector current is given by

$$I_{C2} \simeq \frac{V_{BE2}}{R_3}$$

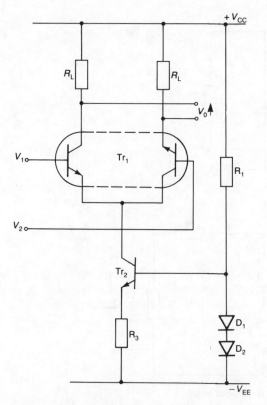

Fig. 2.22 The differential stage with a constant current source

The effective resistance in the emitters of the differential pair is now the output resistance of Tr_2, which can be very high.

In the true differential output mode, assuming both transistors Tr_{1a} and Tr_{1b} and load resistors R_L are perfectly matched and identical, the CMRR should approach infinity. In practice, of course, there will be some mismatch in these components, resulting in a typical CMRR of about 90 dB. In the differential output mode the common-mode voltage gain will be given by:

$$A_{vc} = \frac{g_{m_1} V_{be_1} R_{L_1}}{V_{be_1}(1+g_{m_1}2R_E)} - \frac{g_{m_2} V_{be_2} R_{L_2}}{V_{be_2}(1+g_{m_2}2R_E)}$$

$$= \frac{g_{m_1} R_{L_1}}{1+g_{m_1}2R_E} - \frac{g_{m_2} R_{L_2}}{1+g_{m_2}2R_E}$$

since $g_m 2R_E \gg 1$

$$A_{vc} \approx \frac{R_{L_1}}{2R_E} - \frac{R_{L_2}}{2R_E} = \frac{\Delta R_L}{2R_E} \qquad (2.25)$$

where ΔR_L is the mismatch between the two load resistors. Hence CMRR in differential output mode is:

$$CMRR \approx \frac{2g_m R_E R_L'}{\Delta R_L} \qquad (2.26)$$

Suppose the transistors are run at collector currents of 0.1 mA, and that R_L is 10 kΩ, R_E is 50 kΩ and ΔR_L is 1 per cent; then

$$CMRR = \frac{2 \times 4 \times 10^{-3} \times 10^4 \times 50 \times 10^3}{100} = 92 \, dB$$

The BJT and FET at higher frequencies

So far we have considered the analysis of linear circuits at the low frequency of 1 kHz only, and therefore before we proceed to discuss the important aspects of negative feedback we need to look at the effects of device parameters on the higher-frequency performance of circuits. For a BJT, in common emitter mode, the result of increasing the signal frequency is to cause a fall in current gain, and consequently a reduction in voltage and power gain. It has already been explained in Chapter 1 that this high-frequency roll-off is defined by f_T (the transision frequency) and h_{feo} (the current gain at low frequencies) where

$$f_T = h_{feo} \cdot f_{hfe}$$

Another way to approach the analysis of an amplifier at higher frequency is to use the hybrid–pi equivalent (Fig. 2.23). This model has the transistor capacitance included together with the base spreading resistance $r_{bb'}$, and allows the high-frequency cut-off point for a common emitter amplifier to be reasonably predicted. The analysis that follows assumes that R_L is a relatively low resistance, not more than a few kΩ, and that any capacitance in parallel with R_L, including C_{ce}, is very small. This would normally be the case if high-frequency performance is required. It is the feedback capacitor connected between the collector and the internal base b′ that is most significant in causing loss of voltage gain at higher frequencies, because it is amplified by transistor action and appears in parallel with $C_{b'c}$ to give a much increased input capacitance. This 'amplification' of feedback capacitance is known as the Miller effect,

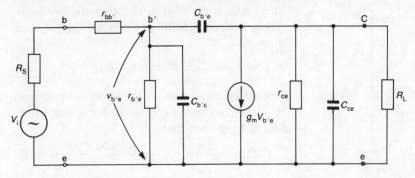

Fig. 2.23 Using the hybrid–pi equivalent

and occurs in all inverting amplifiers (see Appendix B for an explanation).

In this way, the effective input capacitance seen across the base emitter junction is given by:

$$C_{in} = C_{b'e} + C_{b'c}(1 + g_m R_L) \qquad (2.27)$$

Typical values for $C_{b'e}$ and $C_{b'c}$ are 20 pF and 1.5 pF respectively, which might seem relatively small, but if the gain ($g_m R_L$) is about 50, the effective input capacitance becomes:

$$C_{in} = 20 + 1.5\,(1 + 50)\,\text{pF}$$
$$= 96.5\,\text{pF}$$

This capacitance forms a low-pass filter with the input resistance (Fig. 2.24), which reduces the signal reaching the transistor as the frequency is increased. The input resistance is given by:

$$R_{in} = (R_s + r_{bb'})//r_{b'e} \qquad (2.28)$$

When the reactance of C_{in} is equal to R_{in}, the voltage gain will be 3 dB down on its mid-band value.

$$f_h = \frac{1}{2\pi C_{in} R_{in}}$$

The same limitation on high-frequency performance occurs with a FET in common source, for in the FET there is a feedback capacitance between drain and gate (C_{gd}) (Fig. 2.25). For a FET:

$$C_{in} = C_{gs} + C_{gd}(1 + y_{fs} R_L) \qquad (2.29)$$

and $f_L = \dfrac{1}{2\pi C_{in} R_{in}}$.

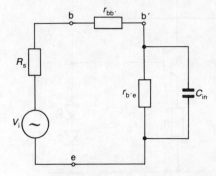

Actual input circuit

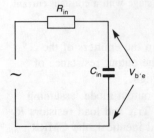

Equivalent input circuit

Fig. 2.24 The low-pass filter at the transistor's input

where R_{in} is the impedance of the signal source as indicated in Fig. 2.25.

Where high voltage gain and good high-frequency performance is necessary, the cascode connection can be used to reduce the effect of feedback capacitance. This is at the expense of using two stages in the amplifier. A typical dual-FET cascode circuit is shown in Fig. 2.25. The first stage is in common source, but since its drain load is the input resistance of the common-gate second stage, the effective first stage gain is unity.

$$A_{v2} = y_{fs}R_L$$

The feed back capacitance between the F_2 drain and F_1 gate can be arranged to be as low as 0.1 pF, which gives the circuit a very high upper cut-off frequency.

A very similar cascode circuit can be used with two transistors.

2.3 Negative feedback

An amplifier or system without any feedback is said to be operating under open-loop conditions. This is because feedback requires a portion of the output signal to be connected and mixed with the input. A feedback loop results, as shown in Fig. 2.28. One of the important results of correctly applied negative feedback is that an accurately defined value of gain is achieved. Other features are that values of input impedance, output impedance and bandwidth can be modified and improved. An open-loop amplifier gives a relatively ill-defined overall value for gain. For example, the voltage gain of a two-stage amplifier without negative feedback might be predicted by analysis to be in the region of 600, but if several versions of the amplifier are built gain values ranging from 400 up to 800 could easily result. These open-loop variations are caused mainly by differences in active component parameters, which can have a wide tolerance. When negative feedback is applied the voltage gain will be reduced, but variations in gain between several versions of the amplifier can be made very small. By using negative feedback it becomes possible to make large numbers of a particular amplifier design, *with all of them having almost the same characteristics*.

The block diagram of an amplifier with negative feedback is given in Fig. 2.29. In this circuit an amplifier with open-loop voltage gain A_{vol} has a portion of its output fed back in series with the input, so that the effective input to the amplifier's terminals is a reduced version of V_i. Note that the amplifier, in this case, has to be a non-inverting type so that V_o is in phase with V_i. The fractional

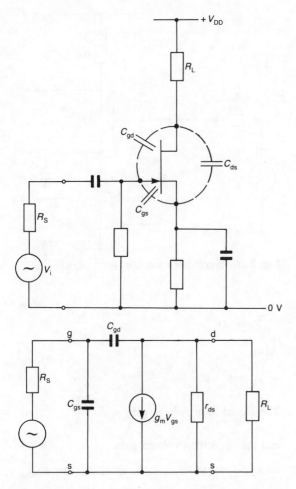

Fig. 2.25 A.c. equivalent at higher frequency for an FET

$$A_{v1} = y_{fs1} R_{in2}$$

But

$$R_{in2} = \frac{i_s}{V_{gs}} = \frac{1}{y_{fs2}}$$

If both FETs are identical

$$A_{v1} \approx 1$$

Therefore $C_{in} = C_{gs} + 2C_{gd}$ (2.30)

which means that the effective input capacitance can be as low as 20 pF.

The voltage gain of the cascode circuit is given by the second stage and is:

gain of the feedback network, normally a passive network of resistors, is called β. At mid-band frequencies where phase shifts are negligible

---

Example

For the circuit in Fig. 2.26, the transistor has the following values:

$r_{bb'}$ 95 Ω
$r_{b'e}$ 2 000 Ω
r_{ce} 40 kΩ
$r_{b'c}$ 1.5 MΩ
$C_{b'e}$ 22 pF
$C_{b'c}$ 1.2 pF

Determine the mid-band voltage gain and the upper cut-off frequency.

Solution

In the analysis both r_{ce} and $r_{b'c}$ can be ignored, since their effect is small when compared with other circuit and parameter values.

In the circuit the d.c. collector current is set by R_2

$$I_C \approx I_E = \frac{V_{EE} - V_{BE}}{R_2}$$

therefore $I_C \approx \dfrac{10 - 0.6}{4.7 \times 10^3} = 2$ mA

Therefore the *gm* for the transistor is about 80 mS.

Mid-band voltage gain is given by:

$$A_{vMB} = g_m R_L \frac{r_{b'e}}{r_{bb'} + r_{b'e} + R_S} = 112$$

Now we proceed to determine the value of the effective input capacitance:

$$C_{in} = C_{b'e} + C_{b'c}(1 + g_m R_L)$$
$$\therefore C_{in} = 22 + 1.2(121)\,\text{pF} = 167.2\,\text{pF}$$

The input resistance is:

$$R_{in} = \frac{(R_S + r_{bb'})\,r_{b'e}}{R_S + r_{bb'} + r_{b'e}} = 135\,\Omega$$

$$\therefore f_h = \frac{1}{2\pi C_{in} R_{in}} = \frac{1}{2\pi \times 167.2 \times 10^{-12} \times 135}$$

$$= 7\,\text{MHz}$$

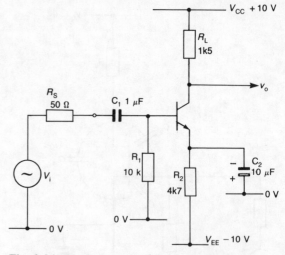

Fig. 2.26 Single-stage amplifier for analysis

$$V_f = \beta V_o$$

Also

$$V_i = V_s + V_f$$

The closed loop voltage gain $A_{vcl} = \dfrac{V_o}{V_i}$

and the open loop voltage gain

$$A_{vol} = V_o/V_s \qquad\qquad \therefore V_o = A_{vol}V_s$$

therefore $A_{vcl} = \dfrac{A_{vol}V_s}{V_s + V_f} = \dfrac{A_{vol}V_s}{V_s(1 + A_{vol}\beta)}$

therefore
$$\boxed{A_{vcl} = \frac{A_{vol}}{1 + A_{vol}\beta}} \qquad (2.31)$$

The product of open-loop gain and β is called the *loop gain*, and the aim in any design should be to make the loop gain much larger than unity. When $A_{vol}\beta \gg 1$

$$A_{vcl} \approx \frac{1}{\beta} \qquad\qquad (2.32)$$

This important result means that the gain with negative feedback is then solely dependent on the components within the feedback loop. Suppose the

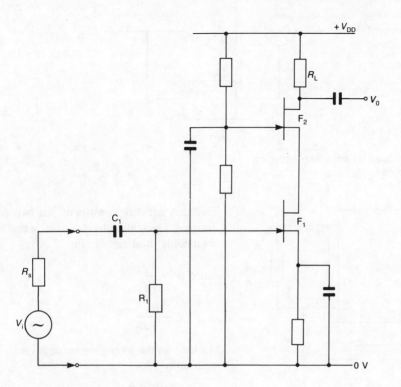

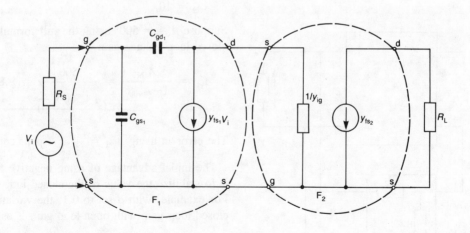

Fig. 2.27 An FET cascode amplifier

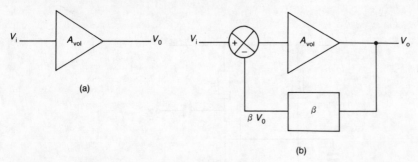

Fig. 2.28 Amplifier systems. (a) open-loop amplifier; (b) negative feedback applied

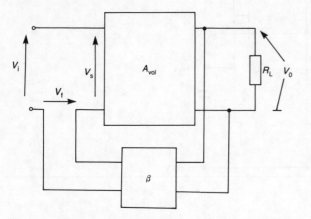

Fig. 2.29 Block diagram of negative-feedback amplifier

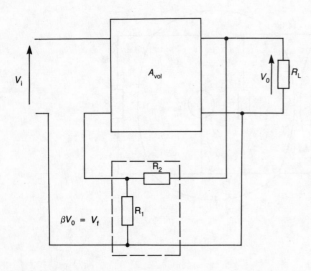

Fig. 2.30 The feedback fraction set by two resistors

feedback network consists of just two resistors forming a potential divider (this is the most commonly used circuit; Fig. 2.30):

since $\beta = \dfrac{V_f}{V_0}$

$$\beta = \frac{R_1}{R_1 + R_2} \qquad (2.33)$$

As long as the loop gain remains much greater than unity

$$A_{vcl} = \frac{R_1 + R_2}{R_1} = 1 + \frac{R_2}{R_1}$$

If, for example, R_1 is $1\,\mathrm{k\Omega}$ and R_2 is $9\,\mathrm{k\Omega}$

$$A_{vcl} = 10$$

Suppose $A_{vol} = 500$; using the full formula for closed-loop voltage gain

$$A_{vcl} = \frac{A_{vol}}{1 + A_{vol}\beta} = \frac{500}{1 + 500 \times \dfrac{1}{10}} = 9.8$$

The error in using $A_{vcl} = \dfrac{1}{\beta}$ is 2 per cent.

The initial advantage of using negative feedback is to stabilize the value of the closed-loop gain. For example, with β set to 0.1, the variation in closed-loop gain with open-loop gain is as follows:

A_{vol}	A_{vcl}
500	9.8
1000	9.9
2000	9.95

Very large changes in open-loop gain result in only fractional changes in closed-loop gain. Negative feedback is therefore widely used, since it results in several important improvements and advantages:

- The closed-loop gain can be closely and accurately defined, and will be a stable value independent of changes caused by variations in component parameters, ageing of components, component replacement and changes due to temperature and power supply variations.
- The frequency response is improved and the bandwidth increased.
- The way in which the feedback signal is derived from the output and applied to the input can be used to modify the input and output impedances of the circuit.
- Internally generated noise and non-linear distortion will be reduced.

The first point on gain stability has already been covered. The improvement in frequency response and the increased bandwidth occurs because variations in open-loop gain with frequency result in much smaller changes in closed-loop gain. This is illustrated in Fig. 2.31, and a proof of this is as follows:

The open loop voltage gain can be represented by the equation

$$A_{vol} = \frac{A_{vol(MB)}}{1 + jf/f_h}$$

where $A_{vol(MB)}$ is the mid-band open-loop gain and f_h is the upper cut-off frequency.

$$\text{Therefore } A_{vcl} = \frac{\dfrac{A_{vol(MB)}}{1 + jf/f_h}}{1 + \dfrac{A_{vol(MB)}\beta}{1 + jf/f_h}}$$

$$= \frac{A_{vol(MB)}}{1 + A_{vol(MB)}\beta + jf/f_h}$$

By dividing by $[1 + A_{vol(MB)}\beta]$ we get

$$A_{vcl} = \frac{A_{vcl(MB)}}{1 + jf/f_h[1 + A_{vol(MB)}]}$$

$$\therefore A_{vcl} = \frac{A_{vcl(MB)}}{1 + jf/f_{hc}}$$

Where f_{hc} is the upper cut-off frequency with negative feedback.

$$f_{hc} = f_h[1 + A_{vol(MB)}\beta] \tag{2.34}$$

In other words, the bandwidth with negative feedback is increased by a factor of $[1 + A_{vol(MB)}\beta]$.

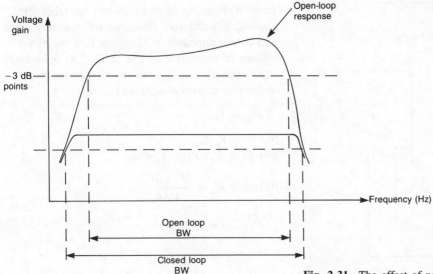

Fig. 2.31 The effect of negative feedback on frequency response

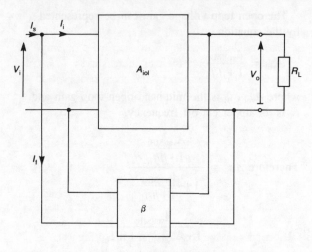

Parallel–voltage feedback

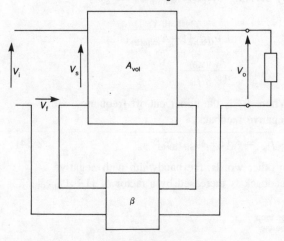

Series–current feedback

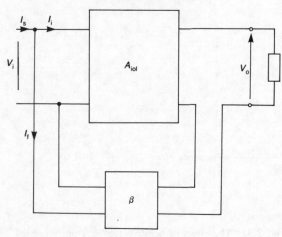

Parallel–current feedback

Another, and simpler, way of looking at this effect is to consider that the gain bandwidth product for a small signal amplifier is almost constant. Therefore

$$A_{vol}(f_h - f_L) = A_{vcl}(f_{hc} - f_{Lc})$$

However, since $A_{vcl} = \dfrac{A_{vol}}{1 + A_{vol}\beta}$

$$(f_h - f_L) = \dfrac{(f_{hc} - f_{LC})}{(1 + A_{vol}\beta)}$$

$$\therefore f_{hc} = f_h(1 + A_{vol}\beta)$$

and $f_{LC} = \dfrac{f_L}{(1 + A_{vol}\beta)}$ \hfill (2.35)

The feedback signal can be derived from the output as either a voltage or as a current (Fig. 2.32) and applied to the input in parallel or in series with the input signal. Thus four possible types of feedback configurations exist.

The block diagram previously given for the analysis of feedback (Fig. 2.28) is for voltage-derived series-applied negative feedback. This is often simply referred to as voltage–series feedback. The other possibilities are:

> parallel–voltage
> series–current
> parallel–current (Fig. 2.32).

Each of these combinations, when the feedback is applied, has different effects on the resulting input and output impedances. Consider first the series–voltage configuration of Fig. 2.33. The open-loop input resistance is R_{in}, but the input resistance under closed loop conditions is:

$$R'_{in} = V_i / i_1$$

but $i_1 = V_s / R_{in}$
and $V_i = V_s + V_f = V_s + \beta V_o$

therefore $R'_{in} = \dfrac{V_s + \beta V_o}{V_s / R_{in}}$

$$\therefore R'_{in} = R_{in}(1 + A_{vol}\beta) \hfill (2.36)$$

Fig. 2.32   Other feedback configurations

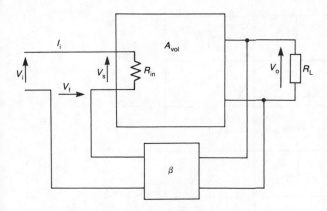

Fig. 2.33 Circuit for determining closed-loop input resistance (series–voltage feedback)

This shows that the input resistance with this type of feedback is increased from the open-loop value by a factor $(1+A_{vol}\beta)$.

To find the closed-loop output impedance the input V_i is assumed to be a short-circuit, the load resistance is removed and an imaginary voltage V is placed across the output terminals, as in Fig. 2.34.

Then $R_o' = V/i$ and $i = \dfrac{V - A_o V_s}{R_o}$

but $V_s = -V_f = -\beta V$

therefore $i = \dfrac{V(1+A_{vol}\beta)}{R_0}$ $\therefore R_o' = \dfrac{R_o}{1+A_{vol}\beta}$

$$(2.37)$$

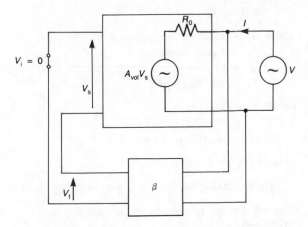

Fig. 2.34 Determining the effect of feedback on closed-loop output impedance

The output resistance is the original open-loop output resistance divided by $(1+A_{vol}\beta)$.

The input and output impedances of a negative-feedback amplifier are either increased by $(1+A_{vol}\beta)$ or decreased by the reciprocal of $(1+A_{vol}\beta)$, depending upon the type of feedback employed.

Feedback type	Input impedance	Output impedance
series–voltage	increased	decreased
parallel–voltage	decreased	decreased
series–current	increased	increased
parallel–current	decreased	increased

Although negative feedback produces highly desirable features, such as a fixed stable value of gain and improved frequency response, there is always a practical limit to the amount of loop gain $(A_{vol}\beta)$ which may be applied in any particular circuit. There will be inevitable phase shifts within the loop, which at some frequency — either at the low-frequency or high-frequency end of the band — add up to 180°. The feedback then changes from negative to positive.

For positive feedback:

$$A_{vcl} = \frac{A_{vol}}{1 - A_{vol}\beta} \qquad (2.38)$$

It can be seen from the formula that if the loop gain equals unity the amplifier is certain to oscillate, since the closed-loop gain is infinite.

In any amplifier the design should ensure that the number of capacitive coupling and decoupling networks is reduced to a minimum and, wherever possible, to use direct coupling, even where this requires more care in the design of the d.c. bias circuit. More than two CR coupling or decoupling networks within the loop will cause low-frequency instability, and if three are used the amplifier is certain to oscillate. There are two methods for investigating the stability of negative-feedback amplifiers; these are to use a Bode plot or a Nyquist diagram.

Bode plot
This plot or diagram is a graphical method for showing how the gain and phase shifts of an

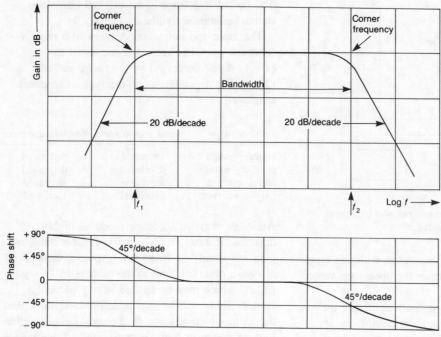

Fig. 2.35 Bode plot for a first-order a.c. coupled amplifier

amplifier vary with frequency. The magnitude of the gain and the amount of phase shift introduced are both plotted against the log of the signal frequency. A typical plot for an a.c. coupled amplifier is shown in Fig. 2.35. At low frequencies, because of the coupling capacitors, the gain is very low and the phase angle of the output relative to the input is leading by 90°. As the signal frequency is increased, the magnitude rises by 20 dB/decade and the phase angle changes by 45°/decade until f_1 is reached. At f_1, which is referred to as the 'corner frequency' or 'low-frequency cut-off point', the magnitude of the gain is $1/\sqrt{2}$, or 3 dB less than its mid-band value, and the phase lead has fallen to 45°. Over the useful frequency range, or bandwidth, the gain and the phase shift of the amplifier remain fairly constant. At f_2, the upper cut-off frequency, the gain is 3 dB down and the phase shift lags by 45°. For this amplifier the gain then falls by 20 dB/decade and the phase angle between output and input increases by −45°/decade to a maximum of −90°. The fall-off in gain and the resulting phase lag are caused by circuit and stray capacitances in parallel

with load resistors. An amplifier with a Bode plot such as this is said to be a first-order system, since the transfer characteristic contains only terms in ω ($\omega = 2\pi f$). The transfer function is said to be 'single-pole'.

A single-pole transfer function is of the form

$$A = \frac{A_0}{1 + jf/f_h}$$

where A = value of the gain at f
 f = signal frequency
 f_h = f_2
 A_0 = mid-band gain

$|A|\,\text{dB} = 20 \log |A|$

$= 20 \log A_0 - 20 \log \sqrt{[1 + f/f_h)^2]}$

Thus if $f/f_h \gg 1$

$|A|\,\text{dB} = 20 \log |A|\,\text{dB} = 20 \log A_0 - 20 \log f/f_h$

showing that the magnitude of the gain falls by 20 dB/decade.

More commonly, at high frequencies the transfer characteristic contains ω^2 or ω^3 terms giving second-order (two-pole transfer function) and third-order (three-pole transfer function) systems.

A two-pole transfer function is represented by

$$A = \frac{A_0}{[1+j(f/f_{h1})]\cdot[1+j(f/f_{h2})]}$$

$$|A| \ \text{dB} = 20 \log A_0 - 20 \log \sqrt{[1+(f/f_{h1})^2]}$$

$$-20 \log \sqrt{[1+(f/f_{h2})^2]}$$

If $f_{h1}=f_{h2}$, then for frequencies $f/f_{h2} \gg 1$, there is a fall-off in gain of 40 dB/decade.

In general, for the three types of system:

System	Gain roll-off	Phase shift
1st order	20 dB/decade	$-45°$/decade
2nd order	40 dB/decade	$-90°$/decade
3rd order	60 dB/decade	$-135°$/decade

Examples of Bode plots for the second and third order systems are shown in Figs 2.36 and 2.37.

The usefulness of Bode plots is in the study of the stability of amplifiers with negative feedback. For an amplifier with negative feedback the closed-loop gain is given by

$$A_{CL} = \frac{A_{OL}}{1+A_{OL}\beta}$$

where A_{OL} = open loop gain (assumed +ve)
β = fraction gain of the feedback network.

The product $A_{OL}\beta$ is called the loop gain, and while this is positive we get negative feedback; in other words, the gain of the amplifier system is reduced and stabilized.

Imagine, though, at some high frequency, that the phase shift approaches 180° while the loop gain is still above unity. If this happens the signal fed back will be in phase with the input, and the overall feedback will be positive, giving instability and possibly oscillations. By plotting the Bode diagram for the open-loop gain of the amplifier — that is, the gain before feedback is connected — the amount of negative feedback that can be applied and give a stable system can be evaluated. For example, in Fig. 2.38 the maximum feedback that can be applied $(1+A_{OL}\beta)$ is 34 dB. In practice it would not be possible to apply 34 dB, since it

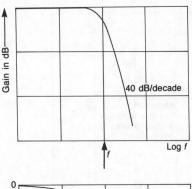

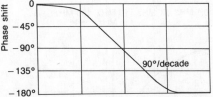

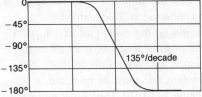

Fig. 2.36 Bode plot for second-order system

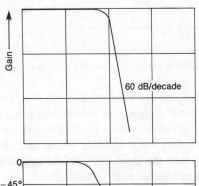

Fig. 2.37 Bode plot for third-order system

would be inevitable that the 180° phase shift would be exceeded by minor deviations in the amplifier or external circuit wiring. Thus the limiting phase has to be chosen as less than 180° by some definite margin to give a stable system. A satisfactory circuit should have a minimum phase margin of 45°; this will give less than 3 dB peaking. This means that only 20 dB of feedback can be safely applied to this amplifier.

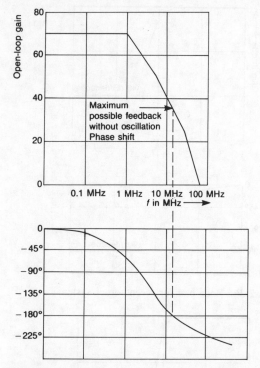

Fig. 2.38 Bode plot showing allowable feedback

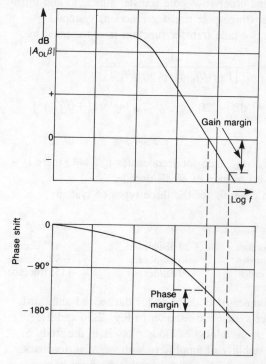

Fig. 2.39 Definition of gain margin and phase margin

An alternative approach in stability investigations is to plot the Bode diagram for the loop gain $A_{OL}\beta$ (Fig. 2.39). If it can be shown that the magnitude of $A_{OL}\beta$ is less than unity when the phase shift of $A_{OL}\beta$ is 180°, then the amplifier with the negative-feedback loop connected will be stable.

The *gain margin* on the Bode plot of $|A_{OL}\beta|$ is the value of the magnitude of $A_{OL}\beta$ in dB at the frequency at which the phase shift is 180°. To give a stable system this must be negative, a typical value being -10 dB. The *phase margin* in degrees is the difference between 180° and the phase shift of $A_{OL}\beta$ when the magnitude of $A_{OL}\beta$ is unity. This should be at least 45°, as stated previously. The meaning of these margins is illustrated in Fig. 2.39.

Suppose the Bode plot of an amplifier shows possible instability; there are then several methods to improve stability. These are basically shaping the response of the open-loop characteristics by inserting a lag, lead, or both, to give a break at a much lower frequency or to modify the feedback network to include reactive elements.

Nyquist diagram
To obtain stability in a negative-feedback amplifier (or control system) the phase shifts occurring in the amplifier must not approach 180° while the loop gain $A_o\beta$ is greater than unity. If this does occur, the feedback becomes positive and the amplifier will oscillate. A Nyquist diagram is one method of investigating the stability of negative-feedback systems by plotting the magnitude and phase of the loop gain on a graph with polar coordinates. This can be achieved by breaking the feedback loop, injecting a signal at the input, and then measuring the amplitude and phase angle of the feedback signal v_f over the whole frequency range.

$$\text{Loop gain } A_o\beta = \frac{v_f}{v_s} \angle \phi$$

A typical plot for an a.c. coupled amplifier is shown in Fig. 2.40.

Nyquist's stability criterion states that a negative-feedback system will be conditionally stable if the plot of the loop gain does not enclose

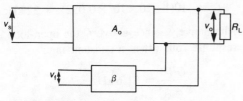

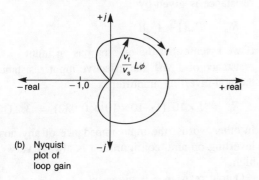

(a) Measurement of $A_o\beta$ (loop gain)

(b) Nyquist plot of loop gain

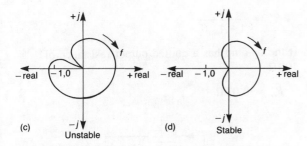

(c) Unstable   (d) Stable

Fig. 2.40 Nyquist plot for a.c. coupled amplifier

the point $(-1, 0)$ while the frequency is increasing.

Noise and distortion in feedback systems

Amplifiers cannot be perfect devices and some additional noise and distortion will always be introduced. In the open-loop amplifier, if this is contained in the later stages, then application of negative feedback will reduce the noise and distortion present in the output signal.

Let an open-loop amplifier have a generator D assumed to be connected to its output, as in Fig. 2.41, and assume that V_i is zero. When a feedback network is connected, the signal fed back will be opposing the noise and distortion. Let the new value of distortion with feedback be D′. There are now two components in the output:

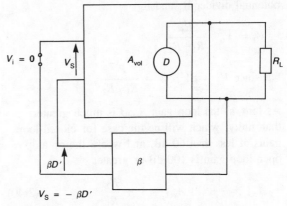

$$V_s = -\beta D'$$

Fig. 2.41 The reduction of internally generated distortion

$$D - A_{vol}\beta D' = D'$$
therefore $\quad D'(1 + A_{vol}\beta) = D$

therefore $\quad D' = \dfrac{D}{1 + A_{vol}\beta}$ (2.39)

Thus the distortion with negative feedback is reduced.

An analysis of some amplifier circuits using negative feedback techniques now follows.

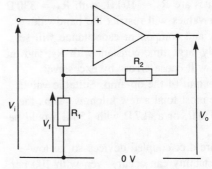

Fig. 2.42 The non-inverting amplifier
$A_{vcl} = 1 + R_2/R_1$

A non-inverting amplifier using an op-amp (Fig. 2.42)

This is a classic connection for an op-amp that gives

- A voltage gain of $A_{vcl} = 1 + \dfrac{R_2}{R_1}$
- A very high input impedance
- A low output impedance.

The circuit uses series—voltage negative via the

potential divider R_1 and R_2

$$V_f = V_o \cdot \frac{R_1}{R_1+R_2}$$

but since $V_f = \beta V_o$ $\beta = \dfrac{R_1}{R_1+R_2}$

As long as the loop gain $A_{vol}\beta$ is much greater than unity, which will be the case for closed-loop gains of less than 60 dB, and where the op-amp open-loop gain is 100 dB or greater

$$A_{vcl} \approx \frac{1}{\beta} \quad \therefore A_{vcl} = 1 + \frac{R_2}{R_1} \qquad (2.40)$$

Suppose a voltage gain of 30 dB is required: 30 dB as a ratio is 31.6, therefore $R_2 = 30.6\,R_1$. All that is necessary is for the designer to select two resistors from the preferred values that fit this ratio. Extremes of values should, however, be avoided. For example:

- $R_2 = 1\,M\Omega$ with $R_1 = 33\,k\Omega$ are values that are too high, and
- $R_2 = 100\,\Omega$ with $R_1 = 3.3\,\Omega$ are values that are too low.

The best values are $R_2 = 10\,k\Omega$, with $R_2 = 330\,\Omega$.

The higher values will restrict the bandwidth because stray and component capacitance will set up a relatively large time constant with R_2, and the lower values will cause errors by excessively loading the output of the op-amp. Suitable values should at the most total a few kilohms. Thus the $10\,k\Omega$ with $330\,\Omega$, or a 4k7 Ω with $150\,\Omega$ would be fine.

Op-amps are d.c. coupled devices so no low-frequency instability can occur, even with 100 per cent feedback where the loop gain is unity. Compensated op-amps are fitted with an internal capacitor that sets the high-frequency cut-off point to a value that ensures a 20 dB roll-off. Therefore it is safe, with these types, to apply negative feedback up to 100 per cent without high-frequency instability or oscillations being set up. Suppose an op-amp has a high-frequency cut-off of 10 Hz, typical for a general purpose op-amp: then

$$f_{hc} = f_h(1+A_{vol}\beta)$$

If $A_{vol} = 1\,000\,000$

$$f_{hc} = 10(1+10\times10^4\times0.032) \approx 32\,kHz$$

Alternatively, since above f_h the open-loop response rolls off at a constant rate:

$$f_{hc} \approx \frac{GBP}{A_{vcl}} = 31.6\,kHz$$

For the circuit under discussion, the input resistance is given by

$$R'_{in} = R_{in}(1+A_{vol}\beta)$$

If we assume that the op-amp has an input resistance of $1\,M\Omega$, the effective input resistance of the non-inverting amplifier is

$$R'_{in} = 1\times10^6(1+10\times10^4\times0.032) \approx 3.2\,G\Omega$$

In other words, the input impedance of any non-inverting op-amp configuration is always very high.

Output resistance is given by

$$R'_o = \frac{R_o}{1+A_{vol}\beta}$$

If the op-amp has a quoted output resistance of $100\,\Omega$

$$R'_o \approx 0.03\,\Omega$$

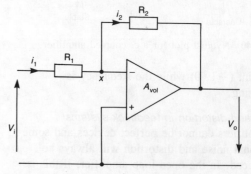

Fig. 2.43 The inverting amplifier $A_{vcl} = -R_2/R_1$

An inverting amplifier using an op-amp (Fig. 2.43)
The circuit uses parallel−voltage feedback to give

- A voltage gain of $A_{vcl} = -R_2/R_1$
- An input resistance of R_1
- A low output resistance.

Point 'x' is a 'virtual earth' since the open-loop gain A_{vol} is extremely large.

Therefore $i_1 = V_i/R_1$

and $\qquad i_2 = -V_o/R_2$

But $\qquad i_1 = i_2$

$$\frac{V_o}{V_i} = -\frac{R_2}{R_1}$$

Therefore $A_{\text{vcl}} = -\dfrac{R_2}{R_1}$

Since the feedback is applied in parallel, the input resistance at point 'x' is given by

$$R'_{\text{in}} = \frac{R_{\text{in}}}{1+A_{\text{vol}}\beta}$$

Suppose $R_2 = 20\,\text{k}\Omega$ $R_1 = 5\,\text{k}\Omega$ Then $\beta = 0.25$

therefore $R'_{\text{in}} = \dfrac{1 \times 10^6}{1+100 \times 10^3 \times 0.25} = 40\,\Omega$

Thus the effective input resistance to the circuit is R_1. Output resistance and bandwidth are determined in the same way as for the non-inverting configuration:

$$R'_o \approx 0.04\,\Omega \text{ (assuming } R_o \text{ is } 100\,\Omega)$$
$$f_{\text{hc}} \approx 250\,\text{kHz (assuming } GBP = 1\,\text{MHz)}$$

A two-stage transistor amplifier

The circuit shown in Fig. 2.44 uses series–voltage negative feedback and represents a standard connection method for small signal voltage amplifiers, where the requirement is for relatively high input impedance and low output impedance. Both stages provide a.c. voltage gain and there are two feedback loops. Direct coupling is used between the stages and d.c. feedback is provided via R_2 and R_3 to stabilize the operating point at the Tr_1 collector to a level of about 6 V. The a.c. feedback loop is from the Tr_2 collector via R_2 and R_1 to the emitter of Tr_1. Thus β, the feedback fraction, is

$$\beta = \frac{R_1}{R_1+R_2}$$

Provided the open-loop gain is large, so that the loop gain is much greater than unity, the closed-loop voltage gain will be:

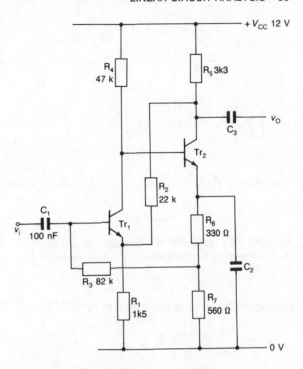

Fig. 2.44 Two-stage transistor amplifier (series–voltage feedback)

$$A_{\text{vcl}} \approx \frac{1}{\beta} = 1 + \frac{R_2}{R_1} = 15.7 \ (\approx 24\,\text{dB})$$

In analysing the circuit we need initially to verify that the loop gain is in fact much greater than unity. To determine the open-loop voltage gain, imagine that a large capacitor is placed across R_1, which will have the effect of eliminating any a.c. feedback signal over the amplifier's passband. The a.c. equivalent circuit, valid for small signals at 1 kHz, is as shown in Fig. 2.45. To find appropriate values for the g_m and r_{be} of each transistor, it is necessary to study the d.c. conditions (see Fig. 2.44). From these

$$I_{C1} \approx 0.2\,\text{mA} \quad \therefore \ g_{m1} \approx 8\,\text{mS}$$
$$\text{and } I_{C2} \approx 1.8\,\text{mA} \quad \therefore \ g_{m2} \approx 72\,\text{mS}$$

The open-loop voltage gain $= A_{\text{v1}} \times A_{\text{v2}}$

where $A_{\text{v1}} \approx g_{m1}R_{\text{L1}}$

and $\quad A_{\text{v2}} \approx g_{m2}R_{\text{L2}}$

R_{L1} is the parallel combination of R_4 and r_{be2}, so an estimate of r_{be2} value is required. Suppose we

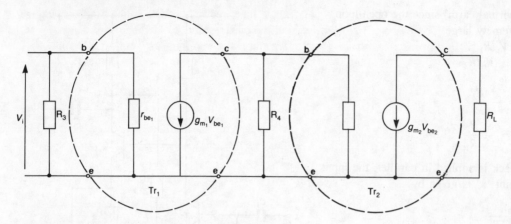

Fig. 2.45 A.c. equivalent for open-loop conditions (R_1 decoupled by large capacitor); $R_L \approx R_5$ in parallel with R_2

assume the h_{fe} of both transistors to be 200, then:

$$r_{be2} = \frac{h_{fe}}{g_{m2}} \approx 2800\,\Omega$$

This is in parallel with R_4 to give a collector load to Tr_1 of about 2600 Ω. Therefore $A_{v1} \approx 21$. The collector load of Tr_2, neglecting any effect of r_{ce}, is 2870 Ω. Therefore $A_{v2} \approx 206$.

Thus a reasonable estimate of the overall open-loop voltage gain of the two stages is 4300 (73 dB). If the full formula is used to calculate the closed-loop voltage gain we get:

$$A_{vcl} = \frac{A_{vol}}{1 + A_{vol}\beta} = \frac{4300}{1 + 4300 \times 0.0638} = 15.61$$

Alternatively, a check on the value of loop gain gives:

$$A_{vol}\beta = 274$$

This is much greater than unity, which is, of course, the essential requirement for a feedback amplifier. The use of the simple closed-loop gain formula is justified.

The open-loop resistance will be r_{be1} in parallel with R_3.

$$r_{be1} \approx \frac{h_{fe}}{g_{m1}} \approx 25\,\text{k}\Omega \quad \therefore \; R_{in} \approx 20\,\text{k}\Omega$$

Open-loop output resistance is R_{L1}, which has been previously determined as 2870 Ω.

The open-loop frequency response is more difficult to evaluate. The low-frequency cut-off point will primarily be set by C_1 and R_{in}, since the only other low-frequency time constants are C_3 and r_{be2}. However, C_3 is a very large-value capacitor. Therefore

$$f_L = \frac{1}{2\pi C_1 R_{in}} = 80\,\text{Hz}$$

The high-frequency cut-off will be set by the capacitive load presented by Tr_2 to the collector of Tr_1 (Fig. 2.46). This will be the case, provided that the source impedance is relatively small.

$$C_{in2} = C_{be} + C_{bc}(1 + A_{v2})$$

It is therefore necessary to arrive at values for Tr_1 capacitances C_{be} and C_{bc}. Suppose these are 20 pF and 4 pF respectively. Then:

$$C_{in2} = 20 + 4(1 + 206)\,\text{pF}.$$
$$= 848\,\text{pF}$$

Thus: $f_h = \dfrac{1}{2\pi R_{L1} C_{in2}}$

therefore $f_h \approx 70\,\text{kHz}$

Having determined the open-loop conditions it is now possible to predict the closed-loop values for R'_{in}, R'_{out} and bandwidth.

$$R'_{in} = R_{in}(1 + A_{vol}\beta) = 20(275)\,\text{k}\Omega = 5.5\,\text{M}\Omega$$

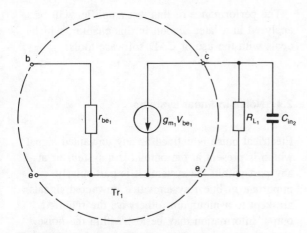

Fig. 2.46 A.c. equivalent for high-frequency analysis of open-loop conditions

Therefore the input resistance of the amplifier will be set by the bias resistor R_3 (82 kΩ)

$$R'_{\text{out}} = \frac{R_{\text{out}}}{1+A_{\text{vol}}\beta} = \frac{2870}{275} = 10.5\,\Omega$$

To determine the bandwidth we might, at first sight, use the following formulae:

$$f'_L = \frac{f_L}{1+A_{\text{vol}}\beta} = 0.3\,\text{Hz}$$
and $f'_h = f_h(1+A_{\text{vol}}\beta) = 19.25\,\text{MHz}$

But in the circuit C_1 is outside the feedback loop and the bias resistor R_3 sets input resistance. Therefore, the low-frequency cut-off is modified to:

$$f'_L = \frac{1}{2\pi C_1 R_{\text{in}'}} = 19.4\,\text{Hz}$$

The upper cut-off calculation is not affected and is the value determined as 19.25 MHz.

Two-stage pair using parallel current feedback (Fig. 2.47)

The circuit, using direct coupling between stages, is designed to give a voltage gain of 10 (20 dB) from a 50 Ω source to a 50 Ω load. The direct coupling provides both a.c. and d.c. feedback. Since the first-stage emitter is connected to ground, V_{B1} will be at 0.6 V and, because Tr_1 base current is very small, this 0.6 V level will appear across R_e. Thus I_{C2} will be given by:

$$I_{C2} \approx \frac{0.6}{R_e} = 8.8\,\text{mA}$$

Therefore $g_{m2} \approx 352\,\text{mS}$ and if an h_{fe} of 200 is assumed, r_{be2} will be approximately 600 Ω.

Under open-loop conditions $A_{v1} = g_{m1}R_{L1}$ where g_{m1} is 172 mS ($I_{C1} = 4.3\,\text{mA}$) and $R_{L1} = R_1//r_{be2} = 430\,\Omega$

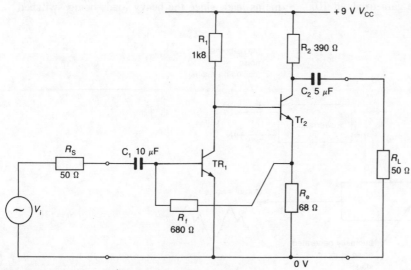

Fig. 2.47 Amplifier using parallel current feedback

Therefore $A_{v1} = 74$

$A_{v2} = g_{m2}R_{L2} = 17.6$

$\therefore A_{vol} = A_{v1} \times A_{v2} \approx 1300$

With the negative feedback applied, the a.c. currents are

$$i_f = \frac{V_i - V_{e2}}{R_f}$$

But V_i must be small since we have just calculated an open-loop voltage gain of 1300.

Therefore $i_f \approx -V_{e2}/R_f$ $\therefore i_f = \frac{(i_o - i_f)R_e}{R_f}$

$$\therefore i_f = \beta i_o = \frac{R_e i_o}{R_e + R_f}$$

$$\therefore \frac{i_o}{i_f} = \frac{R_e + R_f}{R_e}$$

The closed-loop current gain is:

$$A_{icl} = \frac{i_o}{i_f} = \frac{R_e + R_f}{R_e}$$

The closed-loop voltage gain is given by:

$$A_{vcl} = \frac{V_o}{V_i} = \frac{i_o R_L}{i_1 R_S} = A_{icl}\frac{R_L}{R_S}$$

Since R_L and R_S are both $50\,\Omega$, the approximate voltage gain is 11. This figure is modified slightly by the effect of R_2, which shunts the $50\,\Omega$ load reducing the closed loop voltage gain to about 10.

The performance of this last amplifier will be analysed in a later section in this chapter, which deals with the use of CAD software tools.

2.4 Noise in linear systems

Electrical noise is defined as any unwanted signal which is present at the output of a system or at any part within the system. It is particularly important in linear systems that unwanted signals are kept to a minimum, otherwise the required output information may be lost within the noise. Noise is a source of error in both analogue and digital circuits, but the latter is much more tolerant of an electrically noisy environment because in a digital system a wanted signal is either a logic 1 or a logic 0. The difference between a logic level and the threshold gives a barrier to noise, and is referred to as noise margin. This can be as high as 5 V in some CMOS digital systems, but even with TTL is typically 400 mV.

The external noise affecting a system can have several origins. Artificial or man-made sources of noise are, for example, arcing contacts on switches or relays controlling heavy loads such as motors. The spark gives off an electromagnetic radiated signal which is picked up by the input (Fig. 2.48). The interference may also be carried along the mains lead, since the heavy loads being switched

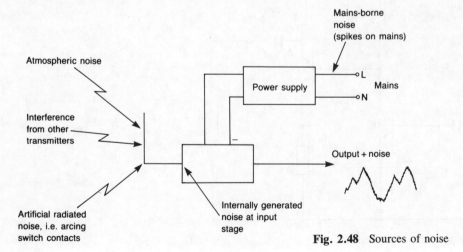

Fig. 2.48 Sources of noise

on and off produce large spikes on the mains which can then be transmitted through the system's power supply. Another source of noise is interference from other systems, from generators or switched power units. The effects of artificial sources can be minimized either by suppression at source (i.e. preventing arcing at switch contacts) or by filters and special shields at the receiver. There are also, of course, natural sources of electrical noise which may also be picked up on the input leads of the system.

The signal arriving at the input of the system will therefore have a small noise superimposed. The system itself now adds more noise in the process of selecting and amplifying the wanted information. Internal noise is mostly the result of that produced in the first stage, and is caused by noise from resistors and semiconductor devices.

Internal noise sources

Thermal agitation or resistance noise

This is produced by the random motion of free electrons in a conductor. RMS noise voltage in a conductor is given by

$$V_n = \sqrt{[4kTBR]} \qquad (2.41)$$

where k = Boltzmann's constant
1.38×10^{-23} J/°K
T = Temperature of conductor in degrees Kelvin
B = Bandwidth in Hz over which the noise is measured
R = Resistance of conductor in circuit.

Example

The noise voltage produced by a 100 kΩ resistor at a temperature of 20°C and over a bandwidth of 100 kHz is

$$V_n = \sqrt{[4 \times 1.38 \times 10^{-23} \times 293 \times 100 \times 10^3} \\ \times 100 \times 10^3]$$
$$= \sqrt{[162 \times 10^{-12}]} = 12.73\ \mu V$$

The available noise power from any resistor is $P_n = KTB$.

Noise in bipolar transistors

This has several components:

(1) *Thermal agitation noise*, developed mostly in the base spreading resistance $r_{bb'}$ of the device, given by

$$V_n = \sqrt{[4kTBr_{bb'}]}$$

(2) *Partition noise*, resulting from the random variations of the emitter current division between base and collector.

(3) *Shot noise*, caused by the random arrival and departure of charge carriers by diffusion across the PN junction.

(4) *Flicker noise* ($1/f$ noise), resulting from changes in the conductivity of the semiconductor material and changes in its surface conduction. This noise is inversely proportional to frequency and is usually negligible above 1 kHz.

To achieve low noise figures from a bipolar transistor it is operated at low values of collector current (a few microamps) and at low voltage.

Noise in FETs

Since an FET is a unipolar device it is inherently less noisy than a bipolar transistor. Only one type of charge carrier is used and only one current flows. The three sources of noise are shot noise, resulting from changes in the small leakage currents in the gate-to-source junction; thermal agitation noise developed in the channel resistance of the device; and flicker noise.

Signal-to-noise ratio

For a quoted input signal power, over a defined bandwidth, the signal-to-noise ratio in an amplifier or receiver is given by

$$\text{S/N ratio} = \frac{\text{Average wanted signal power}}{\text{Average noise power present}}$$
$$= \frac{P_s}{P_n} \qquad (2.42)$$

This is usually expressed in dB as

$$\text{S/N ratio} = 10 \log_{10} (P_s/P_n)$$

Example

At a frequency of 10 kHz the average wanted signal power at the input is 800 μW and the average noise power present is 6 μW. What is the input signal-to-noise ratio?

Input S/N ratio $= 10 \log_{10} (800/6)$
$= 21.25$ dB at 10 kHz

In electronics, voltage ratios are also often used:

S/N ratio $= 20 \log_{10} (V_s/V_n)$ dB

Noise factor (BS 3860)
Used to specify the noisiness of an amplifier or device, noise factor is

$$F = \frac{\text{Total noise power out}}{\text{Power gain} \times \text{Noise power due to source resistor}}$$
$$= P_N/GP_n$$

But since $G = P_{s(o)}/P_{s(i)}$ where P_s is signal power,

$$F = \frac{P_{n(o)}}{\dfrac{P_{s(o)}}{P_{s(i)}} \cdot P_n} = \frac{P_{s(i)}/P_{n(i)}}{P_{s(o)}/P_{n(o)}}$$

$$= \frac{\text{Signal/noise ratio at input}}{\text{Signal/noise ratio at output}} \quad (2.43)$$

Noise figure $= 10 \log_{10} F$ dB.
Thus if the noise figure for a device at a particular frequency is, say, 3 dB, and the input signal-to-noise ratio is 100 : 1 (20 dB), then the resulting signal-to-noise ratio at the output will be 3 dB less at 17 dB (a ratio of 50 : 1).

2.5 Using a CAD software tool

There is a large variety of computer aided design (CAD) tools providing analysis, performance prediction and design enhancement for linear electronic circuits. These CAD packages, most of which run on a PC, have become an essential feature of the electronic design environment, since the correct use of a CAD tool cuts design time to a minimum by avoiding costly prototype breadboarding and associated testing. It is possible to avoid real breadboard testing completely using suitable CAD software to simulate all the possible variations in component parameters. The design is then optimized using the computer software, the PCB layout and artwork are produced, and the completed unit is then ready for production.

Some CAD packages will automatically optimize a design, tailoring voltage gain and/or frequency response under the direction of the user, producing various design versions on screen until the desired target specification is reached. The use of CAD speeds design verification and can often allow the user to check for conditions that might take a large amount of valuable test time; on the other hand, the real world can still present surprises and some additional time spent on producing and testing a prototype is often useful. Oscillations in amplifiers caused by unforeseen capacitance, or higher than expected noise on a power rail, are just some of the hazards that can happen to a computer-only verified design.

The normal procedure in using CAD in electronic design is for the engineer to use a drawing package such as ORCAD to produce a circuit diagram of the required design; this drawing is then transported by software using schematic capture to the CAD tool that is required to carry out the simulation and analysis. SPICE is a typical example of an industry standard. Using the CAD tool it is possible for the user to obtain data on the following:

- Voltage and current gain.
- Frequency and phase response.
- d.c. operating conditions and stability.
- Input and output impedance.

Further features can include Monte-Carlo analysis, where the effects of component variations within their tolerance bands can be examined. The software assumes a set of values within the tolerance band of each component, and then computes the changes in system performance parameters, such as voltage gain and frequency response. The effects are displayed on screen in both tabular form and as a set of graphs. Worst-case analysis, where all components are assumed to be at their extremes of value, all in the wrong direction, can also be made. The time-saving advantages in these processes are obvious. Even with a simple circuit, the time taken to either hand-calculate or — worse still — to check every extreme tolerance change and combination on a prototype, would be very long indeed.

Other software packages, PROMISE being one example, automatically carry out optimization of an initial design, changing the circuit on screen so that the predicted performance gets closer and closer to the target specification.

It is important to realize, however, that the increasing use of CAD packages does not mean that the designer's job is becoming obsolete. The design process is enhanced, but the engineer must produce the initial design and be capable of getting the most from the CAD being used. To do this he must have a clear understanding of the types of models used to represent the components within the software package. Most CAD tools allow the user to specify device parameters and their values, and also to add components to the device library held by the software. An appreciation of these parameters, their effects and the models in which they are used, is essential if the results obtained from the computer analysis are to be considered valid. Most packages use the hybrid–pi or similar model for the BJT, and the sort of model for a FET already described in Chapter 1.

ANALYSER II is a typical low-cost CAD tool. This software can be used for the analysis of linear circuits containing passive components, transformers, FETs, transistors and strip-line radiofrequency components. Circuits with up to 60 nodes can be accommodated.

The best way to appreciate such a tool is to take a relatively simple circuit, since with this type of circuit the results can be verified quickly by hand, and also the use of the tool is not masked by any compilation in the circuit being analysed. Consider the circuit of a single-stage FET common-source preamplifier, as shown in Fig. 2.49. This preamplifier uses the normal bias method found in FET circuits, where a d.c. voltage V_{GG} is set up by a potential divider R_1 and R_2. This bias voltage tends to 'swamp' any changes in V_{GS}, which may vary with devices.

For the bias circuit, neglecting any gate current we get

$$V_{GG} - V_{GS} - V_S = 0$$

Here, $V_{GG} = V_{DD} \dfrac{R_2}{R_1 + R_2}$

and $I_d = V_s/R_4$

therefore $V_{GG} - V_{GS} = I_d R_4$

$$\therefore I_d = \frac{V_{GG} - V_{GS}}{R_4}$$

With V_{GG} set to 3 V and, assuming that V_{GS} is -0.5 V, the drain current will be about 0.7 mA, setting a drain voltage operating point at approximately half the drain supply. Small changes in V_{GS} will not dramatically alter this operating point.

For the a.c. analysis the nodes — points that define a component within the circuit — are added. Before making a selection from ANALYSER II's main menu, it is important to have the circuit diagram sketched out on paper with all the nodes clearly marked, because no circuit schematic is presented on screen with this software tool. The program models the circuit,

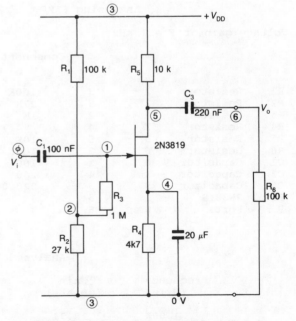

Fig. 2.49 Circuit of an FET preamplifier with nodes marked

```
<1>   START NEW CIRCUIT
<2>   MODIFY CIRCUIT
<3>   ANALYSE CIRCUIT
<4>   SELECT DATA DISC DRIVE
<5>   LOAD CIRCUIT OFF DISC
<6>   SAVE CIRCUIT ON DISC
<7>   LIST CIRCUIT VALUES
<8>   CHANGE CIRCUIT NAME
<9>   CATALOGUE DISC
<0>   RETURN TO DOS
```

Fig. 2.50 Analyser II main menu

producing a netlist of component positions and values, out of the view of the user. The marked-up circuit must include node 0 (usually the input) and consecutive node numbers as required. Since an a.c. analysis is being made, the power rail V_{DD} is given the same node number as the 0 V rail.

Option ⟨1⟩, 'start new circuit', is selected from the main menu (Fig. 2.50), and the program then prompts the user to name the circuit. In this case the name is FAMP. Component references, positions and values are then entered. This can be achieved in a variety of ways, e.g.:

R1,2,3,100E2   c/r

or R1 (space) 2 (space) 3 (space) 100k   c/r

The full list for the circuit is given in Fig. 2.51. The list is completed by entering node numbers for input, output and ground ports as shown. Unless the user wishes to make modifications to correct mistakes or to add components, the netlist is stored on disk and the main menu again presented.

Option 3 is selected to enable the circuit to be analysed and the program responds by outputting prompts for:

"number of steps?"
"start frequency?"
and "end frequency?"

A maximum of 45 steps is allowed, and these can be logarithmic or linear. In this case the number of steps selected is -30 (minus sign indicates logarithmic, which would normally be required for amplifier analysis), the start frequency is 10 Hz and the end frequency 10 MHz.

```
Number One Systems Ltd.  Linear Circuit Analysis Program.  ANALYSER II  (C)198

                     Analysing FAMP     27th February 1992

Voltage gain at F = 1 kHz

                             Component list:

R1     Resistor    2    3     100K
R2     Resistor    2    3     27K
R3     Resistor    1    2     1M
R4     Resistor    3    4        4.70K
R5     Resistor    3    5     10K
R6     Resistor    6    3     100K
C1     Capacitor   0    1     100
C2     Capacitor   3    4     20u
C3     Capacitor   5    6     220.00h
F1     2N3819      1    5     4         3m
P      Ports       0    6     3


                          Analysed Results

          Frequency          Gain           Phase
            (Hz)           (dB abs)          (deg)

           1.00K            28.71          -178.27
```

Fig. 2.51 Component list from Analyser II

Number One Systems Ltd. Linear Circuit Analysis Program. ANALYSER II (C)198

Analysing FAMP 27th February 1992

Frequency response

Component list:

R1	Resistor	2	3	100K	
R2	Resistor	2	3	27K	
R3	Resistor	1	2	1M	
R4	Resistor	3	4	4 70K	
R5	Resistor	3	5	10K	
R6	Resistor	6	3	100K	
C1	Capacitor	0	1	100	
C2	Capacitor	3	4	20u	
C3	Capacitor	5	6	220.00n	
F1	2N3819	1	5	4	3m
P	Ports	0	6	3	

Analysed Results

Frequency (Hz)	Gain (dB abs)	Phase (deg)
10.00	18.50	-87.64
16.10	22.63	-105.99
25.93	25.51	-124.91
41.75	27.23	-141.89
67.23	28.09	-155.04
108.26	28.46	-164.13
174.33	28.62	-170.05
280.72	28.68	-173.80
452.04	28.70	-176.15
727.89	28.71	-177.61
1.17K	28.71	-178.53
1.89K	28.71	-179.10
3.04K	28.71	-179.46
4.89K	28.71	-179.70
7.88K	28.71	-179.87
12.69K	28.71	-180.01
20.43K	28.71	-180.15
32.90K	28.71	-180.32
52.98K	28.71	-180.58
85.32K	28.71	-180.96
137.38K	28.71	-181.57
221.22K	28.71	-182.52
356.22K	28.69	-184.08
573.61K	28.66	-186.54
923.67K	28.58	-190.53
1.49M	28.36	-196.73
2.40M	27.86	-205.85
3.86M	26.80	-218.10
6.21M	24.83	-232.55
10.00M	21.95	-246.35

Fig. 2.52 Print out of frequency response results

A second menu requests the user to select the parameter to be analysed:

⟨1⟩ VOLTAGE GAIN
⟨2⟩ INPUT IMPEDANCE
⟨3⟩ OUTPUT IMPEDANCE

If ⟨1⟩ is selected as in this case, the final menu is presented to allow choice of gain in dB [dB = 20 log A_v] or as a ratio:

⟨1⟩ GAIN (dB absolute)
⟨2⟩ GAIN (dB relative)
⟨3⟩ GAIN (Linear absolute)
⟨4⟩ GAIN (Linear % error)
⟨5⟩ GAIN (real and imaginary)

For the following example option ⟨3⟩ was selected.

After the input of ⟨3⟩ the program then calculates the voltage gain and phase shift of the circuit over the selected frequency range previously input by the user. A print out of the results is given in Fig. 2.52.

Even more useful is the program's ability to graph the frequency and phase response. The result for the preamplifier, using a 2N3819, is shown in Fig. 2.53. This can be produced on a general-purpose n.l.q printer.

Thus in the space of a few minutes we have a frequency response plot of the circuit, which can be seen to have 3 dB points of 15 Hz and 10 MHz

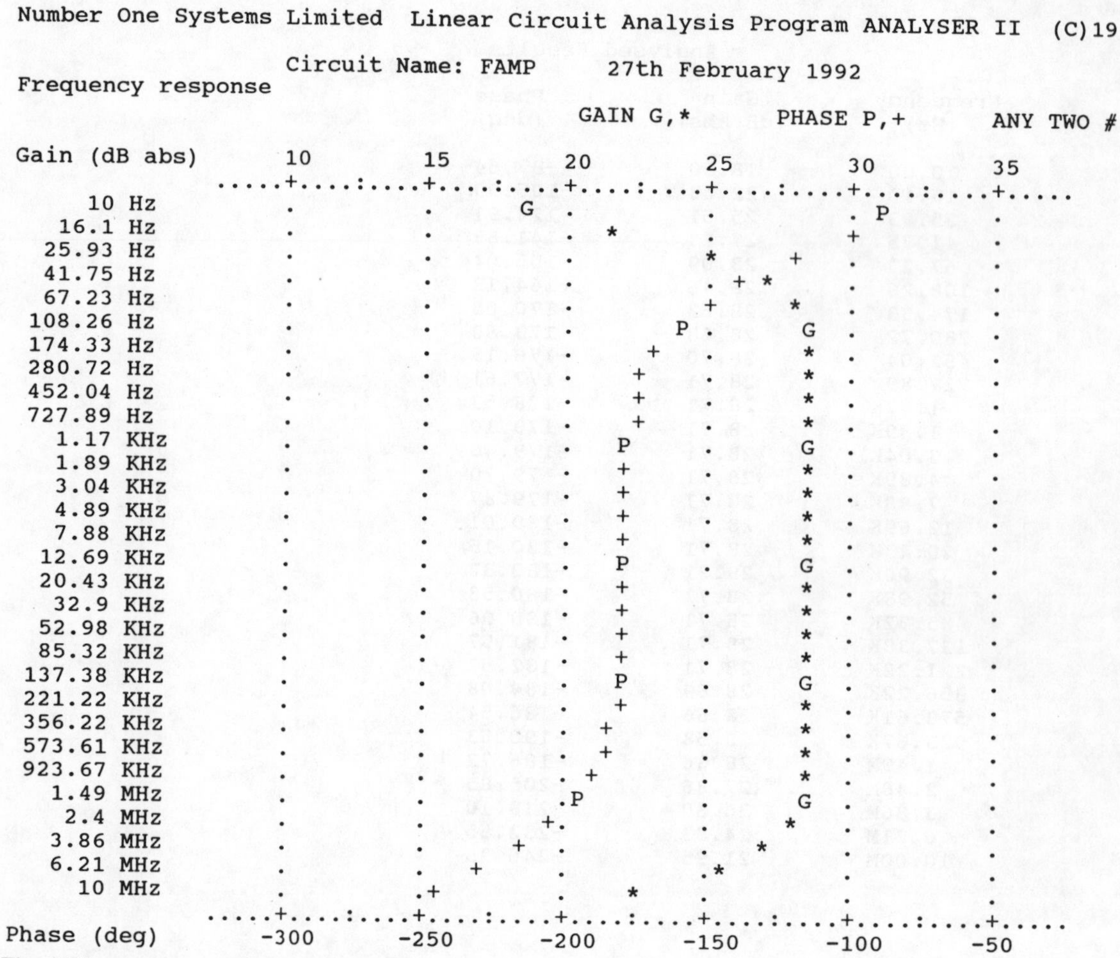

```
Number One Systems Limited  Linear Circuit Analysis Program ANALYSER II   (C)19

                    Circuit Name: FAMP        27th February 1992
Frequency response

                                   GAIN G,*        PHASE P,+        ANY TWO #

Gain (dB abs)       10          15         20          25          30          35
                 ....+....:....+....:....+....:....+....:....+....:....+.....
      10 Hz      .          .      G  .           .          . P         .
    16.1 Hz      .          .         .  *        .          +          .
   25.93 Hz      .          .         .        *      +      .          .
   41.75 Hz      .          .         .          . + *       .          .
   67.23 Hz      .          .         .          +       *   .          .
  108.26 Hz      .          .         .      P .        G     .          .
  174.33 Hz      .          .         .     +      .        *            .
  280.72 Hz      .          .     +        .        *       .          .
  452.04 Hz      .          .     +        .        *       .          .
  727.89 Hz      .          .     +        .        *       .          .
   1.17 KHz      .          .         .  P        .        G .          .
   1.89 KHz      .          .         .  +        .        * .          .
   3.04 KHz      .          .         .  +        .        * .          .
   4.89 KHz      .          .         .  +        .        * .          .
   7.88 KHz      .          .         .  +        .        * .          .
  12.69 KHz      .          .         .  P        .        G .          .
  20.43 KHz      .          .         .  +        .        * .          .
   32.9 KHz      .          .         .  +        .        * .          .
  52.98 KHz      .          .         .  +        .        * .          .
  85.32 KHz      .          .         .  +        .        * .          .
 137.38 KHz      .          .         .  P        .        G .          .
 221.22 KHz      .          .         .  +        .        * .          .
 356.22 KHz      .          .        +         .          * .          .
 573.61 KHz      .          .        +         .          * .          .
 923.67 KHz      .          .       +          .          * .          .
   1.49 MHz      .          .     .P           .        G   .          .
    2.4 MHz      .          .    +.            .        *    .          .
   3.86 MHz      .          .   +       .          *        .          .
   6.21 MHz      .          .  +        .          .*       .          .
    10 MHz      .           .+          .      *   .          .          .
                 ....+....:....+....:....+....:....+....:....+....:....+.....
Phase (deg)     -300       -250       -200        -150       -100        -50
```

Fig. 2.53 Graphical output from software

approximately, and a mid-band gain of just over 27 (28.6 dB).

The value of a CAD package such as this can be illustrated by the speed with which the effects of circuit modifications can be achieved. For example, suppose the source resistance of the generator driving the circuit is assumed to be 2000 Ω, what effect will this have on voltage gain and bandwidth? The modification is achieved by inserting a resistor, R_6, in series with C_1, and

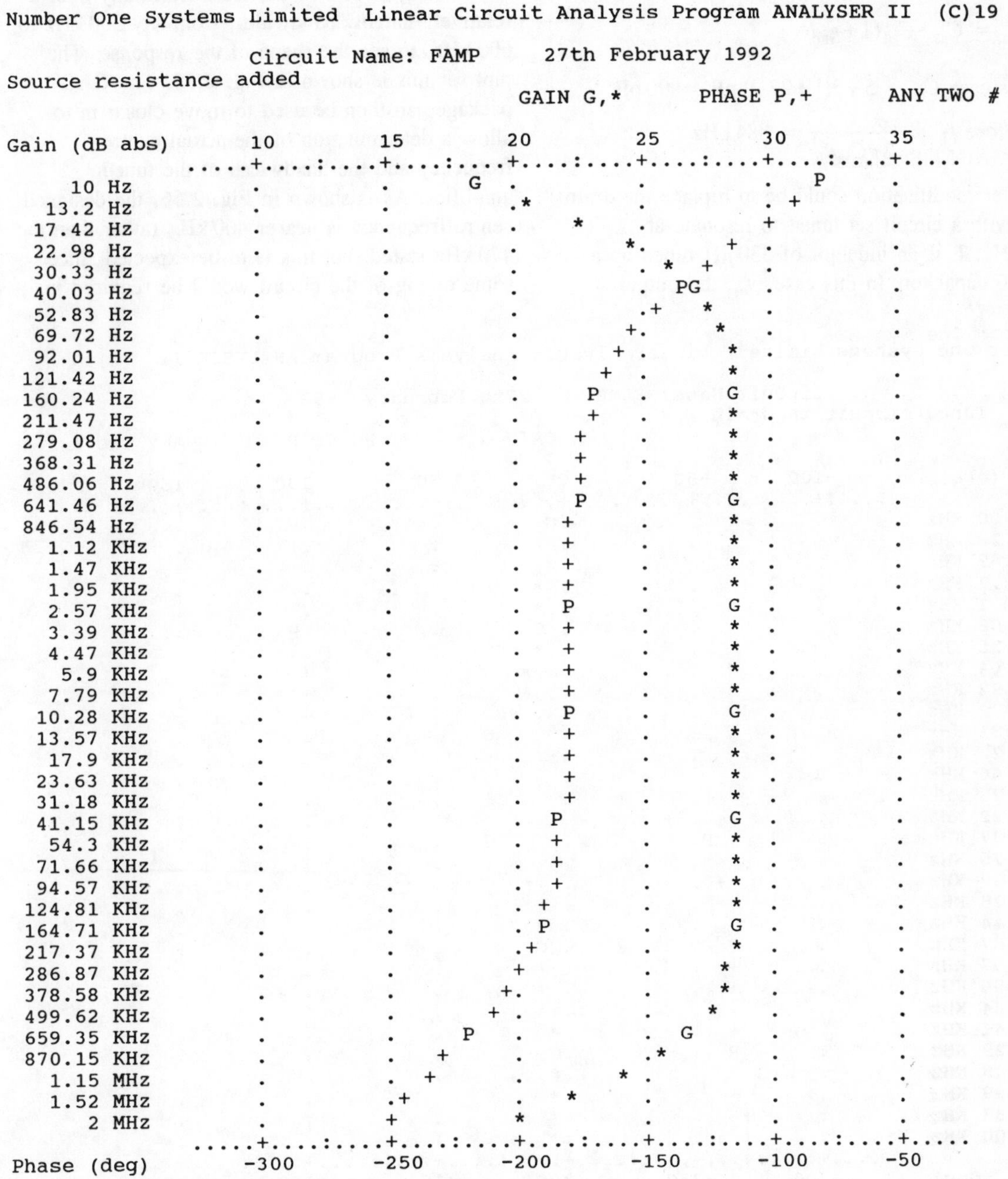

```
Number One Systems Limited  Linear Circuit Analysis Program ANALYSER II   (C)19

               Circuit Name: FAMP      27th February 1992
Source resistance added
                                  GAIN G,*      PHASE P,+      ANY TWO #
Gain (dB abs)   10          15          20          25          30          35
          .....+....:....+....:....+....:....+....:....+....:....+.....
      10 Hz     .           .        G  .           .           . P       .
    13.2 Hz     .           .          .*           .           . +       .
   17.42 Hz     .           .          .        *   .           +         .
   22.98 Hz     .           .          .          *.        +   .         .
   30.33 Hz     .           .          .           . *   +      .         .
   40.03 Hz     .           .          .           .  PG        .         .
   52.83 Hz     .           .          .           .+.     *    .         .
   69.72 Hz     .           .          .         +. .        *  .         .
   92.01 Hz     .           .          .       + .  .        *  .         .
  121.42 Hz     .           .          .     +    . .        *  .         .
  160.24 Hz     .           .          .     P    . .       G  .          .
  211.47 Hz     .           .          .      +   . .        * .          .
  279.08 Hz     .           .          .    +     . .        * .          .
  368.31 Hz     .           .          .    +     . .        * .          .
  486.06 Hz     .           .          .    P     . .       G  .          .
  641.46 Hz     .           .          .   +      . .        * .          .
  846.54 Hz     .           .          .   +      . .        * .          .
  1.12  KHz     .           .          .   +      . .        * .          .
  1.47  KHz     .           .          .   +      . .        * .          .
  1.95  KHz     .           .          .   P      . .       G  .          .
  2.57  KHz     .           .          .   +      . .        * .          .
  3.39  KHz     .           .          .   +      . .        * .          .
  4.47  KHz     .           .          .   +      . .        * .          .
  5.9   KHz     .           .          .   +      . .        * .          .
  7.79  KHz     .           .          .   +      . .        * .          .
 10.28  KHz     .           .          .   P      . .       G  .          .
 13.57  KHz     .           .          .   +      . .        * .          .
 17.9   KHz     .           .          .   +      . .        * .          .
 23.63  KHz     .           .          .   +      . .        * .          .
 31.18  KHz     .           .          .   +      . .        * .          .
 41.15  KHz     .           .          .  P       . .       G  .          .
 54.3   KHz     .           .          .  +       . .        * .          .
 71.66  KHz     .           .          .  +       . .        * .          .
 94.57  KHz     .           .          .  +       . .        * .          .
124.81  KHz     .           .          . +        . .        * .          .
164.71  KHz     .           .          . P        . .       G  .          .
217.37  KHz     .           .          .+         . .        * .          .
286.87  KHz     .           .          +          . .      *   .          .
378.58  KHz     .           .        +.           . .      *   .          .
499.62  KHz     .           .       + .           . .    *     .          .
659.35  KHz     .           .    P    .           . .  G       .          .
870.15  KHz     .           .   +     .           . .*         .          .
  1.15  MHz     .           .  +      .           *. .         .          .
  1.52  MHz     .           .+        .         * .  .         .          .
  2     MHz     .           +         .        *   .  .        .          .
          .....+....:....+....:....+....:....+....:....+....:....+.....
Phase (deg)   -300        -250        -200        -150        -100         -50
```

Fig. 2.54 Graph showing the effect of source resistance

adding another node (7). The gain, as expected and shown in Fig. 2.54, hardly changes at mid-band, but the high-frequency performance is markedly reduced. This effect is explained by R_6, the source resistance, forming a low-pass filter with C_{in}, where C_{in} is given by

$$C_{in} = C_{gs} + C_{gd}(1 + g_m R_L)$$

In this case $C_{in} = 5 + 3(1 + 27.3)\,\text{pF} \approx 90\,\text{pF}$

Therefore $f_L = \dfrac{1}{2\pi C_{in} R_6} = 884\,\text{kHz}$

Another modification could be to replace the drain load with a circuit set tuned to resonate at 470 kHz. L is an inductor of 330 μH tuned by a 330 pF capacitor. In this case, y_{os}, the output admittance of the FET, will have an effect on voltage gain. It can be represented by a 50 kΩ resistor connected between drain and source — this is necessary because the model for the FET used by ANALYSER does not include y_{os}.

The analysis can be carried out initially over a relatively narrow bandwidth, from say 300 kHz to 600 kHz, to see the shape of the response. The plot for this is shown in Fig. 2.55. The CAD package can then be used to move closer in to allow a determination of the actual centre frequency and the bandwidth of the tuned amplifier. As is shown in Fig. 2.56, the designed centre frequency is nearer 400 kHz rather than the 470 kHz stated, but this is to be expected since some tuning of the circuit would be required in

```
Number One Systems Limited  Linear Circuit Analysis Program ANALYSER II   (C)19

                     Circuit Name: FAMP      27th February 1992
          Tuned circuit in drain

                                    GAIN G,*        PHASE P,+      ANY TWO #

Gain (abs)        -100       -50       0          50        100        150
              ....+....:....+....:....+....:....+....:....+....:....+.....
     300 KHz     .         .        .G        .         .P         .
  307.26 KHz     .         .        .*        .         .+         .
  314.69 KHz     .         .        .*        .         .+         .
   322.3 KHz     .         .        . *       .         .+         .
   330.1 KHz     .         .        . *       .         .+         .
  338.08 KHz     .         .        . G       .         .P         .
  346.26 KHz     .         .        . *       .         .+         .
  354.64 KHz     .         .        .  *      .         +          .
  363.22 KHz     .         .        .  *      .         +          .
     372 KHz     .         .        .  *      .         +          .
     381 KHz     .         .        .    G    .       P.           .
  390.22 KHz     .         .        .      *. .   +               .
  399.66 KHz     .         .        .       + .  *                .
  409.32 KHz     .         .      +  .         .  *               .
  419.22 KHz     .        .  +       .      *. .                  .
  429.37 KHz     .      P. .         .    G   .                   .
  439.75 KHz     .    + .             .  *     .                  .
  450.39 KHz     .    + .             . *      .                  .
  461.28 KHz     .    + .             . *      .                  .
  472.44 KHz     .    + .             . *      .                  .
  483.87 KHz     .    P .             . G      .                  .
  495.57 KHz     .    + .             . *      .                  .
  507.56 KHz     .    + .             . *      .                  .
  519.84 KHz     .    + .             .*       .                  .
  532.41 KHz     .    + .             .*       .                  .
  545.29 KHz     .    P .             .G       .                  .
  558.48 KHz     .    + .             .*       .                  .
  571.99 KHz     .    + .             .*       .                  .
  585.83 KHz     .   + .             .*        .                  .
     600 KHz     .   + .             .*        .                  .
              ....+....:....+....:....+....:....+....:....+....:....+.....
Phase (deg)      -300      -250      -200      -150      -100       -50
```

Fig. 2.55 Frequency response with a tuned load

practice. These modification examples do show that CAD can prove very effective in determining likely circuit performance.

Now let us consider a slightly more complicated circuit for which some of the parameter values have already been determined by the traditional method using pen and paper. The amplifier is the one analysed in Section 2.3 on negative feedback, but the circuit is given again in Fig. 2.57, together with the node numbers required for the CAD

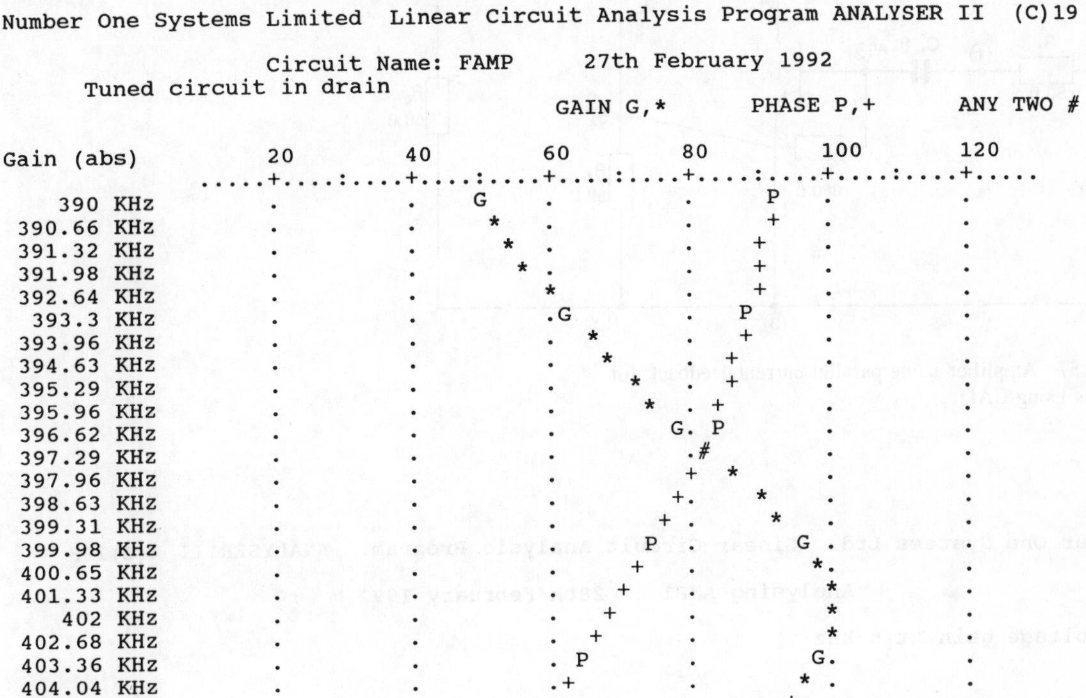

```
Number One Systems Limited  Linear Circuit Analysis Program ANALYSER II  (C)19

                  Circuit Name: FAMP       27th February 1992
       Tuned circuit in drain
                                    GAIN G,*      PHASE P,+     ANY TWO #
Gain (abs)         20          40          60          80         100         120
              .....+....:....+....:....+....:....+....:....+....:....+.....
   390 KHz     .           .    G    .           .      P    .           .
390.66 KHz     .           .  *      .           .      +    .           .
391.32 KHz     .           .*        .           .    +      .           .
391.98 KHz     .           .       *..           .    +      .           .
392.64 KHz     .           .        *.           .    +      .           .
 393.3 KHz     .           .       .G .           P          .           .
393.96 KHz     .           .        . *.          .    +     .           .
394.63 KHz     .           .        .   *.        .  +       .           .
395.29 KHz     .           .        .     *.      .  +       .           .
395.96 KHz     .           .        .       *.    . +        .           .
396.62 KHz     .           .        .       G. P           .           .
397.29 KHz     .           .        .        .# .          .           .
397.96 KHz     .           .        .        + .   *       .           .
398.63 KHz     .           .        .       +.       *     .           .
399.31 KHz     .           .        .      +.   .       *   .           .
399.98 KHz     .           .        .     P .         G . *.           .
400.65 KHz     .           .        .    + .           .  *.           .
401.33 KHz     .           .        .   + .           .   *.           .
   402 KHz     .           .        .  + .            .    *.           .
402.68 KHz     .           .        .   + .           .    *.           .
403.36 KHz     .           .        . P .             .   G.           .
404.04 KHz     .           .        .+.               .  *.            .
404.72 KHz     .           .        +.                . *.             .
 405.4 KHz     .           .        +.                . *.             .
406.09 KHz     .           .       + .             .  *               .
406.77 KHz     .           .      P .               . G               .
407.46 KHz     .           .      + .             . *.                .
408.15 KHz     .           .       + .           . *.                 .
408.83 KHz     .           .      + .           .* .                  .
409.52 KHz     .           .      + .          *  .                   .
410.21 KHz     .      P .           .  G    .                         .
 410.9 KHz     .           +        . *                               .
 411.6 KHz     .           +        .*                                .
412.29 KHz     .         +          *.                                .
412.99 KHz     .         + .        *.                                .
413.68 KHz     .       P    G .                                      .
414.38 KHz     .       + .  *                                        .
415.08 KHz     .       . +  *                                        .
415.78 KHz     .       . + *                                         .
416.48 KHz     .       .+ *                                          .
417.18 KHz     .       .PG                                           .
417.88 KHz     .       .#                                            .
418.59 KHz     .       *+                                            .
419.29 KHz     .       *+                                            .
   420 KHz     .     *+                                              .
              .....+....:....+....:....+....:....+....:....+....:....+.....
Phase (deg)        -300        -250        -200        -150        -100        -50
```

Fig. 2.56 A closer look at the response

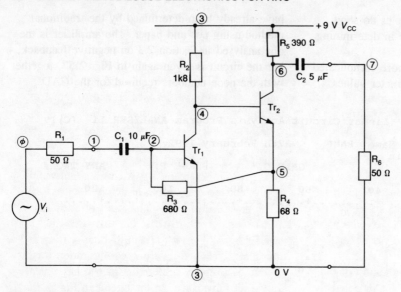

Fig. 2.57 Amplifier using parallel current feedback for analysis using CAD

Number One Systems Ltd. Linear Circuit Analysis Program. ANALYSER II (C)198

Analysing AMP1   28th February 1992

Voltage gain at 5 kHz

Component list:

R1	Resistor	0	1	50			
R2	Resistor	3	4	1.80K			
R3	Resistor	2	5	680			
R4	Resistor	3	5	68			
R5	Resistor	3	6	390			
R6	Resistor	3	7	50			
C1	Capacitor	1	2	10u			
C2	Capacitor	6	7	5u			
QA1	BC108	2	4	3	200	4.30	300
QA2	BC108	4	6	5	200	8.80	300
P	Ports	0	7	3			

Analysed Results

Frequency (Hz)	Gain (dB abs)	Phase (deg)
5.00K	19.20	4.27

Fig. 2.58 Print of net list and the analysed results at one frequency

work. The component values and positions are loaded into the software, but in this case, since BJTs are being used, the package requires the user to define values for h_{fe}, I_c and f_T for both transistors. The d.c. bias currents have been previously determined, h_{fe} values are assumed to be 200, and from the data sheet for a BC108 f_T is 300 MHz. The full component list is shown in Fig. 2.58, together with the computed value for voltage gain in dB. This is 19.2 dB, which is just over 9 as a ratio. In the previous calculation this was found to be about 10. Using the value of gain, the software can be used to plot the frequency response in dB *relative to the mid-band value*. A plot of gain and phase shift over the frequency range 100 Hz−100 MHz is shown in Fig. 2.59. This type of plot allows easy determination of the bandwidth, since the −3 dB points are more easily seen. This is illustrated even more clearly in Fig. 2.60, where the high-frequency end of the response only is plotted, the upper cut-off frequency being clearly shown as between 34 and 39 MHz. Even more detail could be obtained if the frequency range selected is further restricted.

2.6 Op-amp applications

The versatile op-amp is a component that finds applications in a wide variety of circuits, typically d.c. and a.c. amplifiers, oscillators and active filters. An analysis of some of these standard circuits will be given here.

D.C. amplifiers

A d.c. amplifier, normally required for the task of increasing the voltage, current or power level of some slowly varying signal, must of necessity have direct coupling and low drift. Drift is defined as any change in the amplifier's output signal when the input is held at a constant value. Normally drift is referred to the input of the amplifier, since this is where it causes an error. For example, if the input to a d.c. amplifier is 10 mV and the drift referred to the input is 1 mV, then the input drift error is 10 per cent. The major sources of drift are changes in the input circuit bias requirements

with temperature. The input circuit of any d.c. amplifier must therefore be a differential stage, since only with this circuit is it possible to cancel out signals that are common to both inputs. For a transistor or FET differential amplifier, the changes in both input leads will tend to move in the same direction at the same rate with temperature and thus, if both transistors are almost identical, will cancel out. Other causes of drift are variations in power rail levels (which can of course be minimized by using a well regulated supply) and general ageing of active devices.

The most typical application for a d.c. op-amp circuit would be to increase the small slowly varying signal — say a few millivolts — from a transducer. The non-inverting configuration for the op-amp is normally preferred, since it has a very high input impedance. In the circuit in Fig. 2.61, the transducer resistance is represented by R_S and the voltage gain is given by:

$$A_{vcl} = 1 + \frac{R_2}{R_1}$$

Note that a resistor R_3 is included, so that the resistance seen by both inputs is identical.

$$R_3 = R_S - \frac{R_1 R_2}{R_1 + R_2} \tag{2.44}$$

The resistance in both leads is normally required to be matched as closely as possible, so that offsets and offset drifts with temperature due to input bias currents are cancelled.

Apart from drifts there will always be a voltage error, called input offset voltage, that exists at a fixed temperature. Nulling techniques are available to reduce this offset to zero; some of these are shown in Fig. 2.62.

Returning now to the effect of input bias current on the offset voltage, let us take the example circuit and suppose that an op-amp with a bias current of 100 nA is used, and that the parallel combination of R_2 and R_1 is 10 kΩ. In the non-inverting lead a volt drop of 4 mV would be set up by the I_b^+ current flowing through R_S, whereas without R_3 a voltage drop of only 1 mV would occur in the inverting lead. This means that an additional input offset voltage of 3 mV exists.

Number One Systems Ltd.   Linear Circuit Analysis Program.   ANALYSER II   (C)198

Analysing AMP1   28th February 1992

Frequency response relative to 19.2 dB

Component list:

R1	Resistor	0	1	50			
R2	Resistor	3	4	1.80K			
R3	Resistor	2	5	680			
R4	Resistor	3	5	68			
R5	Resistor	3	6	390			
R6	Resistor	3	7	50			
C1	Capacitor	1	2	10u			
C2	Capacitor	6	7	5u			
QA1	BC108	2	4	3	200	4.30	300
QA2	BC108	4	6	5	200	8.80	300
P	Ports	0	7	3			

Analysed Results
Nominal gain is   19.2   dB

Frequency (Hz)	Gain (dB rel)	Phase (deg)
100.00	-11.85	107.54
161.03	-7.32	86.10
259.29	-4.02	64.90
417.53	-1.94	45.67
672.34	-829.34m	30.30
1.08K	-327.00m	19.39
1.74K	-118.57m	12.19
2.81K	-35.72m	7.60
4.52K	-3.41m	4.72
7.28K	9.10m	2.92
11.72K	13.95m	1.79
18.87K	15.82m	1.08
30.39K	16.56m	609.10m
48.94K	16.81m	283.27m
78.80K	16.92m	24.32m
126.90K	16.93m	-230.84m
204.34K	16.86m	-539.08m
329.03K	16.70m	-970.23m
529.83K	16.19m	-1.63
853.17K	14.99m	-2.66
1.37M	11.90m	-4.30
2.21M	3.02m	-6.94
3.56M	-18.52m	-11.22
5.74M	-77.52m	-18.05
9.24M	-242.30m	-29.19
14.87M	-711.33m	-47.37
23.95M	-2.13	-75.08
38.57M	-5.80	-110.99
62.10M	-11.91	-147.45
100.00M	-19.29	-178.58

Fig. 2.59   (a) Results of relative gain

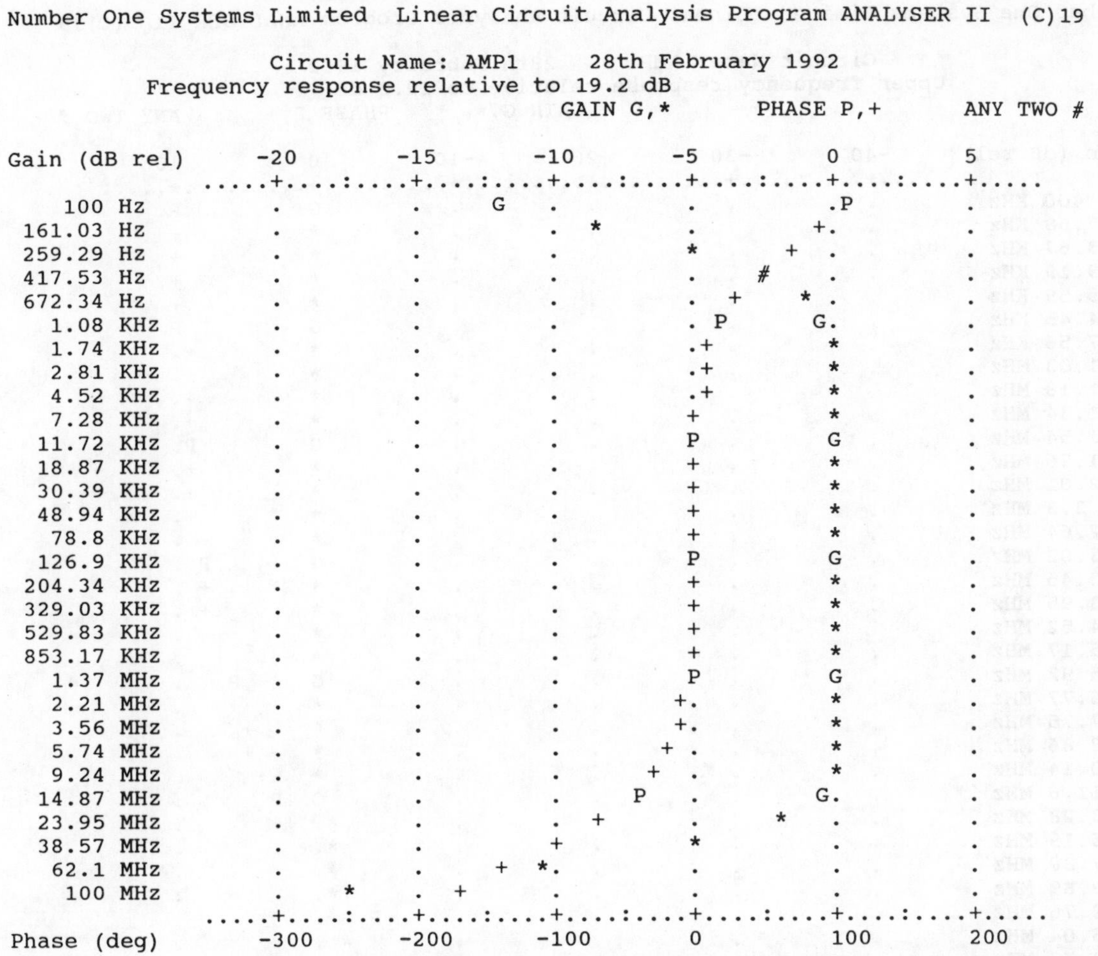

Number One Systems Limited Linear Circuit Analysis Program ANALYSER II (C)19

Circuit Name: AMP1   28th February 1992
Frequency response relative to 19.2 dB

```
                                  GAIN G,*        PHASE P,+        ANY TWO #

Gain (dB rel)    -20       -15       -10        -5         0          5
              .....+....:....+....:....+....:....+....:....+....:....+.....
     100 Hz      .         .      G   .         .         . .P        .
  161.03 Hz      .         .         . *        .         +.          .
  259.29 Hz      .         .         .          *         +  .        .
  417.53 Hz      .         .         .          .        #  .         .
  672.34 Hz      .         .         .          .      +  *  .        .
   1.08 KHz      .         .         .          .  P      G .         .
   1.74 KHz      .         .         .          . +       *          .
   2.81 KHz      .         .         .          . +       *          .
   4.52 KHz      .         .         .          . +       *          .
   7.28 KHz      .         .         .          +         *          .
  11.72 KHz      .         .         .          P         G          .
  18.87 KHz      .         .         .          +         *          .
  30.39 KHz      .         .         .          +         *          .
  48.94 KHz      .         .         .          +         *          .
   78.8 KHz      .         .         .          +         *          .
  126.9 KHz      .         .         .          P         G          .
 204.34 KHz      .         .         .          +         *          .
 329.03 KHz      .         .         .          +         *          .
 529.83 KHz      .         .         .          +         *          .
 853.17 KHz      .         .         .          +         *          .
   1.37 MHz      .         .         .          P         G          .
   2.21 MHz      .         .         .        +.          *          .
   3.56 MHz      .         .         .        +.          *          .
   5.74 MHz      .         .         .       + .          *          .
   9.24 MHz      .         .         .       +  .         *          .
  14.87 MHz      .         .         .     P    .         G.         .
  23.95 MHz      .         .         .  +       .       *            .
  38.57 MHz      .         .         +          *         .          .
   62.1 MHz      .         .     +  *.          .         .          .
    100 MHz      .      *      +     .          .         .          .
              .....+....:....+....:....+....:....+....:....+....:....+.....
Phase (deg)   -300      -200      -100        0         100        200
```

Fig. 2.59 (b) Frequency response relative to 19.2 dB gain

When the resistance in both leads is equalized, in this case by fitting a 30 kΩ in the inverting lead, any offsets due to bias currents are almost cancelled. The offset that does exist due to currents is that set up by the difference between the two input bias currents. This difference is called I_{io}, where

$$I_{io} = I_B^+ - I_B^- \tag{2.45}$$

Thus if I_{io} is, say, 20 nA, the additional offset becomes

$$\begin{aligned} V_{ie} &= I_{io} R_S \\ &= 20 \times 10^{-9} \times 40 \times 10^3 = 0.8 \, mV \end{aligned}$$

Of course any additional offset set up at a fixed

temperature can be easily nulled; the importance of equalizing the lead resistances is in reducing drift with temperature. As with any semiconducting device, the input bias currents and voltages of an op-amp change with temperature, but the rate of change of the difference in the two bias currents will be a fraction of the change in I_b.

For the non-inverting configuration, with the lead resistances equalized, the input offset at a fixed temperature is

$$V_{ie} = V_{io} + I_{io} R_S \tag{2.46}$$

and the temperature coefficient of this input error is given by

$$\frac{dV_{ie}}{dT} = \frac{dV_{io}}{dT} + \frac{dI_{io} R_S}{dT} \, V/°C \tag{2.47}$$

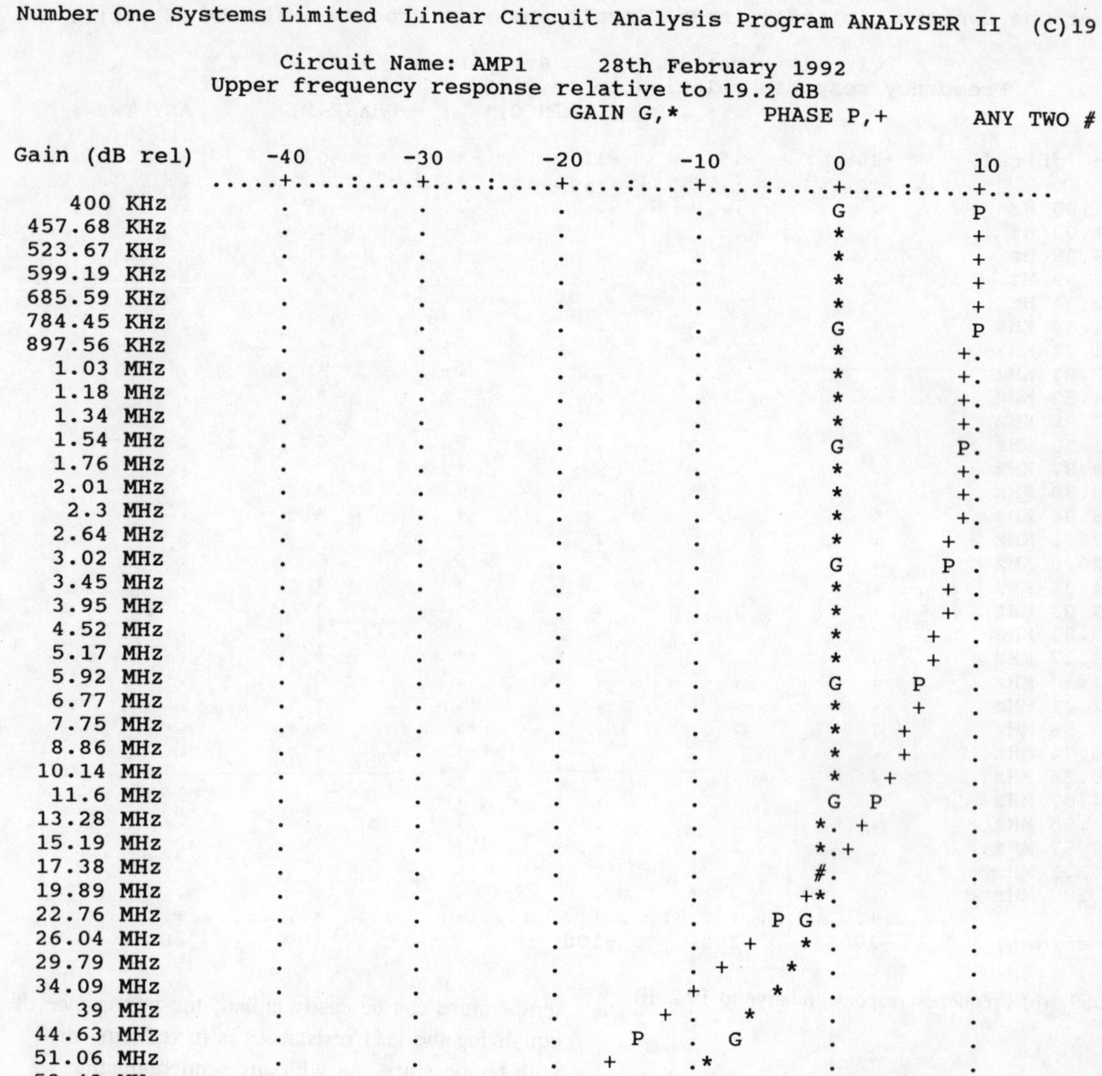

```
Number One Systems Limited  Linear Circuit Analysis Program ANALYSER II   (C)19

              Circuit Name: AMP1      28th February 1992
           Upper frequency response relative to 19.2 dB
                                 GAIN G,*      PHASE P,+      ANY TWO #

Gain (dB rel)    -40        -30        -20        -10         0         10
             .....+....:....+....:....+....:....+....:....+....:....+.....
     400 KHz      .          .          .          .         G          P
  457.68 KHz      .          .          .          .         *          +
  523.67 KHz      .          .          .          .         *          +
  599.19 KHz      .          .          .          .         *          +
  685.59 KHz      .          .          .          .         *          +
  784.45 KHz      .          .          .          .         G          P
  897.56 KHz      .          .          .          .         *         +.
    1.03 MHz      .          .          .          .         *         +.
    1.18 MHz      .          .          .          .         *         +.
    1.34 MHz      .          .          .          .         *         +.
    1.54 MHz      .          .          .          .         G         P.
    1.76 MHz      .          .          .          .         *         +.
    2.01 MHz      .          .          .          .         *         +.
     2.3 MHz      .          .          .          .         *         +.
    2.64 MHz      .          .          .          .         *          +
    3.02 MHz      .          .          .          .         G          P .
    3.45 MHz      .          .          .          .         *          + .
    3.95 MHz      .          .          .          .         *          +  .
    4.52 MHz      .          .          .          .         *           +  .
    5.17 MHz      .          .          .          .         *           +  .
    5.92 MHz      .          .          .          .         G         P
    6.77 MHz      .          .          .          .         *          +
    7.75 MHz      .          .          .          .         *           +
    8.86 MHz      .          .          .          .         *           +
   10.14 MHz      .          .          .          .         *          +
    11.6 MHz      .          .          .          .         G P
   13.28 MHz      .          .          .          .        *. +
   15.19 MHz      .          .          .          .        *.+
   17.38 MHz      .          .          .          .        #.
   19.89 MHz      .          .          .          .       +*.
   22.76 MHz      .          .          .          .     P G .
   26.04 MHz      .          .          .          .    +    * .
   29.79 MHz      .          .          .          .  +     * .
   34.09 MHz      .          .          .          . +     * .
      39 MHz      .          .          .          .+     * .
   44.63 MHz      .          .          .         P .    G
   51.06 MHz      .          .          .      +    .*
   58.42 MHz      .          .          .    +     *.
   66.85 MHz      .          .          .  +     *
   76.49 MHz      .          .          .+     *
   87.52 MHz      .          .         P  G
  100.14 MHz      .          .      +    .*
  114.57 MHz      .          .    +    *.
   131.1 MHz      .          .  +    * .
     150 MHz      .          . +    * .
             .....+....:....+....:....+....:....+....:....+....:....+.....
Phase (deg)    -250       -200       -150       -100        -50         0
```

Fig. 2.60 Upper frequency response

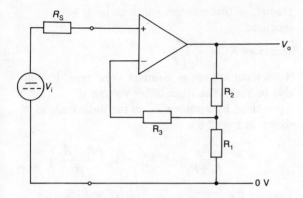

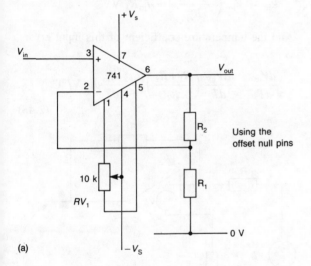

(a)

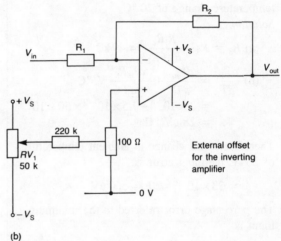

(b)

Fig. 2.61 Non-inverting d.c. amplifier

Using the
offset null pins

External offset
for the inverting
amplifier

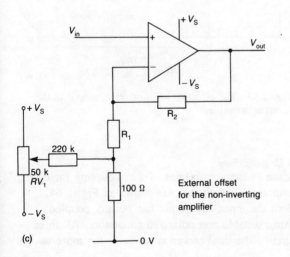

(c)

External offset
for the non-inverting
amplifier

Fig. 2.62 Some offset nulling techniques

Example

A d.c. amplifier using a non-inverting op-amp circuit is used to amplify signals in the range 5–20 mV from a source of 50 kΩ. The voltage gain is set by two resistors of 1 kΩ and 82 kΩ, and the op-amp has the following offset characteristics:

$$\frac{dV_{io}}{dT} = 3\,\mu V/^\circ C \quad \frac{dI_{io}}{dT} = 0.5\,nA/^\circ C$$

Suggest a suitable value for a third resistor to equalize the resistance in the inverting and non-inverting leads, and find the error compared to the minimum input signal for an ambient temperature change of 20 °C.

Solution:

(a) $R_3 = R_S - \dfrac{R_1 R_2}{R_1 + R_2} = 49\,k\Omega$

(b) $\dfrac{dV_{ie}}{dT} = \dfrac{dV_{io}}{dT} + \dfrac{dI_{io} R_S}{dT}$ V/°C

$= 3 \times 10^{-6} + 0.5 \times 10^{-9} \times 50 \times 10^3$

$= 28\,\mu V/^\circ C$

Therefore, for a change in ambient temperature of 20 °C the input error is:

$$V_{ie} = 28 \times 10^{-6} \times 20 = 560\,\mu V$$

The percentage error referred to the minimum input is

$$\text{Error} = \frac{0.56}{5} \times 100\% = 11.2\%$$

In situations where very small d.c. signals are to be amplified, any offset drifts in the op-amp must be small. Special op-amps, called *precision op-amps*, have been developed for this purpose, a good example being the OP-07, which is a pin-for-pin replacement for a 741, but with much reduced values of offset and drift.

The inverting op-amp configuration, which is the preferred method for amplification of current signals, but not often used for voltage amplification, results in a slightly modified equation for input error voltage and input error voltage drift with temperature. Initially a resistor R_3 is required from the non-inverting input pin to

ground, so that resistance in both leads is equalized.

Therefore $R_3 = \dfrac{R_1 R_2}{R_1 + R_2}$

If the input voltage is assumed to be zero, V_o will also be zero. The input offset voltage is represented by a source V'_{io} in the input lead, as shown in Fig. 2.63, where

$$V_{io} = V'_{io}\frac{R_2}{R_1 + R_2} \quad \therefore\ V'_{io} = V_{io}\left(\frac{R_1 + R_2}{R_2}\right)$$

Thus for the inverting d.c. voltage amplifier the input offset at a fixed temperature is

$$V_{ie} = V_{io}\left(\frac{R_1 + R_2}{R_2}\right) + I_{io} R_3\ \text{V}$$

And the temperature coefficient of this input error is

$$\frac{dV_{ie}}{dT} = \frac{dV_{io}}{dT}\left(\frac{R_1 + R_2}{R_2}\right) + \frac{dI_{io}}{dT}R_3\ \text{V/}^\circ\text{C}$$

(2.48)

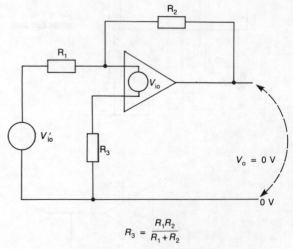

$$R_3 = \frac{R_1 R_2}{R_1 + R_2}$$

Fig. 2.63 The effective input offset generator in the inverting amplifier

A.C. amplifiers

Some of the possibilities of a.c. coupling for op-amp amplifier circuits are shown in Fig. 2.64. Both the input and output can be a.c. coupled using suitable non-polarized capacitors. All three circuits use dual power supplies — the more useful

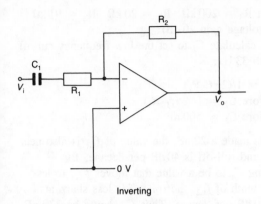

Inverting

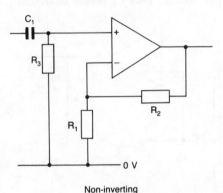

Non-inverting

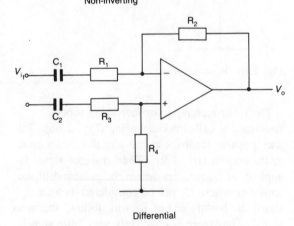

Differential

Fig. 2.64 A.c. coupling for basic op-amp circuits

single-supply circuits are discussed later. In a.c. amplifiers drift of the operating point with temperature — unless excessively high-value resistors are used in the circuit — will not be a problem. The main considerations for an a.c. amplifier using an op-amp are therefore:

- The closed-loop gain.
- The bandwidth.
- Input and output impedance.
- Output amplitude into a stated load.
- The noise level.

In most cases, the non-inverting configuration is the circuit of choice since the feedback resistors R_2 and R_1 can be kept to reasonably low values, which thus ensures that bandwidth restrictions are set by the op-amp itself and not by stray circuit capacitance across R_2. R_3 is an essential signal return path for C_1, and therefore prevents C_1 charging up and causing a latched output condition. It does not affect the voltage gain but does set the effective input resistance. A relatively high value, consistent with the op-amp bias current value, can be used, but in the basic circuit the resistor cannot be too high. For example, suppose that for an op-amp with input bias current of 150 nA R_3 is made 100 kΩ and the parallel combination of R_1 and R_2 is low, at 1 kΩ; an additional input offset of 15 mV will then occur across R_3. If the voltage gain of the amplifier is 100, the d.c. offset at the output is 1.5 V. Such a large d.c. offset of the operating point at the amplifier's output could easily cause distortion in the a.c. signal, especially if low-voltage power rails are used. A better value for R_3 in this example would be 10 kΩ, resulting in only 150 mV of d.c. offset at the output operating point. If high input resistance is required, either an op-amp with lower input bias current must be used, or some form of circuit modification, such as 'bootstrapping' employed.

The input CR network, in this case C_1 and R_3, sets the low-frequency cut-off point.

$$f_L = \frac{1}{2\pi C_1 R_3}$$

The upper cut-off frequency — unless the output is driving a capacitive load — will be set by the GBP of the op-amp. For any amplifier, the magnitude of the open-loop gain at signal frequencies above cut-off is given by

$$|A_{vol}| = \frac{GBP}{f} \qquad (2.49)$$

Suppose an op-amp has a GBP of 10 MHz; the magnitude of the open-loop voltage gain at 200 kHz is

$$|A_{vol}| = \frac{10 \times 10^6}{200 \times 10^3} = 50$$

As a 'rule of thumb', the value of the closed-loop voltage gain at the cut-off point should not exceed 20 per cent of the open-loop gain. Therefore, at 200 kHz a closed-loop voltage gain of 10 would be assured.

There are two techniques for obtaining a high input resistance without setting up too great a change in operating point. The first, shown in Fig. 2.65, is to a.c. couple the feedback signal. The a.c. gain is still set by R_1 and R_2, but the d.c. gain is unity.

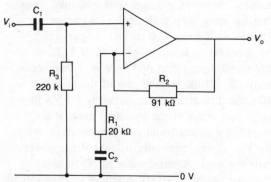

Fig. 2.65 One method of increasing the input impedance

The output offset is now the same value as that set up on the input, i.e. only 15 mV instead of the 1.5 V in the previous example. The penalty is that the roll-off due to C_2 must now be taken into account, and C_2 must be a non-polarized capacitor.

The two low-frequency cut-offs are:

$$f_{L1} = \frac{1}{2\pi C_1 R_3}$$

and $$f_{L2} = \frac{1}{2\pi C_2 R_1}$$

Only one of the reactive networks should be allowed to set the low-frequency cut-off. If they are selected to be values that make f_{L1} equal to f_{L2}, the roll-off at low frequencies will be excessive — 40 dB per decade instead of 20 dB per decade.

With $R_3 = 200\,k\Omega$ $R_1 = 20\,k\Omega$ $R_2 = 91\,k\Omega$ (a.c. voltage gain 20 dB)
Let us calculate C_2 to set the low-frequency cut-off point to 33 Hz:

$$f_{L2} = 1/(2\pi C_2 R_1)$$
Therefore $C_2 = 1/(2\pi f_{L2} R_1)$
Therefore $C_2 \approx 500\,nF$

If C_1 is made a 22 nF, the value of f_{L1} is also near 33 Hz and roll-off is 40 dB per decade. By selecting C_1 to be a value that moves f_{L1}, to less than a tenth of f_{L2}, the roll-off is less sharp at only 20 dB per decade. Thus C_1 should be 220 nF.

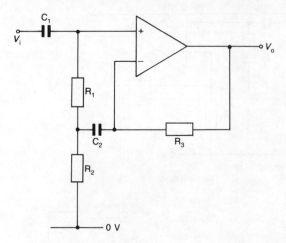

Fig. 2.66 Bootstrapping

The other technique for increasing input resistance is called bootstrapping (Fig. 2.66). This uses positive feedback at just less than unity gain to the bottom end of R_1. When an input signal is applied, at frequencies within the passband of the amplifier where C_2 can be considered as an a.c. short, the bottom end of R_1 will 'follow' the input signal. Thus there is effectively very little signal voltage across R_1, and its a.c. resistance therefore appears to be a much higher value than it actually is. Effective a.c. input resistances of 10 MΩ or higher are possible, even with R_1 equal to a few kΩ. With this circuit, d.c. stability is also high, since the d.c. gain is unity. Both C_1 and C_2 will set the low-frequency cut-off, and the rule of not allowing both to give the same corner frequency applies.

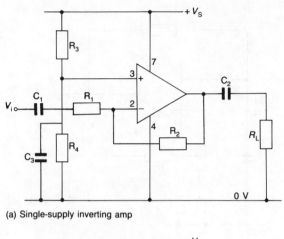

(a) Single-supply inverting amp

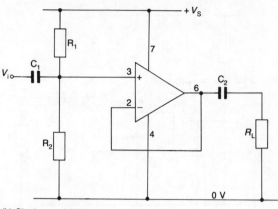

(b) Single-supply follower

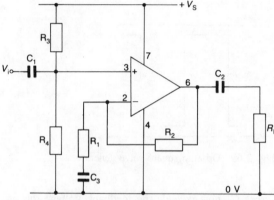

(c) Single-supply non-inverting amp

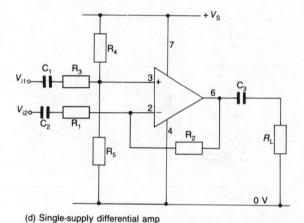

(d) Single-supply differential amp

Fig. 2.67 Single-supply a.c. amplifiers

A.c. coupling also allows the designer to operate the op-amp with a single supply rail, and this is a very useful feature in many applications. The method is to provide bias, usually at half the supply voltage, to *lift* the inputs off ground. A single-supply inverting amplifier with a.c. gain set by R_1 and R_2 is shown in Fig. 2.67. Two equal resistors, R_3 and R_4, bias the non-inverting input to $1/2\ V_S$ and since R_2 gives unity gain d.c. feedback the inverting input and the output will also be at $1/2\ V_S$. A.c. coupling must be used on both the input and output. C_3 can be omitted if the power supply is well regulated; it is there to provide noise and ripple decoupling. R_3 and R_4 should be values that preferably set up the same resistance in both input leads, i.e. $R_3//R_4 \approx R_2$. This will avoid drift of the operating point with

temperature.

Circuits for single-supply follower, non-inverting and differential amplifiers are also shown in Fig. 2.67. In the last circuit, the parallel combination of R_3 and R_4 should be made equal to R_2.

In some single-supply circuits the additional noise introduced by the bias can be overcome by having low-value bias resistors, which are decoupled, and stand-off resistors from the bias point to the op-amp's inputs. Circuits for both the follower and the non-inverting versions are shown in Fig. 2.68.

Oscillator circuits
Op-amps can be used for the generation of sine, square and triangle waveforms, with frequencies

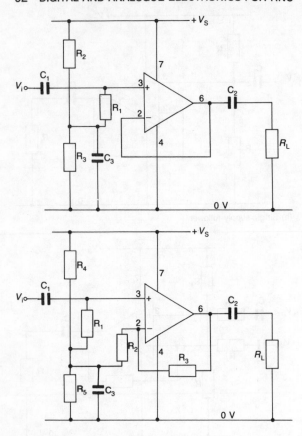

Fig. 2.68 Using stand-off resistors

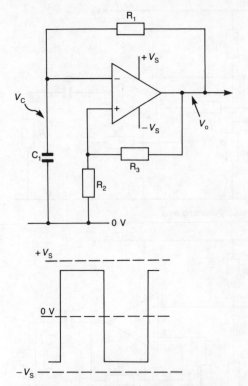

Fig. 2.69 Op-amp square-wave generator

ranging from fractions of a hertz up to several megahertz. Wide bandwidth and very fast slew rate op-amps are required for high-frequency generation, whereas at very low frequencies it is input bias current that becomes the limiting factor. There are, of course, many different circuit variations and therefore only the more basic circuits can be covered in this section.

Fig. 2.69 shows a classic arrangement for a square-wave generator. This is an astable multivibrator which will self-start because of the small offset present in the op-amp and the positive feedback via R_3 and R_2 to the non-inverting input. Assume that the output starts at a high positive state at $V_{o(sat)}^+$ and that the capacitor C_1 is uncharged. A portion of the output is fed back to the non-inverting input pin, and this forces the output to remain in positive saturation. C_1 will then charge towards $V_{o(sat)}^+$, and when the voltage

across C_1 just exceeds the feedback voltage the op-amp output switches rapidly to negative saturation $V_{o(sat)}^-$. C_1 is now discharged via R_1 towards $V_{o(sat)}^-$, and when the voltage across C_1 is just more negative than that on the non-inverting pin, the op-amp output is again forced to switch state. Thus the capacitor is charged and discharged from

$$V_{o(sat)}^+ \left(\frac{R_2}{R_2+R_3}\right) \text{ to } V_{o(sat)}^- \left(\frac{R_2}{R_2+R_3}\right)$$

to give continuous square waves at the output. The waveforms in the circuit are shown in Fig. 2.70.

Since the voltage across a capacitor charging via a resistor is given by

$$v_c = V(1 - e^{-t/CR}) \tag{2.50}$$

in the circuit we get

$$2V_{o(sat)} \left(\frac{R_2}{R_2+R_3}\right) = V_{o(sat)} \left(1 + \frac{R_2}{R_2+R_3}\right) \cdot (1 - e^{-t/C_1R_1})$$

therefore $\dfrac{2R_2}{R_2+R_3} = \left(1 + \dfrac{R_2}{R_2+R_3}\right) \cdot (1 - e^{-t/C_1R_1})$

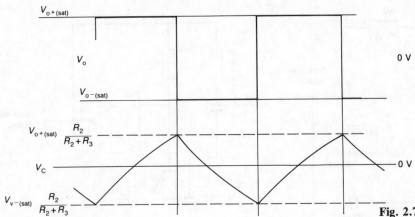

Fig. 2.70 Waveforms in op-amp astable

$$\therefore \frac{2R_2}{R_2+R_3} = \left(\frac{R_2+R_3+R_2}{R_2+R_3}\right) \cdot (1-e^{-t/C_1R_1})$$

$$\therefore e^{-t/C_1R_1} = \frac{R_3}{2R_2+R_3}$$

$$\therefore e^{t/C_1R_1} = \frac{2R_2+R_3}{R_3}$$

$$\therefore t = C_1R_1 \ln\left(1+\frac{2R_2}{R_3}\right)$$

Since the periodic time is $2t$

$$f = \frac{1}{2C_1R_1 \ln\left(1+\dfrac{2R_2}{R_3}\right)} \qquad (2.51)$$

Note that when R_2 is made equal to 0.325R3

$$f \approx \frac{1}{C_1R_1}$$

Two op-amps are necessary for the circuit of a function generator as shown in Fig. 2.71. This circuit gives simultaneous triangle and square-wave outputs. One op-amp is wired as an integrator, with a time constant set by C_1 and R_1, and the other as a level detector. The output of this level detector will switch states from $V_{o(sat)}^+$ to $V_{o(sat)}^-$ when the voltage at its non-inverting pin crosses through zero volts. Thus the output of the integrator, connected to the level detector input, will have an amplitude of $2V_{o(sat)} \cdot R_2/R_3$. Note that in the circuit R_3 must be greater than R_2 or the circuit will latch.

For the integrator using

$$Idt = CdV$$

where in this case

$$I = \frac{V_{o(sat)}}{R_1} \text{ and } dV = 2V_{o(sat)} \frac{R_2}{R_3}$$

we get $t = \dfrac{C_1dV}{I} = \dfrac{2C_1V_{o(sat)}R_2/R_3}{V_{o(sat)}/R_1}$

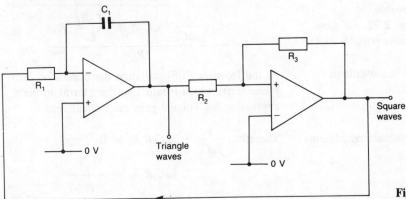

Fig. 2.71 Op-amp function generator

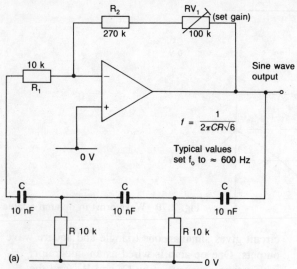

Fig. 2.72   (a) Phase shift oscillator; (b) Wien bridge oscillator

therefore
$$t = 2C_1 \frac{R_1 R_2}{R_3} \tag{2.52}$$

with $R_2 = \dfrac{R_3}{2}$ $t = C_1 R_1$

Therefore
$$f = \frac{1}{2C_1 R_1} \tag{2.53}$$

Several sinewave oscillator circuit configurations using op-amps are possible, most of them capable of generating low-distortion output signals. Typically a phase-shifting circuit is employed to give positive feedback at the frequency of oscillation, and negative feedback, applied to the inverting pin, can be used to stabilize the amplitude of the output. Two possible arrangements are indicated in Fig. 2.72. Of these, the Wien bridge is perhaps the most popular and will be analysed here.

For the phase-shift network of this oscillator

$$V_i = V_o \frac{Z_2}{Z_1 + Z_2} \tag{2.54}$$

Therefore the gain required to maintain oscillations is

$$A_v = \frac{V_o}{V_i} = \frac{Z_1 + Z_2}{Z_2}$$

$$Z_1 = R_1 + \frac{1}{j\omega C_1} \text{ and}$$

$$Z_2 = \frac{R_2 \cdot 1/j\omega C_2}{R_2 + 1/j\omega C_2} = \frac{R_2}{1 + j\omega C_2 R_2}$$

$$\therefore A_v = \frac{R + \dfrac{1}{j\omega C_1} + \dfrac{R_2}{1 + j\omega C_2 R_2}}{\dfrac{R_2}{1 + j\omega C_2 R_2}}$$

$$\therefore A_v = \frac{\left(R_1 + \dfrac{1}{j\omega C_1}\right)(1 + j\omega C_2 R_2) + R_2}{R_2}$$

$$= \frac{R_1 + \dfrac{1}{j\omega C_1} + j\omega C_2 R_2 R_1 + \dfrac{C_2 R_2}{C_1} + R_2}{R_2}$$

At the frequency of oscillation there must be zero phase shift, which means that the j terms in the expression for voltage gain must equal zero.

Therefore $\dfrac{1}{j\omega C_1} + j\omega C_2 R_1 R_2 = 0$

$$\therefore j\omega C_2 R_1 R_2 = -\frac{1}{j\omega C_1} \tag{2.55}$$

$$\therefore \ \omega^2 = \frac{1}{C_1 C_2 R_1 R_2}$$

However, if $C_1 = C_2 = C$
and $\qquad R_1 = R_2 = R$
which is normally the case in this circuit,

$$\omega^2 = \frac{1}{C^2 R^2}$$

$$\therefore f_o = \frac{1}{2\pi CR} \qquad\qquad (2.56)$$

For the oscillations to be just maintained

$$A_v = \frac{R_1}{R_2} + \frac{C_2 R_2}{C_1 R_2} + \frac{R_2}{R_2} \qquad (2.57)$$

with $C_1 = C_2$ and $R_1 = R_2$
$\qquad A_v = 3$

Usually the gain control network is arranged to contain a non-linear device in the feedback loop that varies its resistance with current. This is typically a thermistor, such as the R53, which is a thermistor enclosed in an evacuated glass envelope. Thus as the output amplitude of the oscillator increases, the thermistor's resistance drops slightly and more negative feedback is applied to adjust the gain to exactly 3. An R53 thermistor has a

nominal resistance of $1500\,\Omega$ when the voltage across it is 2 V pk−pk, indicating that a value of about $680\,\Omega$ is ideal for R_3.

$$A_{vcl} = 1 + \frac{R53}{R_3}$$

With $R_3 = 680\,\Omega$ $A_{vcl} = 3.2$

In addition to the features of low distortion levels and stable frequency operation, the Wien bridge oscillator can have its frequency adjusted over a wide range by the use of switched capacitors and a ganged potentiometer, as shown in Fig. 2.73.

Another useful oscillator circuit, which requires two op-amps, is the sine/cosine, or quadrature, waveform generator. In this circuit both amplifiers are connected as integrators, and positive feedback is arranged via an additional CR network. With all capacitors equal in value, and resistors also of equal value, the frequency of oscillation is given by

$$f = \frac{1}{2\pi RC}$$

A typical circuit to give a frequency of 400 Hz is shown in Fig. 2.74.

Active filter circuits

Filter circuits, which can be designed to give low-pass, high-pass, bandpass or band-stop (notch) characteristics, have traditionally been constructed using only passive components; that is, inductors, capacitors and resistors. With an active filter, where an op-amp is used to provide gain, the relatively expensive inductor is no longer needed. This is a real advantage at lower frequencies since the inductor required can be a bulky item. Other advantages of active filters include:

- Almost no insertion loss.
- Relative ease of tuning.
- Good isolation, since the circuits usually have a high input and low output impedance.

Active filters using op-amps are particularly useful at audio frequencies. Other types of filters include ceramic, digital and switched-capacitor filters.

To be really effective a filter needs to have a

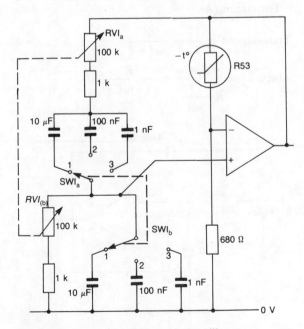

Fig. 2.73 A practical Wien bridge oscillator

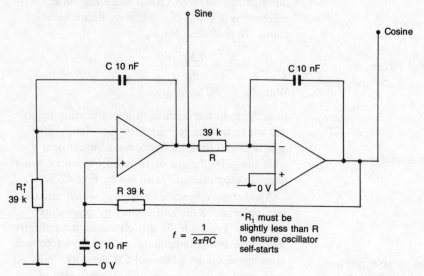

$$f = \frac{1}{2\pi RC}$$

*R_1 must be slightly less than R to ensure oscillator self-starts

Fig. 2.74 Sine/cosine oscillator

sharp cut-off characteristic. The ideal is the 'brick wall' shape, where the signals at frequencies within the pass-band suffer no attenuation, while at the cut-off frequency the attenuation switches to infinity. In practice, a simple design of an active filter may be arranged to give almost zero attenuation in the pass-band, a roll-off of 40 dB per decade from cut-off, and an attenuation in excess of 60 dB at frequencies much higher than the cut-off.

As an introduction to this subject, we shall initially consider two low-pass filter circuits, which are shown in Fig. 2.75. The first is created using passive components only; the inductor passes the

low-frequency signals and as the signal frequency at the input increases the capacitor progressively attenuates the signal. By analysis it can be shown that the active circuit, using the op-amp and CR components, has the same response as the passive version. Thus the inductor can be replaced and the op-amp used to simulate inductive reactance.

For circuit (A):

$$\text{Transmission} = \frac{V_2}{V_1} = \frac{Z}{j\omega L + Z}$$

where $Z = \dfrac{R/j\omega C}{R + \dfrac{1}{j\omega C}} = \dfrac{R}{1 + j\omega CR}$

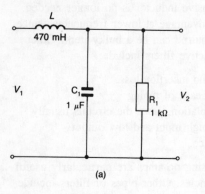

(a)

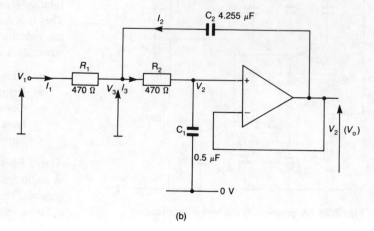

(b)

Fig. 2.75 (a) passive filter; (b) active filter

Number One Systems Limited Linear Circuit Analysis Program ANALYSER II (C)19

Circuit Name: FILT1   19th March 1992

passive filter

```
                                    GAIN G,*      PHASE P,+      ANY TWO #

Gain (dB abs)      -80        -60        -40        -20        0         20
                 .....+....:....+....:....+....:....+....:....+....:....+.....
       10 Hz       .          .          .          .          #          .
     11.7 Hz       .          .          .          .          #          .
    13.69 Hz       .          .          .          .          #          .
    16.02 Hz       .          .          .          .         +*          .
    18.74 Hz       .          .          .          .         +*          .
    21.92 Hz       .          .          .          .         PG          .
    25.65 Hz       .          .          .          .         +*          .
    30.01 Hz       .          .          .          .         +*          .
    35.11 Hz       .          .          .          .         +*          .
    41.08 Hz       .          .          .          .         +*          .
    48.06 Hz       .          .          .          .        P G          .
    56.23 Hz       .          .          .          .        + *          .
    65.79 Hz       .          .          .          .        + *          .
    76.98 Hz       .          .          .          .       +   *         .
    90.06 Hz       .          .          .          .       +   *         .
   105.37 Hz       .          .          .          .     P    .G         .
   123.28 Hz       .          .          .          .    +     .*         .
   144.24 Hz       .          .          .          .  +       .  *       .
   168.76 Hz       .          .          .          .+        .   *       .
   197.45 Hz       .          .          .        +          .     *      .
   231.01 Hz       .          .          .   P    .          .     G      .
   270.28 Hz       .          .          + .          .      .     *      .
   316.23 Hz       .          .      +   .          .        .    *       .
   369.98 Hz       .          .  +     .          .          .   *        .
   432.88 Hz       .          .+         .          .         .  +        .
   506.46 Hz       .        P. .          .          .        G          .
   592.55 Hz       .      + .          .          .          *          .
   693.28 Hz       .     + .          .          .         .*           .
   811.13 Hz       .     + .          .          .        *            .
   949.01 Hz       .     + .          .          .       *            .
    1.11 KHz       .     P .          .          G       .            .
     1.3 KHz       .     + .          .        *          .            .
    1.52 KHz       .     + .          .       *           .            .
    1.78 KHz       .     + .          .      *            .            .
    2.08 KHz       .     + .          .   *             .            .
    2.43 KHz       .     P .        G     .            .            .
    2.85 KHz       .     + .        *.             .            .            .
    3.33 KHz       .      + .      * .             .            .            .
     3.9 KHz       .      + .    * .             .            .            .
    4.56 KHz       .       + .  * .             .            .            .
    5.34 KHz       .       P .  G .             .            .            .
    6.24 KHz       .       + . * .             .            .            .
    7.31 KHz       .        + .  * .             .            .            .
    8.55 KHz       .        + . * .             .            .            .
      10 KHz       .        + . * .             .            .            .
                 .....+....:....+....:....+....:....+....:....+....:....+.....
Phase (deg)       -200      -150       -100       -50        0         50
```

Fig. 2.76 Graph of a passive filter's response

$$\therefore \frac{V_2}{V_1} = \frac{1}{1+j\omega\frac{L}{R}-\omega^2 LC} \quad (2.58)$$

This equation indicates that a resonant condition occurs at a frequency given by

$$f_R = \frac{1}{2\pi\sqrt{LC}} \quad (2.59)$$

and that damping depends upon the relative values of L and R

$$\text{Damping} = \frac{\omega_R L}{2R} \quad (2.60)$$

Consider the following values:

$$L = 470\,\text{mH} \quad C = 1\,\mu\text{F} \quad \text{and} \quad R = 1\,\text{k}\Omega$$

The cut-off frequency is: $f = \dfrac{1}{2\pi\sqrt{LC}} = 232\,\text{Hz}$

The frequency response can be checked using a CAD package, and this is shown in Fig. 2.76, over the frequency range 10 Hz to 10 kHz.

If the value of R is increased to 10 kΩ, the damping will be reduced and a more resonant condition set up; the result is a more pronounced peak in the transfer characteristics, as shown in Fig. 2.77. In this way, by varying the resistance value, the response can be tailored to give a minimum 'peak' and a relatively sharp cut-off.

For the second circuit the analysis is as follows: Since the op-amp is acting as a unity gain follower

$$V_o = V_2$$
$$\therefore I_1 + I_2 - I_3 = 0$$
$$\therefore \frac{(V_1 - V_3)}{R_1} + \frac{(V_2 - V_3)}{Z_2} - \frac{(V_3 - V_2)}{R_2} = 0$$

In this case let $R_1 = R_2 = R$

$$\therefore \frac{(V_1 - V_3)}{R} + \frac{(V_2 - V_3)}{Z_2} - \frac{(V_3 - V_2)}{R} = 0$$

$$\therefore V_1 Z_1 + V_2(R + Z_2) = V_3(R + 2Z_2) \quad (1)$$

Most of the current I_3 flows through C_1 because of the op-amp's high input resistance

$$\therefore \frac{V_2}{V_3} = \frac{Z_1}{R + Z_1} \quad \therefore V_3 = V_2\left(\frac{R + Z_1}{Z_1}\right) \quad (2)$$

Substituting (2) in (1) gives

$$\frac{V_2}{V_1} = \frac{Z_1 Z_2}{R^2 + 2RZ_2 + Z_1 Z_2}$$

putting $Z_1 = \dfrac{1}{j\omega C_1}$ and $Z_2 = \dfrac{1}{j\omega C_2}$ we get

$$\frac{V_2}{V_1} = \frac{1}{1 + j\omega(2RC_1) - \omega^2 R^2 C_1 C_2} \quad (2.61)$$

This equation for transmission is in the same form as that previously derived for the passive circuit (see Eq. 2.58), so it can be said that

$$R^2 C_1 C_2 = LC$$

and

$$2RC_1 = \frac{L}{R_1}$$

(here R_1 = the resistance in the passive circuit)

Let us consider suitable values for the active circuit to give the same performance as before. Initially, a value for one component must be selected so we shall make R equal to 470 Ω. Then, using $LC = 470 \times 10^{-3} \times 1 \times 10^{-6}$
$$= 470 \times 10^{-9}$$

and $\dfrac{L}{R_1} = \dfrac{470 \times 10^{-3}}{1 \times 10^3} = 470 \times 10^{-6}$

Therefore $C_1 = \dfrac{L/R_1}{2R} = \dfrac{470 \times 10^{-6}}{2 \times 470} = 0.5\,\mu\text{F}$

Since $R^2 C_1 C_2 = LC$

$$C_2 = \frac{470 \times 10^{-9}}{(470)^2 \times 0.5 \times 10^{-6}} = 4.255\,\mu\text{F}$$

(see Fig. 2.75).

An analysis of the transmission characteristic of this filter, made on the CAD package over the same frequency range as before, is shown in Fig. 2.78, and apart from very slight differences in phase performance at the higher frequencies, the active circuit produces the same filter characteristics as the passive version.

Filter circuits of high performance can be built using an op-amp as the active element, and a few carefully selected resistors and capacitors. Low-pass, high-pass, band pass and band-stop (notch) circuits are all possible and, since no inductors are

Number One Systems Limited Linear Circuit Analysis Program ANALYSER II (C)19

Circuit Name: FILT1   19th March 1992

passive filter with R equal to 10 k

```
                                    GAIN G,*       PHASE P,+      ANY TWO #

Gain (dB abs)      -60         -40         -20          0           20          40
               .....+....:....+....:....+....:....+....:....+....:....+.....
     10 Hz        .           .           .           G           P            .
  11.52 Hz        .           .           .           *           +            .
  13.26 Hz        .           .           .           *           +            .
  15.28 Hz        .           .           .           *           +            .
  17.59 Hz        .           .           .           *           +            .
  20.26 Hz        .           .           .           G           P            .
  23.34 Hz        .           .           .           *           +            .
  26.88 Hz        .           .           .           *           +            .
  30.95 Hz        .           .           .           *           +            .
  35.65 Hz        .           .           .           *           +            .
  41.06 Hz        .           .           .           G           P            .
  47.29 Hz        .           .           .           *           +            .
  54.46 Hz        .           .           .           *           +            .
  62.72 Hz        .           .           .           *           +            .
  72.24 Hz        .           .           .           *           +            .
   83.2 Hz        .           .           .          .G           P            .
  95.82 Hz        .           .           .          .*           +            .
 110.35 Hz        .           .           .          .*           +            .
 127.09 Hz        .           .           .          .*          +.            .
 146.37 Hz        .           .           .           *          +.            .
 168.58 Hz        .           .           .           G          P.            .
 194.15 Hz        .           .           .           *         + .            .
 223.61 Hz        .           .           .           +         *.             .
 257.53 Hz        .           .     +     .           .         *              .
  296.6 Hz        .        +     .         .           .         *             .
 341.59 Hz        .        P     .           .         G         .             .
 393.41 Hz        .        +     .          *  .                 .             .
 453.09 Hz        .        +     .        *    .                 .             .
 521.83 Hz        .       +      .       *     .                 .             .
 600.99 Hz        .       +      .      *      .                 .             .
 692.16 Hz        .       P     .G            .                  .             .
 797.16 Hz        .       +    *             .                   .             .
 918.09 Hz        .       +   *.             .                   .             .
  1.06 KHz        .       +      *           .                   .             .
  1.22 KHz        .       +        *         .                   .             .
   1.4 KHz        .       P      .   G       .                   .             .
  1.62 KHz        .       +      . *         .                   .             .
  1.86 KHz        .       +      .*          .                   .             .
  2.14 KHz        .       +     .*           .                   .             .
  2.47 KHz        .       +    *             .                   .             .
  2.84 KHz        .       P  G.              .                   .             .
  3.27 KHz        .       + *  .             .                   .             .
  3.77 KHz        .       + *  .             .                   .             .
  4.34 KHz        .       +*   .             .                   .             .
     5 KHz        .       #    .             .                   .             .
               .....+....:....+....:....+....:....+....:....+....:....+.....
Phase (deg)     -200       -150        -100        -50           0           50
```

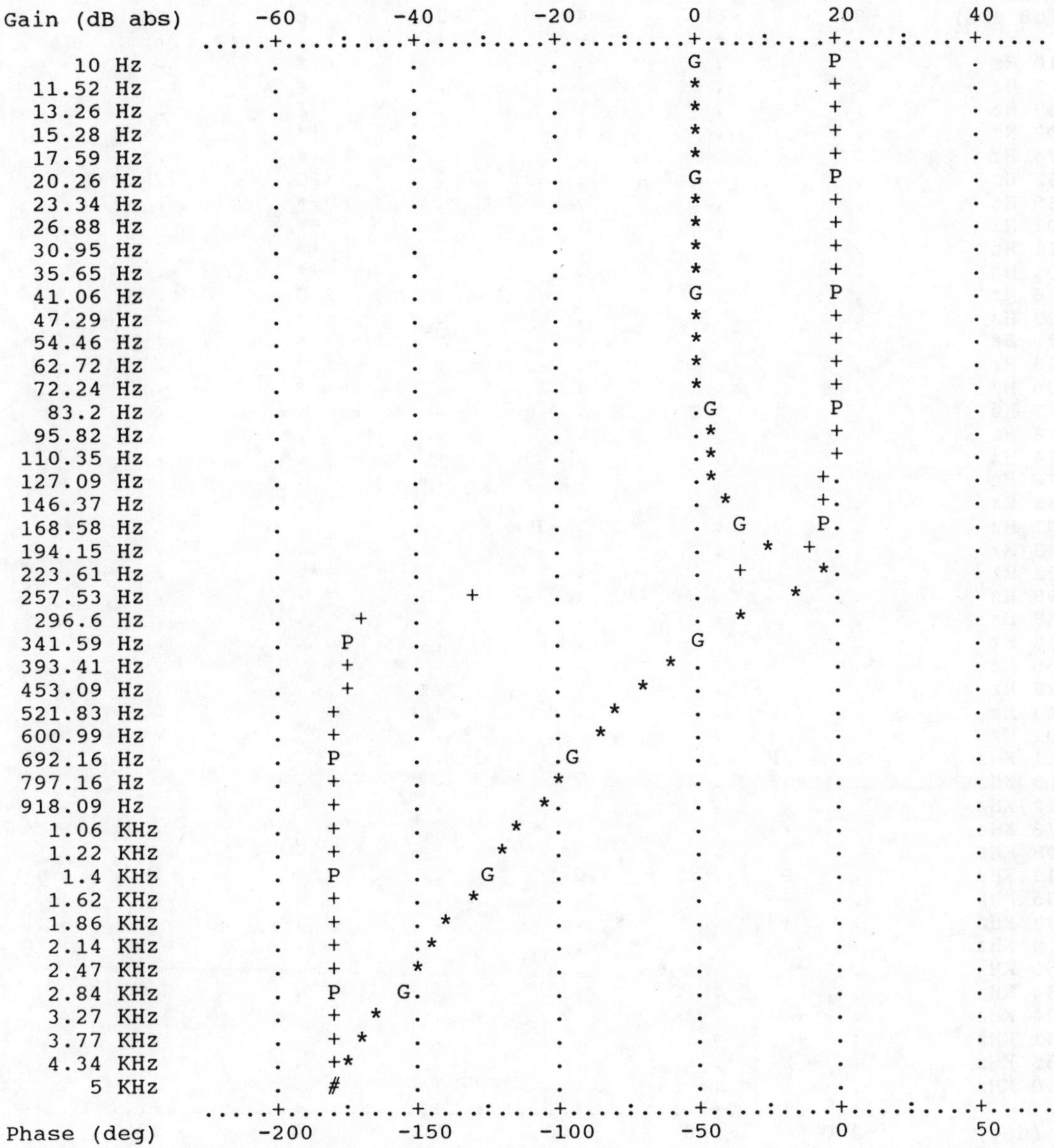

Fig. 2.77 Passive filter response (low damping)

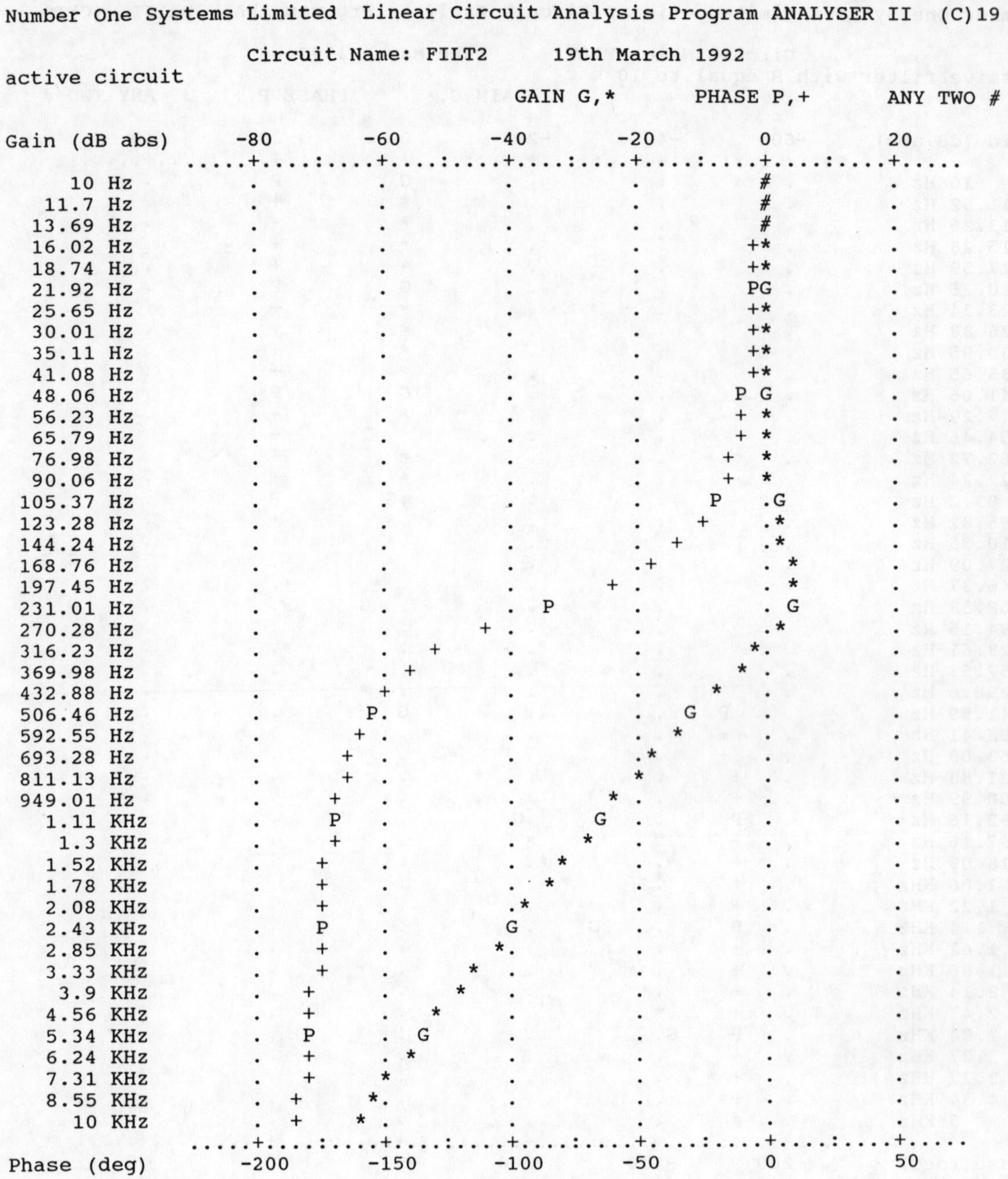

```
Number One Systems Limited  Linear Circuit Analysis Program ANALYSER II  (C)19
                Circuit Name: FILT2      19th March 1992
active circuit
                                     GAIN G,*       PHASE P,+      ANY TWO #

Gain (dB abs)     -80         -60         -40         -20          0           20
             ....+....:....+....:....+....:....+....:....+....:....+.....
     10 Hz       .           .           .           .           #           .
   11.7 Hz       .           .           .           .           #           .
  13.69 Hz       .           .           .           .           #           .
  16.02 Hz       .           .           .           .          +*           .
  18.74 Hz       .           .           .           .          +*           .
  21.92 Hz       .           .           .           .          PG           .
  25.65 Hz       .           .           .           .          +*           .
  30.01 Hz       .           .           .           .          +*           .
  35.11 Hz       .           .           .           .          +*           .
  41.08 Hz       .           .           .           .          +*           .
  48.06 Hz       .           .           .           .         P G           .
  56.23 Hz       .           .           .           .         + *           .
  65.79 Hz       .           .           .           .         + *           .
  76.98 Hz       .           .           .           .        +  *           .
  90.06 Hz       .           .           .           .        +  *           .
 105.37 Hz       .           .           .           .       P  .G           .
 123.28 Hz       .           .           .           .      +   .*           .
 144.24 Hz       .           .           .           .    +     .*           .
 168.76 Hz       .           .           .           .  +       . *          .
 197.45 Hz       .           .           .           .+        . *          .
 231.01 Hz       .           .           .        P   .        . G          .
 270.28 Hz       .           .           .   +        .        .*           .
 316.23 Hz       .           .         +   .          .       *.            .
 369.98 Hz       .           .       +     .          .      * .            .
 432.88 Hz       .           .     +       .          .     *  .            .
 506.46 Hz       .           P.            .          .   G    .            .
 592.55 Hz       .          + .            .          .  *     .            .
 693.28 Hz       .        +   .            .          .*       .            .
 811.13 Hz       .        +   .            .          *        .            .
 949.01 Hz       .       +    .            .        * .        .            .
  1.11 KHz       .       P    .            .      G   .        .            .
   1.3 KHz       .       +    .            .     *    .        .            .
  1.52 KHz       .       +    .            .   *      .        .            .
  1.78 KHz       .       +    .            . *        .        .            .
  2.08 KHz       .       +    .            .*         .        .            .
  2.43 KHz       .       P    .          G .          .        .            .
  2.85 KHz       .       +    .          *.           .        .            .
  3.33 KHz       .       +    .        * .            .        .            .
   3.9 KHz       .      +     .      *   .            .        .            .
  4.56 KHz       .      +     .    *     .            .        .            .
  5.34 KHz       .      P     .  G       .            .        .            .
  6.24 KHz       .      +     .*         .            .        .            .
  7.31 KHz       .      +    *.          .            .        .            .
  8.55 KHz       .     +   *. .          .            .        .            .
    10 KHz       .     +   *  .          .            .        .            .
             ....+....:....+....:....+....:....+....:....+....:....+.....
Phase (deg)      -200        -150        -100         -50          0           50
```

Fig. 2.78   Active filter response

necessary the circuits are less bulky and cheaper than those using just passive components. Also the op-amp provides gain, so there is no insertion loss over the pass-band and the active filter has good isolation. This isolation results from the op-amp's high input impedance and low output impedance. The only drawback is that designs are limited by the frequency characteristics of the op-amp. Therefore most general-purpose op-amps can only be used for filters at audio frequencies.

For low-pass and high-pass filters the most easily designed circuit is the equal-component 'Butterworth' type. These have two CR networks and a voltage gain set to 4 dB (Fig. 2.79); the characteristics are close to those listed previously. Consider the low-pass circuit. Here the two CR networks have the capacitors connecting the signal to a low impedance point, C_2 to ground and C_1 to the output of the op-amp. At low frequencies these capacitors will have a high reactance which allows all the signal through to the op-amp, but as the signal frequency is increased the capacitors shunt more and more of the signal to ground and the output will fall. With $C_1 = C_2$ and $R_1 = R_2$ the attenuation beyond cut-off will increase by 40 dB/decade.

By cascading filters attenuation rates of 60 dB/decade or higher are possible.

For the circuit:

$$f_c = 1/(2\pi \sqrt{R_1 R_2 C_1 C_2}) \quad (2.62)$$

But with $R_1 = R_2$ and $C_1 = C_2$, which is the most convenient design condition, this simplifies to:

$$f_c = 1/(2\pi RC) \quad (1)$$

To set the gain to 1.586 (4 dB) R_4 must be made just over half the value of R_3. Therefore

$$R_4 = 0.586 R_3 \quad (2)$$

Example

Design a low-pass filter with a cut-off frequency of 400 Hz.

Select a standard value for the capacitors.

In this case 22 nF will be suitable. Rearrange equation (1) to make R the subject:
Therefore $R = 1/(2\pi f_c C)$
Therefore $R = 18.08\,k\Omega$ (18 kΩ is nearest preferred value — npv)
Make $R_3 = 56\,k\Omega$
Therefore $R_4 = 0.586 R_3 = 32.82\,k\Omega$ (33 kΩ is npv)

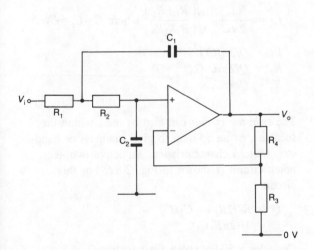

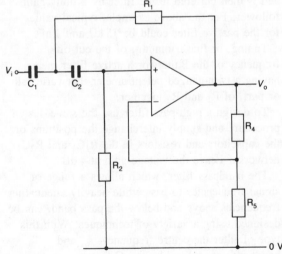

Fig. 2.79 (a) Low-pass; (b) high-pass

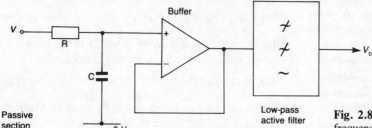

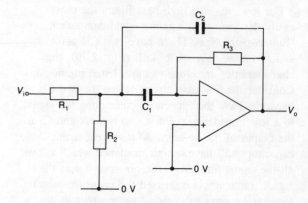

Fig. 2.80 Using a passive filter to improve high-frequency rejection

To obtain the best results from these circuits good-quality close-tolerance components must be used. Since capacitors are relatively bulky and expensive, the values in this design could be reduced to, say, 2.2 nF allowing the use of ± 2.5 per cent tolerance polystyrene types. In that case the two resistors R_1 and R_2 would have to be 180 kΩ ± 1 per cent metal film.

Unless a wide-band op-amp is used the attenuation level will fall above 100 kHz. This is because the open-loop gain of the op-amp falls as the frequency is increased. In other words, the low-pass active filter built with a general-purpose op-amp, such as the 351, has inferior high-frequency rejection. This can be overcome by attenuating the high-frequency components of the signal using a passive filter, as shown in Fig. 2.80. This initial low-pass filter has its cut-off frequency set to ten times that of the active filter, and is then buffered to the filter by a unity gain follower. For the above example, typical values for the passive filter could be 15 kΩ and 1 nF.

Tuning, or fine trimming, of the cut-off frequency of the Butterworth active filter means having a twin-ganged potentiometer that varies all, or part, of R_1 and R_2 together.

To design a high-pass filter use the same design procedure and simply interchange the positions of the capacitors and resistors in the R_1C_1 and R_2C_2 networks. Leave the voltage gain at 4 dB.

The bandpass filter, which allows a range of signal frequencies to pass while heavily attenuating frequencies above and below the pass band, can be designed using a variety of techniques. With this type of filter the centre frequency, f_o, and bandwidth are related by the Q factor.

$$Q = f_o/BW$$

Fig. 2.81 Simple bandpass filter

With a single op-amp used in the multiple-feedback circuit of Fig. 2.81 the value of Q is usually restricted to 5. The gain of the circuit is set by R_3 and R_1, and the centre frequency can be trimmed by R_2. The formulae for the design are:

$$f_o = \frac{1}{2\pi C} \sqrt{\left[\frac{R_1+R_2}{R_1R_2R_3}\right]} \quad \text{where } C=C_1=C_2$$

$$R_1 = Q/2\pi fCG$$
$$R_2 = Q/2\pi fC\,(2Q^2-G)$$
$$R_3 = Q/\pi fC$$

The *twin-tee circuit* can also be used within the feedback of an op-amp to give bandpass or band-stop (notch) characteristics. An active twin-tee notch circuit is shown in Fig. 2.82. For this circuit:

$$Q = R_2/2R_1 = C_1/C_2$$
$$f_o = 1/(2\pi R_1C_1)$$

Consider a 50 Hz notch filter with a Q of 5. Letting $C_1 = 100$ nF

Example

Design a bandpass filter to the following specification:

$f_o = 2\,\text{kHz}$
$BW = 500\,\text{Hz}$
$G = 2$

(1) Choose suitable values for the capacitors. In practice these can be in the range 10–100 nF for audio circuits.

Therefore let C_1 and C_2 be 10 nF

(2) Since the *BW* required is 500 Hz the circuit must have a *Q* of 4.
Therefore $R_1 = 15.9\,\text{k}\Omega$
$R_2 = 1.06\,\text{k}\Omega$
and $R_3 = 63.66\,\text{k}\Omega$

$R_1 = 31.83\,\text{k}\Omega$
Since $Q = 5$ $R_2 = 10R_1$
Therefore $R_2 = 318.3\,\text{k}\Omega$
Finally, since $C_2 = C_1/Q$
$C_2 = 20\,\text{nF}$

The *state variable filter* is a circuit using three op-amps and passive components that can simultaneously give low-pass, high-pass and bandpass characteristics. Basically the circuit consists of a difference amplifier and two integrators (Fig. 2.83). The formulae required for a design are:

$$f_o = 1/(2\pi R_1 C_1)$$

and

$$R_2 = (3Q-1)R_3$$

With this circuit it is possible to achieve a narrow pass band or good high-pass and low-pass response, but not both together.

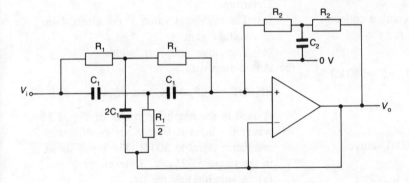

Fig. 2.82 Twin-tee notch filter

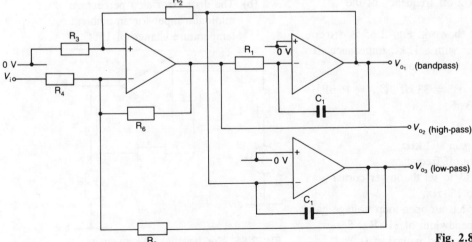

Fig. 2.83 State-variable filter

2.7 Problems

(1) For the circuit in Fig. 2.84, determine a value for C_1 to set the low-frequency cut-off to 15 Hz.

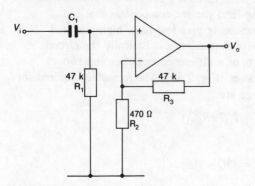

Fig. 2.84 A.c. coupled amplifier

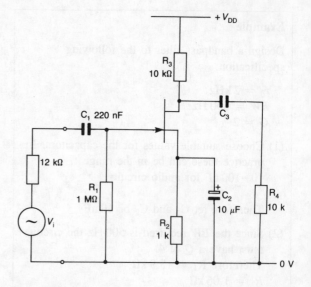

Fig. 2.85 FET common source amplifier

(2) A transistor operated in CE has a d.c. collector bias current of 10 mA and a collector load of 600 Ω. The parameters for the transistor are:

$$r_{bb'} = 85\,\Omega \quad r_{b'e} = 990\,\Omega \quad r_{ce} = 40\,k\Omega$$
$$r_{b'c} = 1500\,k\Omega$$
$$C_{b'e} = 25\,pF \quad C_{b'c} = 2.3\,pF \text{ and}$$
$$C_{ce} = 0.5\,pF$$

The circuit is driven from a 100 Ω source. Determine:

(a) The mid-band voltage gain in dB
(b) The upper cut-off frequency of the amplifier.

(3) The FET circuit shown in Fig. 2.85 is driven from a transducer with a 12 kΩ impedance. If the FET parameter values are:

$$g_{fs} = 4\,mS \quad r_{ds} = 33\,k\Omega \quad C_{gs} = 16\,pF$$
$$\text{and } C_{gd} = 3\,pF$$

determine:

(a) the voltage gain at 1 kHz
(b) the upper cut-off frequency
(c) a value for C_3 to set the lower corner frequency to 150 Hz.

(4) A d.c. amplifier has an open-loop voltage gain of 64 dB and a bandwidth of 31 kHz. Series voltage feedback is used with β of 0.08.

Determine:

(a) The mid-band value of the closed-loop voltage gain
(b) The closed-loop bandwidth.

(5) An op-amp with:

$$dV_{io}/dT = 0.5\,\mu V/°C \text{ and } dI_{io}/dT = 20\,pA/°C$$

is used in the amplifier circuit of Fig. 2.86 where the input is from a sensor of source resistance equal to 50 kΩ. The input signal is in the range 5–25 mV. Determine:

(a) A suitable npv for R_3
(b) The drift error as a percentage of minimum input for an ambient temperature change of 15°C.

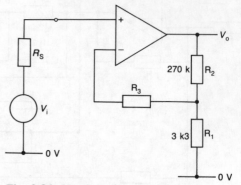

Fig. 2.86 Non-inverting op-amp circuit

2.8   Suggested assignment and project work

(1) The block diagram shown in Fig. 2.87 uses an op-amp in the non-inverting configuration to amplify the signals from a sensor of $2 \, k\Omega$ impedance to the level shown. Design the amplifier and filter circuits.

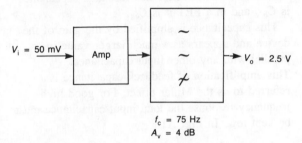

$$f_c = 75 \, \text{Hz}$$
$$A_v = 4 \, \text{dB}$$

Fig. 2.87   Amplifier and filter circuit

(2) A single-supply small signal a.c. amplifier is required to the following specification:

$$V_s = +9 \, \text{V}$$
$$A_v = 40 \, \text{dB} \pm 2 \, \text{dB}$$
$$R_{in} = \text{at least } 40 \, k\Omega$$
$$BW = 15 \, \text{Hz} - 20 \, \text{kHz}$$

Outline the circuit to be used, giving suitable component values. Ensure that only one CR network sets the low-frequency cut-off and select an op-amp that will have the required GBP to give the specified upper cut-off frequency.

(3) Compare a selection of op-amps in terms of the parameters:

A_{vol}, I_b, I_{io}, V_{io}, SR and GBP

(4) Research suitable measurement methods for the key op-amp parameters A_{vol}, V_{io}, I_b, I_{io} and SR.

(5) Compare the use of the 555 timer IC with op-amps in low-frequency square-wave oscillator applications. A list of important parameters for such oscillators will be needed.

(6) A square-wave power generator is to be designed using a power op-amp IC. The specification for the generator is:

$$\text{Frequency} = 400 \, \text{Hz} \pm 10 \, \text{Hz}$$
$$\text{Amplitude} = \pm 5 \, \text{V}$$
$$\text{Load} = 24 \, \Omega$$

Research the available power op-amps, and outline the design. Then design and test the circuit.

(7) A 20 kHz pulse generator giving out $+5 \, \text{V}$ amplitude pulses with a mark-to-space ratio of $1 : 5$ is required by a test department. Produce a suitable design.

(8) Design and test a simple op-amp function generator to give triangle waves at $0.5 \, \text{Hz} \pm 15$ per cent at an amplitude of $\pm 3 \, \text{V}$. Compare your design with at least two other methods used in generating low-frequency triangle waves. (Other methods include using digital ICs or a modified 555 astable.)

(9) The circuit given in Fig. 2.88 is a FET preamplifier with a voltage gain of about 24 dB.

  (a) State the type of feedback used and determine the value of β.

  (b) Estimate the mid-band open-loop voltage gain. You can assume that the FET has $y_{fs} = 1.5 \, \text{mS}$ and that the transistor has an h_{fe} of 200.

  (c) Determine the closed-loop voltage gain

  (d) Using a suitable CAD software tool find mid-band values for A_v, Z_{in} and Z_{out}.

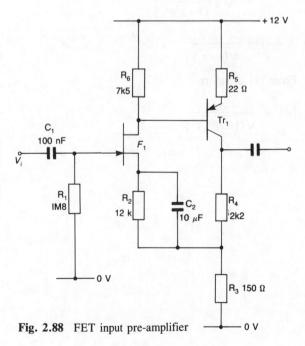

Fig. 2.88   FET input pre-amplifier

Obtain a plot of the frequency response and determine the bandwidth.

(e) Modify the circuit to give a mid-band voltage gain of 20 dB.

Appendix A

If $A = \dfrac{A_o}{1-jf/f_h}$ (1)

take $A = \dfrac{1}{1-jx}$ where $x = f/f_h$

Then $A = \dfrac{1}{(1-jx)} \cdot \dfrac{(1+jx)}{(1+jx)} = \dfrac{1+jx}{1+x^2}$

$\therefore A = \dfrac{1}{(1+x^2)} + j\dfrac{x}{1+x^2}$

$\therefore |A| = \sqrt{\left(\dfrac{1}{1+x^2}\right)^2 + \left(\dfrac{x}{1+x^2}\right)^2}$

$\therefore |A| = \sqrt{\left[\dfrac{1}{(1+x^2)^2} + \dfrac{x^2}{(1+x^2)^2}\right]}$

$= \sqrt{\left[\dfrac{1+x^2}{(1+x^2)^2}\right]}$

$\therefore |A| = \dfrac{1}{\sqrt{(1+x^2)}}$

From (1) therefore

$|A| = \dfrac{A_o}{\sqrt{[1+(f/f_h)^2]}}$

Appendix B

Miller effect

Any inverting amplifier, such as a bipolar transistor connected in common emitter mode, or a FET in common source, will have some small feedback capacitance between its output and input terminals. In a transistor this feedback capacitance is $C_{b'c}$ and in a FET it is C_{gd}.

This capacitance is amplified by the gain of the device and appears as a much larger value in parallel with any other input capacitance. This amplification of feedback capacitance is referred to as the Miller effect. For good high-frequency response the total input capacitance must be kept low. In Fig. A1

$I_1 = I_2 + I_3$
$I_2 = V_i(j\omega C_1)$
$I_3 = (V_i - A_v V_i)j\omega C_f = V_i(1-A_v)j\omega C_f$
$\therefore I_1 = V_i[j\omega C_1 + j\omega C_f(1-A_v)]$

The portion in the square brackets represents the equivalent input capacitance C_{eq}, i.e.

$C_{eq} = C_1 + C_f(1-A_v)$

For example, suppose $C_1 = 22\,\text{pF}$, $C_f = 5\,\text{pF}$ and $A_v = -50$, then

$C_{eq} = 22 + 5(51) = 277\,\text{pF}$

The effect is put to good use in the generation of ramp and triangle waveforms.

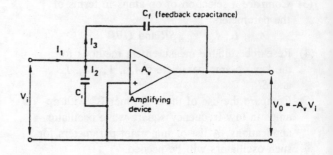

3 Large Signal Amplifiers

3.1 Characteristics and parameters

The large signal or power amplifier circuit is normally designed to deliver a high-power output to a relatively low-impedance load. The most obvious example of this type of amplifier is the output stage of an audio system, where the task of the amplifier is to provide several watts of audiofrequency power to the loudspeaker, with low levels of harmonic distortion. The main specification points for such an amplifier might be stated as shown in Table 3.1.

Table 3.1 Audio power amplifier specification

Maximum power output	40 W into 4 Ω
Efficiency	60 per cent
Bandwidth (BW)	15 Hz–30 kHz
Total Harmonic Distortion (THD)	Less than 0.5 per cent at f=1 kHz and a power output of 30 Watts
Sensitivity	1 V rms

It is worth considering this specification in more detail as a guide to understanding the principles and problems associated with these types of amplifiers. The diagram of the system is shown in Fig. 3.1, where it can be seen that a block for the power supply is included. This is because the power supply must usually be considered as an integral part of the design, since the function of the amplifier is to control the flow of power from the power source to the load. The voltage input to the amplifier is the control input, and is designed in this case to have a sensitivity such that a 1 V rms a.c. input signal at a suitable frequency within the amplifier's bandwidth (1 kHz is a typical test frequency) causes the amplifier to deliver the full rated 40 W output to the 4 Ω load. As the

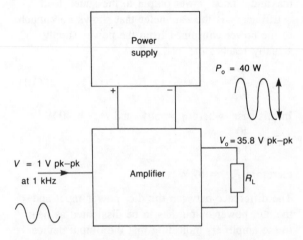

Fig. 3.1 Block diagram of a large signal amplifier

amplitude of the input is varied, so the power output is changed. Although power gain exists in a large signal amplifier it is power output, voltage gain and efficiency that are the key performance parameters. Power output is quoted, unless otherwise stated, as an rms value. If we assume that R_L in the example is resistive, and that a control signal at a frequency of 1 kHz is applied to the input, then the maximum output voltage is given as follows:

$$V_o = \sqrt{P\,R_L} = \sqrt{160} = 12.65 \text{ V rms}$$

Thus the peak-to-peak output voltage is:

$$V_o = 2\sqrt{2}\,\text{Vrms} = 35.8 \text{ Vpk–pk}$$

This voltage signal change across the 4 Ω load indicates that a relatively high supply voltage is required. In the example, a supply of about 48 V($\pm$24 V) is indicated. This illustrates the fact that higher voltage supplies are normally necessary for large signal amplifiers.

Since the sensitivity is 1 Vpk–pk, the voltage

gain required of the amplifier is:

$$A_v = \frac{V_o}{V_i} = 35.8$$

Some negative-feedback loop within the amplifier must be used to set the closed-loop gain to this figure.

Sensitivity is therefore defined as the input voltage value that causes the amplifier to deliver maximum rated power output to the stated load.

Efficiency is the parameter that shows how much of the power consumed from the power supply actually reaches the load.

$$\eta = \frac{P_{ac}}{P_{dc}} \times 100\% \qquad (3.1)$$

In this case, where $\eta = 60\%$ and $P_{ac} = 40\,W$,

$$P_{dc} = \frac{40}{0.6}$$

therefore $P_{dc} = 67\,W$

The difference between the d.c. power input and the a.c. power output has to be dissipated as heat in the amplifier, indicating that the output device or devices must be fitted on an adequate heatsink (see Section 3).

Power loss in amplifier $= P_{dc} - P_{ac}$

It will be appreciated that the higher the efficiency the lower will be the power loss and the smaller the overall size of the amplifier. However, high values of efficiency are not necessarily associated with low levels of distortion, and some increase in size of heatsink may be required in an amplifier designed to achieve a low level of distortion.

Since very large signal level changes will take place in the active devices the analysis of a power amplifier, using models such as the h-parameter or hybrid–pi, is not valid. Graphical analysis using device characteristics is often the preferred method.

Various classes of operation are used in large signal amplifier design, from class A, class B, class AB through to classes C and D. These classes are as follows:

Class A: The output device (transistor, valve or power FET) is biased to the mid-point of its characteristics. Maximum theoretical efficiency is 50 per cent.

Class B: Used in push–pull stages where the two output devices are biased just to cut-off. One conducts on the positive half-cycle of the output signal, the other on the negative half-cycle. Maximum theoretical efficiency is 78.54 per cent.

Class AB: A modified class B, where the two output devices are provided with a small forward bias to reduce the crossover distortion inherent in class B.

Class C: The output device is biased beyond cut-off. This class is used in tuned RF power stages.

Class D: A switching system with devices pulsewidth-modulated to control power output. More complex than class AB, but capable of very high efficiency.

3.2 Class A circuits

Typical circuit arrangements for this type of amplifier are shown in Fig. 3.2. In Fig. 3.2(a) the load is connected directly in the collector circuit, a method that is not normally possible for loads less than $100\,\Omega$. A more usual circuit arrangement for class A uses a transformer to match the load to the transistor's output (Fig. 3.2(b)). A suitable turns ratio in the transformer, causes the load resistance to be reflected back into the primary circuit to appear at a much higher value (Fig. 3.3)).

$$\text{Turns ratio} = \sqrt{\frac{R'}{R_L}} \qquad (3.2)$$

If we consider the output characteristics of the transistor, for the basic circuit the load line can be constructed using the two points A and B, where

point A $\quad I_c = 0$ and $V_{CE} = V_{CC}$

point B $\quad I_c = \dfrac{V_{CC}}{R_L}$ $\quad V_{CE} = 0$

The quiescent operating point (Fig. 3.4) is then selected so that V_{CE} is one-half of V_{CC}. This allows an even voltage and current swing about the operating point. As the input current is varied, a

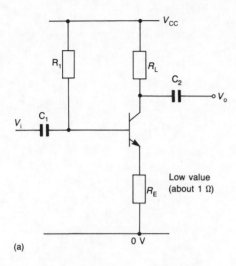

(a)

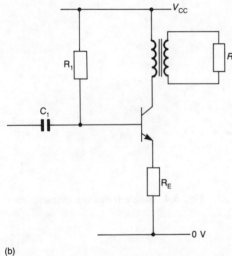

(b)

Fig. 3.2 (a) Class A circuit; (b) class A transformer coupling

much larger change in collector current occurs, setting up a voltage change across R_L.

The maximum theoretical efficiency can be found if we imagine that the whole of the load line is used. In other words, the output voltage change peak-to-peak would be from 0 V to V_{CC}. This, of course, is not possible in a practical circuit.

In determining the maximum theoretical efficiency, the full output characteristics of the transistor are required. For this we assume: (a) that R_E is zero, and (b) that the output can swing fully from 0 V to V_{CC}. For this ideal condition (Fig. 3.5) the maximum a.c. power output is given

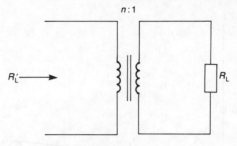

Assuming zero losses
Power in primary = power in secondary

$$\therefore \frac{V_{p2}}{R_L'} = \frac{V_{s2}}{R_L}$$

$$\therefore \frac{V_p}{V_s} = \text{turns ratio} = \sqrt{\frac{R_L'}{R_L}}$$

Fig. 3.3

by

$$P_{ac} = \frac{V_{CC}}{2\sqrt{2}} \cdot \frac{I_{max}}{2\sqrt{2}} \quad \text{W rms}$$

$$= \frac{V_{CC}I_{max}}{8} \quad \text{W rms} \tag{3.3}$$

The d.c. power taken from the supply is

$$P_{dc} = \frac{V_{CC}}{2} \frac{I_{max}}{2} = \frac{V_{CC}I_{max}}{4} \quad \text{W} \tag{3.4}$$

$$\therefore \eta = \frac{P_{ac}}{P_{dc}} \times 100\%$$

$$\therefore \eta = \frac{\dfrac{V_{CC}I_{max}}{8}}{\dfrac{V_{CC}I_{max}}{4}} \times 100\% = 50\% \tag{3.5}$$

Thus the maximum possible efficiency of a class A large signal amplifier cannot exceed 50 per cent.

An exactly similar result is obtained for the transformer coupled class A amplifier. The characteristics and load line are shown in Fig. 3.6.

In this case the operating point is defined by V_{CC} and I_Q, since the d.c. resistance of the transformer primary is considered as almost zero. The theoretical maximum change in collector voltage is therefore from 0 V to 2 V_{CC}. This is because the primary winding presents an inductive load for the transistor.

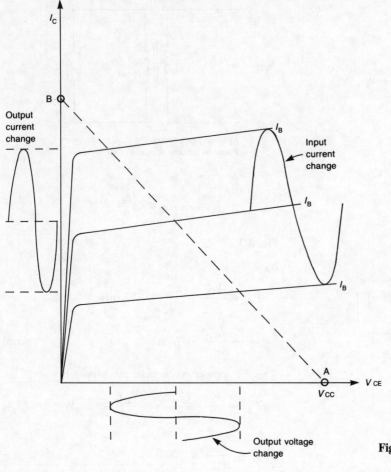

Fig. 3.4 Single transistor characteristics

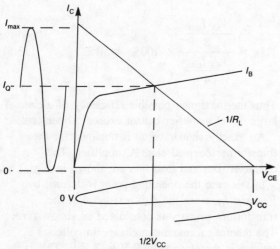

Fig. 3.5 Theoretical maximum efficiency of a simple class A amplifier

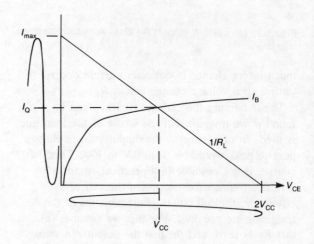

Fig. 3.6 Theoretical maximum efficiency for a transformer coupled class A amplifier

Thus $P_{ac} = 2\dfrac{V_{CC}I_{max}}{8}$ W rms

while $P_{dc} = V_{CC}I_Q = \dfrac{V_{CC}I_{max}}{2}$ W

Thus, as before, $\eta_{max} = 50\%$

In practical circuits efficiencies are often only in the range from 25 to 35 per cent, which can be illustrated by a simple example.

Example

A class A transistor power amplifier is transformer-completed to a $4\,\Omega$ load. Find the required turn ratio and the efficiency of the amplifier.

The characteristics (Fig. 3.7) allow a maximum collector current of 200 mA. V_{CC} is set to $+12\,\text{V}$.

$$R'_L = \frac{24}{0.2} = 120\,\Omega$$

The required turns ratio is

$$n = \sqrt{\frac{R'_L}{R_L}} = \sqrt{\frac{120}{4}} = 5.47 : 1$$

Suppose, for an acceptable distortion level, a collector voltage change of only 18 V pk–pk is allowed.
Then:

$$P_{ac} = \frac{V_o^2}{R'_L} = 337\,\text{mW}$$

However, $P_{dc} = V_{CC}I_Q = 12 \times 0.1 = 1.2\,\text{W}$

$$\therefore \eta = \frac{0.337}{1.2} \times 100 = 28.13\%$$

Such low efficiencies in class A large signal amplifiers indicates that their use is normally restricted to low-power output stages (i.e. less than 1 W). In addition, the transformer has to carry the d.c. operating current I_Q, which means that a relatively large core is necessary for the transformer to prevent it from saturating. However, these problems have not prevented the further development of class A audio power stages, some with significant output levels, with

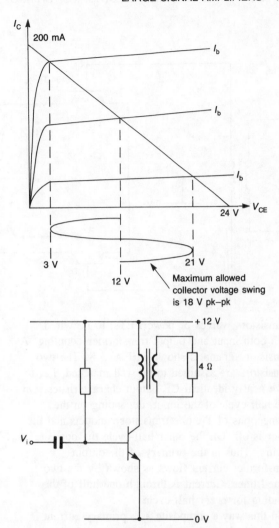

Fig. 3.7 Class A transformer coupled circuit

either thermionic valves or powerFETs being used as the active devices. The additional costs in heatsinks is considered worth it for the benefits of lower distortion and purer sound quality claimed by class A enthusiasts.

3.3 Class B amplifiers

The classic class B arrangement, which makes an excellent starting point for the understanding of the more modern circuits, is for two active devices

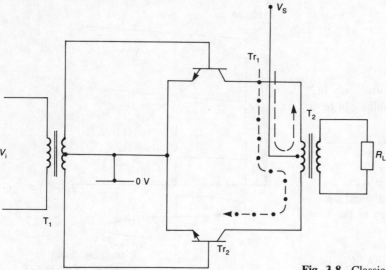

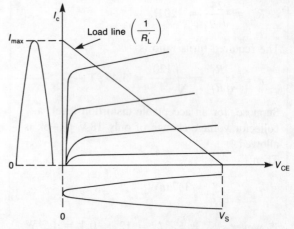

Fig. 3.8   Classic Class B transformer coupled amplifier

(transistors, valves or powerFETs) to be wired with both input and output transformer coupling. A transistor version is shown in Fig. 3.8. The two transistors are assumed to be well matched, i.e. to have nearly identical CE output characteristics. On one half-cycle of the input, depending on the connections of T_1, one transistor conducts and the other is off. On the other half-cycle the opposite occurs. Thus in the primary of the output transformer current flows as shown by the two dotted lines. Current is through one half of the winding for every half-cycle.

In this way a composite a.c. primary current is set up which is transformer coupled to the load. Under no signal conditions both transistors are off so no d.c. current taken from the supply and the transformer can be significantly smaller than for class A. The characteristics for one transistor are shown in Fig. 3.9. When the transistor is off V_{CE} is equal to V_S and I_C is zero. The load line has a slope of $1/R'_L$, where as before

$$R'_L = V_s/I_{max}$$

and $n = \sqrt{\dfrac{R'_L}{R_L}}$

where n is the turns ratio for each half of the primary.

If the whole of the characteristics of both

Fig. 3.9   The characteristics for one transistor in a push–pull amplifier. Note that maximum theoretical current and voltage swings are shown

transistors could be used, the maximum a.c. output power is given by

$$P_{ac(max)} = \frac{V_S}{\sqrt{2}} \cdot \frac{I_{max}}{\sqrt{2}} = \frac{1}{2} V_S \cdot I_{max}$$

To find the power taken from the supply we need the following equation:

$$P_{dc} = V_S \cdot I_{dc}$$

Here the d.c. current is the average of the pulsating current flowing from the V_S connection to the centre tap of the primary.

$$I_{AV} = \frac{2}{\pi} I_{max}$$

therefore $P_{dc} = \frac{2}{\pi} I_{max} V_S$ (3.6)

The maximum theoretical efficiency of the class B circuit is therefore:

$$\eta_{max} = \frac{P_{ac}}{P_{dc}} \times 100\%$$

$$= \frac{\frac{1}{2} V_{S max}}{2/\pi \ I_{max} V_S} \times 100\%$$

$$= \frac{\pi}{4} \times 100\% = 78.54\%$$

This theoretical figure could not be realized in practice, and efficiencies are usually of the order of 60 per cent.

Example

A class B transformer coupled amplifier uses transistors which can be allowed to pass a maximum peak current of 2 A at a V_{CE} of 3 V. The supply is 24 V. Determine the full power output and the efficiency.

A sketch of the output characteristics is given in Fig. 3.10, showing that R'_L is:

$$R'_L = \frac{21}{2} = 10.5 \ \Omega$$

Since $I_{Cmax} = 2$ A and V_{CEmin} is specified as 3 V

$$P_{ac} = V_o I_o = \frac{21}{\sqrt{2}} \cdot \frac{2}{\sqrt{2}} = 21 \ W$$

$$P_{dc} = \frac{2}{\pi} I_{max} \cdot V_S = \frac{2.2}{\pi} \times 24 = 30.56 \ W$$

$$\therefore \eta = \frac{P_{ac}}{P_{dc}} = \frac{21}{30.56} \times 100\% = 68.7\%$$

The typical transformerless class B output stage uses complementary power transistors, as shown in Fig. 3.11.

Two well-matched transistors must be used, to avoid increased distortion, with a suitable driver

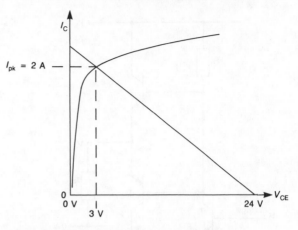

Fig. 3.10 Transistor characteristics showing the practical limits of current and voltage swings

stage included to provide voltage gain. On the positive half-cycles of voltage signal at the driver collector, Tr_2 will conduct and 'push' current into R_L, whereas on the other half-cycle Tr_3 will turn on and 'pull' the current from R_L. Since each transistor could in theory connect a signal of V_S peak across R_L the *maximum theoretical output is given by:*

$$P_{acmax} = \frac{V_S}{\sqrt{2}} \frac{I_{max}}{\sqrt{2}} = \frac{V_S I_{max}}{2}$$

The d.c. power taken from the power supply is

$$P_{dc} = \frac{2}{\pi} I_{max} V_S$$

$$\therefore \eta_{max} = \frac{\frac{V_S I_{max}}{2}}{\frac{2}{\pi} I_{max} V_S} \times 100\%$$ (3.7)

$$= 78.54\% \text{ (as before)}$$

This level of efficiency cannot be achieved in a practical circuit.

With this type of circuit either a single or a split power supply can be used. The latter has the advantage of allowing direct coupling to the load as the quiescent, no-signal operation point at the junction of the two emitters will be 0 V. Alternatively, with a single supply, a coupling capacitor is necessary to isolate the load from the d.c. operating point. This d.c. operating point will be $\frac{1}{2} V_S$ (see Fig. 3.1(b)). Since the load will often

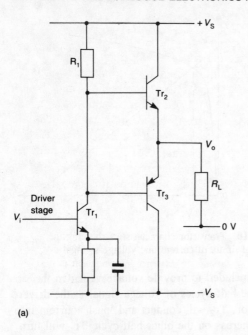

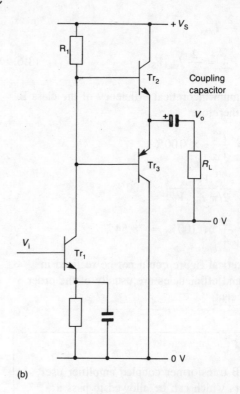

Fig. 3.11 (a) The outline of the basic complementary class B using a split power supply; (b) single supply version

be a low resistance, to ensure good low frequency response, the value of the coupling capacitor needs to be high. For this reason the split-supply d.c. coupled arrangement is often preferred, even though this poses additional protection problems for the load, for with this system if one transistor goes short-circuit, a damaging load current could flow.

The basic complementary class B output stage has several limitations, which can be listed as follows:

(1) Cross-over distortion occurs because each transistor requires at least 600 mV of forward bias before conduction can begin.
(2) Protection of the output transistors and the load must be provided, so that an overload condition does not destroy either of these components or the load.
(3) The d.c. operating point at the junction of the two emitters must be held stable.
(4) On positive half-cycles at the driver collector the voltage across R_1 falls, *reducing* the available current drive to Tr_1

just when it requires its highest value of base current.

The removal of the crossover distortion requires that both transistors (or powerFETs) be given a small forward bias sufficient to just overcome the required V_{BE} or $V_{GS(th)}$ respectively. This changes the class of operation from B to AB, a class which is discussed in the next section. Before we move on to look at the typical class AB circuit in which the solution to the other limitations of class B will also be examined let us work through a class B complementary example.

Example

A complementary class B power output stage uses two transistors to deliver 3 W into a 16 Ω load. If the efficiency is 64 per cent, determine the power supply voltage required.

Since $P_{ac} = 3\,W$
and $P_{ac} = I^2 R$

$$I = \sqrt{\frac{P_{ac}}{R}} = \sqrt{\frac{3}{16}} = 0.433 \text{ A rms}$$

$$\therefore I \text{ peak} = 0.612 \text{ A}$$

$$\eta = \frac{P_{ac}}{P_{dc}}$$

$$\therefore P_{dc} = \frac{3}{0.64} = 4.69 \text{ W}$$

$$\text{But } P_{dc} = \frac{2}{\pi} I_p V_S$$

(Where V_S is the voltage across one transistor)

$$\therefore V_2 = \frac{\pi P_{dc}}{2 I_p}$$

$$= 12 \text{ V}$$

(NB: This is the supply across *one* transistor, therefore the total voltage rail must be either ± 12 V or $+24$ V.)

Fig. 3.12 (a) Simple class AB bias (not recommended see text); (b) improved class AB bias; (c) the V_{BE} multiplier bias circuit

3.4 Class AB amplifiers

To reduce the crossover distortion inherent in the class B amplifier, the d.c. bias voltage applied between Tr_2 and Tr_3 base connections must be just in excess of 1 V. This could be achieved by a simple series resistor placed in the collector of the driver and between the base connections of Tr_2 and Tr_3 (Fig. 3.12(a)). However, this solution is not to be recommended in practice, since under normal operation the two output transistors will heat up, causing the required V_{BE} of both to drop by 2.5 mV per °C. If the bias voltage is fixed, both transistors will tend to pass more current, which will in turn lead to additional heating. The result could be a catastrophic condition called 'thermal runaway', in which the output transistors burn out. This situation is inherent in all class AB complementary stages.

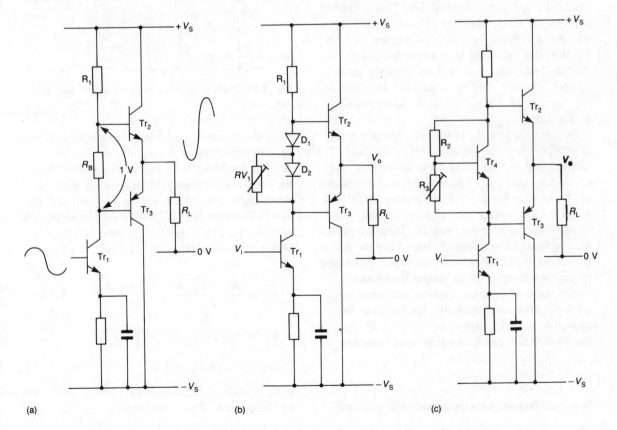

(a)　　　　　　　　(b)　　　　　　　　(c)

A bias circuit is required that sets up the necessary d.c. level but which reduces the applied forward voltage at the same rate with temperature as the output transistors' V_{BE}. One very simple solution is to replace R_B by two diodes (Fig. 3.12(b)), with one diode bridged by a low-value trimpot so that the bias voltage can be trimmed. The two diodes must be in thermal contact with the output transistors, so that as these heat up the diodes also experience the same temperature change. An even better solution, which is standard in most large signal amplifiers, is called the V_{BE} multiplier. This is shown in Fig. 3.12(c). If the current through R_2 and R_3 is made greater than the base current of Tr_4, the resistor chain sets up a voltage across the collector and emitter of Tr_4 that is a multiple of V_{BE}:

$$V_{CE} = V_{BE}\left(1 + \frac{R_3}{R_2}\right) \qquad (3.8)$$

Since the V_{BE} for a silicon transistor is typically 600 mV a ratio of about 0.7 : 1 for R_3 to R_2 will result in a V_{CE} bias voltage of 1 V. This is applied between the base connections of the output transistors to move the class of operation into AB. To allow for variations in components, and to set the bias accurately, part of R_3 is normally made a trimpot. Thermal stability is achieved by clamping the V_{BE} multiplier transistor to the same heatsink as Tr_1 and Tr_2.

Having seen how the crossover distortion effect is greatly reduced in the class AB by the bias arrangement, we can move on to investigate other circuit improvements. The most basic requirements are to stabilize the d.c. operating point at 0 V and to set the a.c. voltage gain to some suitable value. In other words, both d.c. and a.c. feedback paths are required. These feedback loops have the added advantage of further reducing the distortion caused by any non-linearity of the output transistors,* improving the frequency response and increasing the input impedance. Negative feedback can be applied to the driver stage, as in Fig. 3.13, but this method will result in a low input impedance

*It must therefore also further reduce the crossover distortion.

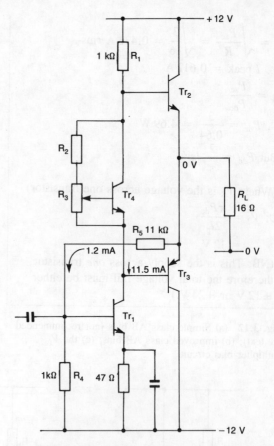

Fig. 3.13 Adding negative feedback to bias the class AB circuit

since the feedback signal from the output is applied in parallel at the input of the driver. Another factor working against this method is that the open-loop voltage gain will not normally be much above 200. In this circuit it is assumed that a +12 V supply is used, so that the output must be held at 0 V. The driver load resistor is 1 kΩ, setting the driver current to 11.5 mA.

$$I_{C_1} = \frac{(V_S^+ - V_{BE_1})}{R_1} = \frac{(12 - 0.6)}{1000} = 11.5 \text{ mA}$$

$$V_{E_1} = I_{C_1}R_4 - V_S^- = -11.4 \text{ V}$$

$$\therefore \ V_{B_1} = -10.8 \text{ V}$$

If R_4 is made at 1k2 Ω then the current via R_5 will be about 1 mA. This is sufficiently large to swamp the small base current required by Tr_3. The value of R_5 is now given by:

$$R_5 = V_{B3}/I_f = 10.8\,k\Omega \text{ (11 k}\Omega \text{ is the npv)}$$

A simple study of the circuit will reveal that the 11.5 mA flowing through Tr_3 will reduce to about 2 mA when Tr_2 base signal is at +10 V. Thus Tr_2 is being starved of base current at the point when it requires the maximum available base drive. Even if half the 2 mA is available for Tr_2, its peak output current, assuming an h_{FE} of 100, cannot be greater than 100 mA. This would imply a load of 94 Ω. The basic circuit is clearly lacking in ability to produce output power. One obvious solution is to use power Darlingtons for Tr_2 and Tr_3, so that a peak output current of 1 A is available. These

Darlingtons can be either as shown in Fig. 3.14(a) or quasi-Darlingtons as in Fig. 3.14(b). The latter require less forward bias than the standard Darlingtons, and therefore provide a slightly more efficient circuit. If we simply consider the circuit of Fig. 3.14(a), we have an amplifier capable of delivering about 5 W into 8 Ω. This is based on the assumption that the voltage at Tr_2 base could rise to 10 V, giving an approximate 9 V maximum peak voltage across R_L. In practice this would not result, because of the current requirements of the Tr_2 Darlington at maximum output. Distortion on the positive half-cycle would set in at a peak positive output voltage of 6 V, restricting the power output to a little over 2 W. Two standard solutions are used to overcome this problem.

Fig. 3.14 (a) Adding Darlington output transistors (b) using quasi-Darlingtons

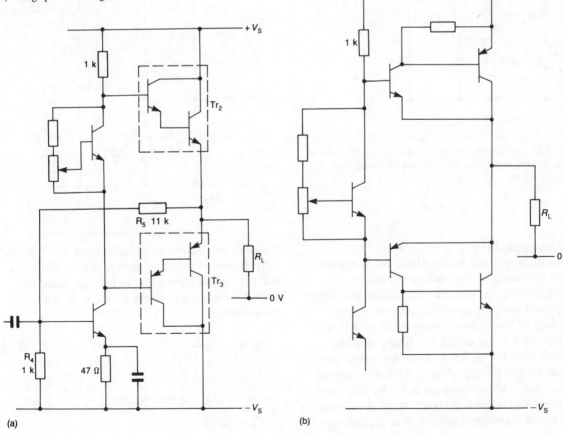

(a)

(b)

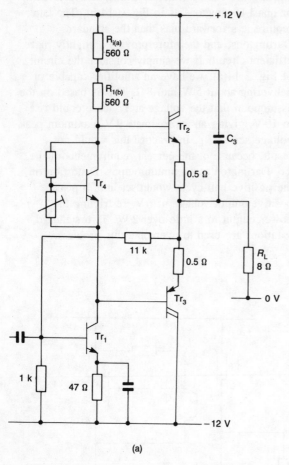

(a)

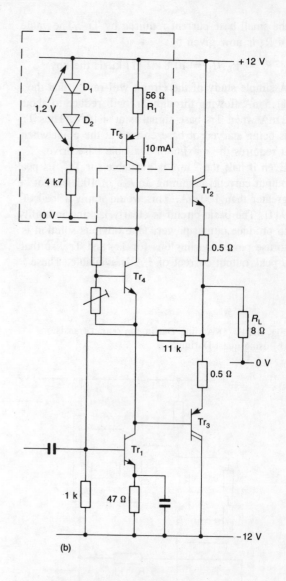

(b)

Fig. 3.15 (a) Bootstrapping to improve output drive & linearity; (b) improving drive by use of a constant current source

Bootstrapping R_1 (Fig. 3.15(a))

Here R_1 is split and positive feedback is applied from the output to the junction of the two resistors. This has the effect of holding the voltage amplitude across $R_{1(b)}$ constant. For example, if the base of Tr_2 increases from $+1$ V to $+10$ V, a change of 9 V, the output will follow this and change from 0 V to $+9$ V. Since the output change is fed back to the top of $R_{1(b)}$, the voltage across $R_{1(b)}$ remains almost constant at 5.5 V. The current through $R_{1(b)}$ remains at about 10 mA even when the top of the positive half-cycle at Tr_1 collector is

reached, thus allowing sufficient drive for Tr_2. The only drawback to this scheme is that an additional CR network is introduced, and the capacitor C_3 must be a low value to maintain low-frequency performance.

$$C_3 = \frac{1}{2\pi f_L \left(\dfrac{R_1}{2} \right)} \tag{3.9}$$

For f_L of 15 Hz in this example:

$$C_3 = 40 \,\mu\text{F}.$$

Providing Tr₁ with a constant current load (Fig. 3.15(b))

This is a more elegant solution. Two diodes are used to give a stable 1.2 V reference which is applied to the base of the PNP transistor Tr_5. The emitter resistor of Tr_5 will therefore have 600 mV across it and its value set the collector current

$$I_{C5} = \frac{V_S - V_{E5}}{R_1} \qquad (3.10)$$

The current through the driver Tr_1 is now fixed, and remains substantially constant over the whole of the cycle, the only drawback being that at least 1.5 V between collector and emitter of Tr_5 is necessary to maintain the current. If the collector voltage of Tr_5, which is directly connected to Tr_1, rises above 10 V, then some distortion in the output will probably occur. In practical circuits the power supply rails are usually well in excess of the +12 V used in this example, so this does not present too much of a disadvantage. In this example:

$P_{out} = 5$ W into 8 Ω

∴ I peak = 1.12 A

∴ $P_{dc} = \dfrac{2}{\pi} \cdot I_p V_S = 8.56$ W

$\eta = 58.5\%$

The problem of low input resistance caused by the type of negative feedback in the basic circuit is eliminated by using a differential input stage before the driver (Fig. 3.16). The open-loop voltage gain is considerably increased by the addition of this stage. Negative feedback is now series-applied, which raises the input resistance of the amplifier and allows the closed-loop gain to be closely defined. This circuit example is designed to deliver an output of 20 W into 8 Ω.

Tr_1 and Tr_2 form the differential input pair with a constant current of 2.2 mA supplied by Tr_3. The collector of Tr_1 is directly coupled to the driver stage Tr_4, which has a constant current of about 11 mA set by Tr_6. The class AB output stage is a matched pair of power Darlingtons Tr_7 (MJ3001) and Tr_8 (MJ2501). D.c. feedback is via R_6 directly to the base of Tr_2, and since the base of Tr_1 is tied to ground via R_1, the output should also be at zero volts. Any offset at the output can be eliminated by using a matched pair for Tr_1 and Tr_2, or by inserting a low-value potentiometer in the common emitters of Tr_1 and Tr_2 (see insert in Fig. 3.16). A.c. negative feedback, which sets the closed-loop voltage gain to approximately 12, is controlled by R_5 and R_6.

$$\beta = \frac{R_5}{R_5 + R_6}$$

$$A_{vcl} \approx \frac{1}{\beta} \quad \therefore A_{vcl} \approx 1 + \frac{R_6}{R_5}$$

At the full power output of 20 W the peak-to-peak a.c. output voltage will be 36 V, so the sensitivity of the amplifier is 1 V rms. The ratio of R_6 to R_5 can be changed to alter this sensitivity. There are two CR networks that affect the low-frequency response of the amplifier and only one must be allowed to dominate the low-frequency roll-off. This will normally be the capacitor in the a.c. feedback loop.

Input capacitor C_1, together with R_1, gives a cut-off of:

$$f_{L_1} = \frac{1}{2\pi C_1 R_1} = 1.6 \text{ Hz}$$

Feedback capacitor C_2, together with R_5, gives a cut-off of:

$$f_{L_2} = \frac{1}{2\pi C_2 R_5} = 12 \text{ Hz}$$

Resistors R_{12} and R_{13} provide some additional linearization to the output, and can also be used to provide an overcurrent protection circuit for the output transistor. The outline of a simple overcurrent limit, together with suitable values for the amplifier of Fig. 3.16, is shown in Fig. 3.17. If a current of more than 5 A is demanded from the output, the voltage across R_{12} will be 1.1 V which, via the potential divider of R_{14} R_{15}, will turn the protection transistor Tr_9 on. This will divert current from the base of Tr_7 and therefore limit the available output current. A similar current-limiting circuit is shown fitted to Tr_8.

Naturally, the heat dissipated by Tr_7 and Tr_8 in the event of a short-circuit output must be safely dissipated. For a short circuit output Tr_7 and Tr_8 will each dissipate a maximum power of

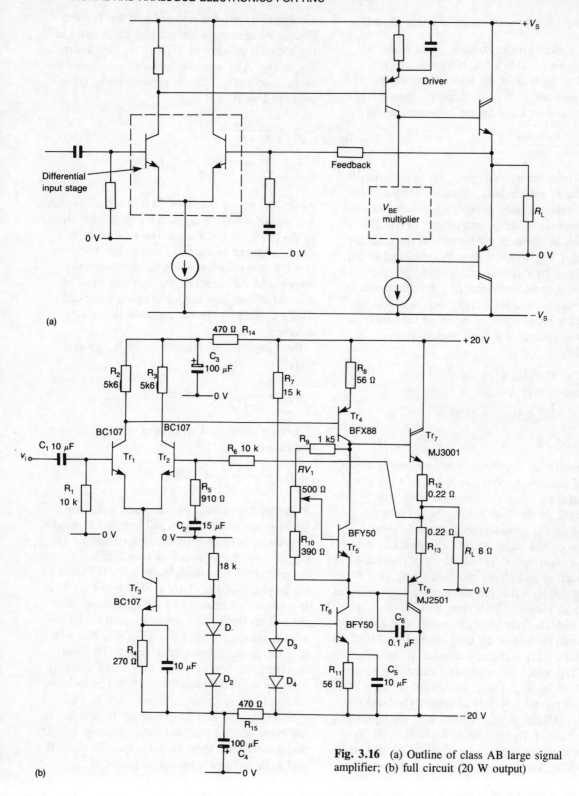

(a)

(b)

Fig. 3.16 (a) Outline of class AB large signal amplifier; (b) full circuit (20 W output)

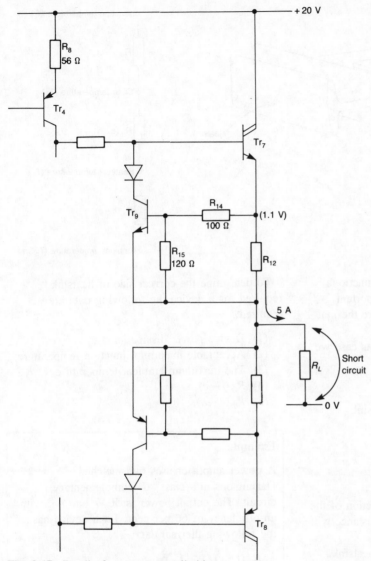

Fig. 3.17 Detail of output current limiting

$$P_{tot(SC)} = V_S . I_{SC} \approx 100\,W$$

This is significantly higher than the power loss of Tr_7 and Tr_8 under normal conditions, where the loss per transistor will be given by

$$P_{tot} = \frac{P_{dc} - P_{ac}}{2}$$

$$P_{tot} = \frac{\dfrac{2}{\pi} I_p V_S - P_{ac}}{2}$$

$$= 18.7\,W$$

3.5 Heatsink calculations

To prevent excessive temperatures in power devices, efficient transfer of the heat generated by the device must be achieved. The standard method of heat transfer is the heatsink, a metal with good thermal transfer properties. For any power device operating at d.c. or low frequencies, the power loss in the collector or drain is given by:

$$P_c = I_C\,V_{CE} \quad \text{(BJT)}$$
$$P_d = I_D\,V_{DS} \quad \text{(FET)}$$

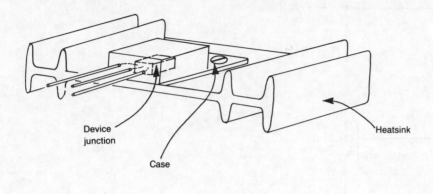

Fig. 3.18 Heatsink calculations

The heat generated causes the internal junction temperature to rise. There are three important thermal resistances (see Fig. 3.18, where thermal resistance is measured in °C/W).

From the internal device junction to its case we have

$R_{th}(j-c)$

From the case of the device to the heatsink

$R_{th}(c-h)$

and from the heatsink to ambient

$R_{th}(h-a)$

$R_{th}(j-c)$ is dependent upon the construction of the device, and a value for this thermal resistance will be quoted on the device data sheet.

The thermal resistance from case to heatsink, $R_{th}(c-h)$, will also be quoted on the data sheet, but depends also on how well the device is thermally connected to the heatsink. To achieve a low value of this thermal resistance, careful mounting techniques to give a tight mechanical joint, with standard heatsink compound between the joint, is essential.

Finally the thermal resistance of the heatsink itself depends upon such factors as size, fin arrangement and material. Typically, black anodized aluminium is used for general-purpose heatsinks. All heatsinks have a quoted value of thermal resistance.

To determine the correct size of heatsink required for a device the following data are required:

(1) Device power dissipation
(2) Acceptable maximum junction temperature
(3) The maximum ambient temperature
(4) $R_{th}(j-c)$
(5) $R_{th}(c-h)$.

Example

A power amplifier uses two matched Darlingtons in a class AB complementary circuit. The output power is 50 W into 4 Ω with an efficiency of 60 per cent. Each device has the following thermal data:

$R_{th}(j-c)$ 1.5 °C/W
$R_{th}(c-h)$ 1.25 °C/W

If the maximum junction temperature after derating is 120 °C, and the circuit has to work in ambient temperatures up to +35 °C, determine a suitable heatsink.

$$P_c = \frac{P_{dc} - P_{ac}}{2}$$

where $P_{dc} = \dfrac{P_{ac}}{\eta} = 83.33\ \text{W}$

$$\therefore\ P_c = 16.7\ \text{W}$$

A full formula for calculating the heatsink thermal resistance is:

$$R_{th}(h-a) = \frac{T_j - T_a}{P_c} - [R_{th}(j-c) + R_{th}(c-h)]$$

$$\therefore R_{th}(h-a) = \frac{120 - 35}{16.7} - (1.5 + 1.25) \ ^\circ C/W$$

$$= 2.34 ^\circ C/W \qquad (3.11)$$

It is often useful to know the expected working temperatures at the device case and at the heatsink. In this case the circuit in Fig. 3.19 can be worked through step by step.

$$T = T_j - P_c . R_{th}(j-c)$$
$$= 120 - (16.7 \times 1.5)$$
$$= 95 ^\circ C$$

$$T_h = T_c - P_c R_{th}(c-h)$$
$$= 95 - (16.7 \times 1.25)$$
$$= 74.1 ^\circ C$$

therefore $R_{th}(h-a) = \dfrac{T_h - T_a}{P_c}$

$$= 2.34 ^\circ C/W \text{ as before}$$

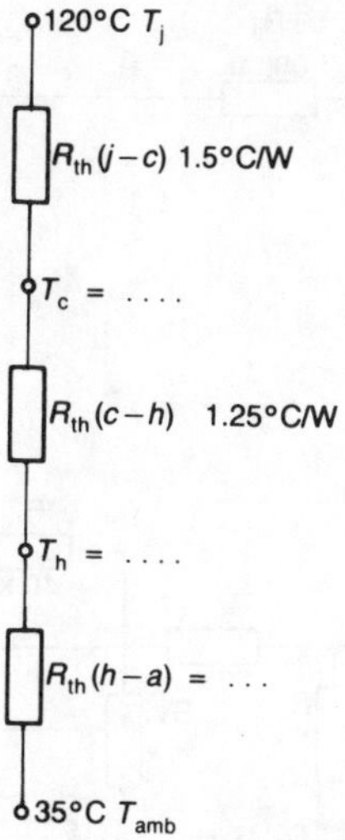

Fig. 3.19 Diagram for example

3.6 PowerFETs in class AB amplifiers

PowerFETs have several advantages compared to the BJT in large signal amplifier design, the most important being the fact that they require a voltage drive between gate and source, and therefore do not greatly load the driver stage; the open-loop gain will therefore be higher and less distortion should result. PowerFETs can also be more easily connected in parallel than BJTs, allowing several devices to be used to generate a high-power output. Also the characteristics tend to be more linear, leading to reduced distortion levels. One disadvantage, however, is that the relatively large value of gate to source threshold voltage could lead to increased crossover distortion and lower efficiency.

One possible example is shown in Fig. 3.20, using two well-matched complementary powerFETs. Matching requires that both $V_{gs(th)}$ and g_{fs} values be nearly identical. The circuit detail is very similar to the previous circuit that used Darlington BJTs, except for the fact that

bootstrapping rather than a constant current source is used. TR_1 and Tr_2 form the differential input circuit, with each transistor passing a quiescent current of about 1 mA. The collector of Tr_1 is directly coupled to the driver stage Tr_3, and the current of this stage is given by

$$I_{C3} = \frac{V_{DD} - V_{GS(th)}}{(R_7 + R_8)} = 5.2 \text{ mA}$$

A V_{BE} multiplier circuit is used to set the bias voltages of the two powerFETs to a value that just equals twice the gate source threshold voltage.

Since $V_{gs(th)}$ is quoted as 2 V minimum for both devices, the values of components are such that when RV_1 is adjusted so that the resistance between the base and emitter of Tr_4 is a maximum (1820 Ω), the resulting bias voltage will be just 4 V.

The circuit is designed to deliver 25 W into 8 Ω; thus the peak currents of both FETs will be

$$I_{peak} = \sqrt{2} \sqrt{(P/R)}$$
$$= 2.5 \text{ A}$$

Power from the d.c. supply will be

$$P_{dc} = \frac{2}{\pi} I_p V_{DD} = 40 \text{ W}$$

giving an efficiency of about 63 per cent.

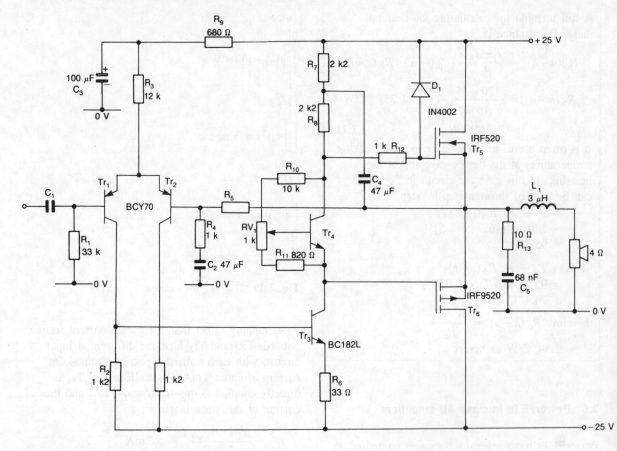

Fig. 3.20 Class AB large signal amplifier using power FETs

In order to produce the peak voltage and current required by the load, a large voltage drive is necessary to the gate of each FET. This is given by

$$I_{d(max)} = g_{fs}\Delta V_{gs} \tag{3.12}$$

where ΔV_{gs} is the voltage change on top of the bias value of $V_{GS(th)}$.

From the data sheets for the IRF520 a g_{fs} of 1.5 S is given as minimum. The IRF9520 device would have to have a g_{fs} that matches this figure. For the IRF9520, g_{fs} minimun is 0.9 S but typically 2S. This is a spread that would allow a match to be made.

Therefore, to achieve the required 25 W into the 8 Ω load, the peak gate drive is given by $V_{pk}+V_{gs}$, where V_{gs} is $\Delta V_{gs}+V_{GS(th)}$. This means that the

gate voltage of the channel FET has to rise to nearly 24 V. Similarly a -24 V peak signal is required at the gate of the P channel device. Bootstrapping via C_4 to the junction of R_7 and R_8 maintains peak drive to the N-channel output FET.

Negative feedback is via R_5 and R_4 setting the voltage gain to about 34. The sensitivity of the circuit is then 400 mV.

3.7 Distortion in large signal amplifiers

The characteristics of transistors and powerFETs cannot be perfectly linear and, where large signal changes are taking place using most of the device's output characteristics, some distortion will inevitably occur.

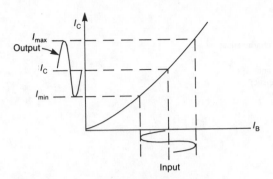

Fig. 3.21 Distorted transfer characteristic

Consider first a class A amplifier and assume that the transistor used has an input/output characteristic that is more of a parabola than a straight line (Fig. 3.21). The instantaneous value of collector current could therefore be represented by:

$$i_c = A_1 i_b + A_2 i_b^2 \qquad (3.13)$$

where A_1 and A_2 are constants. If i_b is a cosine wave, then i_b can be represented by

$$i_b = I_{bmax} \cos \omega t$$
$$\therefore i_c = A_1 I_{bmax} \cos \omega t + A_2 I_{bmax}^2 \cos^2 \omega t \qquad (3.14)$$

But $\cos^2 \omega t = \dfrac{1}{2} + \dfrac{1}{2} \cos 2\omega t$

$$\therefore i_c = A_1 I_{bmax} \cos \omega t + \frac{1}{2} A_2 I_{bmax}^2$$
$$+ \frac{1}{2} I_{bmax}^2 \cos 2\omega t \qquad (3.15)$$

which indicates that the collector current now consists of an amplified version of the input signal, and a d.c. component and a component at twice the input frequency. The latter is referred to as the second harmonic distortion.

In the class A circuit there is already a d.c. component, so we could write:

$$i_c = I_c + B_0 + B_1 \cos \omega t + B_2 \cos 2\omega t \qquad (3.16)$$

where the constants B_0, B_1 and B_2 can be related back to A_1 and A_2.

To evaluate values for the three constants consider the cosine input at various points in the cycle.

(i) When $\omega t = 0$ $i_c = I_{max}$
(ii) When $\omega t = \pi/2$ $i_c = I_c$
(iii) When $\omega t = \pi$ $i_c = I_{min}$

Relating these conditions to equation 3.16 gives:

(i) $I_{max} = I_c + B_0 + B_1 + B_2$ (3.17)
(ii) $I_c = I_c + B_0 - B_2$ (3.18)
(iii) $I_{min} = I_c + B_0 - B_1 + B_2$ (3.19)

From equation 3.18 we obtain

$$B_0 = B_2$$

By subtracting equation 3.19 from 3.17:

$$B_1 = \frac{I_{max} - I_{min}}{2} \qquad (3.20)$$

Using these results in equation 3.17 gives

$$I_{max} - I_c - \frac{1}{2} (I_{max} - I_{min}) = 2B_0$$

$$\therefore B_0 = \frac{I_{max} + I_{min} - 2I_c}{4} \qquad (3.21)$$

Second-harmonic distortion is expressed as the ratio of B_2 to B_1:

$$D = \frac{|B_2|}{|B_1|} \times 100\% \qquad (3.22)$$

As an example, suppose a class A large signal amplifier uses a transistor with the characteristics given in Fig. 3.22.
Here

$$B_0 = B_2 = \frac{(170 + 40) - 200}{4} = 2.5$$

and
$$B_1 = \frac{170 - 40}{2} = 65$$

$$\therefore D = \frac{2.5}{65} \times 100 = 3.85\%$$

The above analysis assumed a parabolic characteristic leading to the distortion. More usually, the transfer characteristic non-linearity is better represented by a power series:

$$i_c = A_1 i_b + A_2 i_b^2 + A_3 i_3^2 + A_4 i_b^4 + \ldots$$

Again, if we assume that the input is a simple cosine wave the value of i_c will be:

$$i_c = I_c + B_0 + B_1 \cos \omega t + B_2 \cos 2\omega t + B_3 \cos 3\omega t + \ldots$$
$$(3.23)$$

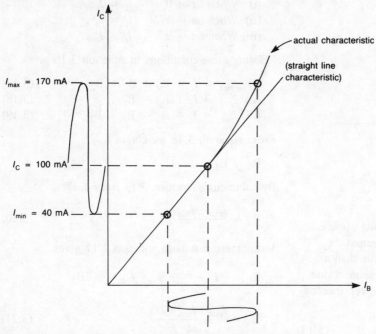

Fig. 3.22 Characteristics (distorted) for example

showing that 2nd, 3rd, 4th, 5th and so on harmonic distortions will be present. Using a similar analysis to that previously shown, the constants can be proved to be as follows:

When $\omega t = 0$ $i_c = I_{max}$
     $\omega t = \pi/3$ $i_c = I_{1/2}$
     $\omega t = \pi/2$ $i_c = I_c$
     $\omega t = \dfrac{2\pi}{3}$ $i_c = I_{-1/2}$

and $\omega t = \pi$ $i_c = I_{min}$

By combining these conditions with equation 3.23, equations containing five unknowns are obtained. A similar solution to that shown previously gives:

$$B_0 = \tfrac{1}{6}(I_{max} + 2I_{1/2} + 2I_{-1/2} + I_{min}) - I_c$$
$$B_1 = \tfrac{1}{3}(I_{max} + I_{1/2} - I_{-1/2} - I_{min})$$
$$B_2 = \tfrac{1}{4}(I_{max} - 2I_c + I_{min})$$
$$B_3 = \tfrac{1}{6}(I_{max} - 2I_{1/2} + 2I_{-1/2} - I_{min})$$
$$B_4 = \tfrac{1}{12}(I_{max} - 4I_{1/2} + 6I_c - 4I_{-1/2} + I_{min})$$

The harmonic distortion is defined as:

$$D_2 = \frac{|B_2|}{|B_1|}$$

$$D_3 = \frac{|B_3|}{|B_1|}$$

$$D_4 = \frac{|B_4|}{|B_1|}$$

where D_n ($n = 2, 3, 4, \ldots$) represents the distortion of the nth harmonic.

The total harmonic distortion can be found using the following:

Output power at the fundamental frequency

$$P_1 = \frac{B_1^2 R_L}{2}$$

Total output power is

$$P = (B_1^2 + B_2^2 + B_3^3 + \ldots)\frac{R_L}{2}$$
$$= (1 + D_2^2 + D_3^2 + \ldots)P_1$$
or $P = (1 + D^2)P_1$

TDH is defined as

$$D = \sqrt{D_2^2 + D_3^2 + D_4^2 + \ldots}$$

In the push–pull amplifier circuits, of either class A or AB, the even harmonic distortion is eliminated, provided of course that both transistors or FETs are well matched.

Consider a push–pull class A circuit with a sinusoidal input, so that the base signal to Tr_1 is

$$i_{b1} = I_{bmax} \cos \omega t$$

and to Tr_2

$$i_{b2} = I_{bmax} \cos (\omega t + \pi)$$

For Tr_1, and using equation 3.23

$$i_{c1} = I_c + B_0 + B_1\cos\omega t + B_2\cos 2\omega t + B_3\cos 3\omega t + \ldots$$

and for Tr_2

$$i_{c2} = I_c + B_0 + B_1\cos(\omega t + \pi) + B_2\cos 2(\omega t + \pi) \\ + B_3\cos 3(\omega t + \pi) + \ldots$$
$$\therefore i_{c2} = I_c + B_0 - B_1\cos\omega t + B_2\cos 2\omega t - B_3\cos 3\omega t + \ldots$$

The total current in the load is given by the difference between these two collector currents.

$$i_L = K(i_{c1} - i_{c2})$$
$$\therefore i_L = 2K(B_1\cos\omega t + B_3\cos 3\omega t + B_5\cos 5\omega t + \ldots)$$

This shows that the push–pull circuit will balance out all even harmonics in the output, leaving the third harmonic term as the main source of distortion.

For a class B push–pull system

$$I_c = 0$$

and $I_{max} = -I_{min}$

$$\therefore \quad B_0 = B_2 = B_4 = 0$$
$$B_1 = \tfrac{2}{3}(I_{max} - I_{1/2})$$

and $B_3 = \tfrac{1}{3}(I_{max} - 2I_{1/2})$

Third-harmonic distortion is given by

$$\text{Distortion} = \frac{|B_3|}{|B_1|}$$

As an example, consider the dynamic transfer characteristic as shown in Fig. 3.23 used in a class B complementary stage. The non-linearity is shown here to be a maximum when the positive peak signal is delivered to the output.

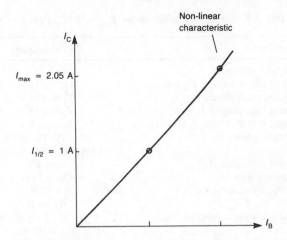

Fig. 3.23 Distortion on transfer characteristics

$$B_1 = \tfrac{2}{3}(2.05 - 1) = 0.7$$
$$B_3 = \tfrac{1}{3}(2.05 - 2) = 0.017$$
$$\therefore D = 2.4\%$$

As shown previously, negative feedback will reduce non-linear distortion provided this distortion is produced in output stages.

$$D' = \frac{D}{1 + A_0 B}$$

In the above case, if we assume an open-loop gain of about 500 and a feedback factor B of 0.03, the overall distortion would be reduced to 0.15 per cent.

3.8 Power op-amp ICs

A wide range of purpose-designed high-power IC op-amps are available, with output powers ranging from a few watts up to 100 W. Most of these ICs use class B or AB outputs, with the internal monolithic circuit following the block diagram given in Fig. 3.24, with a high-gain differential amplifier providing the voltage drive to a class B output stage. A bias circuit, often laser-trimmed by the manufacturer, is included to eliminate crossover distortion in the output stage. Current limiting is always included, and values of the limit are either fixed internally or user-set by two current-limiting resistors.

Table 3.2 Electrical characteristics $T_{amb}=25$ °C. $V_S=\pm 14$ V unless otherwise specified

Parameter	Test conditions	Min.	Typ.	Max.	Unit
Supply voltage V_S		$\pm 6(+12)$		$\pm 18(+36)$	V
Input offset voltage V_{in} (offset)	$V_S=\pm 18$ V		± 2	± 20	mV
Quiescent drain current I_d	$V_S=\pm 18$ V		40	60	mA
Input bias current I_b	$V_S=\pm 18$ V		0.2	2	μA
Input offset current I_{in} (offset)	$V_S=\pm 18$ V		± 20	± 200	nA
Output power P_O	$d=13\%$ $V_S=30$ V		17	21	W
	$f=1$ kHZ $Z_O=4\,\Omega$ $G_V=30$ dB				
Input resistance R_{in}	$=$ve I/P	0.5	5		MΩ
Voltage gain G_V	Open loop		90		dB
Input noise voltage e_n	BW$(-3$ dB$)=22$ Hz to 22 kHZ		3	10	μV
	$R_L=4\,\Omega$				
Supply voltage rejection ratio	$Z_O=4\,\Omega$ $G_V=30$ dB	40	50		dB
	$f_{ripple}=100$ Hz				

Figures in brackets refer to operating limits
Maximum ratings
Supply voltage V_S ± 18V
Input voltage V_{in} V_S
Differential i/p voltage V_{diff} ± 15V
Output peak current (internally limited)   3.5A
Power dissipation at $T_{case}=60$°C P_D 20W
Storage and junction temperature T_1 -40 to $+150$°C
Thermal data
Thermal resistance junction to case   3°C/W max.

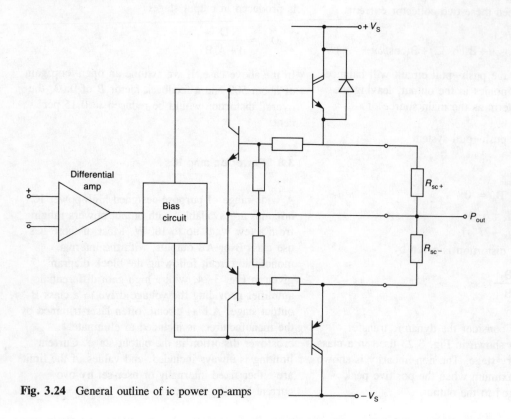

Fig. 3.24 General outline of ic power op-amps

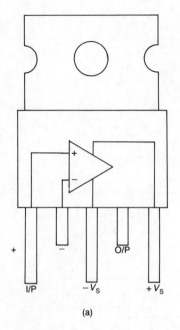

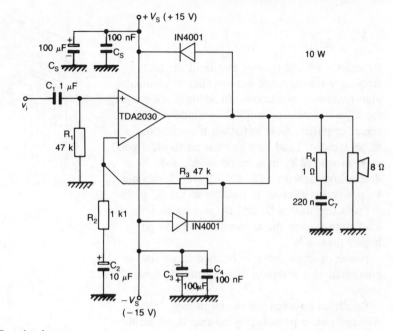

(a)   (b)

Fig. 3.25   (a) pin-out; (b) 10 W amplifier circuit

One typical audio amplifier ic is the TDA 2030 which is capable of an output of 21 W into a 4 Ω load. The outline is given in Fig. 3.25(a). Typical data are shown in Table 3.2.

An example of this use of the IC is indicated in Fig. 3.25(b). Note that a non-inverting mode is used to give high input resistance. We shall design this circuit to have a sensitivity of 200 mV and a power output of 10 W into an 8 Ω load. At this level of power output the THD should be less than 0.1 per cent.

For a 10 W output, the peak output voltage will be 12.6 V, indicating that the d.c. power supply must be ±15 V. Since I_{peak} will be 1.6 A, the d.c. power taken from the power supply will be

$$P_{dc} = 2/\pi\, I_{peak}V_s = 15.3\,\text{W}$$

This indicates that efficiency is approximately 65 per cent. Power loss in the IC is

$$P_{tot} = P_{dc} - P_{ac} = 5.3\,\text{W}$$

Given that the thermal resistances are

$$R_{th}(j-c) \approx 3°\,\text{C/W}$$
$$R_{th}(c-h) \approx 1.5°\,\text{C/W}$$

and if maximum junction and ambient temperatures are 110°C and 35°C respectively, the thermal resistance of an adequate heat sink is

$$R_{th}(h-a) = \frac{110-35}{5.3} - (4.5) = 9.6°\,\text{C/W}$$

R_1 sets the input resistance and, together with C_1, forms a network that restricts the low-frequency response. With $C_1 = 2.2\,\mu\text{F}$ and $R_1 = 47\,\text{k}\Omega$, the low-frequency cut-off due to this input network will be

$$f_{L1} = \frac{1}{2\pi C_1 R_1} = 1.5\,\text{Hz}$$

To give a sensitivity of 200 mV the voltage gain must be 45 (33 dB). Since the open-loop gain for the ic is quoted as 90 dB (32 000 as a ratio) the loop gain will be high — more than sufficient to provide for the sensitivity required. To reduce additional offsets caused by input bias currents and drifts of these with temperature, R_3 should be the same value as R_1.

C_2 sets the low-frequency cut-off. If f_L is to be 15 Hz (ten times higher than f_{L1})

$$C_2 = \frac{1}{2\pi f_L R_2}$$

R_4 and C_7 are components that limit the high-frequency response and are essential to eliminate high-frequency oscillations. In addition, care over the layout of such an amplifier — indeed *all* large signal amplifiers — is important if oscillations are to be avoided. Lead lengths must be short, a good solid ground (0 V) must be provided, and decoupling capacitors C_3, C_4, C_5 and C_6, should be positioned as close as possible to the IC paths.

Protection diodes D_1 and D_2 prevent an inductive load from forcing the ic output voltage to go higher than $\pm V_s$.

Power op-amps can also be used in parallel or connected as a bridge to increase the available output.

Paralleled op-amps are shown in Fig. 3.26. Voltage gain is provided by op-amp A which is wired in the non-inverting configuration, and drives the load through one of the low-value equalizing resistors. The output of A is connected to the input of op-amp B, which is wired as a voltage follower and therefore produces the same output signal as A. The power delivered to the load is doubled.

When connected as bridge amplifiers the power in the load is increased four times. The load is connected between the outputs of two op-amps, *not* connected to ground (Fig. 3.27).

Op-amp A provides gain set by R_2 and R_1, and the output of this amplifier is connected to the input of op-amp B, which is wired as a unity gain invertor. The load thus receives twice the voltage swing, and a four fold increase in power output is available without the corresponding increase in power supply rail voltage.

3.9 Switch-mode large signal amplifiers

Linear large signal amplifiers, even the class AB types, do not possess high efficiency. Class B, for example, cannot have an efficiency of greater than 78.5 per cent. In practical circuits, efficiencies of 50 per cent are more typical. This means that, for a large output power, considerable power is lost

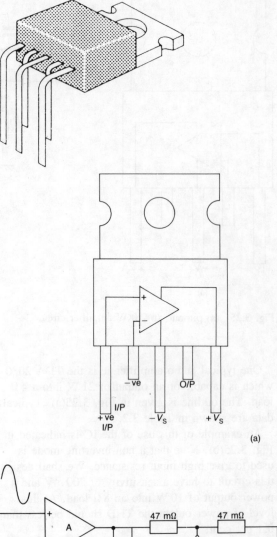

(a)

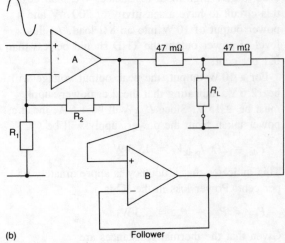

(b)

Follower

Fig. 3.26 (a) TO 220 package (Tab connected to $-V_S$); (b) connection method for paralleled op-amps

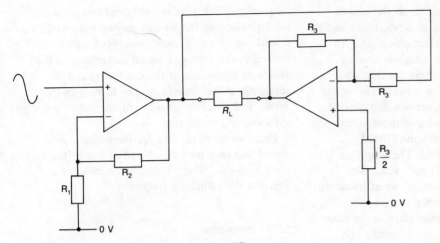

Fig. 3.27 Bridge connection for power amplifiers

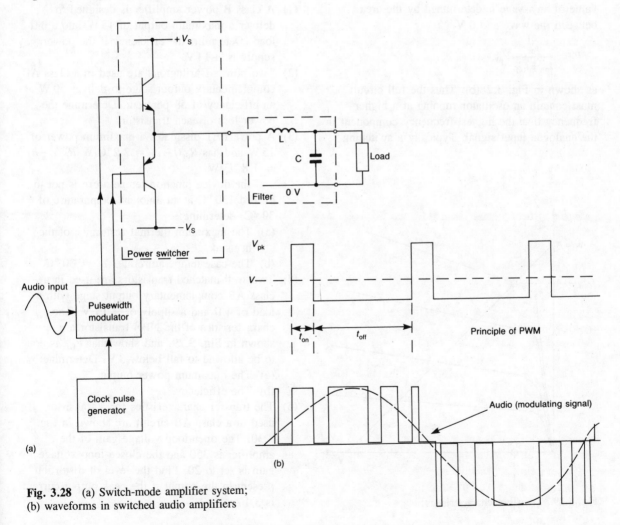

Fig. 3.28 (a) Switch-mode amplifier system;
(b) waveforms in switched audio amplifiers

(as heat) in the amplifier itself. Both the power supply and the amplifier have to be designed and built to take account of this poor efficiency. An alternative approach is to use a high-frequency digital switching technique, where the output devices — power transistors or powerFETs — are switched on and off for time periods that depend upon the lower-frequency analogue input signal. Essentially a pulsewidth modulation (PWM) technique is used (Fig. 3.28(a)). The amplifier is said to be operated in class D and, since the output devices are either off or on, an efficiency in excess of 90 per cent is possible.

With switch-mode power amplifiers, as in many switch-mode power supplies, the principle of operation is PWM. In this system the average value of any wave is determined by the area between the wave and 0 V.

$$V = \frac{t_m}{t_{on} + t_{off}} V_{pk}$$

as shown in Fig. 3.28(b). Thus the full circuit must contain an oscillator running at a higher frequency than the highest-frequency component in the analogue input signal. Typically a switching

frequency of 100 kHz is used, and this oscillator must produce an output that can be pulsewidth modulated by the incoming analogue signal. Basically, the analogue signal is sampled at the switching frequency of the oscillator, and the amplitude at that instant is used to control the width, and possibly polarity, of the output pulse to the switching transistors.

These switches operate for the defined time period and output of a pulse of power to the load via a high-pass filter. This filter removes the signal at the switching frequency.

3.10 Problems

(1) A class B power amplifier is designed to deliver a maximum output of 15 W into a 3 Ω load. Determine the efficiency if the power supply is ± 14 V.

(2) Two power Darlingtons are used in a class AB complementary output stage to deliver 50 W at an efficiency of 58 per cent. Determine the power loss of each transistor.

(3) A powerFET dissipates a maximum power of 15 W and has $R_{th}(j-c) = 2.2\,°C/W$ $R_{th}(c-h) = 1.8\,°C/W$.

 If the device junction temperature is not to exceed 120 °C at an ambient temperature of 30 °C, determine:

 (a) The maximum thermal resistance of the heatsink.

 (b) The case temperature at $T_{amb} = 30\,°C$.

(4) Two well-matched transistors are used in a class AB complementary output stage with a load of 4 Ω and a supply of ± 15 V. The characteristics of the NPN transistor are shown in Fig. 3.29, and show that V_{CE} is not to be allowed to fall below 3 V. Determine:

 (a) The maximum power output.

 (b) The efficiency.

(5) The transfer characteristics for a transistor used in a class AB circuit are shown in Fig. 3.30. The open-loop voltage gain of the amplifier is 350 and the closed-loop voltage gain is set to 20. Find the level of distortion present in the output if the peak output current is 3.1 A.

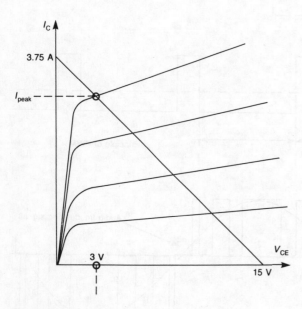

Fig. 3.29 Transistor characteristics

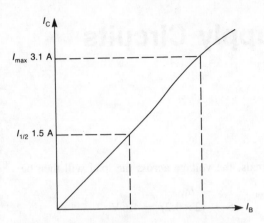

I_C

I_{max} 3.1 A

$I_{1/2}$ 1.5 A

I_B

Fig. 3.30 Transfer characteristic with distortion

3.11 Suggested assignment and project work

(1) Using a TDA2030 audio amplifier IC, design an amplifier to the following specification:

P_{out}: 8 W into 4 Ω
R_{in}: 22 kΩ
Sensitivity: 250 mV
f_L: 10 Hz
T_{amb}: 40 °C

Your design should include the specification for the power suppply and any heatsink necessary for the IC. Assume an efficiency of 60 per cent and a maximum device junction temperature of 100 °C.

(2) Research the testing methods required for the key parameters and characteristics of large signal amplifiers.

In each case give details of the test set-up, test procedure, test equipment and any precautions required.

4 Regulated Power Supply Circuits

4.1 Introduction

Every electronic system needs a power source of some kind, which usually has to be a well-regulated and stabilized d.c. voltage that can provide the required load current. The basic methods for deriving the d.c. supply from the a.c. mains are shown in Fig. 4.1, and include:

(a) An unregulated supply followed by a linear regulator (discrete or IC version).
(b) A switched-mode system using secondary switching.
(c) A switched-mode system using primary switching (often referred to as direct off-line switching).

All of these regulators must have a low output resistance. The need for this can be seen from Fig. 4.2, where a power supply has an open circuit voltage of 5 V and an output resistance of 0.2 Ω. If a load of 2 A is connected across the output terminals, the voltage across the load will then be

$$V_{out} = V_{oc} - Ir_0$$
$$= 5 - (2 \times 0.2) = 4.6 \, V$$

Clearly, if the need is to hold the load voltage almost constant with changes in load current, the power supply must possess a much lower output resistance than 0.2 Ω. D.c. power supplies are specified using the following key parameters:

- Load regulation
- Line regulation or stability factor
- Efficiency
- Noise and ripple level
- Stability
- Transient response
- Short-circuit or overload current.

Load regulation indicates how much the output voltage changes from zero to full load current while the input voltage to the power supply is held constant.

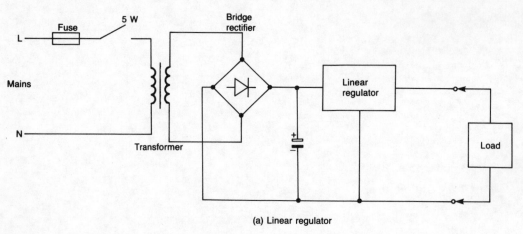

(a) Linear regulator

Fig. 4.1 Basic methods for achieving a regulated d.c. supply

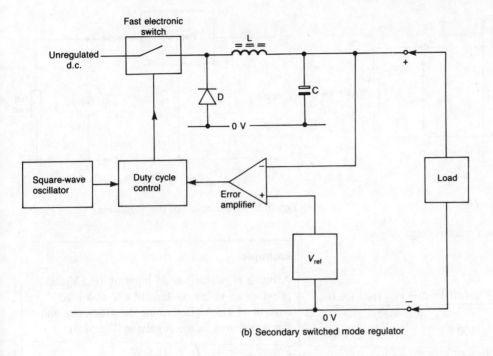

(b) Secondary switched mode regulator

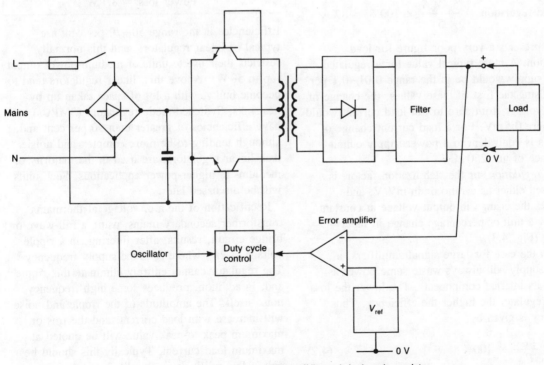

(c) Direct off-line switched mode regulator

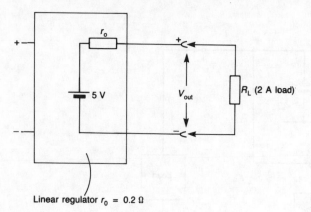

Fig. 4.2 Regulator with relatively high output resistance

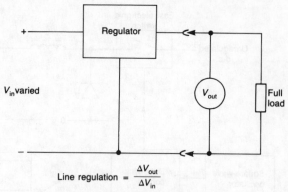

Fig. 4.3 Measurement of line regulation

$$\text{Load regulation} = \frac{V_{out}\,(\text{off load}) - V_{out}\,(\text{full load})}{V_{out}\,(\text{off load})} \times 100\% \qquad (4.1)$$

In the previous example (Fig. 4.2) the value of load regulation would be:

$$\text{Load regulation} = \frac{5 - 4.6}{5} \times 100\% = 8\%$$

This represents a very poor figure for load regulation. A more typical value for a regulated power supply would be in the range 0.01–0.1 per cent. Using the first of these values, the change in output voltage from zero to full load current would be a mere 0.5 mV. For a load current change of 2 A this is equivalent to a power supply output resistance of just 250 $\mu\Omega$.

Line regulation, or the stabilization factor, is expressed either as a ratio or in mV/V, and indicates the change in output voltage at constant load for a unit or percentage change in input voltage (Fig. 4.3).

As in the case for large signal amplifiers, a power supply will always waste some power as heat in its internal components. The lower the loss in the regulator the higher the efficiency. Thus *efficiency* is given by:

$$\eta = \frac{P_{out}}{P_{in}} \times 100\% \qquad (4.2)$$

Example

A linear regulator has an input of 10.5 V and provides an output voltage of 6 V at a load current of 1.8 A. Determine the efficiency and the power loss in the regulator (Fig. 4.4).

Power in $= V_{in} . I_L = 18.9$ W
Power out $= V_{out} . I_L = 10.8$ W
$\therefore$ Efficiency $= 57\%$
Power loss $= 8.1$ W

Efficiencies in the range 50–70 per cent are typical of linear regulators, and this normally restricts their use to units of medium-power output (up to 50 W). Above this, linear regulators tend to become bulky, with a lot of space taken up by heatsinks. Switched-mode regulators (SMPUs) can have efficiencies of greater than 90 per cent and, although tending to be more complex and noisier than linear regulators, are used in the majority of medium- to higher-power applications. Such units will be discussed later.

Rectification of the a.c. voltage at the mains transformer secondary mains, using a full-wave or bridge circuit, results, after filtering, in a ripple voltage at $2f_S$, where f_S is the supply frequency. The regulator cannot entirely eliminate this ripple and, in addition, produces some high-frequency noise itself. The amplitude of the ripple and noise will increase with load current, and the rms or maximum peak-to-peak value will be quoted at maximum load current. Typically this should be only a few millivolts in amplitude.

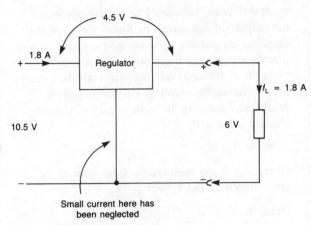

Fig. 4.4 Efficiency in a linear regulator

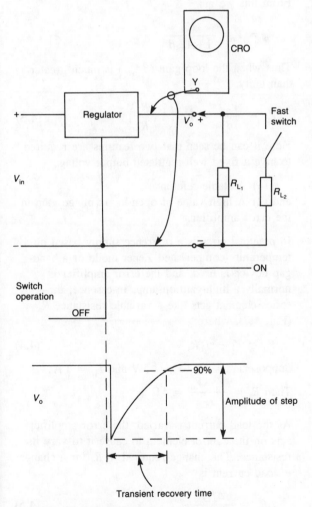

Fig. 4.5 Measurement of transient response

Most loads for power supply units are not static, where the load current is constant, but dynamic consisting of complex switching circuits. The power supply regulator must be able to respond to sudden rapid changes in load current without variations in output voltage. Transient response is the parameter that states how fast the power unit's output voltage recovers when the load is rapidly switched from one value to another. This is illustrated in Fig. 4.5.

At a constant load, and with the input held steady, the output voltage of a power unit will still vary slightly with time as components age and change their characteristics and also, more importantly, with temperature. For the short term (24 hours) it is the effects with temperature that predominate and the parameter of interest is then the temperature coefficient.

Example

A regulator has the following specification:

V_{in} = 15 V nominal
V_o = 9 V at 2 A
Load regulation: 0.02 %
Line regulation: 2 mV/V
Temperature coefficient: -50 ppm/°C

Determine the overall change in output voltage if the following occur simultaneously:

(a) The load current is reduced to 1 A.
(b) The input voltage rises by 0.3 V.
(c) The ambient temperature drops by 10 °C.

Change due to ΔI_L

$$= \frac{0.01 \times 9}{100} = +0.9 \, \text{mV}$$

Change due to ΔV_{in}
$$= 2 \times 10^{-3} \times 0.3 = +0.6 \, \text{mV}$$

Change due to ΔT
$$= -50 \times 10^{-6} \times 9 \times (-10) = +4.5 \, \text{mV}$$

$\therefore$ The total change is 6 mV

It can be seen from this example that good performance in terms of load and line regulation can easily be masked by changes in output with temperature unless good temperature stability is built into the design. As we shall see later, achieving a good temperature characteristic is usually dependent on the stability of the reference supply within the regulator.

4.2 Linear Regulators

These can be designed using discrete components, or are readily available on IC form as three terminal regulators. The basic portions of a linear regulator are:

(1) A fixed stable reference supply
(2) An element to sample the output voltage
(3) An error amplifier
(4) A series control element (see Fig. 4.6).

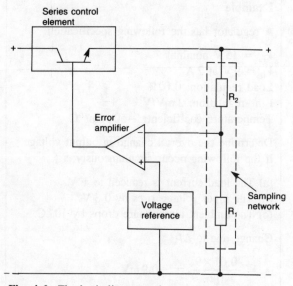

Fig. 4.6 The basic linear regulator

The reference is the input to one pin of the error amplifier, and a sampled portion of the output voltage, dependent upon R_2 and R_1, is connected to the other input pin. Any difference between these two input levels is amplified and applied to the base of the series element. In this example a BJT is connected as an emitter follower. Thus if the output voltage falls with increased load, the

small difference between V_{ref} and the portion of the output voltage across R_1 forces the amplifier output to go positive, driving the transistor on and therefore supplying more power to the output.

As far as the amplifier is concerned, the circuit uses series-applied—voltage-derived negative feedback. Assuming the voltage gain of the series element to be unity.

$$V_o = A_{vol} . V_i$$

where A_{vol} is the open-loop voltage gain of the error amplifier and $V_i = V_{ref} - V_f$

therefore $V_o = A_{vol} (V_{ref} - \beta V_o)$

where $\beta = R_1/(R_1 + R_2)$
From this we get

$$V_o = V_{ref} . \frac{A_{vol}}{1 + A_{vol}\beta}$$

Thus when the loop gain (βA_{vol}) is much greater than unity

$$V_o \approx \frac{V_{ref}}{\beta} \approx V_{ref}\left(1 + \frac{R_2}{R_1}\right) \qquad (4.3)$$

Here it can be seen that two features are required to give a fixed well-regulated output voltage:

(1) A stable reference
and (2) A high value of open-loop voltage gain in the error amplifier.

In practical circuits a reference supply based on a temperature-compensated Zener diode or a band-gap device is used, and the error amplifier is normally a high-gain op-amp. In essence, the series element acts like a variable resistance R_s (Fig. 4.7), where:

$$V_o = V_i - I_L R_s \qquad (4.4)$$

Suppose $V_i = 9\,V$ $V_o = 5\,V$ and $I_L = 1\,A$
Then $R_s = \dfrac{V_i - V_o}{I_L} = 4\,\Omega$

As the load current is varied, the error amplifier acts on the control element to cause it to vary its resistance. The change required in R_s for a change in load current is

$$\Delta R_s = \frac{\Delta I_L R_s}{I_L + \Delta I_L} \qquad (4.5)$$

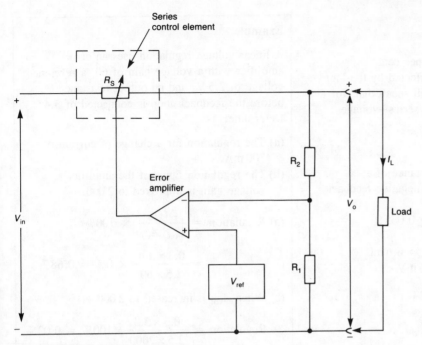

Fig. 4.7 Simple model for a linear regulator

If I_L increases to 1.5 A

$$\Delta R_s = \frac{0.5 \times 4}{1.5} = 1.33 \, \Omega.$$

Therefore, the new value of R_s must be set by the circuit to 2.7 Ω.

The ability of the circuit to both accurately and rapidly change R_s to the required value, and thus to hold the output voltage constant, determines the performance characteristics of the power supply.

To understand the features more closely, consider the basic circuit shown in Fig. 4.8. Here, a simple regulator using a 2.5 V reference is set to give a 7.5 V output from a 12 V input:

$$\beta = \frac{R_1}{R_1 + R_2} = \frac{1}{3}$$

Suppose A_{vol} (error amplifier gain) is only 100; then

$$V_o = V_{ref} \cdot \frac{A_{vol}}{1 + A_{vol}\beta} = 7.28 \, \text{V}$$

The error in required output is 3 per cent. The loss in required output is due to the input difference signal required at the error amplifier.

The voltage between the amplifier terminals is

$$V_s = V_{ref} - \beta V_o$$

where $V_{ref} - \beta V_0 = V_0 / A_{vol}$
therefore $V_s = 72.8 \, \text{mV}$

If, however, the error amplifier's gain is 1 000, we get

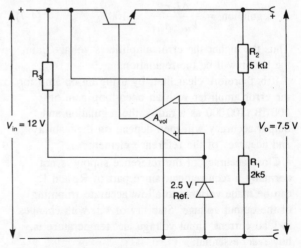

Fig. 4.8 A simple regulator designed to give a 7.5 V output

$$V_0 = V_{ref} \cdot \frac{A_{vol}}{1+A_{vol}\beta} = 7.48\,\text{V}$$

The error in output is now 0.3 per cent.

The regulation is also greatly affected by the loop gain. From earlier work you will recall that, for a negative feedback circuit of the series–voltage type

$$r'_o = r_0/(1+A_{vol}\beta) \tag{4.6}$$

If, for example, the output resistance of a regulator before the controlling negative feedback loop is connected is $2\,\Omega$.

With $A_{vol}\beta = 30$ $r'_o = 2/31 = 0.065\,\Omega$

For $\Delta I_L = 1\,\text{A}$ $\Delta V_o = 65\,\text{mV}$

But if $A_{vol}\beta = 300$ $r'_o = 2/30 = 6.6\,\text{m}\Omega$

and for $\Delta I_L = 1\,\text{A}$ $\Delta V_o = 6.6\,\text{mV}$

Since $\Delta V_o = \Delta I_L r'_o = \dfrac{\Delta I_L r_o}{1+A_{vol}\beta}$

and regulation $= \dfrac{\Delta V_o}{V_0} \times 100\%$

we can determine a general equation for regulation. From previous work.

$$V_o = V_{ref}\frac{A_{vol}}{1+A_{vol}\beta}$$

$$\text{regulation} = \frac{\dfrac{\Delta I_L r_o}{1+A_{vol}\beta}}{V_{ref}\dfrac{A_{vol}}{1+V_{vol}\beta}} \times 100\%$$

$$\therefore \text{regulation} = \frac{\Delta I_L r_o}{V_{ref} \cdot A_{vol}} \times 100\% \tag{4.7}$$

Thus the higher the error amplifier's voltage gain the better will be the regulation.

It is therefore clear that, by using an op-amp for the error amplifier with an open-loop gain of 100 dB (100 000 as a ratio), the regulation and output accuracy will then depend on the stability and accuracy of the reference element.

Close accuracy of the reference supply is not normally a requirement, since part of R_1 and R_2 can be made variable to allow accurate trimming of the output voltage. Stability of V_{ref} with changes in load current, input voltage and temperature is, however, essential.

The dynamic resistance of the reference supply is required to be as low as possible. In Fig. 4.9 a

---

Example

A linear voltage regulation uses an error amplifier with a voltage gain of 60, a reference voltage of 2.5 V, and an output resistance before the feedback loop is connected of $3.4\,\Omega$. Determine:

(a) The regulation for a change of current of 300 mA.
(b) The regulation figure if the amplifier's voltage gain is improved to 2 000.

(a) Regulation $= \dfrac{\Delta I_L r_o}{V_{ref} \cdot A_{vol}} \times 100\%$

$$= \frac{0.3 \times 3.4}{2.5 \times 60} \times 0\% = 0.68\%$$

(b) When A_{vol} is increased to 2 000

$$\text{Regulation} = \frac{0.3 \times 3.4}{2.5 \times 2000} \times 100\% = 0.02\%$$

---

simple zener reference supply is considered. R_S determines the value of zener current:

$$I_z = \frac{V_{in} - V_z}{R_s}$$

and the zener's dynamic resistance determines the stability of the reference voltage with changes in V_{in}:

$$\Delta V_{ref} = \Delta V_{in} \cdot \frac{r_z}{r_z + R_S} \tag{4.8}$$

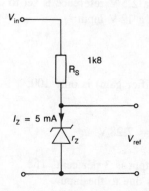

Fig. 4.9 Simple zener reference

Suppose we pick a zener with the following specification:

V_z: 5.1 V ±5% at I_z: 5 mA
r_z: 38 Ω
V_{in}: 15 V ±2 V

Here $R_S = \dfrac{V_{in} - V_z}{I_z} = 1\,980\,\Omega$ (1k8 is npv)

Using R_S as 1k8

$$\Delta V_{ref} = \Delta V_{in}\, \frac{r_z}{r_z + R_S} = 41.3\,\text{mV}$$

This may not appear excessive but would represent an unacceptable shift in reference voltage for most linear regulators. The solution is to either choose a zener or reference device that has a much lower value of dynamic resistance, or to design the reference using two zener diodes, so that a pre-regulator is used to supply the main reference diode (Fig. 4.10).

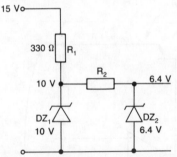

Fig. 4.10 Improved zener reference

Here, DZ_1 can be a general-purpose zener and DZ_2 a temperature-compensated zener such as the 1N827. With the values shown, DZ_1 is supplied with a current of about 8 mA and DZ_2 with the design value of 7.5 mA. Therefore with V_{in} at 15 V ±2 V:

$$R_1 = \frac{V_{in} - V_{z1}}{I_{z1} + I_{z2}} = 330\,\Omega$$

$$R_2 = \frac{V_{z1} - V_{z2}}{I_{z2}} = 500\,\Omega$$

ΔV_{ref} is now found using

$$\Delta V_{ref} = \Delta V_{z1}\, \frac{r_{z2}}{R_2 + r_{z2}} \approx \Delta V_{z1}\, \frac{r_{z2}}{R_2}$$

Where $\Delta V_{z1} \approx \Delta V_{in}\, \dfrac{r_{z1}}{R_1}$

$$\therefore \Delta V_{ref} = \Delta V_{in}\, \frac{r_{z1}\, r_{z2}}{R_1\, R_2} \tag{4.9}$$

Since $\Delta V_{in} = 2\,\text{V}$ ∴ $\Delta V_{ref} \approx 7\,\text{mV}$
(NB. This assumes r_{z1} to be 38 Ω as before)

Reference circuits using band-gap devices would further improve the reference stability and regulation, and they also exhibit much lower noise voltages than zener diodes. The device is based on the fact that the base−emitter voltage of a silicon integrated transistor can be readily predicted. The circuit is shown in Fig. 4.11 and consists of three transistors. From this circuit

$$V_{ref} = V_{BE(Tr3)} + I_2 R_2 \tag{4.10}$$

The values of R_1 and R_2 are set during the fabrication of the IC so that the collector currents of Tr_1 and Tr_2 are significantly different. Normally I_1 is made ten times greater than I_2. This current difference means that the V_{BE} of Tr_1 will always

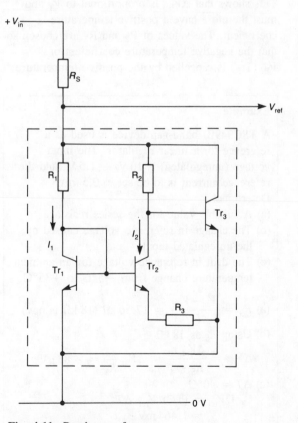

Fig. 4.11 Band-gap reference

be larger than the V_{BE} of Tr_2:

$$V_{R3} = V_{BE(Tr_1)} - V_{BE(Tr_2)}$$

$$\therefore I_2 = \frac{V_{BE(Tr_1)} - V_{BE(Tr_2)}}{R_3}$$

Substituting for I_2 in equation 4.10 gives

$$V_{ref} = V_{BE(Tr_3)} + \left[\{V_{BE(Tr_1)} - V_{BE(Tr_2)}\} \cdot \frac{R_2}{R_3} \right]$$

or $V_{ref} = V_{BE(Tr_3)} + \left[\Delta V_{BE} \cdot \frac{R_2}{R_3} \right]$ (4.10a)

The collector currents of the two silicon transistors TR_1 and Tr_2 are given by:

$$I_{C1} = I_{ES1} \, e^{V_{BE1}/V_T}$$
$$\text{and } I_{C2} = I_{ES2} \, e^{V_{BE2}/V_T}$$
where $V_T = KT/q$

Thus $\dfrac{I_{C1}}{I_{C2}} = e^{\Delta V_{BE}/V_T}$

or $\Delta V_{BE} = V_T \ln \left(\dfrac{I_{C1}}{I_{C2}} \right)$ (4.11)

This shows that ΔV_{BE} is proportional to V_T and must therefore have a positive temperature coefficient. The values of R_2 and R_3 are chosen so that the negative temperature coefficient of $V_{BE}(Tr_3)$ is cancelled by the positive temperature

---

Example

A TSC949BJ band-gap device is used as a reference for a linear regulator. The input voltage (unregulated) is $10\,V \pm 1.5\,V$, and the reference current is to be set to 0.5 mA. Determine:

(a) A suitable value for the series resistor.
(b) The change in reference voltage caused by the unregulated input.
(c) The drift in reference voltage for an ambient temperature change from $-5°C$ to $+35°C$.

(a) $R_S = \dfrac{V_{in} - V_{ref}}{I_{ref}} = 17.56\,k\Omega$ (18 kΩ is npv)

(b) Using R_S as 18 kΩ

$$\Delta V_{ref} = \frac{\Delta V_{in}\, r_d}{R_S + r_d} \approx \Delta V_{in} \frac{r_d}{R_S} = \pm 83\,\mu V$$

(c) $\Delta T = 40°C$

$\therefore \; DV_{ref} = (TC) \cdot V_{ref} \cdot \Delta T$
$\qquad = 1.464\,mV$

---

coefficient of the term in the bracket of equation (4.11). A $10:1$ ratio is normal since ΔV_{BE} is about 70 mV, with a TC of $+0.24\,mV$ per °C. Typically V_{ref} is 1.26 V.

The TSC949BJ is a standard device with the following specification:

V_{ref} ($I_R = 0.5\,mA$) = 1.22 V
Dynamic impedance = $1\,\Omega$
Reference current = $50\,\mu A - 5\,mA$
Temperature coefficient = 30 ppm/°C
Noise voltage = $5\,\mu V$ rms (10 Hz–10 kHZ)

Protection circuits
The linear series regulator can easily be damaged by an overload current. In Fig. 4.12, if we assume a fault condition in the load puts a short-circuit across the output terminals, the power dissipation of the series element would be

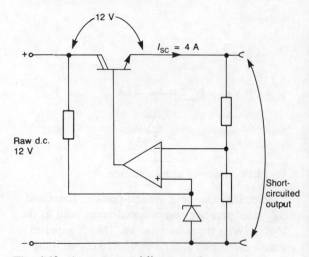

Fig. 4.12 An unprotected linear regulator

$$P_{SC} \approx V_{in} \cdot I_{SC}$$
$$\approx 48\,W$$

If the series element with its heatsink is designed to dissipate just a few watts, the overload will almost certainly destroy the series transistor. In the worst case this transistor could melt and reduce itself to one piece of low-resistance silicon, with an almost-short circuit between its collector and emitter. If the original fault is now removed, the output voltage will rise to the same value of the

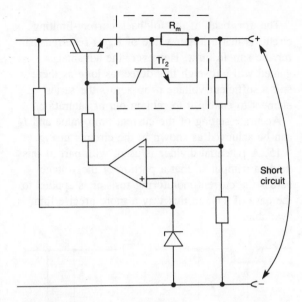

Fig. 4.13 A simple current limit

unregulated input. This in turn could place an overvoltage on the load, leading to more damage. Thus two protection circuits are essential in power supply units. These are an overcurrent limit, and an overvoltage trip or limit.

The most simple current-limit circuit is shown in Fig. 4.13 and consists of a current-monitoring resistor R_m and a transistor Tr_2. Note that R_m is within the feedback loop of the regulator, so that it

does not degrade the regulation of the circuit. If the load current increases beyond a value set by R_m, Tr_2 is forced to conduct and diverts current from the base of Tr_1.

Thus $I_{SC} \approx \dfrac{V_{BE(2)}}{R_m}$ (4.12)

To limit the output current to 1.25 A:

$$R_m = \frac{600}{1.25}\,m\Omega = 0.48\,\Omega\ (470\,m\Omega\ \text{is npv})$$

Although this simple circuit performs well, it has two major defects:

(1) Under short-circuit conditions the dissipation of the series element may still rise to an unacceptable level, since nearly the full unregulated voltage appears across it.
(2) The value of I_{SC} cannot be accurately set and depends on the tolerance of R_m and the V_{BE} of Tr_2.

A foldback current-limiting circuit overcomes the first limitation; this is shown in Fig. 4.14.
For Tr_2 the V_{BE} will be given by:

$$V_{BE(2)} = I_L R_m - V_{R1}$$
$$= I_L R_m - (V_o + I_L R_m)\,\frac{R_1}{R_1 + R_2}$$

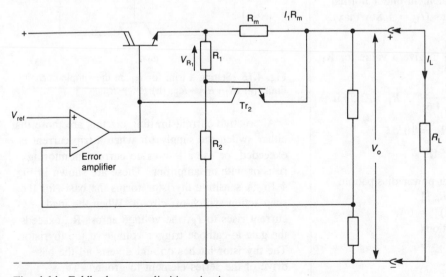

Fig. 4.14 Foldback current-limiting circuit

Rearranging gives

$$I_L = \frac{V_{BE(2)}(R_1+R_2)+V_0R_1}{R_mR_2} \qquad (4.13)$$

Since $V_{BE} = 0.6\,V$ at I_k (the knee current) we get

$$I_L = I_K = \frac{0.6(R_1+R_2)+V_oR_1}{R_mR_2} \qquad (4.14)$$

When the output is short-circuited, $I_L = I_{SC}$ and $V_o = 0$

therefore $I_{SC} = \dfrac{0.6(R_1+R_2)}{R_mR_2} \qquad (4.15)$

Using the equations 4.14 and 4.15

$$\frac{I_K}{I_S} = \frac{0.6(R_1+R_2)+V_oR_1}{R_mR_2} \cdot \frac{(R_mR_2)}{0.6(R_1+R_2)}$$

therefore $I_K = I_{SC}\left[1+\dfrac{V_oR_1}{0.6(R_1+R_2)}\right] \qquad (4.16)$

and from the equation for I_{SC} we get:

$$R_m = \frac{0.6(R_1+R_2)}{I_{SC}.R_2} \qquad (4.17)$$

Example

A 9 V regulator with $V_{in} = 15\,V$ has a foldback current limit with $I_{SC} = 0.5\,A$ and $I_K = 2\,A$. Given that R_2 is a $10\,k\Omega$ resistor, determine the values for R_m and R_1. Hence determine the power loss in the series element under normal and short-circuit conditions ($I_L = 1.8\,A$ max).
Using equation 4.16

$$I_K=I_{SC}\left[1+\frac{V_oR_1}{0.6(R_1+R_2)}\right] \text{ to give a value for } R_1$$

we get $\dfrac{2}{0.5} = 1+\dfrac{9R_1}{0.6R_1+6} \quad \therefore R_1 = 2.5\,k\Omega$

Using $R_1 = 2.5\,k\Omega$ and $R_2 = 10\,k\Omega$

$$R_m = \frac{0.6(12.5)}{0.5.10} = 1.5\,\Omega$$

The normal series element power dissipation:
$$P_C = I_L[V_{in}-(V_o+I_LR_m)]$$
$$= 1.8[15-(9+2.7)] = 6\,W$$
Under short-circuit conditions
$$P_C = I_{SC}[V_{in}-R_mI_{SC}]$$
$$= 0.5[15-0.75]$$
$$= 7.125\,W$$

The drawback of the foldback current-limiting circuit is that a larger value of R_m is required than for the simple limit. However, the advantages gained will outweigh this defect as long as there is still a sufficient voltage drop across the series element to enable it to remain out of saturation.

Accurate setting of the current limit value and I_K can be achieved as shown in the circuits in Fig. 4.15. A potential divider is used, with part of this made a trimpot so that a portion of the voltage across the current-monitoring resistor is applied to the base of Tr_2. In this way a more precise limit is available.

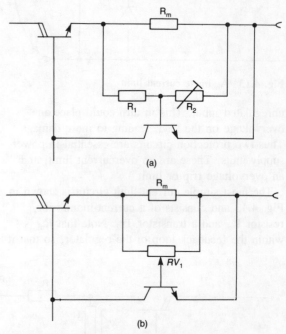

Fig. 4.15 Setting a trim for I_{SC} in the simple current limit. (a) $(R_1+R_2)\gg R_m$; (b) $RV_1 \gg R_m$

Alternative current-limiting circuits are those that either switch the supply off when a trip current is exceeded, or use a low-value current-monitoring resistor with an amplifier. These are shown in Fig. 4.16. A sensitive thyristor forms the basis for the snap-action switch-off circuit. When the load current rises to I_K, the voltage across R_m exceeds the gate-to-cathode trigger voltage of the thyristor. The thyristor latches on and diverts all the base drive of the series element to ground. The regulator is therefore turned off completely, and

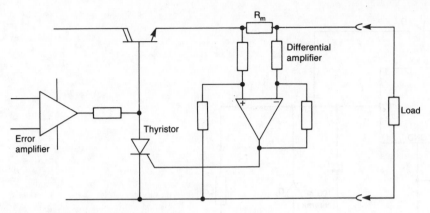

Fig. 4.16   Over current trip circuit

can only be restarted after the unit is switched off and the fault removed. The thyristor trip circuit also forms the basis of overvoltage protection. The circuit is usually referred to as a *crowbar*, and it consists of an output voltage sensing circuit and a fast trigger device. The voltage-sensing circuit, connected directly across the load or the power supply output terminals, is a zener within a potential divider chain. A portion of the sensed output voltage is used to trigger the thyristor. An outline is given in Fig. 4.17. If the output voltage rises above a predetermined level (V_T) the zener conducts and the voltage across R_2 just exceeds the V_{GT} of the thyristor. The thyristor switches and

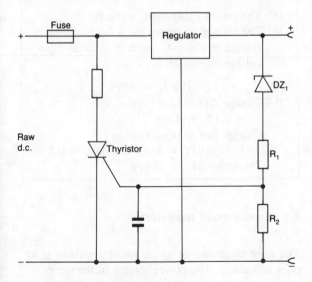

Fig. 4.17   Over-voltage protection

forces the unregulated input voltage towards zero volts, so that after a short interval the fuse blows.

A sensitive thyristor with low values of gate trigger current and voltage is required.

From the circuit, assuming that I_{GT} is small:

$$V_{GT} = (V_T - V_z) \cdot \frac{R_2}{R_1 + R_2}$$

Rearranging to make V_T the subject gives

$$V_T = V_z + V_{GT}\left(\frac{R_1 + R_2}{R_2}\right) \tag{4.18}$$

Example

A TIC106 thyristor with $V_{GT} = 800\,\text{mV}$ and $I_{GT} = 0.2\,\text{mA}$ is used in a crowbar circuit to protect a 5 V output. The trip value is to be 6.5 V. Determine suitable component values. First select a suitable zener voltage: this could be 5.1 V.

Using 4.18, find the ratio of R_1 and R_2:

$$R_1/R_2 = 0.75$$

It is important, however, that the actual values of R_1 and R_2 are such that the current through them when V_T is reached is substantially more than I_{GT}.

Make $I_R = 10\,I_{GT} = 2\,\text{mA}$ in this case
$$R_1 + R_2 = 700\,\Omega$$
Using $R_1 = 0.75\,R_2$ gives
$$R_2 = 400\,\Omega \text{ and } R_1 = 300\,\Omega$$

Values of 390 Ω and 300 Ω would be suitable.

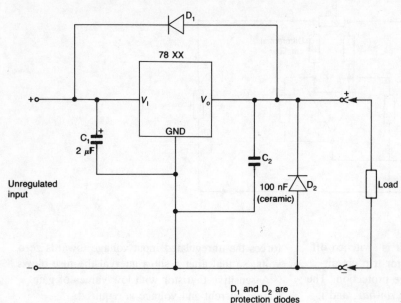

Fig. 4.18 Wiring for a regulator IC

Three-terminal regulator ICs have all the necessary series regulator parts, including overload protection, all built into one package. Types include fixed positive and negative regulators, with voltages of 5 V, 6 V, 12 V and 15 V, and standard current ratings of 0.1 A, 0.3 A, 1 A and 3 A, and adjustable regulators such as the 723 and the 317M/K.

Typical performance parameters for the 78/79 range are

(7805)

Input voltage	$= 7-25$ V
Output voltage	$= 5 2$ V
Output current	$= 1$ A
Load regulation	$= 0.2\%$
Line regulation	$= 0.2\%$
Ripple rejection	$= 70$ dB
Noise (10 Hz$-$100 kHz)	$= 0.04$ mV
I_{sc}	$= 750$ mA

The devices are very simple to use but must normally be provided with external decoupling capacitors, as shown in Fig. 4.18.

Example
A 7805 regulator is used to supply a 5 V load at 500 mA. The input is nominally 9 V. Determine:

(a) The power dissipation of the IC.
(b) The change in output for a load current change of 250 mA, together with an input voltage change of 0.5 V.

(a) $P_{tot} = (V_{in} - V_o).I_L = 2$ W
(b) Change due to load current
   $= 0.1\% = 4$ mV
Change due to input voltage
   $= 10$ mV/V $= 5$ mV for $\Delta V_{in} = 0.5$ V
Therefore $\Delta V_o = 10$ mV.

4.3 Switch-mode regulators

The main disadvantage of the linear regulator is its poor efficiency. The power wasted in the series element means that large heatsinks are required

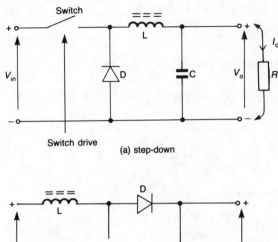

Fig. 4.19 Basic switching circuits

even for units of moderate power output. Switch-mode regulators are very efficient, and therefore require far less space than the linear types. There are two basic forms for the SMPU: secondary switched-mode regulators, and direct off-line switching regulators. In the first type (Fig. 4.1(b)) a fast electronic switch (a BJT or powerFET) is driven on and off at a frequency above audio to connect an unregulated d.c. voltage to the load via an LC filter: step-down, step-up and inverting designs are possible. For the step-down (Fig. 4.19), when the switch is on power is applied to the load, and when this switch is off the flywheel diode keeps the current flowing and maintains the output voltage. The filter has the task of removing the switching frequency to give a smooth d.c. output. Control of this output is achieved by feeding back a portion of the output voltage, comparing it with a stable reference and using the amplified error to alter the mark-to-space ratio of the switching waveform.

Let us assume initially that V_o is constant; then, for the basic circuit with the switch on for time t_1 (see waveform diagram in Fig. 4.20)

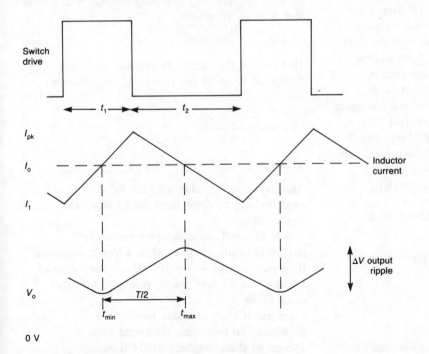

Fig. 4.20 Waveforms in the step-down circuit

$$(V_{in} - V_o) = L\frac{dI}{t_1} \qquad (4.19)$$

where $dI = (I_{pk} - I_1)$

When the switch is off, for time t_2, the almost instantaneous action of the switch forces the inductor to reverse its voltage. It then acts as a generator, supplying current as its magnetic field collapses. The flywheel diode conducts clamping the voltage across the inductor to almost $-V_o$. Again, if we assume V_o hardly changes, we have:

$$-V_o = -L\frac{dI}{t_2} \qquad (4.20)$$

Using the two equations gives

$$\frac{t_1}{t_2} = \frac{\dfrac{LdI}{(V_{in} - V_o)}}{LdI/V_o} = \frac{V_o}{V_{in} - V_o}$$

$$\therefore \frac{V_o}{V_{in}} = \frac{t_1}{t_1 + t_2} = \frac{t_1}{T} \qquad (4.21)$$

or $V_0 = V_{in} \cdot t_1/T$

The output voltage cannot be greater than V_{in}, and its value depends upon the mark-to-space ratio of the switching waveform. This is the basis for the circuit of a step-down regulator. To control the actual value of the output voltage the frequency can be held constant and the mark-to-space ratio altered, or the mark can be held fixed and the frequency varied. Both methods are used in conventional secondary switching regulators.

The proof that V_o depends on the mark-to-space ratio assumed that V_o remained constant. The smoothing capacitor has the job of doing this, but naturally some ripple voltage will be present. The magnitude of this ripple voltage can be approximated from a study of the switching waveforms (Fig. 4.20).

From t_{min} to t_{max} the charge added to C is:

$$Q = C\Delta V$$

where ΔV is the peak-to-peak ripple voltage

therefore $I_C \dfrac{T}{2} = C\Delta V$

since $(t_{max} - t_{min}) = \dfrac{T}{2}$

The current charging the capacitor over the time period t_{min} to t_{max} is

$$I_C = \tfrac{1}{2}(I_{pk} + I_o) - I_o = \tfrac{1}{2}(I_{pk} - I_o) \qquad (4.22)$$

But $I_{pk} = I_o + \dfrac{(I_{pk} - I_1)}{2}$

Rearranging gives $I_o = \tfrac{1}{2}(I_{pk} + I_1)$

$$\therefore I_C = \tfrac{1}{2}(I_{pk} - \tfrac{1}{2}\{I_{pk} + I_1\})$$

$$= \frac{(I_{pk} - I_1)}{4}$$

$$\therefore \Delta V = \frac{(I_{pk} - I_1)}{8C}T$$

However $(I_{pk} - I_1) = \dfrac{(V_{in} - V_o)}{L}t_1$

$$\therefore \Delta V = \frac{(V_{in} - V_o)t_1 T}{8LC}$$

Using $t_1 = T\dfrac{V_o}{V_{in}}$ in the above gives

$$\Delta V = \frac{T^2}{8LC}\frac{V_o}{V_{in}}(V_{in} - V_o)$$

$$\therefore \Delta V = \frac{T^2}{8LC}V_o\left(1 - \frac{V_o}{V_{in}}\right) \qquad (4.23)$$

In designing the filter circuit the initial values of V_{in}, V_o and I_o will be known. The minimum value of L will be given by assuming that $I_{pk} = 2I_o$, and that $I_1 = 0$. Therefore

$$L_{min} = \frac{t_1(V_{in} - V_o)}{2I_o}$$

However, if the change in inductor current is limited to about 50 per cent of I_o, the inductor value is

$$L = \frac{t_1(V_{in} - V_o)}{\Delta I_L}$$

where $\Delta I_L = (I_{pk} - I_1) = 0.5I_o$.

Then by using equation 4.23 the value of the capacitor can be determined for an acceptable ripple voltage.

Note that both these components can be physically small and that, when a higher switching frequency is used — say $100\,kHz$ — the values of L and C can be even lower, resulting in further space saving.

Several ICs are available for the task of switching and regulating the output voltage. Typical of these are the LT1074 (Linear Technology), the 78S40 (Fairchild) and the TL594

Example

Determine the filter components for a step-down switching regulator where:

$$V_{in} = 12\ V\ V_0 = 6\ V\ f = 20\ kHz\ V_R = 40\ mV\ pkpk$$
and $I_o = 1.5\ A$

$$T = 1/f = 50\ \mu s\ \therefore\ t_1 = T\frac{V_o}{V_{in}} = 25\ \mu s$$

Since $I_o = 1.5\ A\quad \Delta I_L = 0.5(I_o) = 0.75\ A$

$$\therefore\ L = \frac{t_i(V_{in} - V_o)}{\Delta I_L} = 200\ \mu H$$

Since $\Delta V = 40\ mV\ pk-pk$ (this is the allowable ripple)

$$C = \frac{T^2}{8L\Delta V}\ V_o\left(1 - \frac{V_o}{V_{in}}\right) = 117\ \mu F$$

(Texas Instruments). Each of these ICs has a built-in oscillator, precision reference, pulsewidth modulation control and a fast switch transistor (BJT or MOSFET). The block diagram of the 74S40 is shown in Fig. 4.21, together with a typical circuit example to give a 25 V output from a 5 V input. This is step-up mode.

The LT1074 family of step-down switching regulators are newer devices that require even fewer external components. The controlled saturation Darlington output switch has an on-chip current monitor, and the switch output is floating, allowing output voltage swings of up to 40 V below the ground pin. An internal oscillator, running at 100 kHz, drives the Darlington switch through a control latch. PWM control of the switching signal is achieved by comparing a portion of the output voltage with the internal 2.21 V reference. Frequency compensation has to be set by the user by an RC network from the error amplifier's output to ground. A typical example of the use of this IC is shown in Fig. 4.22. The input voltage is 12 V and the output 5 V at 5 A. Since $V_{ref} = 2.21$ V, the actual output is given by the formula

$$V_o = V_{ref}\left(1 + \frac{R_2}{R_1}\right)\ For\ V_o = 5\ V\ R_2 = 1.26\ R_1$$

Suitable values are 1.2 kΩ for R_1 and 1.5 kΩ for R_2, as shown. As with any switching regulator

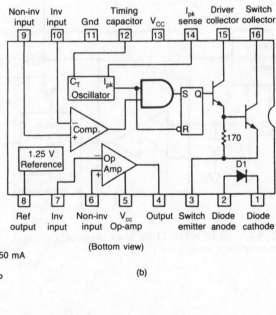

Fig. 4.21 (a) 78S40 connections for a step-up switching regulator; (b) block diagram of the 74S40

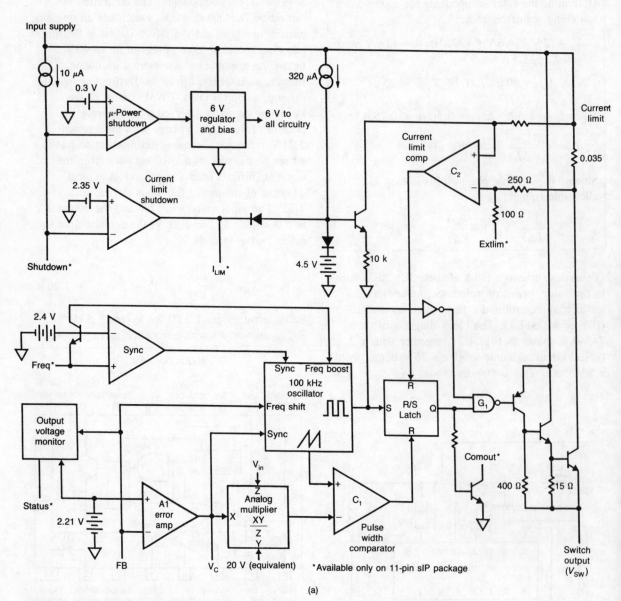

(a)

Fig. 4.22 (a) LT1074/LT1076 block diagram; (b) step-down regulator using the LT1074

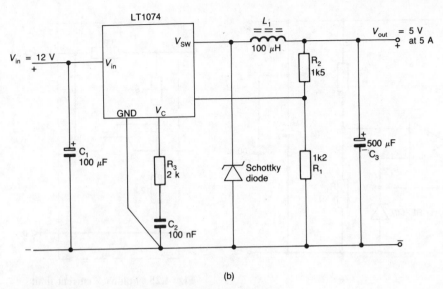

(b)

great care has to be taken over the layout, to avoid excessive spikes on the output and the generation of radiated signals. A good solid earth point is essential, plus additional decoupling at the input ($C_1 = 100\,\mu F$) and output with 100 nF ceramic compacitors.

4.4 Problems

(1) A linear regulator has the following specification:

$V_{in} = 22\,V$ d.c. nominal
$V_{out} = 15\,V$ at 3 A load current
$I_o = 3\,A$ (max)
$I_{sc} = 0.5\,A$ (foldback)
Load regulation = 0.005%
Line regulation = 5 mV/V
Temperature coefficient = 33 ppm/°C.

Determine:

(a) The efficiency of the power supply at full load.
(b) The approximate power dissipation of the unit.
(c) The change in output voltage if simultaneously V_{in} rises by 0.4 V, the load current is reduced to 1 A and the ambient temperature falls by 12°C.

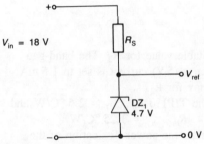

Fig. 4.23 Reference circuit

(2) The reference supply in Fig. 4.23 uses a 4.7 V zener which has a quoted dynamic resistance of 22 Ω at an I_z of 7.5 mA. Calculate a suitable value for R_s, and determine the change in reference voltage for a 1 V change in V_{in}.

(3) A linear regulator is designed to the following specification:

$V_{in} = 15\,V$ nominal
$V_{out} = 9\,V$
$I_o = 2\,A$
Load regulation = 0.2%
Line regulation = 5 mV/V
Ripple and noise = 25 mV pk–pk
Temperature coefficient = ± 200 ppm/°C

An outline of the circuit is shown in Fig. 4.24.

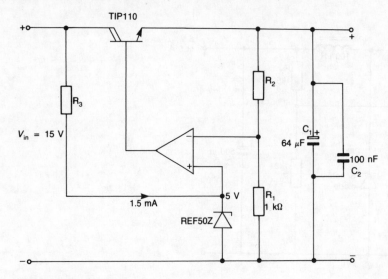

Fig. 4.24 Linear regulator

Fig. 4.25 Foldback current limit

Determine:

(a) A suitable value for R_3. The band-gap reference (5 V) current is set to 1.5 mA.

(b) The npv for R_2.

(c) For the TIP110 $R_{th(j-c)} = 2.5$ °C/W and
$$R_{th(c-h)} = 1.25 \text{ °C/W}$$
Calculate the power dissipation of the device at maximum load current and then determine the thermal resistance of the heatsink. Assume that the ambient temperature is a maximum of 35 °C, and that the junction of the device must not be allowed to rise above 120 °C.

(d) If the open-loop output resistance (R_o) of the circuit is approximately 5 Ω, and the open-loop gain of the error amplifier is 10 000, determine the load regulation of the circuit.

4.5 Suggested assignment work

(1) Research the test methods necessary for the measurement of load regulation in power units. Give details of the test set-up and an estimate of the measurement accuracy.

Tests on a power supply for load regulation give the following results:

V_{out}	6.024	6.012	6.001	5.993	5.984	V
I_{out}	5	200	400	600	800	mA

Determine the load regulation.

(2) Design a simple current limit for the circuit given in Fig. 4.24 to operate at 2.2 A. Given that the short circuit current will be 2.25 A, comment on any other changes required in the design.

(3) A foldback current limit with values given in Fig. 4.25 is used to protect a regulator. Calculate the values of the knee and short-circuits' output currents.

(4) A filter circuit is required for a step-down SMPU. The switching frequency is 50 kHz, V_{in} is 18 V and V_{out} 9 V. Load current is 1.5 A and I_L is set to 50 per cent of I_o. Ripple in the output is not to exceed 25 mV pk−pk.

5 Digital Electronics

5.1 Introduction to logic circuits

Digital circuits can be broadly separated into two main categories: combinational logic and sequential logic.

Combinational logic (sometimes called combinatorial logic) is where a specific combination of input states must be present simultaneously to give the desired output. An example is indicated in Fig. 5.1, where the output state F is related to the input states by the Boolean equation

$$F = A.\bar{C}. (\overline{D + B})$$

Only when $A = 1$, $C = 0$ and both D and B are 0 will F, the output, be at logic 1. Typical examples of combinational circuits are encoders, decoders, multiplexors, demultiplexors and comparators.

Sequential logic (or state logic) are digital circuits containing a memory. These have an output state that is a function of both the current input and the internal memory state of the circuit.

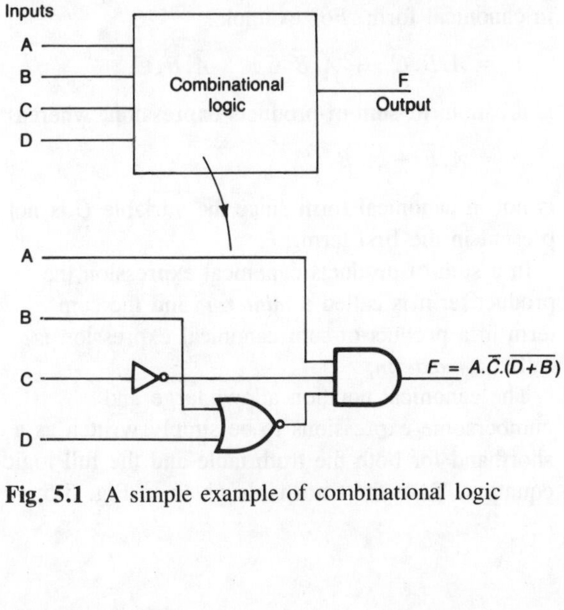

Circuits such as registers, counters, memories and microprocessors are typical examples of sequential logic.

As we shall see later, sequential logic circuits can be further classified by the way in which they are driven, either synchronously with a master clock, asynchronously, or by separate memory and combination logic sections. Thus to gain a full understanding of the more complex sequential circuits it is essential to have a knowledge of combinational logic.

The way in which a particular logic function is to be implemented varies with requirements, and could be in CMOS, TTL, ECL, programmable logic (PLD) or even in an ASIC (application-specific IC); using SSI, MSI, LSI or VLSI technologies. The parameters and key features of the various logic families are covered in earlier chapters to which the reader should refer.

A basic knowledge of gate functions (AND, OR, NOT, NAND, NOR and EXCLUSIVE OR) is assumed, but device symbols are given in Fig. 5.2 and Boolean laws in Fig. 5.3 for easy reference.

Inputs

A
B — Combinational logic — F Output
C
D

A

B

C — [NOT] — [NAND] — $F = A.\bar{C}.(\overline{D+B})$

D — [NOR]

Fig. 5.1 A simple example of combinational logic

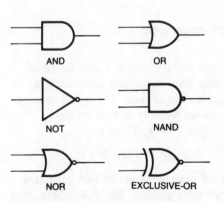

AND   OR

NOT   NAND

NOR   EXCLUSIVE-OR

Fig. 5.2 Standard ANSI gate symbols

Commutative law

A + B = B + A
A.B = B.A

Associative law

A + B + C = A + (B + C) = (A + B) + C
A.B.C = A.(B.C) = (A.B).C

Distributive law

A.(B + C) = (A.B) + (A.C)
A + (B.C) = (A + B).(A + C)

This law implies that expressions can be factorized.
i.e.   (A.B) + (A.C) + (A.D) = A.(B + C + D)
and also (A + B).(A + C).(A + D) = A + (B.C.D)

AND rules

A.0 = 0
A.1 = A
A.A = A
A.$\overline{A}$ = 0

OR rules

A + 0 = A
A + 1 = 1
A + A = A
A + $\overline{A}$ = 1

Double-not rule

$\overline{\overline{A}}$ = A

De Morgans theorem

$\overline{A + B}$ = $\overline{A}.\overline{B}$

$\overline{A.B}$ = $\overline{A} + \overline{B}$

$\overline{\overline{A}.\overline{B}}$ = $A + B$

$\overline{\overline{A} + \overline{B}}$ = $\overline{A}.\overline{B}$

Redundancy theorem

In a 'sum of products' Boolean expression, a product that contains *all* the factors of another product is redundant.

A + (A.B) = A
also A + ($\overline{A}$.B) = A + B

Fig. 5.3 Summary of the laws of Boolean algebra

5.2 Combinational logic

This is the type of logic where a specific set of input conditions must be present simultaneously to give the required output state. The initial example of Fig. 5.1 allows for only one set of input conditions to give $F = 1$. These are:

$$A = 1 \quad C = 0 \quad D = 0 \text{ and } B = 0$$

A more typical example might be that generated from the truth table given in Fig. 5.4, where three possible combinations of the input variables *ABC*

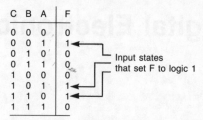

C	B	A	F
0	0	0	0
0	0	1	1
0	1	0	0
0	1	1	0
1	0	0	0
1	0	1	1
1	1	0	1
1	1	1	0

Input states that set F to logic 1

Fig. 5.4 Truth table example: $F = A.\overline{B}.\overline{C} + A.\overline{B}.C + \overline{A}.B.C$

result in the output *F* being high. From the truth table the full Boolean expression for this example is given as:

$$F = A.\overline{B}.\overline{C}. + A.\overline{B}.C. + \overline{A}.B.C.$$

An expression such as this is called a sum-of-products expression, since the variables are first connected by AND operators and the resulting terms are then connected together using OR operations. An alternative expression for *F* would be to first connect the variables together using the OR operator, and then to AND the resulting terms together. This is called a product-of-sums expression. For our example, the product-of-sums (OR-AND) expression can be found for not F ($\overline{F}$) by inversion of the AND-OR equation:

$$\therefore \overline{F} = \overline{A.\overline{B}.\overline{C}. + A.\overline{B}.C. + \overline{A}.B.C.}$$
$$\therefore \overline{F} = \overline{A.\overline{B}.\overline{C}.} \cdot \overline{A.\overline{B}.C.} \cdot \overline{\overline{A}.B.C.}$$
$$\therefore \overline{F} = (\overline{A} + B + C) \cdot (\overline{A} + B + \overline{C}) \cdot (A + \overline{B} + \overline{C})$$

When each of the terms in a logic expression contain every variable the expression is said to be in canonical form. For example.

$$F = A.\overline{B}.\overline{C}. + A.\overline{B}.C. + \overline{A}.B.C.$$

is a canonical sum-of-products expression, whereas

$$F = A.\overline{B} + A.B.\overline{C}$$

is not in canonical form since the variable *C* is not present in the first term.

In a sum-of-products canonical expression the product term is called a *minterm*, and the sum term in a product-of-sum canonical expression is called a *maxterm*.

The canonical notation allows large and cumbersome expressions to be simply written as a shorthand for both the truth table and the full logic equation. Take the truth table given in Fig. 5.5;

	D	C	B	A	F
0	0	0	0	0	0
1	0	0	0	1	1
2	0	0	1	0	0
3	0	0	1	1	1
4	0	1	0	0	0
5	0	1	0	1	1
6	0	1	1	0	0
7	0	1	1	1	1
8	1	0	0	0	0
9	1	0	0	1	0
10	1	0	1	0	1
11	1	0	1	1	0
12	1	1	0	0	0
13	1	1	0	1	0
14	1	1	1	0	0
15	1	1	1	1	0

Fig. 5.5 Truth table for $F(D,C,B,A) = \Sigma(1,3,5,7,10)$

the canonical sum-of-products expression is:

$$F = A.\bar{B}.\bar{C}.\bar{D} + A.B.\bar{C}.\bar{D} + A.\bar{B}.C.\bar{D} + A.B.C.\bar{D} + \bar{A}.B.\bar{C}.D$$

This can be written as

$$F(D,C,B,A) = \Sigma(1,3,5,7,10)$$

where A is considered the least significant bit or variable in the expression. Conversely, if:

$$F(C,B,A) = \Sigma(1,2,4)$$

the full expression can be directly written as:

$$F = A.\bar{B}.\bar{C} + \bar{A}.B.\bar{C} + \bar{A}.\bar{B}.C$$

Note that a sum-of-products expression not in canonical form can be converted by multiplying each term by $(A + \bar{A}).(B + \bar{B}).(C + \bar{C}). \ldots$ where ABC are the variables in the original expression. Thus $F(C,D,A) = A.\bar{B}. + C.B$ is expanded as follows, to give the full canonical expression:

$$F(C,B,A) = A.\bar{B}.(C+\bar{C}) + C.B.(A+\bar{A})$$
$$= A.\bar{B}.C + A.\bar{B}.\bar{C} + A.B.C + \bar{A}.B.C$$

As can be seen from the above, most sum-of-product canonical expressions can be simplified, allowing fewer gates to be used in a design. The techniques used in logic expression simplification and minimization include:

- use of the Boolean laws
- Karnaugh mapping
- The Quine–McCluskey tabular method.

A simple example using just three variables will illustrate the uses of two of the above methods. The truth table is shown in Fig. 5.6(a).

Where $F(C,B,A) = \Sigma(2,3,4,6,7)$
$$\therefore \quad F = \bar{A}.B.\bar{C} + A.B.\bar{C} + \bar{A}.\bar{B}.C + \bar{A}.B.C + A.B.C$$

This expression, in its unsimplified form, would require a logic circuit using six invertors, five three-input AND gates and one five-input OR gate. The purpose of the simplification process is to reduce the expression to its minimal form, so that the lowest number of logic gates is used.

Using the Boolean laws (showing all steps)
$$F = \bar{A}.B.\bar{C} + A.B.\bar{C} + \bar{A}.\bar{B}.C + \bar{A}.B.C + A.B.C$$
The distributive law allows factorization.
$$\therefore F = B.\bar{C}(\bar{A}+A) + \bar{A}.\bar{B}.C + B.C(\bar{A}+A)$$
From the OR rules $(\bar{A}+A) = 1$
$$\therefore F = B.\bar{C}.1 + \bar{A}.\bar{B}.C + B.C.1$$
But $A.1 = A \therefore B.\bar{C}.1 = B.\bar{C}$ and $B.C.1 = B.C$
$$\therefore F = B.\bar{C} + \bar{A}.\bar{B}.C + B.C$$

Further factorizing gives

$$F = B.(\bar{C}+C) + \bar{A}.\bar{B}.C$$
$$\therefore F = B + \bar{A}.\bar{B}.C$$
However, since $A + \bar{A}.B = A+B$
$$\therefore F = B + \bar{A}.C.$$

The circuit requires only three gates and is shown in Fig. 5.6.

	C	B	A	F
0	0	0	0	0
1	0	0	1	0
2	0	1	0	1
3	0	1	1	1
4	1	0	0	1
5	1	0	1	0
6	1	1	0	1
7	1	1	1	1

(a)

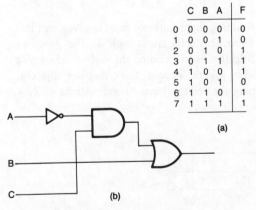

(b)

Fig. 5.6 (a) Truth table for example; (b) logic circuit after simplification

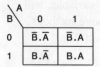

Two-variable map

C\BA	00	01	11	10
0	$\bar{C}.\bar{B}.\bar{A}$	$\bar{C}.\bar{B}.A$	$\bar{C}.B.A$	$\bar{C}.B.\bar{A}$
1	$C.\bar{B}.\bar{A}$	$C.\bar{B}.A$	$C.B.A$	$C.B.\bar{A}$

Three-variable map

DC\BA	00	01	11	10
00	$\bar{D}\bar{C}\bar{B}\bar{A}$	$\bar{D}\bar{C}\bar{B}A$	$\bar{D}\bar{C}BA$	$\bar{D}\bar{C}B\bar{A}$
01	$\bar{D}C\bar{B}\bar{A}$	$\bar{D}C\bar{B}A$	$\bar{D}CBA$	$\bar{D}CB\bar{A}$
11	$DC\bar{B}\bar{A}$	$DC\bar{B}A$	$DCBA$	$DCB\bar{A}$
10	$D\bar{C}\bar{B}\bar{A}$	$D\bar{C}\bar{B}A$	$D\bar{C}BA$	$D\bar{C}B\bar{A}$

Four-variable map

Fig. 5.7 Karnaugh maps for two, three and four variables

Using a Karnaugh map

The Karnaugh map is a graphical representation of all the combinations of the variables involved in a logic expression. Maps for two, three and four variables are shown in Fig. 5.7. The map is the graphic representation of the minterm canonical form of the logic expression, where each minterm is represented by one cell.

Take the example

$$F = \bar{A}.B.\bar{C} + A.B.\bar{C} + \bar{A}.\bar{B}.C + \bar{A}.B.C + A.B.C$$

The resulting three-variable map is given in Fig. 5.8. Here, five cells are at logic 1. The process of simplification is to examine the cells marked with 1s and to join or 'couple' those that are adjacent, grouping the cells in binary combinations of 2, 4,

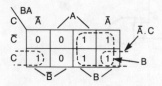

Fig. 5.8 Three-variable map for the expression
$F = \bar{A}.B.\bar{C} + A.B.\bar{C} + \bar{A}.\bar{B}.C + \bar{A}.B.C + A.B.C$

8 etc. From the map we can see that all the cells containing B are filled, showing that four of the terms can be replaced by the single variable B. Cells on the edge of the map can also be considered as adjacent. Thus from the map a 'couple' can be made of the cells $\bar{A}.\bar{B}.C$ and $\bar{A}.B.C$, to give the simplification of $\bar{A}.C$.

From the maps the simplification is $F = B + \bar{A}.C$ as before.

Mapping will often yield a result more quickly than simplification based on Boolean algebra alone. Suppose we take a four-variable expression

$$F = A.B.\bar{C}.\bar{D} + A.B.C.\bar{D} + A.B.C.D$$
$$+ A.\bar{B}.\bar{C}.\bar{D} + A.\bar{B}.C.\bar{D}$$
$$+ A.\bar{B}.C.D + \bar{A}.\bar{B}.C.D$$

The simplification using the laws of Boolean algebra will obviously be lengthy and could lead to errors, whereas the map shown in Fig. 5.9 can be readily used to give the simplification of

$$F = A.C + A.\bar{D} + \bar{B}.C.D$$

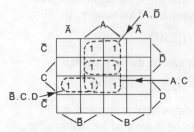

Fig. 5.9 Map for the expression $F = \Sigma(1, 3, 5, 7, 12, 13, 15)$

Karnaugh maps can be used for expressions of more than four variables, as illustrated in Fig. 5.10, but beyond this number it becomes advisable to use a tabular method (Quine–McCluskey) run by a software package.

Where a function is not in canonical form the expression can either be expanded, as shown earlier, by multiplying terms by $(A + \bar{A}).(B + \bar{B}).(C + \bar{C}) \ldots$ and then mapping, or by mapping each term directly and placing a term with one variable missing on to two adjacent cells, a term with two variables missing on to four cells, and so on. Thus $F = A.\bar{B} + A.B.D$ would be mapped directly as shown in Fig. 5.11, where the expansion is

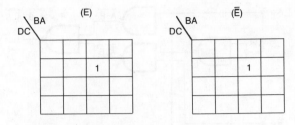

Fig. 5.10 Maps for five variables. Here $F = A.B.C.\bar{D}.E + A.B.C.\bar{D}.\bar{E}$ overlay the maps to simplify to $F = A.B.C.\bar{D}$

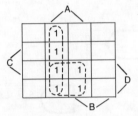

Fig. 5.11 Map for $F = A.\bar{B} + A.D$

$$F = A.\bar{B}.(C+\bar{C}).(D+\bar{D}) + A.B.D\ (C+\bar{C})$$
$$= A.\bar{B}.(C.D + C.\bar{D} + \bar{C}.D + \bar{C}.\bar{D})$$
$$\quad + A.B.D.C + A.B.D.\bar{C}$$
$$= A.\bar{B}.C.D + A.\bar{B}.C.\bar{D} + A.\bar{B}.\bar{C}.D$$
$$\quad + A.\bar{B}.\bar{C}.\bar{D} + A.B.C.D + A.B.\bar{C}.D$$

The simplification is, of course,

$$F = A.\bar{B} + A.D$$

5.3 Combinational logic design techniques

Various techniques exist for the design of combinational logic, depending on the complexity of the circuit. These include:

- SSI using simple gate functions with either AND-OR gates, NAND gates, or a mix of logic functions.
- MSI chips
- ROMs and multiplexors
- Programmable logic devices (PLDs).

The important features of any design, from the smallest circuit of a few gates upwards, are *testability*, *reliable operation*, and *ease of fault location*. We shall start by considering relatively simple circuits using low-level gate functions. Since most logic expressions are in the sum-of-product form, AND-OR gates can be used effectively to create designs. For example if:

$$F = \overline{A.B + C.D}$$

an AND-OR IC such as the TTL 7450 can be used directly to implement the functions, as shown in Fig. 5.12.

De Morgan's laws have to be used if a logic circuit needs to be devised using NAND-only or NOR-only gates. Using one type of gate, or universal logic set (ULS), was at one time the most convenient method of realizing logic, simply because the major logic families offered a limited range of gate functions. If one has only NAND gates available it is possible to produce all other gate functions. For example:

$$\overline{\overline{A.B}} = \bar{\bar{A}} + \bar{\bar{B}} = A + B \ \text{(OR)}$$
$$\overline{\overline{\overline{A.B}}} = A + B \qquad \text{(NOR)}$$
$$\overline{\overline{A.B}} = A.B \qquad \text{(AND)}$$

and similarly the EXCLUSIVE-OR can be created using

$$\bar{F} = \overline{A.\bar{B} + \bar{A}.B}$$
$$\therefore F = \overline{\overline{A.\bar{B}}.\overline{\bar{A}.B}}. \qquad \text{(Fig. 5.13(a))}$$

The process of producing a NAND-only design from a logic expression where the expression is in sum-of-product form, is to use double inversion, as indicated above.

Suppose $F = A.\bar{B} + C$

then $\quad \bar{\bar{F}} = \overline{\overline{A.\bar{B} + C}}$

$\therefore \quad F = \overline{\overline{A.\bar{B}}.\bar{C}}$

See Fig. 5.13(b) for the NAND-only circuit.

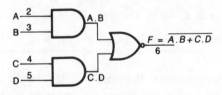

Fig. 5.12 Using $\frac{1}{2}$ 7450

In practice, however, it is often better to use standard logic functions so that the resulting logic circuit diagram is in an easy-to-read form; this improves testability and makes for easier fault diagnosis.

Example

(1) Given that a logic expression is in the form
$F(D,C,B,A) = \Sigma (0, 2, 8, 10, 11)$
  (a) Simplify the expression and draw the logic circuit.
  (b) Design an all-NAND gate solution.

(a) Here $F = \bar{A}.\bar{B}.\bar{C}.\bar{D} + \bar{A}.B.\bar{C}.\bar{D} + \bar{A}.\bar{B}.\bar{C}.D + \bar{A}.B.\bar{C}.D + A.B.\bar{C}.D$
The Karnaugh map is shown in Fig. 5.14(a), giving the simplification of:
$F = \bar{A}.\bar{C} + B.\bar{C}.D$
or $F = \bar{C}.(\bar{A} + B.D)$
Two possible logic circuits are those shown in Fig. 5.14(b).
(b) Since $F = \bar{A}.\bar{C} + B.\bar{C}.D$
$\bar{\bar{F}} = \overline{\overline{\bar{A}.\bar{C} + B.\bar{C}.D}}$
$\therefore F = \overline{\overline{\bar{A}.\bar{C}}.\overline{B.\bar{C}.D}}$
This NAND-only version is given in Fig. 5.14(c).
(2) A logic circuit is required that gives an output logic 1 only when three or more of its four inputs are high. Devise a logic solution using NAND gates only. The logic expression for this majority logic circuit is

$F = A.B.C.\bar{D} + A.B.\bar{C}.D + A.\bar{B}.C.D + \bar{A}.B.C.D + A.B.C.D$

After mapping (Fig. 5.15) the minimum gate form is given by

$F = A.B.C + A.B.D + B.C.D + A.C.D.$
$\therefore \bar{\bar{F}} = \overline{\overline{A.B.C + A.B.D + B.C.D + A.C.D}}$
$\therefore F = \overline{\overline{A.B.C}.\ \overline{A.B.D}.\ \overline{B.C.D}.\ \overline{A.C.D}}$

The all-NAND circuit is shown in Fig. 5.16.

Before we proceed to the study of other design methods, we need to investigate the causes of false ouputs in logic circuits. Race hazards in combinational logic will sometimes arise, causing

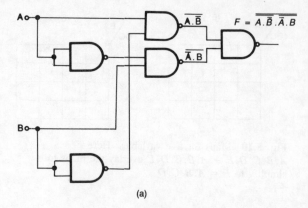

(a)

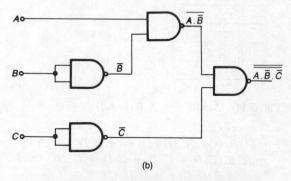

(b)

Fig. 5.13 (a) Creating the EXCLUSIVE-OR using NAND gates; (b) circuit for $F = A.B + C$

short-duration false pulses (glitches) at gate outputs. A race hazard is primarily caused by signals arriving at the inputs to a gate at slightly different times. Delays in signals can be set up by different path lengths in the layout, or can be inherent in the design. The latter, referred to as *static race hazards*, are caused by an additional gate in the path of one signal. This gate delay can normally be detected and eliminated. As an example, suppose we require the following function:

$F = \bar{A}.B + A.C$

The logic circuit for this, together with a timing diagram, is shown in Fig. 5.17. This illustrates one of the glitches that can be caused when B and C inputs are at logic 1 and A changes state from 1 to 0. Because of the delay in the extra inverter, necessary to generate $\bar{A}$, both A and $\bar{A}$ signals will be low for the brief time period of one gate delay. (NB: In the diagram other delays have been

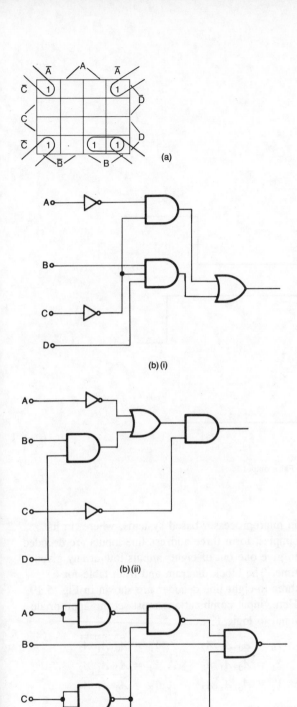

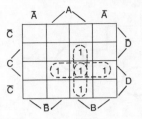

Fig. 5.15 Map for a four-input majority logic circuit

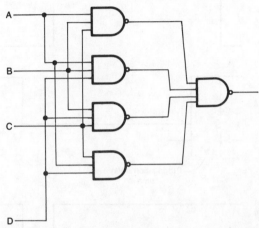

Fig. 5.16 NAND circuit for majority logic problem

Fig. 5.14 (a) K-map for the function $F(D,C,B,A) = \Sigma(0,2,8,10,11)$. Simplification is: $F = \bar{A}.C + B.\bar{C}.D$; (b) two possible logic circuits; (c) a NAND-only gate solution

ignored.) The classic method for eliminating this delay was to study the map for the function. This is given in Fig. 5.18(a), where it can be seen that the couple $B.C (A + \bar{A})$ is not included in the simplification.

If this additional term is included, one of the race hazards present in the original circuit is eliminated. The new circuit would have to conform to the Boolean expression:

$$F = \bar{A}.B + A.C + B.C. \quad \text{(see Fig. 5.18(b))}$$

As we shall see later, in the section on the use of software digital simulator tools, the above method, which was considered sufficient to eliminate all glitches, does not in fact achieve this end, and other more obvious techniques are often more successful.

Returning to digital design techniques, we have so far considered simple gate circuits with just one output. In practice, combinational logic circuits may have several inputs and several outputs. A good example is an address decoder circuit, used

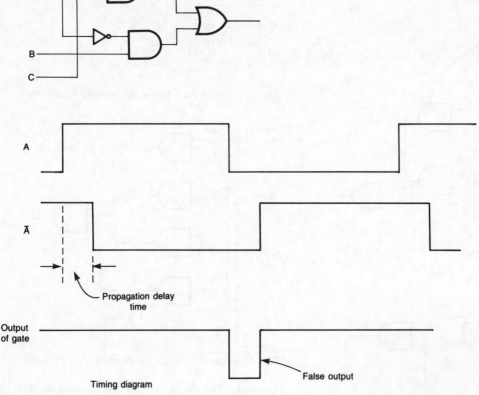

Fig. 5.17 Logic circuit for $F = \bar{A}.B + A.C$

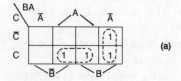

(a)

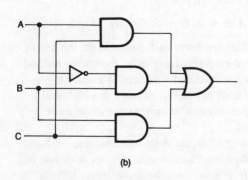

(b)

Fig. 5.18 (a) Map for $F = \bar{A}.B + A.C$ (b) circuit supposed free of static race hazard

in microprocessor-based systems, where, in its simplest form three address line inputs are decoded to give one out of eight outputs low at any given time. The block diagram and truth table for a three-to-eight line decoder are shown in Fig. 5.19. Here, input combinations must set the appropriate input to logic 1. i.e.

$$\bar{Y}_0 = \bar{A}_0.\bar{A}_1.\bar{A}_2 \quad \therefore Y_0 = \overline{\bar{A}_0.\bar{A}_1.\bar{A}_2}$$
$$\bar{Y}_1 = A_0.\bar{A}_1.\bar{A}_2 \quad \therefore Y_1 = \overline{A_0.\bar{A}_1.\bar{A}_2}$$
$$\bar{Y}_2 = \bar{A}_0.A_1.\bar{A}_2 \quad \therefore Y_2 = \overline{\bar{A}_0.A_1.\bar{A}_2}$$

and so on.

The logic circuit required is a collection of inverters and NAND gates, as indicated in Fig. 5.19(c). However, since this address decoding is a commonly required function in logic circuits, several standard MSI devices exist to perform the task. One such IC in TTL is the 74138, which has the logic circuit already discussed plus additional

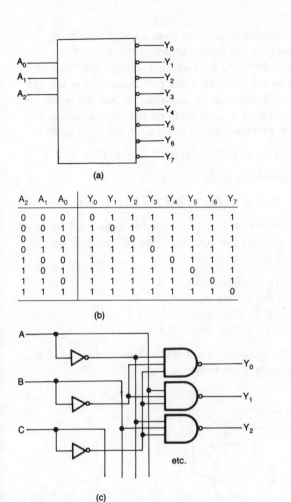

Fig. 5.19 (a) 3-to-8 line decoder; (b) truth table; (c) resulting logic circuit

enable inputs (G, $\overline{G_2A}$ and $\overline{G_2B}$) allowing the IC to be cascaded. Wherever possible a solution using standard parts should be used in a design, even if this requires some small modifications, since this reduces chip count and cost.

5.4 Combinational designs using multiplexors and ROMs

The digital multiplexor or data selector is a combinational circuit that can often be put to use in realizing a logic design. Data selector ICs include 4-to-1, 8-to-1, and 16-to-1 devices.

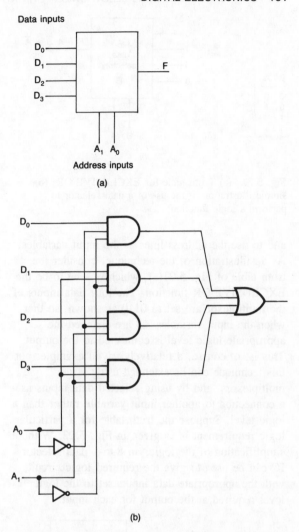

Fig. 5.20 (a) 4-to-1 data selector; (b) logic circuit for a 4-to-1 data selector

Consider the relatively simple 4-to-1 data selector: this has four data inputs, D_0, D_1, D_2 and D_3, one output F and two address lines A_0 and A_1. The operation is such that, depending on the state of A_0 and A_1, only one data input line is connected to the output (Fig. 5.20(a)). Therefore the logic expression for F is:

$$F = \overline{A}.\overline{B}.D_0 + A.\overline{B}.D_1 + \overline{A}.B.D_2 + A.B.D_3$$

resulting in the logical diagram of Fig. 5.20(b). With a multiplexor it is possible to set the data inputs to 1s and 0s as required by a truth table,

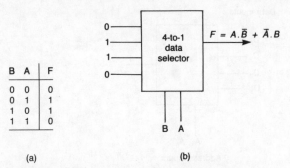

Fig. 5.21 (a) Truth table for EXCLUSIVE-OR; (b) simple illustration of the use of a data selector to perform a logic function

and to use the address lines as the input variables. As an illustration of the technique, consider the truth table of Fig. 5.21(a), which is seen to be the EXCLUSIVE-OR function. The four data inputs of the multiplexor are set to 0110 as shown, so that when the input variables AB are changed the appropriate logic level is connected to the output. This is, of course, a relatively trivial example, but this technique can be extended using larger multiplexors, and by using selected data inputs as a connection to another input variable rather than a logic level. Suppose the truth table for a particular logic requirement is as given in Fig. 5.22. Without simplification of the logic, an 8-to-1 data selector IC can be used to give the required logic circuit, with the appropriate data inputs set to the logic level required at the output for each input

combination, and the three address lines being used for the input variables (Fig. 5.22(b)). Alternatively, a 4-to-1 data selector can be used, with selected data input pins connected to one of the variables or its complement, and the others to logic 0 or 1, depending on the logic equation. In the example, the equation from the truth table is:

$$F = \bar{A}.B.\bar{C} + \bar{A}.\bar{B}.C + A.\bar{B}.C + A.B.C$$

Factorizing gives

$$F = B.\bar{C}.(\bar{A}) + \bar{B}.C.(\bar{A}+A) + B.C.(A)$$

However $A + \bar{A} = 1$. Therefore the four possible conditions for input variables BC must be set as follows:

$(\bar{B}.\bar{C})$ Data input $= 0$
$(B.\bar{C})$ Data input $= \bar{A}$
$(\bar{B}.C)$ Data input $= 1$
$(B.C)$ Data input $= A$

The resulting circuit required using a 4-to-1 data selector IC is shown in Fig. 5.23.

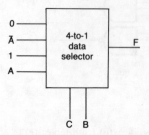

Fig. 5.23 A better solution using one 4-to-1 data selector (here A is called the data variable)

In the above example, the variables B and C will be called the *select* variables, while A is called the *data* variable. Of course we need not have chosen A as the data variable. Suppose we make C this variable; then from the initial equation we get

$$F = A.B\,(C) + A.\bar{B}\,(C) + \bar{A}.B\,(\bar{C}) + \bar{A}.\bar{B}\,(C)$$

The circuit is shown in Fig. 5.24. In the same way we could pick B as the data variable. In practice, the variable selected to be used on the data input is the one that often has its complement also present, since this arrangement will not force the designer into the use of an extra inverter gate. From the above it can be seen that a 4-to-1 data selector can

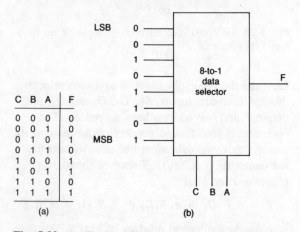

Fig. 5.22 (a) Truth table for example; (b) using an 8-to-1 data selector to realize the logic required from the truth table

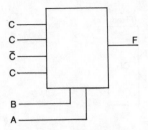

Fig. 5.24 Using C as the data variable

be used to realize any function of three variables, an 8-to-1 data selector can be used for up to four variables, and a 16-to-1 IC can be used to create logic designs with up to five variables.

An alternative in combinational designs, which is particularly useful in situations where there are multiple inputs and multiple outputs, is the ROM. Typical examples where a ROM can be used effectively are in special-purpose code convertors where the required output code is programmed into the memory chip and is accessed by the input code applied to the address lines. In ROM, PROM, EPROM and EAROM, the memory is either arranged in words of 1, 4, 8 and 16 bits, so that if eight outputs are required and the input variables total say five, a ROM with a minimum memory size of 256 bits is indicated (Fig. 5.25). Thus a relatively small ROM would be used to carry out a conversion from 4-bit binary to 4-bit Gray code.

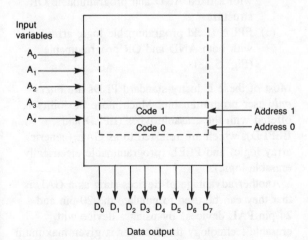

Fig. 5.25 Using a ROM as a 5-bit to 8-bit code convertor

The four bits of the binary would be used as the address input, and for each combination of the binary input the Gray code, previously stored in the ROM, would be output on the four data lines — a 64-bit ROM is necessary (Fig. 5.26).

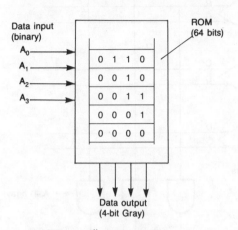

Fig. 5.26 4-bit binary-to-Gray code convertor

Data inputs				Data outputs			
A_3	A_2	A_1	A_0	D_3	D_2	D_1	D_0
0	0	0	0	0	0	0	0
0	0	0	1	0	0	0	1
0	0	1	0	0	0	1	1
0	0	1	1	0	0	1	0
0	1	0	0	0	1	1	0
			etc.				etc.

5.5 Combinational circuit design using programmable logic devices (PLDs)

Reducing the chip count of a system improves reliability and lowers the time that has to be spent on testing. Thus the move in design has been away from SSI devices, firstly to MSI, and then wherever possible to use LSI and VLSI chips. Custom-designed ICs or ASICs (application-specific integrated circuits) are a possible route for the medium- to high-volume producer of digital equipment, since these manufacturers can afford the very high investment necessary. A less costly and somewhat faster design approach is to use PLDs. The basic principle of a PLD is to have programmable AND-OR arrays (either one or both functions programmable depending on the type of PLD) within one IC. This structure is used

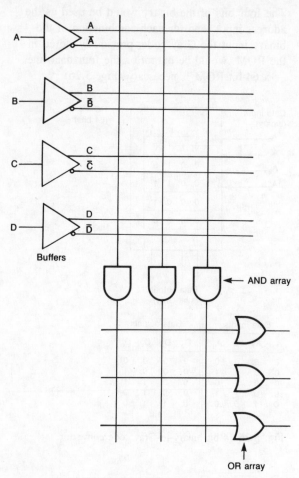

Fig. 5.27 Typical PLD structure

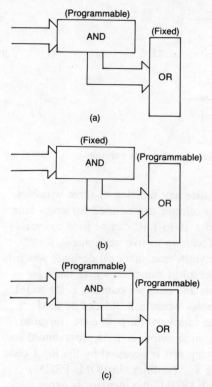

Fig. 5.28 Types of PLD in common use. (a) PAL; (b) PROM; (c) FLPA

because the majority of logic equations required for a design are either in sum-of-product form or can be converted to it, i.e.

$$F = A.B.C + \bar{A}.B.C + A.\bar{B}.\bar{C} + \ldots$$

The simplest type of PLD consists of a set of buffered inputs which give the true and the complement of each input, a rank of AND gates so that various combinations of the inputs can be ANDed together to give *product terms*, and then a bank of OR gates to allow selected product terms to be combined into output signals or sums-of-products (Fig. 5.27).

There are basically three main types of PLD:

(1) PAL (programmable array logic) using a programmable AND and fixed OR structure.

(2) PROM (programmable read-only memory) with a fixed AND and programmable OR structure.

(3) FPLA (field programmable logic array) with both AND and OR programmable (Fig. 5.28).

Most of these industry-standard PLDs are *once-only* user programmable. Much more flexibility is offered with the erasable types (EPLD and EEPLD), which are referred to as GAL (generic array logic) and PEEL (programmable electrically erasable logic).

Another advantage of devices such as a GAL is that they can be used to emulate the 20-pin and 24-pin PAL devices. By using a device with erasable technology the designer is given maximum flexibility — the design does not have to be right first time.

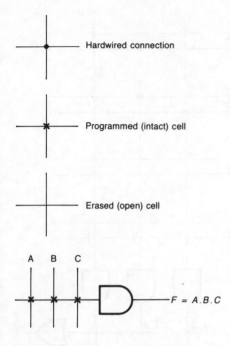

Hardwired connection

Programmed (intact) cell

Erased (open) cell

A   B   C

$F = A.B.C$

Fig. 5.29 PLD connections

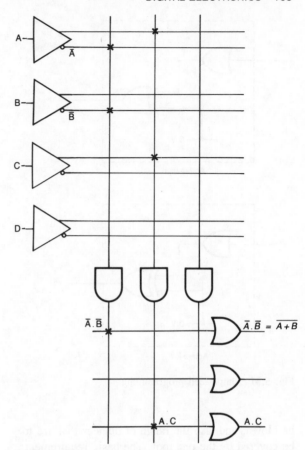

$\overline{A}.\overline{B}$

$\overline{A}.\overline{B} = \overline{A+B}$

$A.C$

$A.C$

Fig. 5.30 An illustration of logic equation creation

PLDs use a slightly different notation from normal logic. The connection method is shown in Fig. 5.29, where a programmed — i.e. intact — cell is shown with an 'X' at the intersection. An erased or open connection is shown without this 'X'. The AND gate in the diagram will therefore have the output $A.B.C$. Let us take this a step further and look at a typical FPLA structure (both AND and OR programmable). Figure 5.30 shows a portion of an FLPA programmed to give two outputs; one a NOR function $(\overline{A+B})$ where only the connections $\overline{A}$ and $\overline{B}$ have been left intact to one AND gate, and only that AND output is connected to the OR gate, and one AND function $(A.C)$.

Programming is slightly more complicated than this, since the OR gates that give the sum-of-product terms can themselves be programmed to be active-high or active-low (Fig. 5.31). In the device this is achieved by incorporating an EX-OR gate on the output of each OR. If the programmable input to this EX-OR is left intact (i.e. connected to logic 0) the EX-OR acts as a non-inverting buffer (active-high) whereas if the connection is 'blown' the EX-OR input goes to

logic 1 and the gate acts as an invertor (active-low). A simple example using this principle is given in Fig. 5.32, where the EXCLUSIVE-OR and EXCLUSIVE-NOR of AB is developed, and also the NAND output $\overline{A.B.C}$.

The design process for PLDs requires the generation of the full functional specification, and the Boolean equations or state diagrams needed to implement the specification. The design should preferably then be verified by logic simulation. Only then should programming the device take place. This is obviously very important for devices such as PALs, which are once-only programmed. Any mistakes in design, which could have been picked up by simulation and verification, can be rather costly.

The tools required for the design and blowing of PLDs depend on the complexity of the devices to

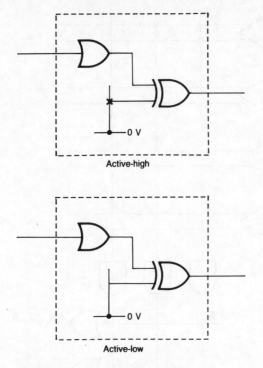

Fig. 5.31 Output-cell programming

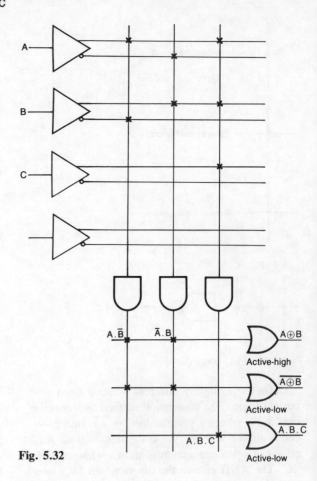

Fig. 5.32

be blown, and also the range of devices that are to be covered by the one tool. The basic requirement is for software to enable the user to select the device being used (i.e. a PAL, GAL, PEEL etc.) and which will accept Boolean equations that define what the programmed IC has to do. The software must then assemble the text file containing the user-defined data (Boolean equations/state diagrams) and produce a fuse map that can be 'blown' into the device. Additional hardware is necessary to translate this fuse map into signals that will enable the software to download the correct pattern to the IC. The IC will be connected to a zero insertion force (ZIF) socket and via a cable or link to the programming hardware.

Most manufacturers of PLD devices have developed software packages that can be used to program their devices, these often being free to the user. The user then has to purchase the appropriate hardware programmer. Typical software packages are:

AMAZE (Signetics/Mullard) ⎫ Both of these are
PALASM (AMD)   ⎭ assemblers

ABEL (Data I/O)   ⎫ These are
CUPL (Logical devices)   ⎭ compilers

Assembly-based software requires the user to define input and output pins and the desired Boolean logic equations, whereas with the compiler packages the user has only to define the truth table or the state diagram for the proposed design.

We will consider the use of a typical assembler-based package, the Power Logic Development System produced by MPE Ltd. This consists of a PC plug-in card, a small programming pod with a ZIF socket and GAL/EPLD assembler software. The system is designed for programming erasable programmable logic devices, i.e. the 16V8 or the

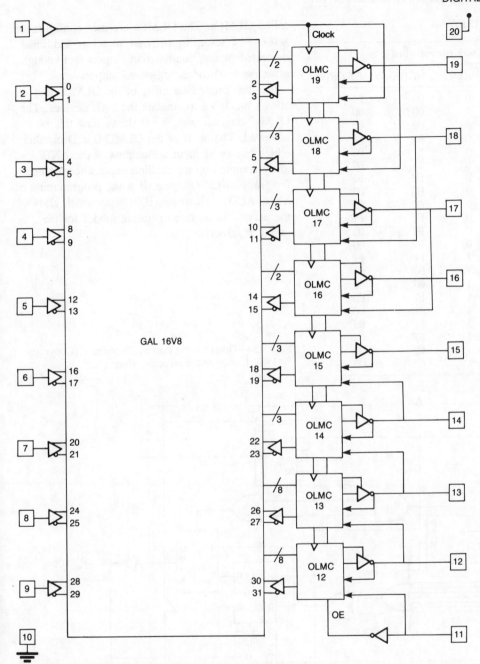

Fig. 5.33 Block diagram of 16V8 (Copyright © 1988 Lattice Semiconductors Corp.)

EP300, and since the GAL 16V8 and the EP300 can be used to emulate many of the PAL devices (see Table 5.1) this approach, although limited, is an excellent starting point. Before discussing the operation of the software tool we should look at the architecture of the GAL 16V8.

The GAL 16V8 is a Lattice Semiconductor electrically erasable programmable logic device. It has 20 pins (Fig. 5.33), of which eight are inputs and eight are connected to output logic macro cells

Table 5.1 Lattice GAL 16V8

Pal type	Architecture control word			
	SYN	AC0	AC1(n)	EX-OR(n)
10H8	1	0	00	FF
10L8	1	0	00	00
10P8	1	0	00	00
12H6	1	0	81	FF
12L6	1	0	81	00
12P6	1	0	81	00
14H4	1	0	C3	FF
14L4	1	0	C3	00
14P4	1	0	C3	00
16H2	1	0	E7	FF
16L2	1	0	E7	00
16P2	1	0	E7	00
16H8	1	1	FF	FF
16R8	0	1	00	00
16RP8	0	1	00	00
16L8	1	1	FF	00
16R6	0	1	81	00
16RP6	0	1	81	00
16P8	1	1	FF	00
16R4	0	1	C3	00
16RP4	0	1	C3	00

called OLMCs. The OLMCs are user-configurable and can be set up by software to act as additional dedicated inputs, combination outputs (active-high or active-low), or as registered outputs.

It is this programmability of the OLMCs that allows the 16V8 to emulate the PAL devices. The OLMC diagram (Fig. 5.34) shows how this is achieved. The heart of the OLMC is a D-bistable which has as its input the outputs of the AND array summed by the multiple input OR gate and fed from an EX-OR gate. It is the programming of SYN, ACO, ACI(n) and EX-OR(n) which allows the user to select five operating modes for the output macrocell.

Fig. 5.34 Output logic macrocell structure (Copyright © 1988 Lattice semiconductors Corp.)

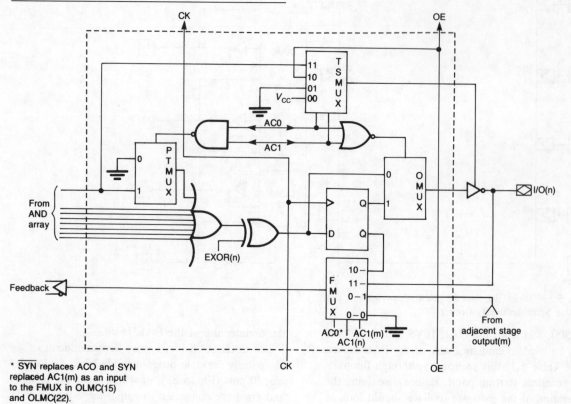

* SYN replaces ACO and SYN replaced AC1(m) as an input to the FMUX in OLMC(15) and OLMC(22).

Mode	SYN	ACO	ACl(n)	EX-OR(n)	Function
1	1	0	1	—	dedicated input
2A	1	0	0	0	combinational output (active-low o/p)
2B	1	0	0	1	combinational output (active-high)
3A	1	1	1	0	combinational output using the enable input (active-low)
3B	1	1	1	1	combinational output using enable (active-high)
4A	0	1	1	0	combinational output with clock (active-low)
4B	0	1	1	1	combinational output with clock (active-high)
5A	0	1	0	0	Registered output (active-low)
5B	0	1	0	1	Registered output (active-high)

These various modes are illustrated in Fig. 5.35.

The actual programming of the function for the OLMCs is done by the software, using selected bits of an 82-bit control word in location 60. An additional feature of the GAL 16V8 is the use of a security cell in row address 61. If this is programmed no-one is able to read the device. This prevents others from (a) discovering the logic design and (b) reprogramming the device.

Within the software of the MPE Power Logic Development System the user can either define the mode in which the GAL/EPLD device is to be used, or define the PAL type that it is required to emulate. For example, suppose we wish to make the GAL 16V8 emulate a PAL 16L8, a combinational device only with active-low outputs. The Lattice GAL architecture control word could be set up as follows:

$$SYN \quad = 1$$
$$ACO \quad = 1$$
$$ACI(n) \quad = FF$$
$$EX\text{-}OR(n) = FF$$

Alternatively, an initial statement in the text file can be:

Lattice
PAL 16L8

where this statement instructs the software to program the Lattice GAL 16V8 as a PAL 16L8.

Let us now look at a specific example using this development tool to set up a GAL 16V8 to carry out the task of the logic circuit in Fig. 5.36. In this circuit you will see that there are three inputs of *ABC* and four active-high outputs of *WXY* and *Z*. The Boolean equations for the four outputs are:

$$W = A.B.\bar{C} + \bar{B}.\bar{A}$$
$$X = A.\bar{C} + B.\bar{C}$$
$$Y = \bar{A}.\bar{B}.\bar{C}$$
$$Z = A.\bar{B}.C$$

As you can see from the circuit, 10 two-input NAND gates and three three-input NAND gates are required to complete the circuit in SSI. This relatively simple example will only be using about one-third of the available circuitry on the 16V8, but it will demonstrate that the four SSI ICs required for the circuit in TTL or CMOS can be replaced by one GAL IC.

The MPE power logic card must be previously installed in a spare slot in the PC (location 0300 Hex is normally used, but the user is allowed to change this), and the assembler software on the hard disk. The development tool can be put to use. The main menu is called by typing cd PLDs, then PLDs to run the software. The layout of the main menu is shown in Fig. 5.37, where the Edit File has been named TEST1. DCF.

A DCF (device configuration file) will consist of three sections:

Device configuration
Pin names
Equations.

From the main menu the options can be selected either using the mouse or the ⟨up⟩ and ⟨down⟩ keys to move the highlighted yellow marker to the required option. Alternatively, the key which is shown highlighted will also select the option: i.e. for 'select device Type' — press the key T.

The first step is to edit the file. In this case, the editor used is LANCS\ASS68000\EC.EXE, but other user editors are allowed, e.g.

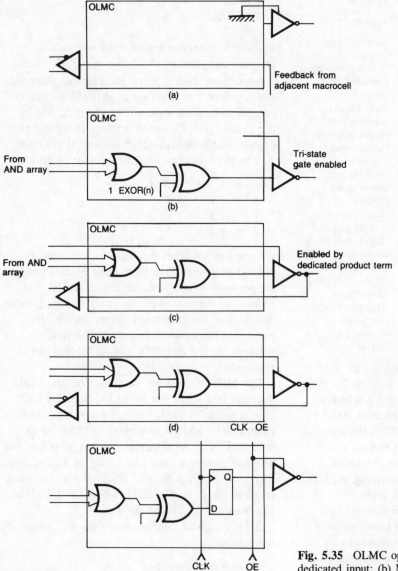

Fig. 5.35 OLMC operating modes. (a) Mode 1: dedicated input; (b) Mode 2 (EXOR(n) sets output active state; (c) Mode 3; (d) Mode 4; (e) Mode 5

EDITORS\WS\EXE. Within the configuration option the user can set up the editor of his choice — no text editor is provided with the Power Logic software. After selection *F* (edit the file) the text is entered. The text file Printout is shown in Fig. 5.38. Here, the device selected is a Lattice emulating a PAL 16H8 (active-high output combinational device). Pin definition follows and then the Boolean equations that state the relationships between the outputs and the inputs.

As in logic expressions:

$$\cdot \ = \text{and}$$
$$+ \ = \text{or}$$
but $\ / \ = \text{complement}$

Therefore W is typed as:

$$W = a.b./c + /b./a \ ;$$

the statement is ended with a semicolon. Comments on each line can be added following a

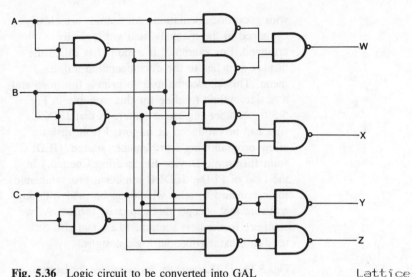

Fig. 5.36 Logic circuit to be converted into GAL

PowerLogic Development System   v2.0
© MicroProcessor Engineering Ltd., 1989

Edit File	PLD.DCF	
Assemble file		
Edit fuse Map		
Program device		
		Device at top of socket
Select device Type	GAL16V8	Family: Lattice
Erase device		Checksum: 10F1
Bland check		Security fuse: OFF
Read device		Fam/Pinout: 3655
Verify device		Signature: '.....'
Set security fuse		Erase cycles: 255
		MASTER
Device Identification menu		
JEDEC file menu		
Configuration menu		
Documentation Utilities		
DOS commands		
Quit		

Fig. 5.37 PLDS main menu

```
Lattice
pal 16h8

pins

pin 1 = clk
pin 2 = a
pin 3 = b
pin 4 = c
pin 19 = w
pin 18 = x
pin 17 = y
pin 16 = z

equations

w = a.b./c + /b./a ;
x = a./c + b./c ;
y = /a./b./c ;
z = a./b.c ;
end
```

Fig. 5.38 Printout of list and equations

slash, e.g.

    pin 2 = a   \input sensor A
and y = /a./b./c ; \output to motor drive

The text file is terminated with the END statement and saved on disk. The user then returns from his text editors to the PLDS main menu. Option A, assemble file, is then used to assemble the text file to produce the fuse pattern necessary to program the selected device. All that is required from the user is to select option P to do this.

Programming takes only a few seconds. The GAL 16V8 is then ready for use in the circuit, replacing the four TTL/CMOS ICs previously specified for the logic circuit. Since the GAL is CMOS *all unused inputs must be disabled by being connected to 0 V or* V_{CC}, whichever is more convenient.

In this brief introduction to PLDs it is not possible to cover all the features of a particular development system. The software described is very user-helpful, simple to operate, and comes

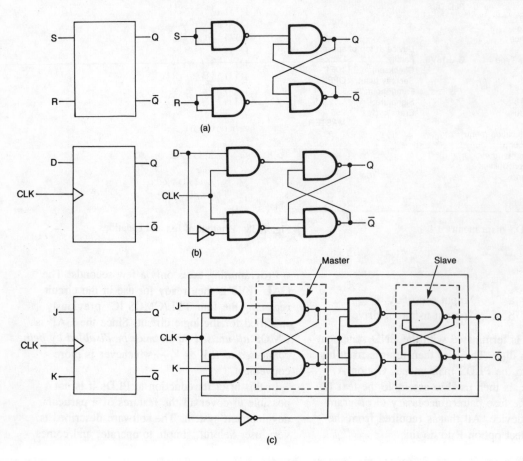

CLK	1		20	
	2		19	W
A				
B	3		18	X
C	4		17	Y
	5		16	Z
	6		15	
	7		14	
	8		13	
	9		12	
	10		11	

with good documentation. All options are clearly explained in the manuals, and are logically arranged. For example, if option U is called the display switches to the documentation utilities menu. This allows the user to print a fuse map and a device outline (outline for this example in Fig. 5.39). Another important feature is that JEDEC files can be produced or imported from disk to allow programming from another source. (JEDEC: Joint Electronic Device Engineering Council.) In the case of PLDs, JEDEC implies a programmable logic standard format, which can be used with any software that accepts this approved format. As we shall see in the next section, PLDs can also be used to create sequential logic designs.

Fig. 5.39 PLD assembler device outline for lattice GAL 16V8. (PowerLogic Development System, MicroProcessor Engineering Ltd. © 1978,88,89)

Fig. 5.40 Bistables. (a) RS type; (b) data latch (d) type; (c) master–slave JK type

(a)

(b)

Master   Slave

(c)

5.6 Sequential logic

Sequential digital circuits are circuits with state, and can be classified as:

- Event-driven — where the circuit elements respond directly to changes in their inputs and no clock-synchronizing signal is used.
- Clock-driven — a master clock generator, or state generator, controls the operation of all devices in the system.
- Pulse-driven — circuits where input signals do not overlap and where a very fast response is possible.

In most sequential designs it is the clock-driven circuits, where the operation of all units within the system is synchronized with a master clock generator, that is the standard design method, because the generation of false states is thereby minimized.

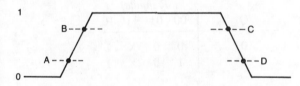

Fig. 5.41 Clock timing in the JK master—slave bistable

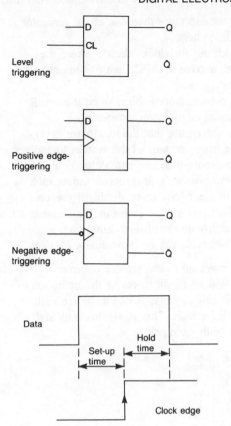

Fig. 5.42 Bistable clocking methods

Circuits with state are built up using the building blocks of bistables (flip-flops), i.e. the RS, clocked RS, D and JK types (Fig. 5.40). In most cases the D and JK bistables are preferred, since with these there can be no indeterminate states, and when using the JK it is advisable to rely on the master—slave versions, since the feedback loop is effectively disconnected when the master is isolated from the slave. In the JK master—slave bistable the clock signal on the rising edge first isolates the master, then allows JK inputs and the previous state to force a change of state to the master. On the clock falling edge any JK data are prevented from further changing the state of the master, and finally the master is reconnected to the slave and the Q, $\bar{Q}$ outputs can assume the new state. This timing is illustrated in Fig. 5.41. One of the important aspects of synchronized sequential design is the clocking method. Bistables can be

level-triggered, where data will be accepted all the time the clock is at the logic level (0 or 1), or edge-triggered. In edge-triggering, which can be on the positive or the negative edge, the data must be present on the inputs for a minimum specified time (the set-up time) before the clock edge arrives, and held there for a minimum specified time (the hold time) after the clock appears. Fig. 5.42 shows the various methods.

To avoid confusion in a design it is normal to have one form of clocking throughout, i.e. either positive edge-triggering or negative edge-triggering, rather than mixing methods. Some general rules for sequential logic designs are therefore:

- Use synchronized design wherever possible.
- Have all circuits triggered on the same edge of the clock — usually the positive edge.

- Do not use more than one clock generator in the system.
- Watch out for clock 'skew', where the clock arrives at a PCB with additional delay.
- Do not use monostables, since these will generate edges asynchronously.
- Try and ensure that the maximum delay time from one part of the system to another is not more than one gate delay time.
- Where bistable asynchronous inputs such as set or clear have to be disabled, use one pull-up resistor for each pin. This assists testability and hardware debugging, since each bistable can be individually checked.

Before we move on to study more complex circuits, it will be useful to revise the operation of the basic bistable circuits. All of them are built around the RS circuit. This is asychronous and follows the truth table below:

S	R	Q	Qn
0	0	0	0
0	0	1	1
0	1	0	0
0	1	1	0
1	0	0	1
1	0	1	1
1	1	0	X) indeterminate
1	1	1	X) state

From this table a state diagram, called the Moore model state diagram, can be drawn. The large circles represent the states, which are labelled 1 and 2, and the lines between the states represent the transitions from one state to the other. Each of these lines is assigned the input RS conditions that force a change of state. With the RS, as for any bistable, some input conditions will not force a change of state; these are indicated by a line that simply connects to the same state circle (Fig. 5.43(a)).

Using the state diagram a state table can be constructed that lists the current state and the next state for all possible new input conditions. In this case the *SRQ* variables are assigned their logic values.

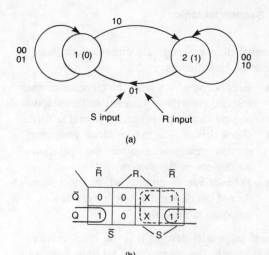

(a)

(b)

Fig. 5.43 (a) Moore model state diagram for the RS bistable; (b) Karnaugh map for RS bistable

Present state	Next state (SR inputs)			
Q	00	01	11	10
0	0	0	X	1
1	1	0	X	1

This is, of course, just another way of drawing the truth table, and it shows that the Q output will move from a 0 state to 1 when S = 1 and R = 0 and will change from 1 to 0 when S = 0 and R = 1. when both inputs are 1 an indeterminate state is indicated by X. The Karnaugh map for Qn can be drawn directly from the state table, where Qn is the new state. From the map in Fig. 5.43(b):

$$Qn = Q.\bar{R} + S$$

The two common logic circuits to implement this expression are using cross-coupled NAND gates, and using cross-coupled NOR gates.

For the NAND circuit

$$Qn = \overline{Q.\bar{R} + S}$$
$$= \overline{\overline{Q.\bar{R}}.\bar{S}} \qquad \text{(Fig. 5.44(a))}$$

For the NOR circuit

$$\bar{Q}n = \overline{Q.\bar{R} + S}$$

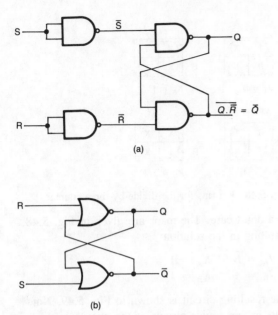

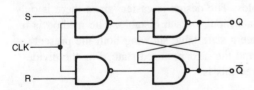

Fig. 5.44 Commonly used circuits for the RS bistable.
(a) RS NAND circuit (set and reset with logic 1s); (b)
RS NOR circuit

But $Q.\bar{R} = \overline{\bar{Q} + R}$

$\therefore \quad \overline{Qn} = \overline{\bar{Q} + R} + S$ (Fig. 5.44(b))

A synchronous RS bistable, which had the
advantage of input clocking with a master timing
pulse, is a simple extension of the basic NAND
circuit to provide gating on the input NANDs (Fig.
5.45). The circuit still has the drawback of giving
indeterminate outputs when both R = 1 and S = 1
while the clock signal is applied. The JK and D
bistables, as stated previously, overcome this
disadvantage.

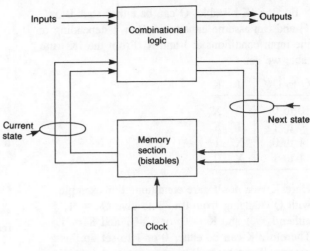

Fig. 5.45 The clocked RS bistable

Bistables are the basic building blocks of all
sequential circuits. Groups of bistables are linked
together to create registers, shift registers, counters

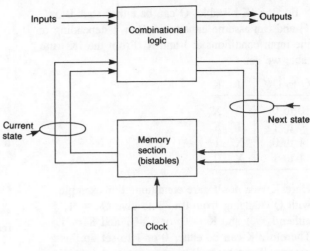

Fig. 5.46 State machine model

and sequence generators and so on. As indicated,
in the example of the bistable circuit, the analysis
of sequential logic requires the use of additional
tools such as state diagrams and state tables. The
standard model for a state machine is shown in
Fig. 5.46. This consists of a number of inputs and
outputs, and is divided into a combinational logic
section and a memory (state) section. The circuit
exists in a particular state defined by the internal
signals, which are referred to as *state variables* or
present-state variables. For example, with two
state variables and two bistables there could be
four different states. In a state machine each
subsequent state is a consequence of both input and
current state. Consider the simple example of a
divide-by-three synchronous counter. Suppose it is
designed using JK master−slave bistables. Two
bistables are necessary and the states required are:

State	B	A
0	0	0
1	0	1
2	1	0

These three states must be generated sequentially
with clock input. Note that one state — when A
and B are both 1 — is not valid.

For the JK bistable, Q can be either state 0 or 1, and can assume either state 0 or 1 depending on the input conditions at J and K. From the JK truth table we get:

Q to Q_N	J	K
0 to 0	0	X
0 to 1	1	X
1 to 0	X	1
1 to 1	X	0

Here X = a don't care condition. For example, with Q changing from 0 to 1 to give Qn = 1, either J = 1 and K = 0, or J = 1 and K = 1. Therefore K can be either 0 or 1 to set up this change. The table will be required in determining the required J and K inputs for the counter.

From the original table for the divide-by-three, a state diagram can be produced; this is virtually a flow chart of the required states, and is given in Fig. 5.47. The example is, of course, very simple, since the circuit moves from state 0 $(\bar{B}.\bar{A})$, to 1, to 2 and then back to 0 without jumping any states. Each of the states is then assigned the value of the variables AB (A is the least significant bit).

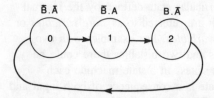

Fig. 5.47 State diagram for a divide-by-three counter

State 0 requires $\bar{A}.\bar{B}$
State 1 requires $A.\bar{B}$
State 2 requires $\bar{A}.B$

The required inputs to the J and K pins of each bistable to force the counter to divide by three can be found by a study of the transition between every state. For example, from state 0 we have $\bar{A}.\bar{B}$ moving to $A.\bar{B}$ at state 1. Q_A is required to change from a 0 to 1, which means that J_A must be 1 and K_A a don't care (X). Karnaugh maps can be drawn for the required J and K values for both bistables from a study of the state diagram.

In these diagrams the missing state AB is marked

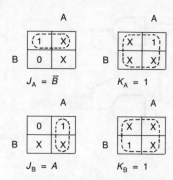

Fig. 5.48 K maps for the divide-by-three counter

as a don't care. The maps are given in Fig. 5.48, resulting in the solution:

$$J_A = \bar{B} \quad K_A = 1$$
$$J_B = A \quad K_B = 1$$

The resulting circuit is shown in Fig. 5.49. Note that, in this simple circuit, if the missing code was generated by noise, after one clock pulse the counter would return to state 0. A further study of missing and invalid codes will be made later.

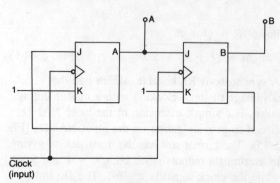

Clock
(input)

Fig. 5.49 Circuit for the divide-by-three counter

Now consider the divide-by-three using D bistables. The design is easier, since there is only one data input to each bistable. The method is to produce a state table showing both the present state and the next required state. For the divide-by-three this is:

Present state		Next state	
B	A	Bn	An
0	0	0	1
0	1	1	0
1	0	0	0

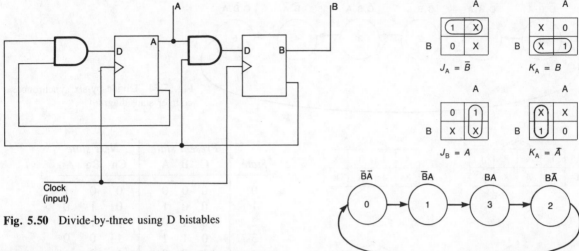

Fig. 5.50 Divide-by-three using D bistables

Fig. 5.51 State diagram and maps for a 2-bit Gray code counter using JKs

For the next state to be logic 1 the D input must be set to logic 1 before the arrival of the clock pulse.

thus $D_A = \bar{A}.\bar{B}$
and $D_B = A.\bar{B}$

The circuit is shown in Fig. 5.50.

Consider now the task of creating a 2-bit Gray code counter using first JK bistables and then D bistables. The required table is:

| Current state | | Next state | |
B	A	Bn	An
0	0	0	1
0	1	1	1
1	1	1	0
1	0	0	0

The state diagram is given in Fig. 5.51, together with the maps required for J_A, K_A, J_B and K_B. From the maps:

$J_A = \bar{B}$ $K_A = B$
$J_B = A$ $K_B = \bar{A}$

and the resulting circuit is given in Fig. 5.52, which can be seen to be a two-stage Johnson (twisted ring) counter.

If D bistables are to be used the D inputs are given from the next state in the state table.

$An = \bar{A}.\bar{B} + A.\bar{B} = \bar{B}(\bar{A} + A) = \bar{B}$
and $Bn = A.\bar{B} + A.B = A$

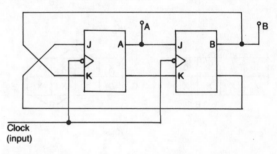

Fig. 5.52 Circuit for 2-bit Gray code counter

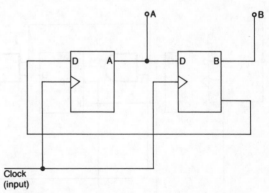

Fig. 5.53 2-bit Gray code counter using D bistables

The circuit is shown in Fig. 5.53.

Let us extend the design technique further with the design of a divide-by-six synchronous counter. The state table is:

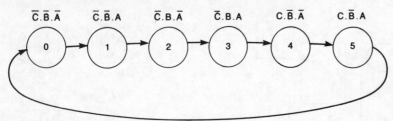

Fig. 5.54 Divide-by-six synchronous counter state diagram

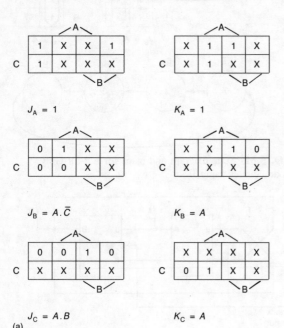

State	Present state			Next state		
	C	B	A	Cn	Bn	An
0	0	0	0	0	0	1
1	0	0	1	0	1	0
2	0	1	0	0	1	1
3	0	1	1	1	0	0
4	1	0	0	1	0	1
5	1	0	1	0	0	0

and the state diagram is given in Fig. 5.54.

If JK bistables are to be used, the maps for the three J and K inputs must be drawn. Since there are two unused states — 6 and 7 — these can initially be mapped as don't cares. From the maps we get:

$$J_A = 1 \qquad K_A = A$$
$$J_B = A.\bar{C} \qquad K_B = A$$
$$J_C = A.B \qquad K_C = A$$

leading to the circuit in Fig. 5.55.

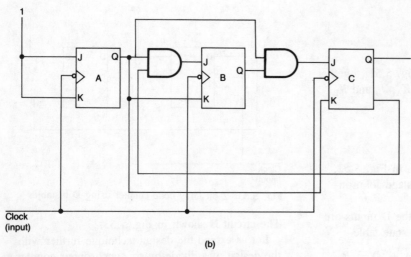

Fig. 5.55 (a) K-maps for the divide-by-six using KJs; (b) resulting circuit for the divide-by-six

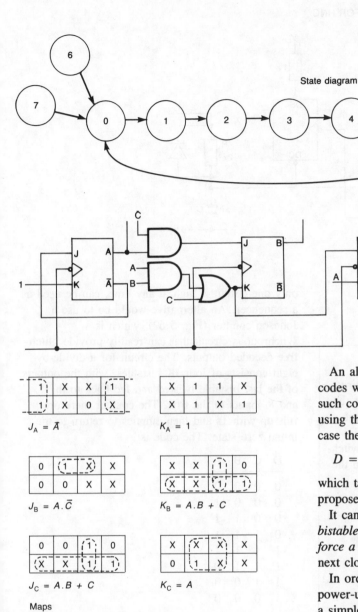

Maps

Fig. 5.56 Synchronous logic design example

Unused codes or states in a counter constructed using JK bistables could lead to a latched condition or the generation of false outputs. One method of eliminating the possibility of false codes is to ensure that, if they did occur, the counter switches to the 0 state on the next clock pulse. The state diagram modified for this condition, together with the maps and resulting circuit, is shown in Fig. 5.56.

An alternative method to eliminate any invalid codes would be to set up a detection circuit for such codes and then force each bistable to reset, using the asynchronous reset input pins. In this case the detection circuit would be:

$$D = \bar{A}.B.C + A.B.C = B.C$$

which takes less logic than the method already proposed.

It can be seen that a *real advantage of using D bistables* is that any *invalid codes generated will force a counter to return to the zero* state on the next clock pulse.

In order for a counter to assume the 0 state at power-up, the reset pins can be initialized by using a simple circuit as shown in Fig. 5.57. Any unused set and reset inputs should be properly disabled if the correct operation of counters and registers is to be achieved.

Counters and shift registers are often used as code generators, as in the last example, and also for generating timing signals. For example, a recirculating register can be used for this purpose. If a serial-in/serial-out 8-bit shift register is initially loaded with 00000001, the application of eight shift pulses will cause the 1 to travel through the register (Fig. 5.61). This sort of circuit, where

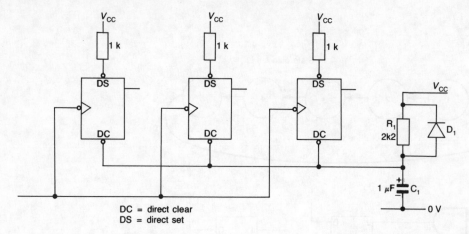

DC = direct clear
DS = direct set

Fig. 5.57 Power-up initialization

Example

A counter circuit using JK bistables is required, that gives the arbitrary code pattern given in the following table. Design a synchronous circuit with all invalid codes eliminated. Any invalid code that might be caused by noise or at switch-on must be arranged to reset the counter on the next clock pulse.

C	B	A
0	0	0
0	1	0
1	0	1
1	0	0
1	1	0

Solution

The state diagram is given in Fig. 5.58, with the invalid states 1, 3 and 7 arranged to reset the counter. Three JK bistables are needed, and the maps for the appropriate J and K inputs are shown in Fig. 5.59. These give:

$$J_A = A + B.\bar{C}. \qquad K_A = 1$$
$$J_B = \bar{A} \qquad K_B = 1$$
$$J_C = A.B \qquad K_C = A.B$$

resulting in the circuit diagram in Fig. 5.60.

only one output is high at any time, can be used as a sequencer. An alternative would be to use a Johnson counter (Fig. 5.62), which is a synchronous circuit that can readily provide glitch-free decoded outputs. The circuit for a divide-by-eight consists of four JK bistables, with the outputs of the last bistable twisted and fed back to the J and K inputs of the first. The counter therefore fills up with 1s and then empties to return to the initial zero state. The code is:

D	C	B	A
0	0	0	0
0	0	0	1
0	0	1	1
0	1	1	1
1	1	1	1
1	1	1	0
1	1	0	0
1	0	0	0

Eight two-input AND gates are needed for the decoder, where:

$$0_0 = \bar{A}.\bar{D}$$
$$0_1 = A.\bar{B}$$
$$0_2 = B.\bar{C}$$
$$0_3 = C.\bar{D}$$
$$0_4 = A.D$$
$$0_5 = \bar{A}.B$$
$$0_6 = \bar{B}.C$$
$$0_7 = \bar{C}.D$$

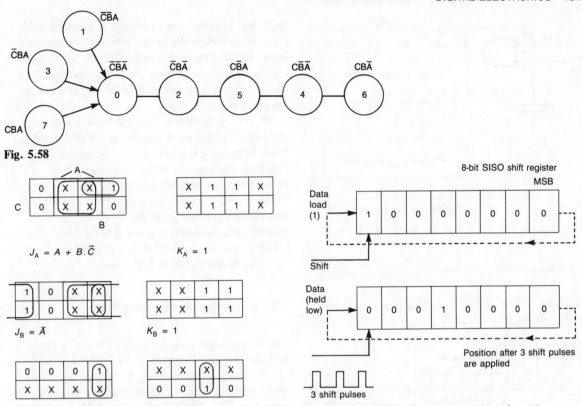

Fig. 5.58

Fig. 5.59

$$J_A = A + B.\bar{C}$$ $$K_A = 1$$

$$J_B = \bar{A}$$ $$K_B = 1$$

$$J_C = \bar{A}.B$$ $$K_C = A.B$$

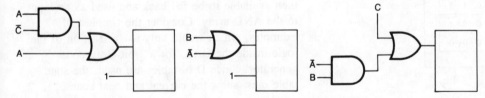

Fig. 5.60

8-bit SISO shift register

MSB

Data load (1)

Shift

Data (held low)

Position after 3 shift pulses are applied

3 shift pulses

Fig. 5.61 Using a recirculating register for code generation or timing signals

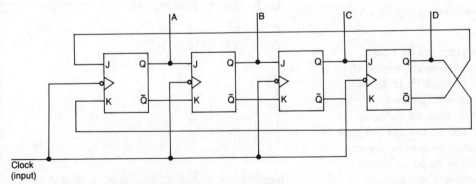

Fig. 5.62 Divide-by-eight Johnson counter

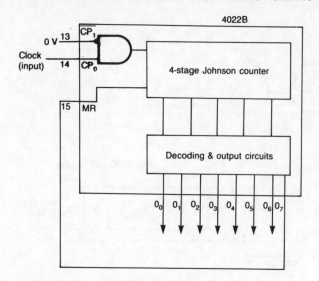

Fig. 5.63 A CMOS 4022B modified to give a seven-stage sequence

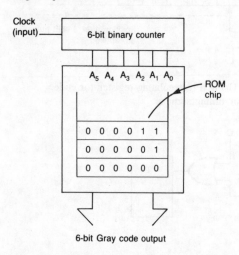

Fig. 5.64 Outline for method of generating a 6-bit Gray code

Because the Johnson counter can be readily decoded to give glitch-free outputs, variations of it are used in MSI chips, particularly in CMOS logic. One example is the 4017, a divide-by-ten (decade) Johnson counter, with the decoding on chip to give one out of ten high at any one time. MSI or LSI devices should be used wherever possible in place of designs based on simple bistables and logic. Suppose a seven-stage sequencer is required: better solutions to using

gates and bistables are to modify a standard MSI chip, or to design the circuit into programmable logic. In the first case a 4022 CMOS divide-by-eight synchronous counter could be modified to divide by seven by connecting the eight-output to the reset pin (Fig. 5.63).

For code generators, where there are a large number of variables, a counter and ROM can be used. Suppose a 6-bit Gray code generator is required: the solution could be to use a 6-bit counter with its outputs driving the address lines of a ROM, and the Gray code then held in ROM, so that address 000000 gives the Gray outputs 000000, address 000001 gives 000001 and 0000010 giving the Gray output 000011, and so on. This is illustrated in Fig. 5.64.

5.7 Sequential design using PLDs

The output logic macro cell (OLMC) of a GAL and the registered outputs of PALs have a built-in D bistable. It is then relatively easy to program these types of PLD to act as state machines. In the case of a GAL 16V8 mode 5 (see table on page 169) would be selected during programming to give registered outputs, and the $\bar{Q}$ of the bistable is then available to be fed back and used as an input to the AND array. Consider the simplest of examples, which would only use a fraction of the logic inside the GAL, for a 3-bit Gray code generator. Since D bistables are used, the state table must show the current and next states.

Current state			Next state		
C	B	A	Cn	Bn	An
0	0	0	0	0	1
0	0	1	0	1	1
0	1	1	0	1	0
0	1	0	1	1	0
1	1	0	1	1	1
1	1	1	1	0	1
1	0	1	1	0	0
1	0	0	0	0	0

Therefore $An = \bar{A}.\bar{B}.\bar{C} + A.\bar{B}.\bar{C} + \bar{A}.B.C + A.B.C$ which simplifies to $An = B.C + \bar{B}.\bar{C}$

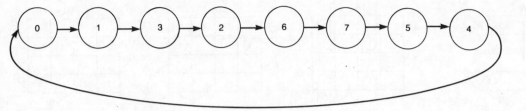

Fig. 5.65 State diagram for 3-bit Gray code counter

Similarly $Bn = A.\bar{C} + \bar{A}.B$
and $\qquad Cn = A.C + \bar{A}.B$ $\qquad$ (Fig. 5.65).

The text file for the GAL using the PDLS software package previously described is

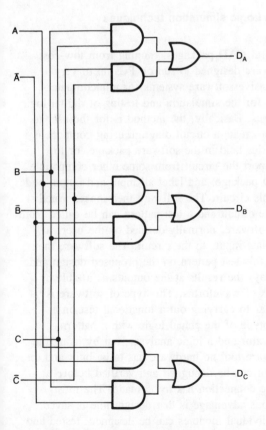

Fig. 5.66 Logic required to implement the 3-bit Gray code counter (plus three bistables)

Lattice
Pal 16R8 $\qquad$ \emulating a registered PAL

Pins
Pin 1 $\quad$ = Clk \clock input
Pin 19 = c
Pin 18 = b
Pin 7 $\quad$ = a

Equations

a = b.c + /b./c ;
b = a./c + /a.b ;
c = a.c + /a.b ;
end

The logic circuit of Fig. 5.66 can thus be replaced by one PLD.

Now let us consider the slightly more complex circuit for a divide-by-12 synchronous counter. This will more fully utilize the flexibility within a PLD. The state table is:

D	C	B	A	Dn	Cn	Bn	An
0	0	0	0	0	0	0	1
0	0	0	1	0	0	1	0
0	0	1	0	0	0	1	1
0	0	1	1	0	1	0	0
0	1	0	0	0	1	0	1
0	1	0	1	0	1	1	0
0	1	1	0	0	1	1	1
0	1	1	1	1	0	0	0
1	0	0	0	1	0	0	1
1	0	0	1	1	0	1	0
1	0	1	0	1	0	1	1
1	0	1	1	0	0	0	0

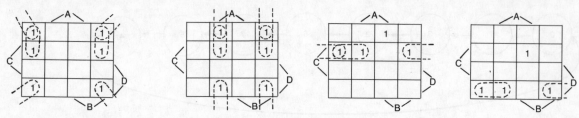

$$An = \bar{A}.\bar{C} + \bar{A}.\bar{D} \quad Cn = A.B.\bar{C}.\bar{D} + \bar{B}.C.D + \bar{A}.C.\bar{D} \quad Dn = A.B.C.\bar{D} + \bar{B}.\bar{C}.D + \bar{A}.\bar{C}.D$$

$$Bn = A.\bar{B}.\bar{D} + \bar{A}.B.\bar{D}$$
$$+ A.\bar{B}.\bar{C} + \bar{A}.B.\bar{C}$$

Fig. 5.67 K maps for the divide-by-12 counter

From this table and the Karnaugh maps of Fig. 5.67 we obtain the simplifications:

$$An = \bar{A}.\bar{C} + \bar{A}.\bar{D}$$
$$Bn = A.\bar{B}.\bar{D} + A.\bar{B}.\bar{C} + \bar{A}.B.\bar{D} + \bar{A}.B.\bar{C}$$
$$Cn = A.B.\bar{C}.\bar{D} + \bar{B}.C.\bar{D} + \bar{A}.C.\bar{D}$$
$$Dn = A.B.C.\bar{D} + \bar{B}.\bar{C}.D + \bar{A}.\bar{C}.D$$

Using SSI, this divide-by-12 would require four bistables and a relatively complex combinational logic circuit. All of this can be fitted into one PLD. Using a GAL the text file would be:

Lattice
Pal 16R8

Pins
Pin 1 = Clk \clock input
Pin 19 = d
Pin 18 = c
Pin 17 = b
Pin 16 = a

Equations

a = /a./c + /a./d ;
b = a./b./d + a./b./c + /a.b./d + /a.b./c ;
c = a.b./c./d + /b.c./d + /a.c./d ;
d = a.b.c./d + /b./c.d +/a./c.d ;
end

When this file is assembled and the fuse map created and downloaded to the GAL, we would have a divide-by-12 synchronous counter all contained in one package.

Note that when using PLDs it is essential to obtain the minimized logic form, to avoid cumbersome equations and — more importantly —

to reduce the risk of running out of space in the device map. The use of D bistables in the output circuit of register-type PLDs also has the important advantage of the safe elimination of invalid states.

5.8 Logic simulation techniques

Several CAD packages, ranging from low-cost software designed to run on PCs up to very expensive software systems for minicomputers, exist for the simulation and testing of digital logic designs. Basically, the method is for the user to either create a circuit diagram using component libraries held in the software package, or to transport the circuit from some other compatible CAD package, and label all input and output nodes on this circuit. The software then makes a netlist of the circuit and a test pattern can be called from the software, normally defined by the user, to simulate inputs to the circuit. The software then runs this test pattern on the proposed design and displays the results at the outputs as a table or series of waveforms. This type of software is similar to carrying out a functional test on a prototype of the actual logic with a pattern generator and a logic analyser, but by using the software tool no hardware has to be built and the design can be debugged and verified before a single connection has to be made. The most obvious advantage is that design time is saved.

Individual modules can be designed, tested and verified and their output patterns used to test the next modules in the system. The pattern of signals used for the simulation can be varied to give any combination of 1s and 0s, as well as variations in clock width and speed. In this way the response of the design to unusual input states, or even an entirely random input pattern, can be assessed.

One typical PC logic simulation tool is MICRO-LOGIC II, which operates as described in the previous paragraph. A flow chart of the required user actions for this package is shown in Fig. 5.68.

Consider the very simple example of simulating a 4-bit binary-to-Gray convertor. A circuit for this is given in Fig. 5.69. Using the drawing facility of MICRO-LOGIC II, an EOR gate package is selected from the library and placed on the screen using the mouse. The mouse is then used to place two more EOR gates on the screen. If these placements are not exactly as required, a MOVE facility is available which enables a component to be repositioned on the screen. The circuit has four inputs and so four separate data generators are selected from the component library and suitably placed on the screen. Connecting lines and nodes are then made using the ADD and LINE commands from the menu. Finally the nodes are labelled using the ADD and TEXT facility. In this case the input nodes are labelled B_0, B_1, B_2 and B_3, and the outputs are OUT_0 to OUT_3.

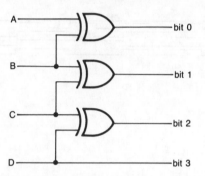

Fig. 5.69 4-bit binary-to-Gray convertor

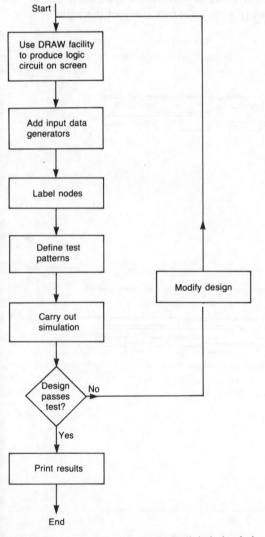

Fig. 5.68 User actions for a CAD digital simulation package

The editor pop-down menu can then be used to define a pattern generator required by the user. The simulation option can now be selected from the menu, and within this portion of the software the signal patterns for the selected data generators used in the design can be set up. In this example, a binary pattern is selected for the 4-bit input. The simulation is run and the inputs and outputs displayed on the screen. A hard copy of the result can then be obtained.

Simulation has important advantages in detecting glitches caused by race hazards and those generated in decoding circuits. A simple example is shown in Fig. 5.70 for a combinational logic circuit consisting of four two-input NAND gates.

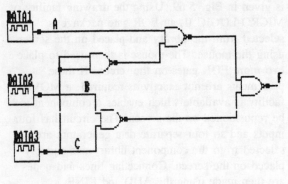

Fig. 5.70

The output of the circuit is seen to be

$$F = \overline{\overline{A.\overline{C}}.\overline{B.C}}$$

The design is verified by the MICRO-LOGIC II package by applying three data inputs to the inputs *A, B* and *C*. If an ascending binary pattern is selected for the three inputs and a simulation run made, the output conforms to the required Boolean expression and no glitches are apparent. The printout for this simulation run is shown in Fig. 5.71(a). However, if input *B* is held high and a random pattern is selected for both inputs *A* and *C*, short-duration glitches are apparent in the output (Fig. 5.71(b)). A study of the logic

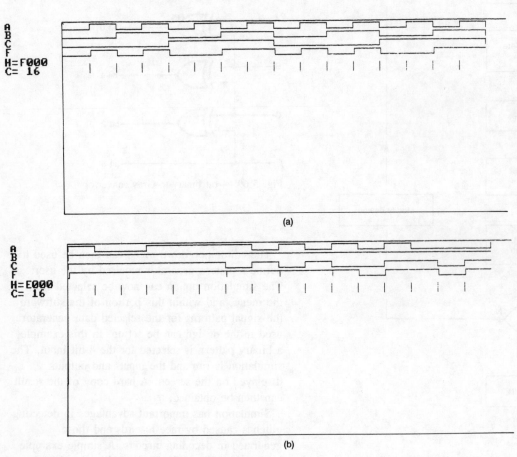

(a)

(b)

Fig. 5.71 (a) Binary input pattern applied: (b) glitch generation

$$F = \overline{\overline{A.\overline{C}.B.C}}$$
$$\therefore F = A.\overline{C} + B.C$$

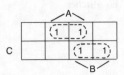

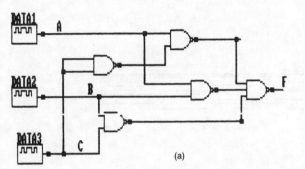

Fig. 5.72 K map for logic

equation gives:

$$F = \overline{A.\overline{C}} + \overline{\overline{B.C}} = A.\overline{C} + B.C$$

resulting in the Karnaugh map of Fig. 5.72, where it can be seen that the classic method for producing a race-free output would be to include the couple $A.B$. This results in:

$$F = A.\overline{C} + B.C + A.B$$

or $F = \overline{\overline{A.\overline{C}}.\overline{B.C}.\overline{A.B}}$

This modified and supposedly race-free circuit is shown in Fig. 5.73, together with simulation printouts using the similar pattern generators that were used to test the original circuit. The glitches have not all been eliminated. One particular glitch occurs when A is a don't care condition and both B and C are returning simultaneously from a 1 to

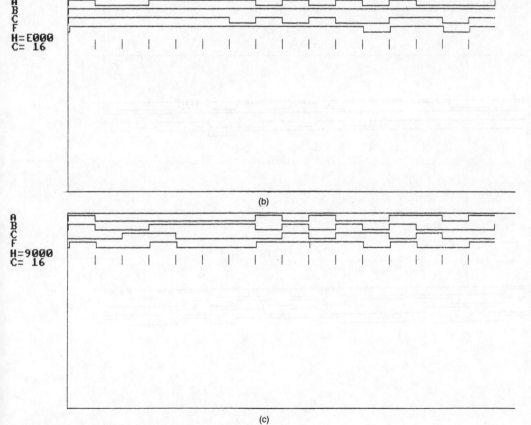

Fig. 5.73 (a) Modified circuit intended to eliminate glitches; (b) test for glitches; (c) glitch present

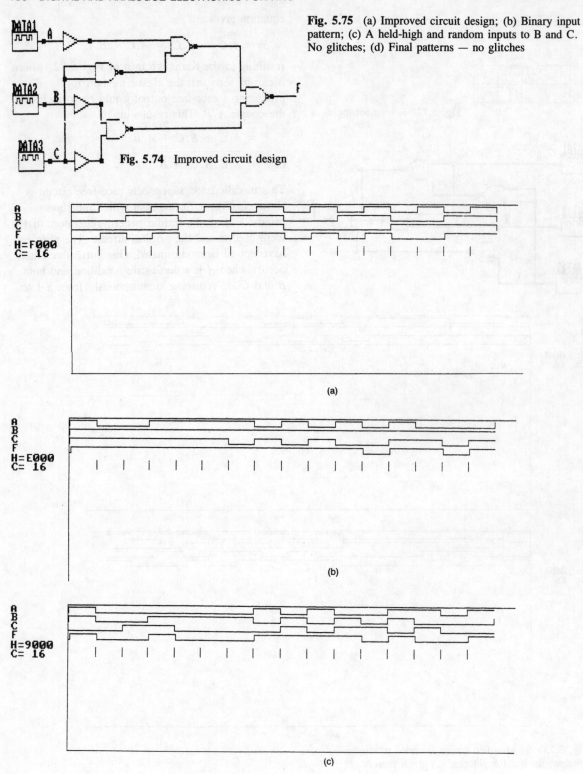

Fig. 5.75 (a) Improved circuit design; (b) Binary input pattern; (c) A held-high and random inputs to B and C. No glitches; (d) Final patterns — no glitches

Fig. 5.74 Improved circuit design

(a)

(b)

(c)

a 0 state. The signal delay present on C sets all three inputs of the final NAND gate high for one gate delay period. A short-duration glitch is produced from 1 to 0 at this output. An improved method is required to eliminate any possible false output in this circuit, and therefore other similar combinational circuits. Two possible methods exist:

(1) To provide a synchronizing clock or strobe pulse to interrogate the output of the final gate.
(2) To ensure that all signal paths to output gates have the same number of gate delays.

The latter method, which is inherent in PLD circuit structures, requires the inclusion of non-inverting buffer gates in those variables that are not complemented. Thus the original circuit is modified as shown in Fig. 5.74, with non-inverting buffers in the signal paths of all three variables A, B and C to compensate for the delay generated by the inverter that is necessary to give the A signal. This circuit, as shown by the simulator printouts, is glitch-free see Fig. 5.75.

Logic simulation techniques can thus be an invaluable aid in testing designs before committing them to hardware. In the case of most non-reprogrammable PLDs (PAL for example) extensive simulation is vital to eliminate bugs in the design before the circuit is downloaded into the IC.

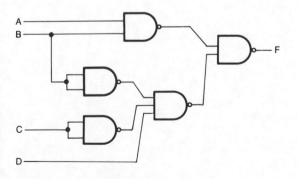

Fig. 5.76 Logic circuit

5.9   Problems

(1) Design NAND-only gate solutions for the following Boolean expressions:
(a) $F_1 = A.\bar{B} + C.A$
(b) $F_2 = \overline{A + B}.C.D$
(c) $F_3 = R + \overline{S}.T + \bar{S}$

(2) From the following truth table obtain a minimized Boolean expression and produce a logic design using basic gate functions:

C	B	A	F
0	0	0	0
0	0	1	1
0	1	0	0
0	1	1	0
1	0	0	1
1	0	1	1
1	1	0	1
1	1	1	0

(3) A logic circuit has four inputs and two outputs where:

$$F_1(D,C,B,A) = \Sigma(1,4,5,9,12,13)$$
$$F_2(D,C,B,A) = \Sigma(1,3,9,11,13,15)$$

Find minimized expressions for both outputs and design the logic using:
(a) Inverters and AND-OR ICs
(b) NAND ICs
Determine which of the circuits is the most economical.

(4) The circuit of Fig. 5.76 is suspected of producing a static race hazard. Prove that this is the case and modify the circuit to eliminate the hazard.

(5) For the next truth table, design a logic circuit using a 4-to-1 data selector. Make C the data variable.

C	B	A	F
0	0	0	1
0	0	1	0
0	1	0	0
0	1	1	1
1	0	0	1
1	0	1	1
1	1	0	0
1	1	1	0

(6) A logic circuit is required with four inputs (D,C,B,A) and three outputs where:

Output F_1 is high when three or more inputs are high.

Output F_2 is high when input A is the same as input D.

Output F_3 is high when more than two inputs are at logic 0.

Deduce the minimized logic expressions for the three outputs, and write a text file suitable for a software package so that a GAL 16V8 can be used for the circuit.

(7) Design a divide-by-five synchronous counter using JK master—slave bistables. In this case,

any missing codes can be considered as don't cares.

(8) Modify the design for problem (7) so that all invalid states reset the counter to the zero state on the next clock pulse.

(9) Produce a design, using JK bistables, for an arbitrary code generator with states 1, 3, 0, 2.

(10) A divide-by-nine synchronous counter is to be designed using a PLD. Produce the minimized logic equations for the inputs to the D bistables, and write the text file suitable for the circuit to be implemented in a GAL 16V8.

6 Signals and System I/O

6.1 Signals and signal processing

Much of the earlier work in this book has been concerned with the operation and theory of devices and circuits, where in most cases the analogue and digital parts of electronics have been dealt with separately. However, in real situations a system may often contain a mix of analogue and digital portions, or a digital system may need to respond to analogue inputs and give output-controlling signals to drive analogue load devices. Electronics can itself be described or defined as concerning the detection, manipulation, processing, storing and use of electrical signals. Thus a study of signals in their various forms is an important area of electronic engineering. This chapter is an attempt to integrate a simple treatment of signal theory with some aspects of system design.

In its most basic form a system may require just one input signal — the stimulus — and from the value of this signal produces a suitable output effect. The characteristic of the input signal being used by the system could be its voltage or current amplitude, its phase relationship to a reference frequency, its frequency or its shape. Let us consider the case of a signal from a thermocouple with a typical sensitivity of 41 μV/°C, being used to measure temperature in the range from 0°C up to +250°C. Imagine that the thermocouple is designed to obtain the temperature profile of the interior of a pipe by moving the sensor on an automatic trolley at a uniform rate through the pipe. The signal from the thermocouple, which will be a slowly changing voltage, could be a maximum of 10.25 mV. This level would result from a pipe temperature of 250°C. The rate of the sensor travel through the pipe and the temperature gradient would result in a maximum frequency component in the sensor signal. If this is limited to

5 Hz we now have both the voltage amplitude and the expected bandwidth of the input signal defined. Since any thermocouple has a low resistance, a brief specification of the sensor signal would be:

$V_s = 0-10.25$ mV
$f_{max} = 5$ Hz
$R_s = 50\,\Omega$
Sensitivity $= 41\,\mu$V/°C

The signal now has to be processed by some measurement system, which we shall consider as comprising an amplifier and an analogue-to-digital convertor (ADC) arranged so that the output of the system will be digitized values of the temperature profile along the pipe. These digitized values could be stored in a memory for later evaluation or printout (Fig. 6.1).

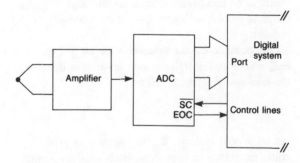

Fig. 6.1 Outline of system input

The input circuit must be an amplifier with a voltage gain that increases the sensor signal to a level that fits the input span of the ADC:

$$A_{vcl} = \frac{V_{FS(ADC)}}{V_{smax}} \qquad (6.1)$$

where $V_{FS(ADC)}$ is the full-scale input, or span, of the ADC. Thus in this case the closed-loop voltage gain has to be approximately 200.

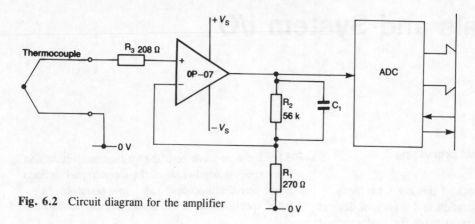

Fig. 6.2 Circuit diagram for the amplifier

Apart from voltage gain, other important features of the amplifier are going to be a low noise value and low drift. This is because the input signal is relatively small. Suppose it is necessary to resolve a one-degree change of temperature inside the pipe; the added noise and drift referred to the input must be much less than the 41 μV sensitivity obtained from the thermocouple. A low-noise low-drift precision op-amp is essential for the input stage. This signal from the amplifier also needs to be bandwidth-limited so that higher-frequency noise — above f_s — is substantially reduced.

One possible circuit solution is given in Fig. 6.2, where an OP-07 precision op-amp is used in the non-inverting mode. Here:

$$A_{vcl} = 1 + (R_2/R_1)$$
$$A_{vcl} = 207$$

An additional resistor, R_3, is essential to give equal resistance in both input leads of the op-amp. This reduces voltage drift at the amplifier's inputs caused by bias current changes with temperature, as explained in Chapter 2. In this case

$$R_3 = \left(\frac{R_1 R_2}{R_1 + R_2} \right) - R_s$$

$$\therefore R_3 \approx 208 \, \Omega$$

The resistance in each lead is then equal to R_3 plus R_s, and the drift error caused by ambient temperature changes around the system is given by:

$$\text{Drift error at input} = \left[\frac{dV_{io}}{dT} + \frac{dI_{io}}{dT}(R_3 + R_s) \right] \Delta T$$

for the OP-07 $\dfrac{dV_{io}}{dT} = 0.5 \, \mu V/°C$

and $\dfrac{dI_{io}}{dT} = 12 \, pA/°C$

Thus for a 20°C change in ambient temperature (ΔT) we get

$\text{Drift error at input} = [0.5 \times 10^{-6} + 12 \times 10^{-12} \times 270]20 \ V$
$= 10 \, \mu V$

This is equivalent to a measured temperature change, at the thermocouple, of 0.25°C. The use of a circuit based on the OP-07 should therefore meet the requirement. This can be compared (by the reader) with the drift from the same circuit but with a general-purpose op-amp such as the 741 in place of the OP-07.

To bandwidth-limit the input, a suitable capacitor could be placed in parallel with R_2 to increase negative feedback at higher frequencies. In that case:

$$f_h = \frac{1}{2\pi C_1 R_2}$$

A value of 330 nF for C_1 would set the upper 3 dB point of the amplifier's response to about 8 Hz, which is above the maximum signal frequency expected from the thermocouple. However, the roll-off from this cut-off will only be 20 dB per decade. A better method would be to include an

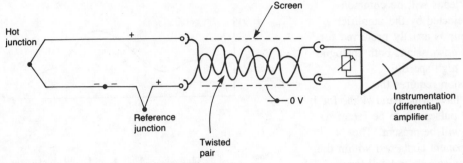

Fig. 6.3 Improved temperature measuring system

active filter between the amplifier and the ADC. Even a simple equal-component filter based on one op-amp would improve the roll-off to 40 dB per decade.

The resolution of the whole system, neglecting the effects of noise and drift, will be determined by the number of bits used in the ADC. An 8-bit ADC with 256 levels would allow a resolution of $\pm 1°C$, whereas a 10-bit ADC with 1024 levels would theoretically give a $\pm 0.25°C$ resolution. If a 10-bit ADC is used, then an input amplifier circuit giving even lower noise and drift becomes essential.

Questions now arise as to what sampling rate is necessary to collect sufficient data on the pipe's temperature, and how will the conversion speed of the ADC affect system accuracy? If the sensor speed through the pipe is a maximum of 10 cm/s and the temperature gradient within the pipe is not expected to be more than 20 °C/cm, then the rate of signal change will be a maximum of about 8 mV/s. A sampling rate of 10 Hz, 10 conversions per second, would give readings for every centimetre of the pipe.

As will be proved later, the conversion time of the ADC affects the maximum-frequency component that can be allowed in the sensor signal. For errors to be less than ± 0.5 LSB (least-significant bit), the relationship between conversion time (t_c) and f_{max} is given by

$$f_{max} = \frac{1}{2\pi t_c 2^n} \qquad \text{(see Appendix A)} \qquad (6.2)$$

where n is the number of bits used in the ADC. If f_{max} from the sensor is assumed to be 5 Hz, and

the ADC has 8 bits, the conversion time of the ADC must be better than 125 μs for errors to be less than ± 0.5 LSB.

It can be seen that, in order for the integrity of the digitized values of temperature to be maintained, several factors must be taken into consideration at the design stage of this data collection system. These factors, which apply equally to most similar data collection circuits, are:

- Noise and drift reduction
- Filtering and bandwidth limiting
- Sampling rate
- Conversion speed
- Resolution
- Linearity.

Looking back at the example, it can be seen that even if a low-noise low-drift amplifier is used, the noise level — within the restricted bandwidth — picked up on the input lead must be kept lower than 20 μV if errors of less than ± 0.5 LSB are to be maintained. This might prove a difficult task involving the screening of the whole lead down the length of the pipe. In a simpler situation — for example, where the sensor is not required to move — it would be possible to use a differential arrangement with two thermocouples connected as shown in Fig. 6.3. Here the thermocouples' signals oppose each other, so that the output signal is proportional to the temperature difference between the hot and reference junctions. A shielded twisted pair of signal lines can be used with an instrumentation amplifier to provide gain. The advantage of this circuit is that any noise picked up on the input leads will be common-mode, and should be rejected by the amplifier. This differential principle is usually preferred for many forms of signal transmission, both analogue and digital, at low and high speed.

Digital data transmission requires the transmission system to have wide bandwidth, for if the edges of the digital pulses are to be retained, high-frequency signals will be present. The highest-frequency component contained within the pulse is related to the pulse rise and fall times:

$$f_h \approx \frac{0.35}{t_r} \tag{6.3}$$

Thus a TTL-type digital pulse with rise and fall times of less than 10 ns contains frequencies up to

$$f_h = \frac{0.35}{10 \times 10^{-9}} \approx 35\,\text{MHz}$$

At such frequencies it is best to treat the signal path as a transmission line which must be properly terminated to avoid reflections. A poorly terminated transmission line sets up distortions and ringing in the pulse signal.

A differential line-driver IC is used at the sending end of the link, and a differential amplifier at the receiver. In this way common-mode noise will be almost eliminated. The received pulse can then be reshaped by a Schmitt trigger-type gate. These 'snap-action' switching gates have built-in hysteresis and wider noise margins than standard gate-type ICs, and are therefore widely used for digital signal reshaping (Fig. 6.4).

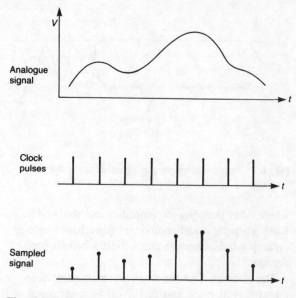

Fig. 6.5 Initial sampling waveforms

6.2 Sampling and sample-and-hold

One common situation in modern electronics is where an analogue — that is, a continuous-type — signal is required to be converted into digital form. This encoding process means that the analogue signal must first be sampled at regular intervals. An example of this is shown in Fig. 6.5, where the analogue is shown initially converted into a discrete form, resulting in pulses of varying height, each representing the amplitude of the analogue at the instant each sample is taken.

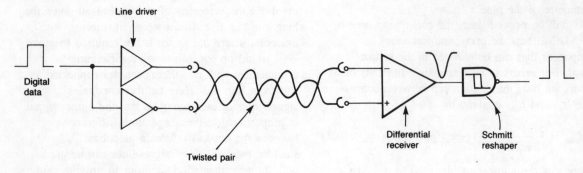

Fig. 6.4 Digital transmission

Obviously the sampling rate must be high enough to capture sufficient detail of the analogue input signal. The actual minimum sampling rate is determined by **Shannon's sampling theorem**, which can be stated as: 'a continuous signal containing frequency components up to some maximum frequency f_1 may be completely represented by regularly spaced samples taken at a rate set to be just greater than $2f_1$ samples per second'.

This is illustrated in Fig. 6.6, and a typical example of the use of this theorem in practice is in telephony, where the analogue speech bandwidth is first limited to 3.4 kHz and then sampled at 8 kHz, before being encoded into digital and then transmitted. An important feature of any sampling system is that the input signal must be bandwidth-limited before being sampled. This prevents higher-frequency signals — those above f_1 — being sampled and 'moved down' into the bandwidth of the system. This adverse effect, called *aliasing* (Fig. 6.7), causes any signals at frequencies above f_1 to appear as if they are at some lower frequency, within the bandwidth of the system but at the same amplitude as the original, non-required signal. An anti-aliasing bandwidth-limiting filter becomes an essential feature of most data acquisition systems. Another block often required within such a system is called a sample-and-hold.

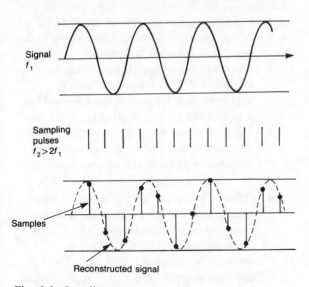

Fig. 6.6 Sampling rate

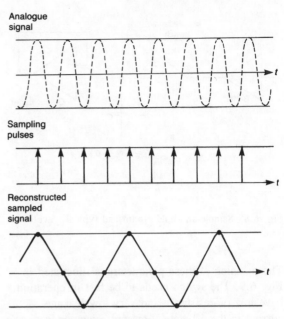

Fig. 6.7 Illustration of aliasing

This type of circuit will be necessary if the process of converting the height of the sampled analogue signal — that is, the impulse-type signal shown in Fig. 6.5 — requires more time than the width of the sampled pulse allows. In other cases the sampling may be carried out by an ADC acting directly on the analogue input signal, and if the analogue value is not held steady during the conversion time required by the convertor, then the digital output from the convertor will be in error. A sample-and-hold, which has an output with what is called a zero-hold characteristic, consists of a fast electronic switch, a hold capacitor and a buffer amplifier, as shown in Fig. 6.8. The switch, usually a MOSFET, is closed by the sample pulse for a short time to allow the hold capacitor to charge to the value of the analogue input. When the S/H input to the circuit is taken low, between samples, the switch opens and the capacitor holds the analogue value, keeping it steady while the ADC carries out the conversion. Important parameters of a sample-and-hold circuit are:

- Acquisition time
- Droop rate
- Hold step.

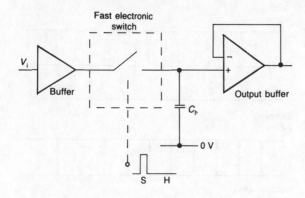

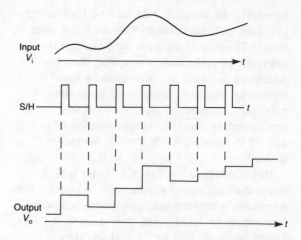

Fig. 6.8 Sample-and-hold circuit and typical waveforms

The meaning of these parameters is illustrated in Fig. 6.9. The switch needs to be fast in operation, have low on-resistance and very low leakage current in the off state. Low on-resistance is necessary so that the capacitor is rapidly charged to give low acquisition time. With typical IC sample-and-hold devices the hold capacitor is specified in the range 100 pF up to 10 nF, and acquisition times are typically a few microseconds. During the hold mode the charge on the capacitor must not be allowed to leak away, and therefore both the buffer amplifier and the switch must have low bias and leakage current values respectively. Usually a MOSFET op-amp and a MOSFET switch are specified, giving droop rates of better than 1 mV/s. Hold step refers to the output amplitude when the analogue input is held at 0 V. Any offsets present in the switch and the op-amp, together with dielectric hysteresis in the hold capacitor, will set up a small output signal, as shown previously in Fig. 6.9. A good-quality low-hysteresis low-leakage capacitor, such as a polystyrene, is needed for the C_h position and a low offset is necesary in the op-amp to ensure that the hold step amplitude is kept to a small value.

We have now seen that data acquisition of analogue signals may often require amplification, a bandwidth-limiting filter and a sample-and-hold before conversion into digital form can take place (Fig. 6.10). The next sections deal with this conversion process. Because the digital-to-analogue convertor often forms an integral part of some

analogue-to-digital convertors, the DAC will be examined first.

6.3 Digital-to-analogue convertors (DAC) (Fig. 6.11)

The DAC is a circuit that takes an n-bit digital input word and produces an analogue value, as a current or a voltage, equivalent to the weight of the digital word. The various parameters used to specify a DAC are as follows:

- *Resolution* The number of bits used (n).
- *Non-linearity* The maximum amount by which any point on the transfer characteristic deviates from the ideal straight line. Non-linearity is usually expressed as a fraction of the LSB and has a typical value of $\pm\frac{1}{2}$LSB (Fig. 6.11).
- *Differential non-linearity* An error between the value of any one of the analogue step outputs compared to the others. Again, this has a typical specified value of $\pm\frac{1}{2}$LSB.
- *Offset* The small value of analogue output voltage (or current) which appears at the output when all digital inputs to the DAC are at logic 0 (Fig. 6.12). This can normally be trimmed out at the buffer amplifier stage (Fig. 6.12). A typical value of offset is 5 mV.

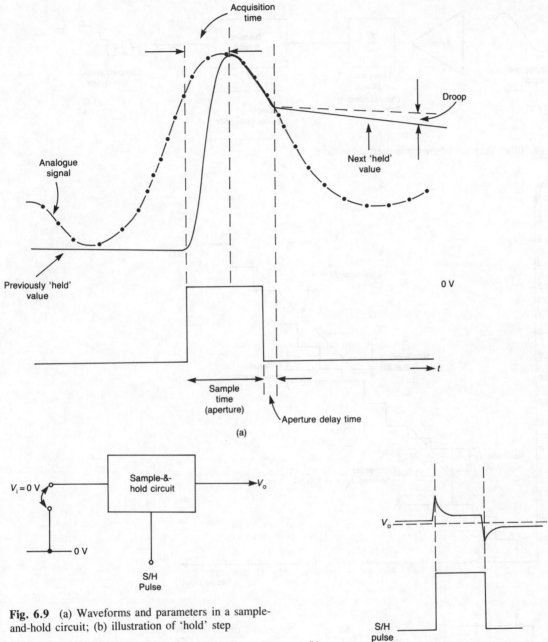

Fig. 6.9 (a) Waveforms and parameters in a sample-and-hold circuit; (b) illustration of 'hold' step

- *Offset error temperature coefficient* The rate of change of offset voltage (or current) with temperature. Typically $5 \, \mu\text{V}/°\text{C}$.
- *Settling time* The time taken for the analogue output to settle to within $\pm\frac{1}{2}\text{LSB}$ following a change in the digital input code. The worst-case change is when all the bits switch from 1 to 0 or vice versa (1111 to 0000 or from 0000 to 1111 for a 4-bit DAC). Settling times vary from 2 ns to 2 μs. (In some specifications settling time is quoted for an LSB change, which produces the best figure for this parameter).

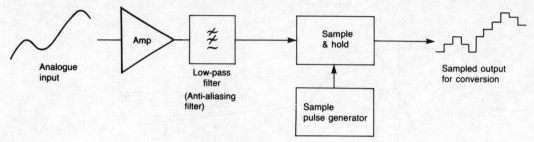

Fig. 6.10 Block diagram of analogue data acquisition system

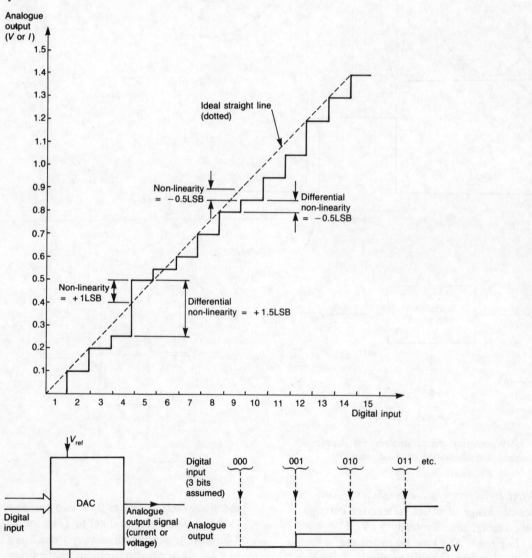

Fig. 6.11 Principle of digital-to-analogue conversion (DAC) and non-linearity in a DAC response

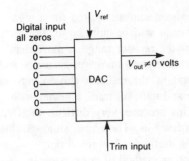

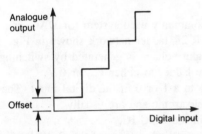

Fig. 6.12 Offset error in a DAC

Buffer amplifier (if $R_1 = R_2$ Gain = 2)

Set all bits of digital input to 0
and adjust RV_1 until V_{out} = 0 V

Removal of offset error

- *Analogue output resistance* The resistance at the analogue output seen looking back into the DAC. A typical value is 5 kΩ. This means that some sort of external buffer amplifier is essential.

The general equation for a digital-to-analogue convertor is

$$V_{out} = V_{ref}\left[\frac{B_{n-1}}{2} + \frac{B_{n-2}}{4} + \frac{B_{n-3}}{8} \ldots + \frac{B_0}{2^n}\right] \tag{6.4}$$

where B_0 is the least significant bit (LSB)
B_{n-1} is the most significant bit (MSB)
n is the number of bits involved
V_{ref} is a stable reference voltage.

Therefore, in a 4-bit DAC ($n=4$):

$$V_{out} = V_{ref}\left[\frac{B_3}{2} + \frac{B_2}{4} + \frac{B_1}{8} + \frac{B_0}{16}\right]$$

If $V_{ref} = +5$ V and the digital input is 1011:

$$V_{out} = 5(\tfrac{1}{2} + 0 + \tfrac{1}{8} + \tfrac{1}{16}) = 3.4375 \text{ V}$$

The maximum output from a DAC is called the *full-scale output* (V_{FSO}). V_{FSO} occurs when all n-bits of the digital word are at logic 1. For a 6-bit example with $V_{ref} = +5$ V:

$$V_{FSO} = 5\left[\frac{1}{1} + \frac{1}{4} + \frac{1}{8} + \frac{1}{16} + \frac{1}{32} + \frac{1}{64}\right]$$

$$= 4.922 \text{ V}$$

$$\therefore V_{FSO} = V_{FS}\left(\frac{2^n - 1}{2^n}\right) \tag{6.5}$$

V_{FSO} cannot equal V_{FS} (the full-scale output) and is always 1 LSB less than V_{FS}.

The essential elements of a DAC are:

- A set of electronic switches
- A network of resistors
- A stable reference supply (V_{ref}) (Fig. 6.13).

The simplest method of building a DAC is to use a weighted-resistor network, a summing amplifier and a set of electronic switches (Fig. 6.14). Each of the resistors has to be weighted in value in a binary sequence, i.e. R, 2R, 4R, 8R, etc. The digital word to be converted is used to operate the

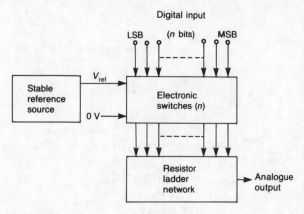

Fig. 6.13 The elements used in a DAC

electronic switches to connect these resistors to V_{ref} if the bit is 1, and to 0 V if the bit is 0. Suppose the digital input for the 4-bit DAC example is 1010; then switches 1 and 3 are operated to connect two of the resistors to the 5 V reference. The output from the summing op-amp will be

$$V_o = \frac{R_f}{R} \cdot V_{ref}(1 + \tfrac{1}{4}) = 3.125 \text{ V}$$

Similarly, if the digital input changes to 0110, then

$$V_o = \frac{R_f}{R} \cdot V_{ref}(\tfrac{1}{2} + \tfrac{1}{4}) = 1.875 \text{ V}$$

and $V_{FSO} = \frac{R_f}{R} \cdot V_{ref}(1 + \tfrac{1}{2} + \tfrac{1}{4} + \tfrac{1}{8}) = 4.375 \text{ V}$

The only problem with this simple circuit is that

the range of resistor values required for a high-resolution convertor will be quite large. For a 12-bit convertor the resistor range is more than 2000 : 1. To achieve good linearity, accuracy and monotonic operation, the resistors chosen must be close-tolerance and must all track together with temperature. This becomes very difficult for DACs of more than a few bits. Therefore, although this simple circuit is useful for low-resolution convertors, another method of conversion is preferred.

The most commonly used system for DACs is based on the R-2R ladder network shown in Fig. 6.15. The output voltage is generated by switching sections of the ladder to either V_{ref} or 0 V, corresponding to a 1 or 0 of the digital input. The switches are electronic and are usually incorporated in the DAC IC.

There are several advantages of the R-2R ladder compared to the weighted-resistor network:

● Only two values of resistors are used.
● It can easily be extended to as many bits as desired.
● The absolute value of the resistor is not important — only the ratio needs to be exact.
● The resistor network can be readily manufactured as a film network or in monolithic form. In this way the temperature characteristics of the resistors will all be very similar.

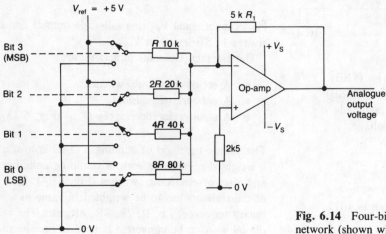

Fig. 6.14 Four-bit DAC using a binary weighted network (shown with the input set to 1010)

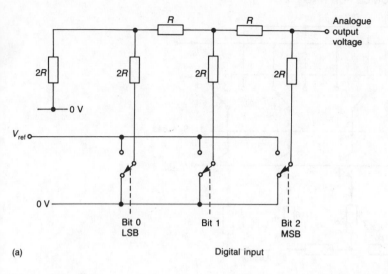

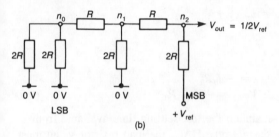

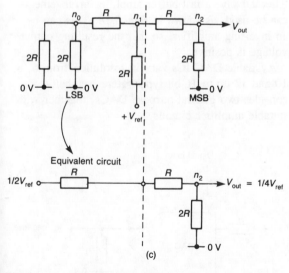

Fig. 6.15 (a) R-2R ladder (3-bit DAC shown); (b) 3-bit-ladder with only the MSB = 1; (c) only bit 1 set to 1

Consider the case of a simple 3-bit ladder, as shown in Fig. 6.15(a). At any node point except the MSB, the resistance seen looking in any direction will be $2R$. Now consider the situation when the MSB of the digital input is high while the other two bits are low at logic 0. This is shown in Fig. 6.15(b), and it can be seen that at node n_2 the resistance seen looking into the network is $2R$. Therefore V_{out} must equal $1/2\ V_{ref}$.

If we now consider bit 1 of the digital input at logic 1 while the other two bits are at 0, we get the circuit shown in Fig. 6.15(c). By viewing the network to the left of the dotted line and using Thevenin's theorem, the voltage at n_1 will be $1/2\ V_{ref}$ and the effective resistance equal to R. Thus at the output of the ladder the voltage will be $1/4\ V_{ref}$.

By the same analysis the voltage at the output, due to only the digital LSB being high, will be $1/8\ V_{ref}$.

For an n-bit ladder, the output level due to each bit follows the equation:

$$V_{out} = V_{ref}\left[\frac{B_{n-1}}{2} + \frac{B_{n-2}}{4} + \frac{B_{n-3}}{8} + \ldots\frac{B_0}{2^n}\right] \quad (6.6)$$

as required for a DAC.

Current-output DACs, which are generally faster than voltage-output types, also use an R-2R ladder network and switches. A reference current is set up inside the IC — the value usually adjustable by

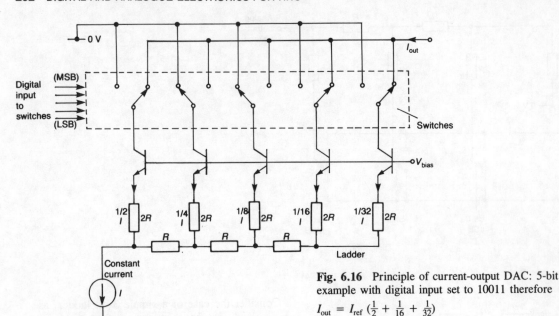

Fig. 6.16 Principle of current-output DAC: 5-bit example with digital input set to 10011 therefore

$$I_{out} = I_{ref} \left(\tfrac{1}{2} + \tfrac{1}{16} + \tfrac{1}{32} \right)$$

a user external voltage and trim resistor — and applied to the resistor ladder as shown in Fig. 6.16. The binary weighted values of current are summed from the collectors of NPN transistors, all operated from the same bias voltage, via the switches. The switches, operated by the digital input levels, connect each current to either the common current output (I_o) or to ground. At each node in the ladder the current is divided by two, since at any node, travelling from the MSB, the resistance seen looking into the ladder or towards a switch via one transistor is $2R$. In this way the currents in each transistor collector starting from the MSB are $1/2\,I_{ref}$, $1/4\,I_{ref}$, $1/8\,I_{ref}$, and so on down the chain. Settling time is fast because the currents do not change in value — a current is either switched to the output or to 0 V. This differential principle means that internal capacitances do not have to be continually charged and discharged by changing current values, as is the case with the voltage-output DAC. The output current can be converted into an analogue voltage by simply placing a load resistor at the output of the DAC, as shown in Fig. 6.17. Since I_o is a sink current and flows back into the DAC, this output voltage will be negative:

$$V_{out} = -I_o R_L$$
$$\therefore\; V_{FSO} = -I_{FSO} R_L \qquad (6.7)$$

To maintain the fast settling time available from the current-type DAC, the load resistor value must be low — typically a few hundred ohms. Alternatively, a fast-buffer amplifier arrangement can be used, as shown in Fig. 6.18. This can be an inverting amplifier, so that the resulting output voltage is positive.

Available DAC ICs vary in resolution from 6, 8, 10 and 12 up to 16-bit types. Here we shall consider two general-purpose DACs, together with suitable amplifier circuits.

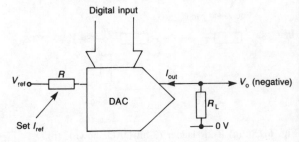

Fig. 6.17 Obtaining a voltage output from the current DAC

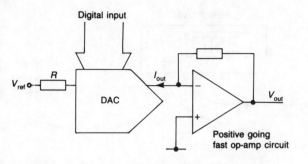

Fig. 6.18 Using an inverting amplifier to convert the current output into voltage

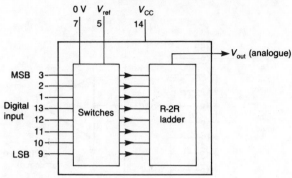

Fig. 6.19 The ZN429 DAC (8 bits)

The GEC-Plessey ZN429 is a good example of DAC design. It contains the required electronic switches and an 8-bit R-2R ladder network. An external voltage reference supply must be provided by the user, which must be stable and have a low slope resistance (Fig. 6.19):

Resolution	= 8 bits
Non-linearity	= ±0.5 LSB (max)
Differential non-linearity	= ±0.5 LSB (typ)
Offset voltage V_{os}	= 8 mV max
dV_{os}/dT	= 5 μV/°C
Settling time	= 1 μs 1 LSB step
	2 μs Full step

Analogue output resistance	= 10 kΩ
Power supply V_{CC}	= 4.5–5.5 V max
I_{CC}	= 9 mA max
Reference supply	= 2–3 V

A typical circuit arrangement is shown in Fig. 6.20, where the precision band-gap device REF25Z sets the reference voltage to 2.500 V ±10 mV, and the analogue output from the DAC on pin 4 is buffered and amplified to a V_{Fs} value of +5 V by a non-inverting op-amp circuit. The voltage gain required is 2, and RV_2 allows this gain figure to be set precisely. Since the output resistance of the ZN429 is specified as 10 kΩ, the

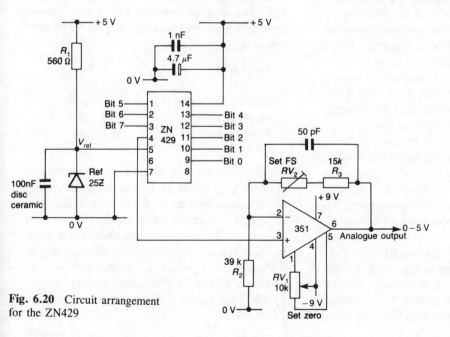

Fig. 6.20 Circuit arrangement for the ZN429

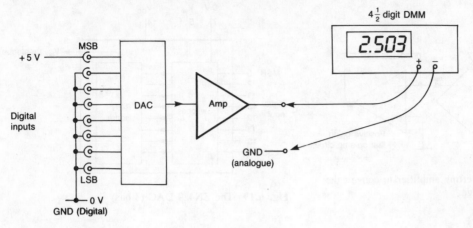

Fig. 6.21 Test set-up for DAC adjustment (digital input shown set to 10000000)

resistance in the inverting lead is also arranged to be about 10 kΩ, so that input bias current-induced drifts are minimized. Offset and zero adjustment is made using RV_1. A low-value capacitor — 50 pF in the circuit — is connected across the feedback resistors to limit overshoot and ringing in the analogue output.

The complete circuit can be tested and set up using the following procedure (Fig. 6.21).

(1) Set zero output by connecting all digital inputs to logic 0 (0 V). RV_1 should be adjusted until the output voltage from the op-amp is 0 V ± 10 mV, where the 10 mV represents $\pm 1/2$ LSB.

(2) Set full-scale output (V_{FSO}) by connecting all digital inputs to logic 1 (+5 V). RV_2 should then be adjusted until the op-amp output voltage is 4.980 V ± 10 mV.

(3) Half-full scale can then be checked by setting the MSB of the digital input to logic 1 and all other bits to logic 0. The output should be 2.500 V ± 10 mV. If necessary, steps (1) and (2) can be repeated until V_{FSO}, $1/2$ V_{FS} and zero output are all within the specification.

(4) Test settling time, using a fast CRO and the suggested test set-up in Fig. 6.22. In this circuit all digital bits of the input are tied together and driven from a TTL generator at a frequency of about 40 kHz. All bits of

the digital input will be forced to change state, and the low-to-high and the high-to-low settling times can be displayed on a suitable wideband CRO. A typical waveform example showing how this measurement is made is also given in Fig. 6.22.

The second example is a convertor using the 3410 DAC. This is a 10-bit device which uses current switching and has a fast settling time of 250 ns. The block diagram, together with a semi-schematic circuit, is given in Fig. 6.23. For the 3410 the typical specification is:

Resolution	= 10 bits
I_{ref}	= 2.00 mA
Relative accuracy	= 1/4 LSB
Relative accuracy drift	= 2.5 ppm/$^\circ$C
Monotonicity	= 10 bits
Settling time	= 250 ns.

The IC has four segment current sources, which are used to generate the two most significant bits of the output, and an R-2R precision ladder for scaling the remaining 8 bits required in the conversion. As previously described, the currents in the ladder are switched either differentially to the output or to ground. I_{out} is arranged to be a maximum of twice the reference current less 1 LSB. Thus I_{FSO} is 3.996 mA for an I_{ref} of 2.000 mA.

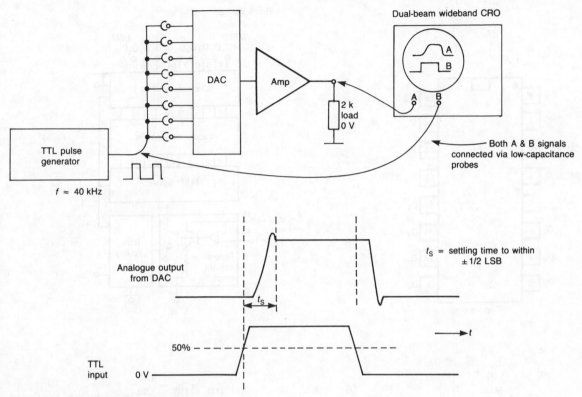

Fig. 6.22 Testing DAC settling time

An internal fast slew rate reference current amplifier drives the segment decoder and the ladder. The user is required to provide a fixed reference voltage and a precision resistor to convert this reference voltage into the current needed by the DAC. Inside the IC a current mirror is used to double I_{ref}, and it is this value that is supplied to the segment decoders, and hence to the ladder. For example, if the external voltage reference is 2.00 V, a resistor of 1 kΩ is necessary to set I_{ref} to 2 mA. It is obviously important that both the external voltage reference and the resistor provide a stable value of reference current, otherwise the full 10-bit accuracy of the DAC cannot be used. The output current, a maximum of $2I_{ref}\left(\dfrac{1023}{1024}\right)$, can be converted into a negative voltage signal by connecting a suitable low-value resistor from pin 3 — I_{out} — to ground, a 50 Ω load giving a -200 mV maximum output. Another method is to use a wideband op-amp in the inverting mode, with the load resistor in the feedback loop.

Where the number of digital output lines from a system is restricted, an alternative type of DAC, using series techniques, can be used. Such DACs are necessarily slower in operation than the parallel types, and have a settling time that is not constant but dependent upon the time taken to fill an n-bit serial input shift register or an n-bit counter. For n bits, where the LSB takes x μs to load into the counter, the overall settling time of a serial DAC will be

$$t_S \approx \frac{(2^n - 1)}{2} x \, \mu s \qquad (6.8)$$

The principle of operation is illustrated in Fig. 6.24. Only two data lines are required from the digital system, these being *count* and *clear*. The outputs of the n-bit counter are connected to an R-2R ladder, which converts the counter state to the required analogue value. Initially, the counter

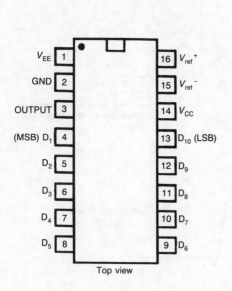

Top view

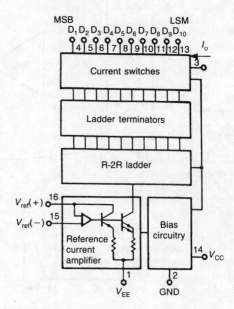

Block diagram

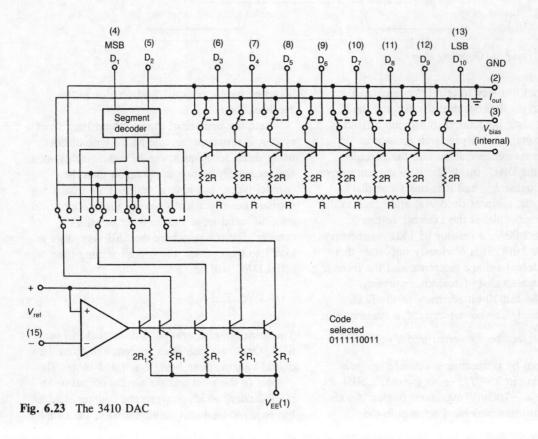

Fig. 6.23   The 3410 DAC

Code
selected
0111110011

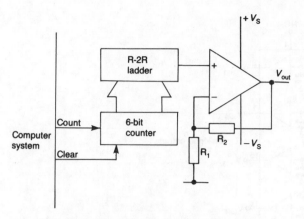

Fig. 6.24 Block diagram of a serial-type DAC

Where several analogue outputs are needed, it is not always necessary to provide a convertor for each: one DAC can be multiplexed instead of each analogue being tied to its own DAC. An outline of the circuit technique is given in Fig. 6.26. One n-bit DAC output is multiplexed using a fast electronic switch IC to four analogue channels, with each of the channels provided with a sample-and-hold circuit made up of a 1 nF hold capacitor and a precision-buffer op-amp.

is cleared by a short-duration pulse on the clear input. This sets the counter outputs to logic 0, and thus the analogue output is also zero. If a full-scale output is required, then $2n-1$ pulses must be applied to the count input. The counter accumulates these pulses and the analogue output ramps up to the V_{FSO} value. For any desired analogue output the number of digital input pulses must be adjusted to the correct value, and between the groups of pulses needed for any analogue value a clear pulse must be sent. For example, if $n=6$ the required pulses for full-scale output will be 63, half-full scale needs 32 pulses, and quarter-full scale 16. One of the advantages of serial convertors is that the digital inputs can be more easily isolated from the analogue circuit. In the example, only two inputs require isolation (Fig. 6.25), whereas for a parallel DAC all digital input lines would have to be isolated.

6.4 Analogue-to-digital conversion

An ADC takes the instantaneous value of an analogue input signal and then produces as its output a coded digital word with a weight that corresponds to the level of the analogue. The process is therefore the opposite to that of the DAC but, unlike the DAC, an ADC will always contain some uncertainty over the conversion. This is because the analogue input is a continuous signal and can take any value within a defined range, whereas the digital output can only exist as a fixed number of codes. The uncertainty for an ADC is called quantizing error, and will be $\pm 0.5\,LSB$. Consider a simple 4-bit ADC with an input span of 5 V. The digital output, a 4-bit code, can take values from 0000, 0001, 0010, and so on up to 1111, which means that it has 16 quantization levels. Suppose the analogue input is 1.25 V, then the digital code is 0100. When the input is 1.5625 V this digital code changes to 0101, i.e.

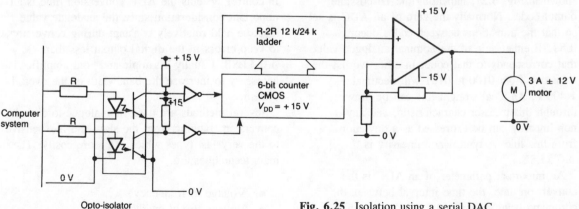

Fig. 6.25 Isolation using a serial DAC

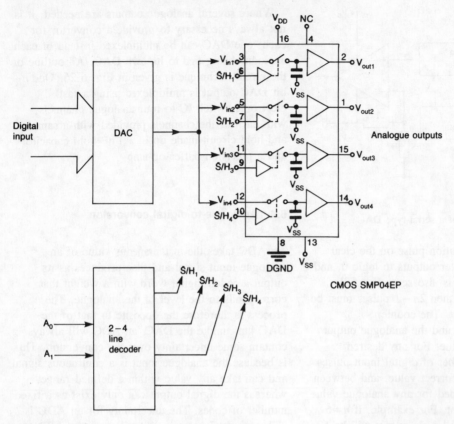

Fig. 6.26 Outline of multiplexed DAC outputs

one LSB step. However a value of 1.406 V, halfway between 1.25 V and 1.5625 V, could give a digital code of 0100 or 0101. This is what is meant by the uncertainty of an ADC.

The transfer characteristic for a 4-bit ADC is shown in Fig. 6.27, indicating the 16 possible output codes. Normally the zero of an ADC is set so that the transitions between codes occur 0.5 LSB either side of the nominal analogue value that corresponds to that code. In other words, the transition from 0100 to 0101 will occur at 1.406 V. An ideal straight line can be drawn through this transfer characteristic, and any non-linearity can be expressed as a deviation from this line. A typical non-linearity is ±0.5 LSB.

An important parameter of an ADC is the conversion time: the time interval between the command being given to the ADC to begin the

conversion and the appearance at the output of the complete digital equivalent of the input value. The speed of conversion varies with the type of ADC, and can be as short as a few nanoseconds for the ultra-fast types, or as slow as several milliseconds. In control systems the ADC conversion time is an important consideration since the analogue value must be held relatively constant during conversion, to keep errors in the digital output less than ±0.5 LSB. Usually a sample-and-hold amplifier is necessary to increase the bandwidth of the overall system.

Several methods are used in analogue-to-digital conversion, ranging from the slow and inexpensive to the very fast types which are more costly. The main techniques are:

- Voltage to frequency
- Voltage to pulsewidth

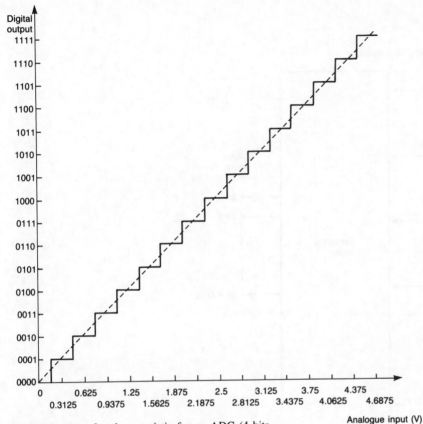

Fig. 6.27 Transfer characteristic for an ADC (4 bits only shown)

- Parallel or flash conversion*
- Single ramp and counter*
- Dual/triple ramp
- Tracking conversion*
- Successive approximation*

The four marked with an asterisk are some of the most commonly used systems and will be covered here.

Parallel or flash convertor

With this type all the bit values for the digital representation of the analogue input level are determined simultaneously. The method is therefore very fast, and a flash-type ADC may be capable of sampling at speeds of 50 MHz or higher. The analogue input voltage, as shown in Fig. 6.28, is applied to a parallel bank of voltage comparators, each of which has its reference input

tied to a discrete voltage level. For example, in a 3-bit* flash convertor the comparators would respond to the following voltage levels:

$$V_{\text{ref}}/2^{n+1}, \; 3\,V_{\text{ref}}/2^{n+1}, \; 5\,V_{\text{ref}}/2^{n+1}, \; \ldots \text{ up to } 13\,V_{\text{ref}}/2^{n+1}$$

The comparator outputs are connected to encoding logic, so that the states of the comparator outputs can be converted to the appropriate n-bit binary code. Suppose, for the 3-bit example, that the analogue input voltage just exceeds $5\,V_{\text{ref}}/2^{n+1}$; the outputs of comparators A, B and C will then switch low, while the outputs of comparators D, E, F and G will remain high. The encoding logic must set the binary word at 011 $(=3_{\text{IO}})$ for the

*A 3-bit convertor is only used here as an example; most practical ADCs are 6, 8, 10, 12 or 16-bit.

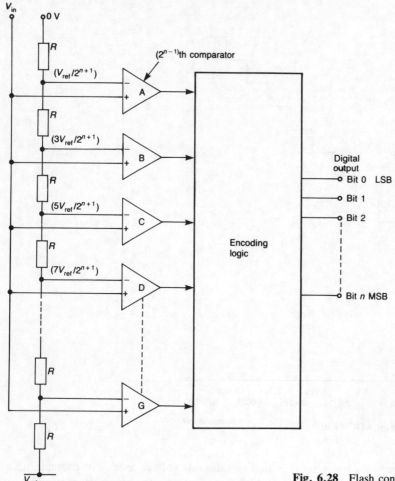

Fig. 6.28   Flash convertor

comparator outputs of $\overline{A}.\overline{B}.\overline{C}.D.E.F.G$. Other codes would be similarly created.

This method, although fast, requires 2^{n-1} comparators plus a complex logic encoding circuit. A 6-bit flash ADC must have at least 63 comparators. The use of large-scale integrated (LSI) circuits had made more of these devices available but they remain expensive.

Single ramp and counter (Fig. 6.29)
This type of ADC uses an *n*-bit counter with an internal DAC, some control logic and a fast comparator. When the start conversion pulse is received, the counter is initially cleared and the logic set so that clock pulses are allowed through to the counter. As the counter counts up, the DAC generates a rising-staircase ramp which is applied to one input of the comparator. During the time that the ramp is less than the value of the input, clock pulses continue to be fed to the counter, but at the instant that the ramp value just exceeds V_{in}, the control logic cuts off the supply of clock pulses. The counter stops and its content is proportional to the value of the analogue input. The Ready line indicates that valid data are available.

This method is very useful for medium accuracy and slow speed. The conversion time (t_c), which may be several milliseconds, is basically set by the

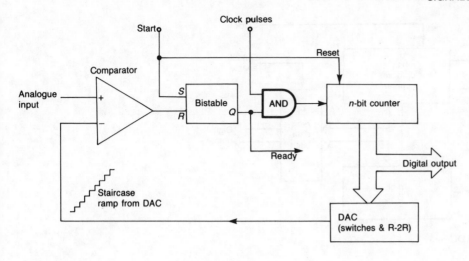

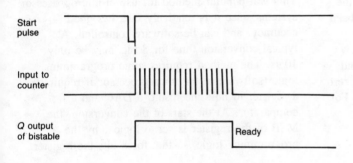

Fig. 6.29 Single ramp and counter ADC

clock frequency. The upper limit to the clock frequency is itself dictated by the speed of the comparator and logic. With a clock of 100 kHz, a full 8-bit conversion will take 2.55 ms. A clock frequency in the range of 100–500 kHz is typical.

The accuracy of this method is limited by the linearity of the ramp (which can be good if the internal DAC has good linearity) and input offset drift in the comparator.

Tracking convertor (Fig. 6.30)
This is an improved version of the single ramp and counter method, that enables a changing input signal to be rapidly followed. The tracking ADC uses a window comparator, an up/down counter

and a DAC. The DAC continuously outputs a tracking signal, in the form of a staircase waveform, for as long as the analogue input is outside the narrow window set by the comparator. Suppose the analogue input changes to a new positive value; the window comparator switches the counter to the up mode and clock pulses are accumulated. The state of the counter is converted by the internal DAC until the tracking signal equals the analogue. The counter is then stopped. Since the comparator can output up or down control levels to the counter, the output from the DAC follows the analogue input. The counter is stopped when the DAC output is within 0.5 LSB of the analogue value.

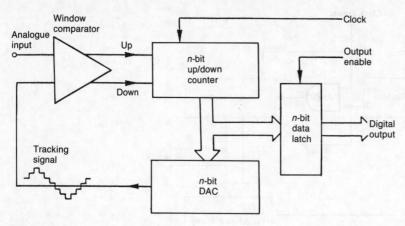

Fig. 6.30 The tracking ADC

A tracking convertor is inherently faster than a single ramp and counter ADC because, once the first conversion — starting from zero — has been carried out, all further conversions require only that number of clock pulses necessary to follow any rise or fall in the input. With the ramp and counter ADC, all conversions are made from zero and the counter is reset between conversions. For the tracking type and the clock set to 1 MHz, conversions can be carried out in a few microseconds.

Successive approximation convertor (Fig. 6.31) This is a popular method for use in microprocessor systems since it is relatively fast, has good accuracy, and can be software-controlled. A typical conversion time for 8 bits may be only 10 μs. The method requires some programming logic (software in the microprocessor if required), a register to hold the result, a DAC and a fast comparator. At the start of the conversion, the MSB of the register is set to logic 1 by the programming logic, so that for 8 bits the register

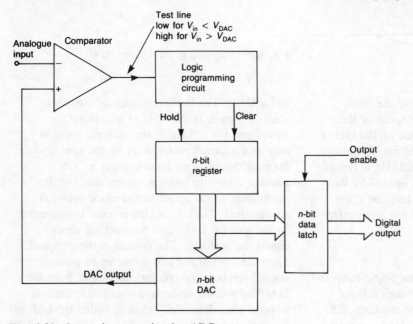

Fig. 6.31 Successive-approximation ADC

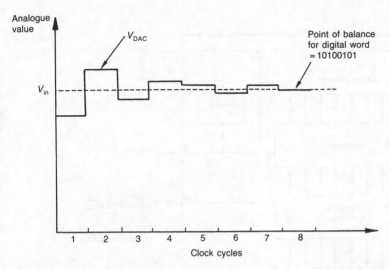

Analogue value

V_{DAC}

V_{in}

Point of balance for digital word = 10100101

1   2   3   4   5   6   7   8

Clock cycles

Fig. 6.32 Successive-approximation cycle

reads 10000000. This is converted by the DAC and the output value compared with the analogue input. If the output by the DAC is larger than V_{in}, the logic 1 is removed from the MSB and placed in the next most significant bit; the register now holds 01000000. This in turn is converted by the DAC and the value compared with the analogue input. Suppose it is less than V_{in}: the logic 1 in that position is retained and the next most significant bit is also set to 1 (register holds 01100000) and used for comparison.

This process continues until all bits have been tried and a point of balance is reached; that is, when V_{in} is just greater than the DAC output voltage. A successive approximation cycle, often called a put and take, is shown in Fig. 6.32. The ZN427E 8-bit successive approximation ADC is a good example. This chip has all the necessary logic, a DAC, a 2.5 V precision reference and a fast comparator. Only a few external components are required to create an accurate, high-speed ADC. Conversion time can be as fast as 10 μs. In addition, tri-state output buffers are included to allow direct connection to the data bus of a system. The block diagram of the chip, together with a circuit diagram showing external components, is given in Figs 6.33 and 6.34. This ADC is shown connected to the ports of a micro system. In this case the start conversion pulse is derived under software control from bit 0 on Port

B and the end of conversion signal is detected on bit 1 of Port B. A gated clock pulse generator set to run at approximately 500 kHz is formed from two of the gates inside a 74132 dual NAND Schmitt TTL IC. Brief specification details on the ZN427E are:

Resolution	= 8 bits
Linearity error	= ±0.5 LSB max
Internal voltage reference	= 2.560 V type
	$\left(\begin{array}{l} R_{ref}=390\,\Omega \\ C_{ref}=4\,\mu7F \end{array}\right)$
	2.475 V min
	2.625 V max
Slope resistance of V_{ref}	= 2 Ω max
V_{ref} temperature coefficient	= 50 ppm/°C
Maximum clock frequency	= 900 kHz
Start conversion pulsewidth	= 250 ns
Conversion time	= 10 μs (clock set to 900 kHz)

Conversion is initiated by a negative-going start conversion ($\overline{SC}$) pulse. This sets the MSB to 1. There are certain restrictions on the time between the leading edge of the $\overline{SC}$ pulse and the first active edge ($\curvearrowright$) of the clock pulse. This negative edge should not occur until at least 1.5 μs after the negative edge of the $\overline{SC}$ pulse. In this circuit arrangement, since the clock generator is gated with the $\overline{SC}$ pulse, the first clock pulse active edge

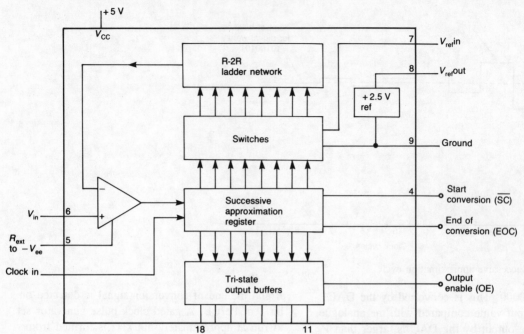

Fig. 6.33 ZN427E successive-approximation ADC: block diagram

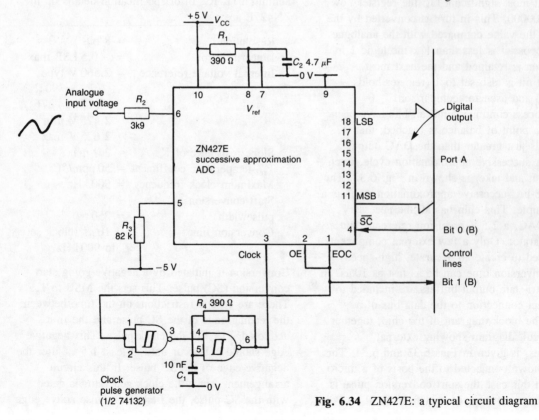

Fig. 6.34 ZN427E: a typical circuit diagram

will occur some $4-5\,\mu s$ after the leading edge of the $\overline{SC}$ pulse. This timing takes into account the time taken for the instructions CLR PORTB and INC PORTB to be fetched and executed, and for bit 0 on Port B to respond.

After nine pulses have been delivered by the clock, the end of conversion (EOC) line goes high and this is used to gate the tri-state outputs by pulling the output enable pin (EO) high. Data is then available for the microcomputer on Port A.

6.5 Convertor noise

The quantization process inherent in an ADC must inevitably add noise to the input signal of a sampled data system. This is because of the uncertainty (an error of ± 0.5 LSB) that always exists in the conversion. If the noise present in the signal at the ADC input is much less than the quantization level, then the noise introduced by quantization will be the limiting factor on the resolution of the system. However, in those situations where the *rms noise* in the signal to the ADC exceeds the quantization, the effect of convertor noise is to add an additional *white-noise* component into the signal. This added component has an amplitude given by

$$\text{Convertor noise } v_n = V_q / \sqrt{12} \qquad (6.9)$$

where V_q is the quantization level.

Take an example of a 10-bit ADC with a span of 5 V (V_{FS}). Suppose the noise presented in the signal to this ADC is 6 mV rms. The total noise is calculated as follows:

$$V_q = V_{FS}/2^n = 4.883\,\text{mV}$$
$$v_n \text{ due to ADC quantization} = 4.883\,\text{mV}/\sqrt{12}$$
$$= 1.41\,\text{mV}$$
$$\therefore \text{ Total rms noise} = 7.41\,\text{mV}$$

6.6 Interfacing techniques

Any link between two systems or subsystems conveying signals between the two parts can be considered as an interface. Ensuring that the signal

integrity across the link is maintained without altering the bias conditions at the sender and receiver is essential. Interfacing can therefore involve one or more of the following techniques:

- Impedance matching and buffering
- Isolation
- Signal conditioning
- Level shifting
- Encoding or decoding.

Consider the simple example of matching the voltage output of a sensor to the input of an ADC. The ADC input resistance may be only $5\,\text{k}\Omega$, which means that signal loss and distortion will occur if the output resistance of the sensor is more than a few hundred ohms. A direct connection between the sensor and the ADC is not usually possible. One simple solution is to use a unity gain buffer amplifier between the sensor and the ADC, as shown in Fig. 6.35. If, however, some gain is required, additional matching of impedance levels may be necessary. Suppose the sensor output resistance is $40\,\text{k}\Omega$ and the amplifier has to provide a voltage gain of 5. In the non-inverting amplifier of Fig. 6.36, the resistor values must be selected

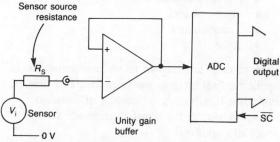

Fig. 6.35 Matching the high source resistance of a sensor to the relatively low input resistance of an ADC

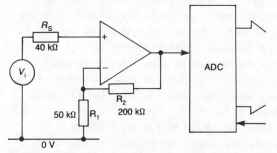

Fig. 6.36 Providing matching and voltage gain (in this case $A_{vce} = 5$)

to meet two conditions:

$$\frac{R_1 R_2}{R_1 + R_2} = R_5 \qquad (6.10)$$

and $\quad 1 + \dfrac{R_2}{R_1} = 5 \qquad (6.11)$

From equation (6.11) we get $R_2 = 4R_1$.
Substituting this result in equation (6.10) gives

$$\frac{4R_1^2}{5R_1} = 40$$

(where values are in kΩ).
Therefore $4R_1 = 200$
$\therefore \qquad R_1 = 50\,\text{k}\Omega$
Since $R_2 = 4R_1 \qquad R_2 = 200\,\text{k}\Omega$

These two values in a circuit ensure that the correct voltage gain is set and that the resistance in each input lead of the op-amp is identical. The latter point minimizes current-induced drifts.

Isolation is a protective technique that is essential where voltage levels and ground system on either side of a link must be kept separate. Several methods can be used, including:

- Isolation amplifiers
- Opto-isolators
- Transformers
- Relays.

Each of these has its own merits and particular application advantages, but in any isolated link the important features are the amount of isolation voltage provided, the transfer efficiency and the speed of response.

The optocoupler shown in Fig. 6.37(a) can be used to illustrate these features. In this type of isolator the input and output voltage supplies and ground systems are completely isolated, since the signal path is the infrared optical link between the input LED and the photodetector. This photodetector can be diode, phototransistor, photosensitive thyristor, or even a detector with an associated Triac. Some of these possibilities are shown in Fig. 6.37.

Since the optical path in these devices can be several millimetres, the isolation voltage can be as high as 4 kV. With the single phototransistor opto-isolators, such as the MCT2E, the transmission

efficiency (h_{ctr}) is not high: 20 per cent is the quoted minimum value for this device. Transfer efficiency is defined in an opto-isolator as the ratio of output collector current to input diode current times 100 per cent. Thus:

$$h_{\text{ctr}} = \frac{I_C}{I_F} \times 100\% \qquad (6.12)$$

For the MCT2E, when I_F, the diode forward current, is set to 10 mA, the collector current of the output phototransistor will be a minimum of 2 mA.

Other types of opto-isolator have Darlington output stages and these can have transfer efficiencies of up to 500 per cent.

Example

A 6N139 opto-isolator is to be used to interface TTL signals to a circuit which uses a 12 V supply. Design the link to give an output current of 20 mA. Brief specification details of the 6N139 are:

$$\begin{aligned}
I_{F\text{max}} &= 20\,\text{mA} \\
V_{R\text{max}} &= 5\,\text{V} \\
V_{CC\text{max}} &= 18\,\text{V} \\
I_{o\text{max}} &= 60\,\text{mA} \\
h_{\text{ctr}} &= 400\%\ \text{min}\ 900\%\ \text{typ} \\
&\quad\ \text{at}\ I_F = 0.5\,\text{mA}
\end{aligned}$$

Propagation delay times $= t_{\text{PHL}}\ 60\,\mu\text{s}$
$t_{\text{PLH}}\ 100\,\mu\text{s}$

The circuit outline is given in Fig. 6.38.

Since the output current is to be 20 mA, the minimum value of I_F for the input LED is:

$$I_F = \frac{I_{\text{out}}}{h_{\text{ctr(min)}}} = \frac{20}{400}\,\text{mA} = 0.05\,\text{mA}$$

$$\therefore R_{1\text{max}} = \frac{V_{\text{OH}} - F_V}{I_F} = \frac{2.4 - 2}{0.05 \times 10^{-3}}\,\Omega = 8\,\text{k}\Omega$$

$\therefore$ Make R_1 6 k8

$$R_L = \frac{V_{CC}}{I_{\text{out}}} = 600\,\Omega$$

The data transmission rate will be relatively low with this arrangement, since the internal receiver photodiode cannot rapidly switch off

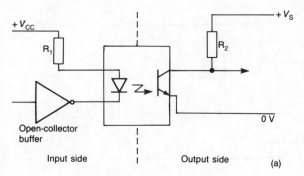

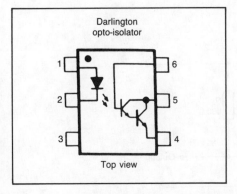

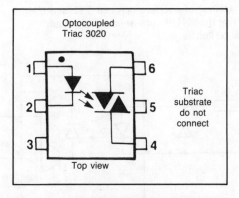

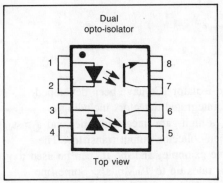

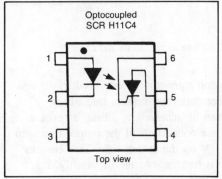

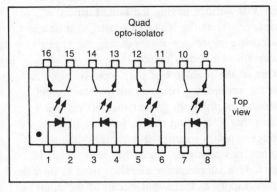

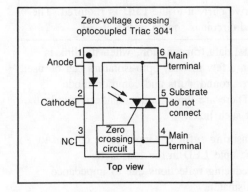

(b)

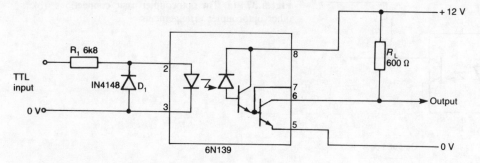

Fig. 6.38 Outline of interface between TTL and CMOS (+12 V) using the 6N139 opto-isolator, maximum data rate ≃ 60 kbits/s

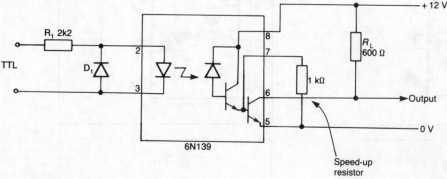

Fig. 6.39 Data rate increased to 500 kbits/s

the Darlington transistors. Faster switch-off and hence higher data transmission rate (up to 1 Mbit/s) can be achieved by fitting a resistor from the base connection of the output transistor (pin 7) to 0 V on the output side. This ensures that the final transistor turns off smartly, but also reduces the transfer efficiency. Higher input drive current to the LED is required. The modified circuit is shown in Fig. 6.39.

In digital data transmission, when the link is more than a few metres, opto-isolators can be used to remove ground shifts and common-mode signals. There are three main considerations in the design of such links:

(1) Ensuring sufficient input drive current to the opto LED in the 'on' state.
(2) Reducing reflections due to impedance mismatch.
(3) Achieving a high data rate.

Several opto-isolator ICs have been developed which have integrated detectors including a photodiode, a high-gain linear amplifier and a fast Schottky open-collector output transistor. The 6N137 is one example, and the IC can be used to achieve data rates up to 10 Mbits/s. Some line termination methods are indicated in Fig. 6.41. Note that a diode having the same turn-on characteristic as the IC LED is used to maintain a reasonable impedance match during the negative excursion of the data input.

One of the problems of basic opto-isolators is that the breakdown voltage rating of the output transistor is often not greater than 30 V, which means that interfacing to d.c. loads in higher voltage supplies requires that some additional limiting power supply circuit has to be used. In Fig. 6.42 a simple zener circuit is used to provide a 12 V supply to the output circuit of the opto-isolator, while the load is connected in a 100 V

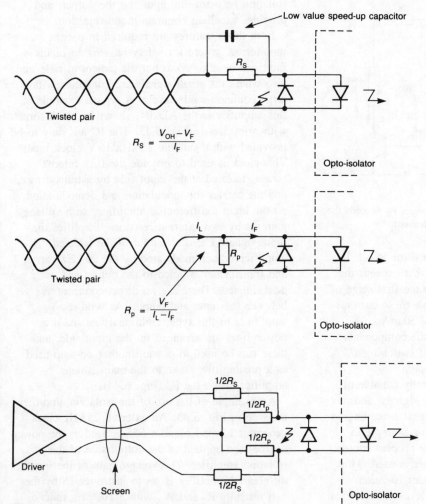

Low value speed-up capacitor

R_S

Twisted pair

Opto-isolator

$$R_S = \frac{V_{OH} - V_F}{I_F}$$

I_L I_F

R_p

Twisted pair

Opto-isolator

$$R_p = \frac{V_F}{I_L - I_F}$$

$1/2R_S$

$1/2R_p$

Driver

$1/2R_p$

Screen

$1/2R_S$

Opto-isolator

Fig. 6.40 some termination methods for data links to opto-isolators

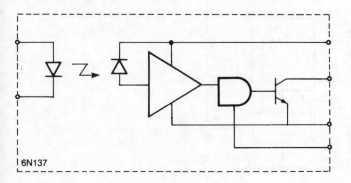

6N137

Fig. 6.41 The 6N137 high-speed opto-isolator

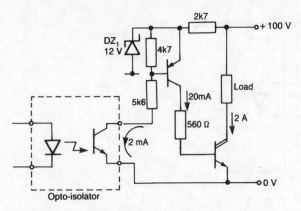

Fig. 6.42 Output circuit design when V_S exceeds the breakdown voltage of the output transistor

d.c. supply. While the optotransistor is off, the zener current must be a value that exceeds the opto output current and that in the first stage of the switch. Since in the example these currents total 22 mA, a zener current of 30 mA is sufficient. With the values of the components shown, the circuit is capable of switching a 2 A resistive load in the 100 V supply.

The optocoupler is not generally capable of faithfully transmitting analogue signals, and in applications where analogue signal isolation and amplification are essential — for example in patient monitoring and in many process control systems — an isolation amplifier is used. This amplifier, which uses transformer isolation techniques, ensures very high levels of electrical isolation between the input and the output, and provides excellent common-mode rejection.

Both these features are required in patient monitoring, where for safety reasons no mains fault can be allowed to put the patient at risk, and also where the small signals are contained within large common-mode levels. A typical example of this amplifier is the AD204, shown in block form with brief data in Fig. 6.43. The IC has only to be provided with a suitable 25 kHz 15 V clock input. This clock is used to provide the IC's internal power, isolated at the input side by a transformer, and the carrier for modulation and demodulation. At the input a differential amplifier, with voltage gain set by two external resistors, amplifies the input signal. The d.c. output of the isolated amplifier is then modulated by the 25 kHz carrier and transformer coupled to the output and demodulated. There are no direct connections between the input and output. As with most amplifiers of this type, additional isolated d.c. power lines are arranged on the input side, and these can be used to power another op-amp used as a preamplifier stage to the main isolated amplifier inside the IC (Fig. 6.44).

An example of the use of the isolation amplifier is given in Fig. 6.45. An external 25 kHz clock generator formed round a 555 is used as the power source, and applied to the output side of the isolation amplifier. The voltage gain of the input differential amplifier is set to just over 15 by the two resistors R_1 and R_2, with a 100 pF capacitor

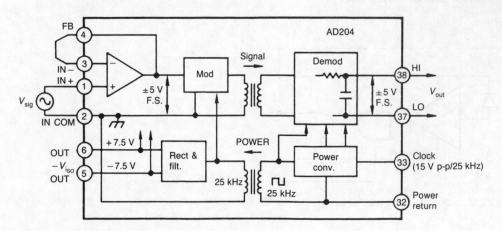

Fig. 6.43 AD204 functional block diagram

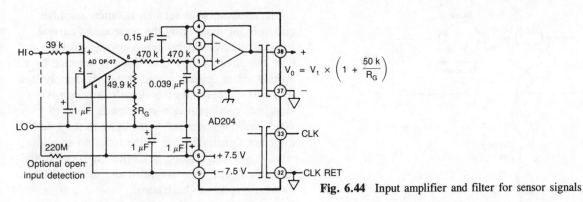

$$V_0 = V_1 \times \left(1 + \frac{50\,k}{R_G}\right)$$

Fig. 6.44 Input amplifier and filter for sensor signals

connected from the feedback pin to the common
pin on the input side. With the isolated input at
zero, the noise level at the output will be almost
entirely composed of carrier ripple at 25 kHz and
multiples of this frequency. This ripple is typically
a few millivolts, but it can be reduced still further
by following the output with an active filter.

Careful layout and screening is usually required,
and the power lines to the oscillator must be
separated from those to the filter, otherwise
switching spikes will appear at the filter output.
All lead lengths must be kept short, and proper
decoupling must be provided. These points are
indicated in the figure.

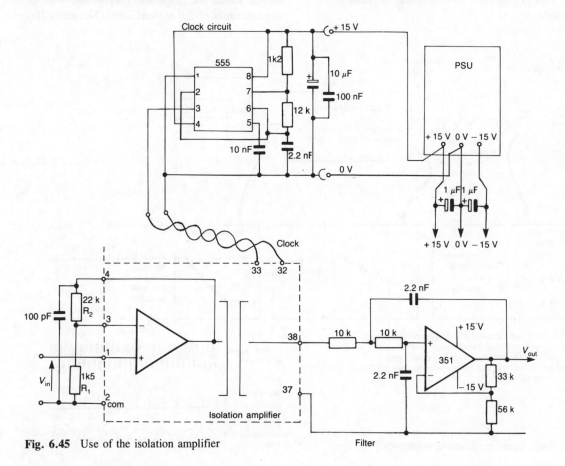

Fig. 6.45 Use of the isolation amplifier

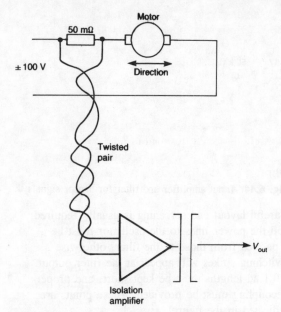

Fig. 6.46 Using an isolation amplifier to detect direction

One application of such an isolation amplifier circuit is for monitoring the presence of current flow in relatively high-voltage circuits. In Fig. 6.46 the direction of a d.c. motor is detected by a current series resistor placed within the supply lead of a 100 V circuit. As the motor's direction is switched, common-mode step signals of up to 100 V will be generated, in addition to the small direction signal. The use of the isolation amplifier, with its very high value of CMRR, will enable the direction signal to be amplified and the common switching spikes to be ignored.

6.7 Signal conditioning

In the context of electronic systems the expression signal conditioning covers the shaping, amplification and filtering of a signal so that it comes within the range and bandwidth requirements of the system input. Normally this

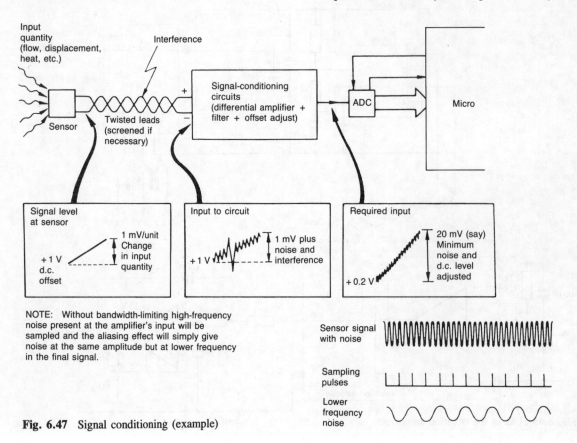

NOTE: Without bandwidth-limiting high-frequency noise present at the amplifier's input will be sampled and the aliasing effect will simply give noise at the same amplitude but at lower frequency in the final signal.

Fig. 6.47 Signal conditioning (example)

entails bringing a sensor's signal level up to the input span of an ADC, typically 0 V to +5 V (Fig. 6.47). One of the features of many sensors is that the resulting electrical output per unit change of the quantity being sensed is invariably tiny. It will be either some tens of microvolts or, at best, a few millivolts. This small, possibly slowly varying, signal will be contained within noise and interference signals. Any amplifier, which must often be a d.c. type, will require a high common-mode rejection ratio (CMMR) and very low values of drift with temperature and time. The bandwidth of the sensor signal must also be limited to reduce and minimize any aliasing effect. This can occur in a sampled data system because noise signals at frequencies of $0.5f_s$ and above (*see* sampling theorem, p. 195) will appear as low-frequency noise at the input of the system. It follows that the design of any signal conditioning circuit has to be tailored to suit a particular sensor application, and also requires a very careful consideration if the overall resolution of the system is not to be degraded. There are several well established techniques for these design requirements. They include:

- Conversion (i.e. changes of resistance into voltage signals)

- Amplification and buffering
- Bandwidth limiting
- Interference reduction
- D.c. offsetting, or zero adjust.

Let us consider the problem of obtaining a useful signal from a platinum RTD (temperature sensor) so that temperatures in the range 50–150 °C can be brought within the span of an 8-bit ADC. We shall assume that the ADC requires a maximum input of 5 V, so that 1 LSB is equivalent to a d.c. change at the ADC input of nearly 20 mV. In order to resolve temperature changes of 1 °C, the final output from the circuit must be at least 20 mV or greater per °C change, and errors due to drift, non-linearity, noise and interference must be less than 10 mV at this point (i.e. less than $\frac{1}{2}$LSB).

A typical platinum resistance temperature sensor has the following specification:

Range	$= -50$ °C to $+500$ °C
Resistance	$= 100\,\Omega \pm 0.1\,\Omega$ at 0 °C
Temperature coefficient	$= +0.385\,\Omega$ per °C
Self-heating	$= 0.2$ °C/mW in still air
	0.005 °C/mW with
	infinite heatsink.

Therefore at   50 °C, $R_{T1} = 119.25\,\Omega$
and at   150 °C, $R_{T2} = 157.75\,\Omega$

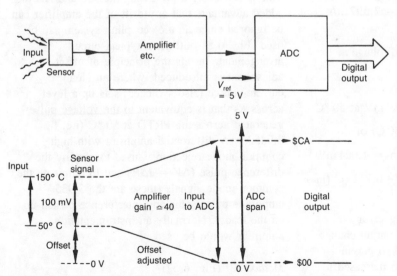

Fig. 6.48 Signal amplification and d.c. offset adjustment for a PRTD to provide input to an ADC

The requirement is for the range of temperature to use the full span — or as much as possible — of the ADC. Thus any circuit must provide some means of offset, or zero adjust, so that at 50 °C the digital output of the ADC is $00. The gain of the amplifier for, say, 1 mV/°C output from the sensor must then be approximately 40, which will give an output from the ADC of about $CA when the temperature is 150 °C (Fig. 6.48).

Two methods of obtaining an output voltage from the sensor are:

(1) To supply it with a constant current.
    Then $V_o = I\Delta R_T$ where $\Delta R_T = 0.385\,\Omega/°C$.
(2) To wire the sensor into one arm of a Wheatstone bridge.

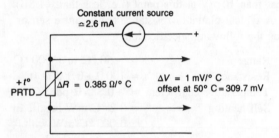

Fig. 6.49 Using a constant-current supply to obtain voltage signals for a PRTD

Method (1) (Fig. 6.49)

For $V_o = 1\,\text{mV/°C}$ $I = \dfrac{V_o}{\Delta R_T} = 2.597\,\text{mA}$

This current would set up an offset voltage at 50 °C of

Offset = IR_{T1}
         $\therefore$ d.c. offset = 309.69 mV at 50 °C

and a dissipation at R_{max} (R_{T2} at 150 C) of

$P = I^2 R_{T2}$ $\therefore$ power dissipation = 1.064 mW

which gives a self-heating error of +0.212 °C (in still air) at 150 °C.

This is not insignificant; self-heating error introduced at 150 °C occurs for an output change of only 1 mV/°C. Suppose we tried to get an output of 10 mV/°C; then I must be increased to 25.97 mA, resulting in a dissipation of 106 mW, giving in turn a self-heating error of 21.27 °C!

A tenfold increase in current produces a hundredfold increase in dissipation and self-heating error.

However, in a sampled data system there is no need for the current to be supplied continuously and a high current can be applied by pulsing the sensor (usually called pulse excitation) at a very low duty cycle (Fig. 6.50). For example, by pulsing the sensor with a current of 33 mA at a duty cycle of 1 per cent we would get the following results:

$V = I\Delta R$ $\therefore$ $V = 12.70\,\text{mV}$
$P = (I_{AV})^2 R_{T2}$ Power dissipation = 17.2 μW
Self-heating error   +0.003 °C at 150 °C

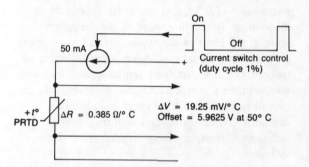

Fig. 6.50 Pulsed excitation

This is obviously a promising method and has the added advantage that any drift of the amplifier can be ignored since an a.c. coupling system can be used. Fig. 6.51 outlines a typical circuit arrangement. In this the principle of offset adjustment is introduced, where an identical current source (also switched) sets up a level across R_2 that is equivalent to the voltage pulse generated across the PRTD at 50 °C (i.e. 3.935 V). A differential amplifier with high common-mode rejection is used to amplify the difference pulse ($\Delta V = I\Delta R$) and to eliminate the common-mode signals (these are the 3.935 V amplitude pulses plus any interference picked up on the leads). Normally an instrumentation amplifier would be used.

Method (2) (Fig. 6.52)
Here the PRTD is connected into one arm of a bridge and the circuit is supplied with a voltage

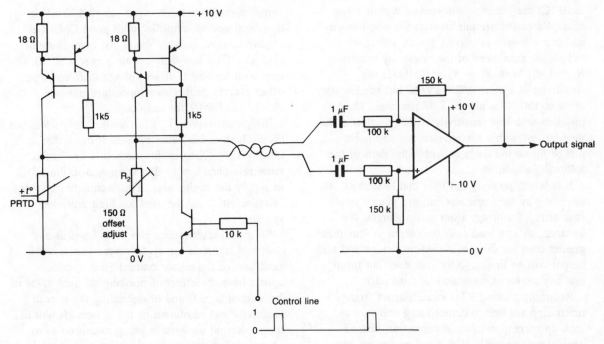

Fig. 6.51 Detector with simple amplifier unit

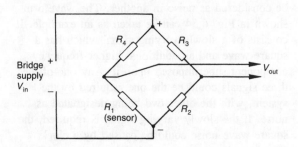

Fig. 6.52 Sensor bridge arrangement

V_{in}. For the bridge:

$$V_{out} = \left(\frac{R_1}{R_1+R_4}\right)V_{in} - \left(\frac{R_2}{R_2+R_3}\right)V_{in} \qquad (6.13)$$

$$V_{out} = \frac{(R_1/R_4)-(R_2/R_3)}{[(1+R_1)/R_4][(1+R_2)/R_3]}V_{in} \qquad (6.14)$$

At balance, when $R_1/R_4 = R_2/R_3$, $V_{out} = 0$ (null). As R_1 varies with temperature, the bridge becomes unbalanced and a small output voltage is generated. Two points arise from this:

(1) The output is not independent of the bridge supply (V_{in}), which must therefore be a stable source.

(2) The output is not linear unless the deviation of the sensor's value is kept small; for example, if $V_{in} = 10$ V and $R_3 = R_4 = 10\,000\,\Omega$ ($R_2 = R_1$ at 50 °C) the non-linearity error introduced at 150 °C is -2.7 per cent, i.e. the output from the bridge should be 0.385 mV/°C, but at 150 °C this has changed to 0.375 mV/°C. Take the case of a bridge with all resistances equal, and one deviating from the value R by a factor $(1 + X)$: from equation (6.13)

$$V_{out} = \frac{R(1+X)}{R+R(1+X)}V_{in} - \frac{R}{2R}V_{in}$$

$$\therefore V_{out} = \left(\frac{2+2X-2-X}{2(2+X)}\right)V_{in}$$

$$\therefore V_{out} = \left(\frac{X}{1+\frac{1}{2}X}\right)\frac{V_{in}}{4}$$

Thus only if $X \ll 1$ will V_{out} remain a reasonably linear function of X. If $X = \pm 0.02$ (equivalent to a temperature change for the PRTD of just

±10 °C) the linearity will remain within 1 per cent. We can either put up with the non-linearity and use software to correct for the effect, or reduce the sensitivity of the bridge by increasing R_3 and R_4. With $R_3 = R_4 = 20\,000\,\Omega$ the sensitivity is a mere $192.5\,\mu\text{V}/°\text{C}$ but the linearity error at 150 °C is now -1.37 per cent. The problem with low sensitivity is that resolution may then be lost within the interference and noise picked up on the leads or within the drift of the following amplifier.

It is worth pointing out here that if sensors, all deviating by the same amount, are placed in all four arms of a bridge (four strain gauges, for instance, as in a load cell) the output is four times greater than for the single-element bridge and this output will be linear. (NB: This does not mean that any sensor non-linearity is reduced.)

Returning to the PRTD circuit, apart from linearizing the bridge output using software (a look-up correction table or correction factor applied automatically within the program), one analogue method available for non-linearity correction is to feed back a signal to modify the bridge excitation voltage (V_{in}). The principle is illustrated in Fig. 6.53, where a small portion of the amplifier's output voltage (βV_o) is used to vary the reference voltage to the bridge supply. As the output voltage increases, a small change in V_{in} occurs that compensates for the non-linearity.

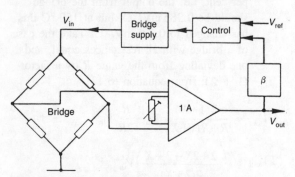

Fig. 6.53 Non-linearity correction method

Offset adjustment in a bridge arrangement is straightforward, since either R_2 or R_3 can be trimmed so that at the reference point (50 °C for the example) the output from the bridge is exactly zero volts. There will, however, be an appreciable common-mode voltage output (about 120 mV in this case) and an amplifier with good CMRR is required. Also, because the signal level is small ($385\,\mu\text{V}/°\text{C}$) a low-drift circuit is essential. An op-amp with low-input offset voltage drift and input offset current drift with temperature must be chosen (an OP-07 for example).

Bridge excitation (V_{in}) can be d.c. or pulsed, but should be a stable value because it has a direct effect on V_{out}. One useful method is to use the same reference supply that is applied to the ADC to supply the bridge also. This technique, known as ratiometric, can be used for high-precision systems.

Noise and interference can be defined as any electrical signal at the system input that is not a valid part of the sensor output. Such spurious signals have the effect of masking the real value of the wanted signal, and of degrading the overall sensitivity and resolution of the system. It will of course depend on what is being measured as to what is called the noise in a system; what might constitute a useful signal for one circuit could well be considered as noise in another. The waveform shown in Fig. 6.54 can be taken as an example. It consists of a slowly varying signal which has a square wave and an additional higher-frequency component superimposed upon it. Any one of the three signals could be the one required by the system, with the other two being designated as noise. If the slowly varying signal is required, the square-wave noise could be caused by a clock waveform being cross-coupled on to the sensitive input lead, and the third waveform could be due to some other interference. In this case the noise could be reduced by screening out the interference effect (moving cables for example) and/or bandwidth-limiting the signal by a filter circuit. Filtering would have the additional advantage of reducing the aliasing effect when the signal is sampled.

On the other hand, suppose the square wave is the wanted signal and the low-frequency variations are caused by short-term drift in the sensor and amplifier. The problem then centres on reducing this drift to eliminate the noise effect.

All disturbances can be lumped together under the general heading of noise, but it is better to

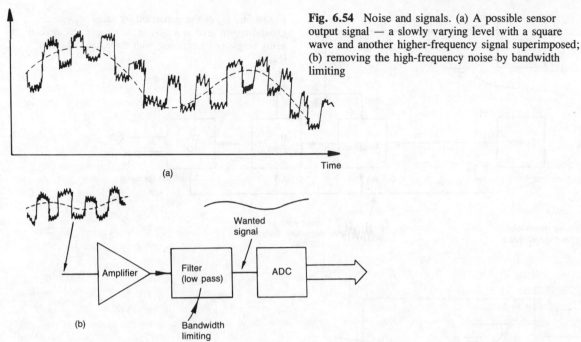

Fig. 6.54 Noise and signals. (a) A possible sensor output signal — a slowly varying level with a square wave and another higher-frequency signal superimposed; (b) removing the high-frequency noise by bandwidth limiting

separate out the main categories of noise to enable proper consideration of total noise reduction to be made. Interference or environmental noise originates from electrical sources that radiate electromagnetic signals (Fig. 6.55). These signals may be

- Generated locally
- Communicated within the subsystem via ground loops or on power lines

- Picked up by any conductor at the input acting as an aerial.

We shall deal briefly with these in turn.

Locally generation interference is mostly at very low frequency and is caused by thermocouples set up in the signal path. Any combination of wire, connectors, solder and so on can easily generate unwanted thermoelectric voltages which then contribute to the overall drift with temperature.

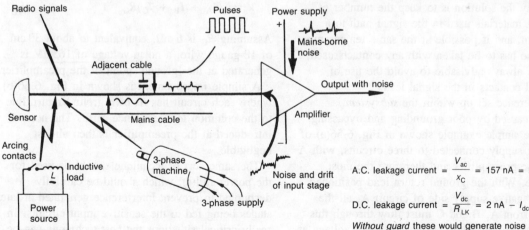

Fig. 6.55 Some sources of environmental noise

A.C. leakage current $= \dfrac{V_{ac}}{x_C} = 157\,nA = I_{ac}$

D.C. leakage current $= \dfrac{V_{dc}}{R_{LK}} = 2\,nA - I_{dc}$

Without guard these would generate noise as follows:
a.c. signal $= I_{ac}R_S = 40\,mV$ of 50 Hz hum
d.c. drift $= I_{dc}R_S = 500\,\mu V$

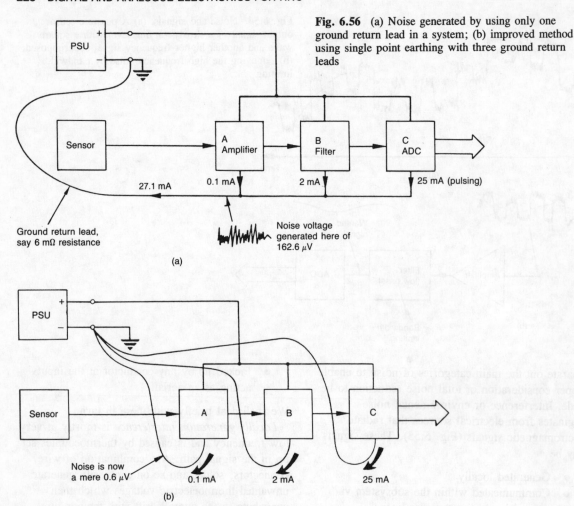

Fig. 6.56 (a) Noise generated by using only one ground return lead in a system; (b) improved method using single point earthing with three ground return leads

Generally the solution is to keep the number of different materials used in the signal path to a minimum, and if possible at the same temperature. Care also has to be taken with any contacts used, and it is always advisable to avoid the use of switched contacts in the signal lead.

Interference set up within the *subsystem* is usually caused by poor grounding and bypassing. Take the simple example shown in Fig. 6.56(a) of a power supply connected to three circuits, with A being the preamplifier and therefore the most sensitive. With the ground return lead positioned to the negative supply side of circuit A, all the current from A, B and C must flow through this lead back to the supply earth. The noise voltage at A is therefore

$$V_n = (I_A + I_B + I_C)R_G$$

Assuming R_G is $6\,\text{m}\Omega$, equivalent to about $30\,\text{cm}$ of 18-gauge wire, a noise voltage of $163\,\mu\text{V}$ is generated at the 'ground' point of the preamplifier.

A simple improvement is shown in Fig. 6.56(b), where each circuit has its own ground return line to the common low-resistance earth. The noise introduced at the preamplifier is then almost negligible.

The same sort of technique should be used for the power rail(s), which should be carefully decoupled to prevent interference generated at later stages being fed to the sensitive input circuits. In really critical situations the best technique can be to use separate power supplies, with one good solid ground plane to which all return lines are taken.

The most common causes of interference picked up on sensitive input leads are the a.c. mains (240 V, 50 Hz UK, and 110 V, 60 Hz USA) and arcing contacts used to switch inductive loads. Any source that is being rapidly switched can generate an electromagnetic wave that can be radiated as a radio signal or be capacitively coupled to the input. In addition, interference can result from relatively high voltage sources (a.c. or d.c.) feeding leakage currents to an unguarded input.

The main methods of reducing these effects, in addition to careful layout, are to use one or a combination of

- Twisted pairs and differential inputs
- Shielding and guarding techniques
- Bandwidth limiting (covered earlier in this chapter).

A twisted pair of wires carrying the sensor signal will be subject to the same interference. Thus any induced signal (noise) will be common to both, and by using a differential amplifier with high CMRR the noise effects can be substantially reduced.

A shield is a conductive covering round a sensitive circuit point, and is connected to ground potential. Any radiated signal is absorbed by the shield and prevented from having too large an effect on the lead. The shield, if used on a cable, should be connected to the source end only.

A guard is a conductive ring placed around a sensitive input to absorb stray currents from local high-voltage sources. The guard is maintained near the potential of the input pin(s) but is at a much lower impedance, and should ideally completely enclose the point being protected. Fig. 6.57 illustrates a simple example of a guard on a unity gain buffer amplifier where the guard is connected to the low-impedance output of the amplifier and absorbs leakage current from adjacent sources. Without the guard the leakage currents would flow into the high-impedance input lead and develop 0.5 mV of d.c. error and 39 mV of a.c. hum.

6.8 Problems

(1) A 10-bit successive approximation ADC requires an initial reset pulse of $0.5\ \mu s$, and thereafter each cycle takes $0.75\ \mu s$. Determine:
  (a) The conversion time.
  (b) The maximum-frequency component allowed in the analogue input if errors are not to be greater than ± 1 LSB.

(2) The noise level of a signal presented to the input of an 8-bit ADC is 5 mV rms. Determine the value of quantization noise and the total noise of the system. The ADC span is 2.500 V.

(3) The output of a DAC with a V_{FS} equal to 2.00 V is to be increased to 5 V. The DAC ladder output resistance is 20 kΩ. Design a suitable amplifier using npv resistors.

(4) A sensitive opto-isolator is to be used as shown in Fig. 6.58 to interface from CMOS logic ($V_{DD} = 5$ V) to a 24 V 5 A resistive load. Determine the values of all resistors.

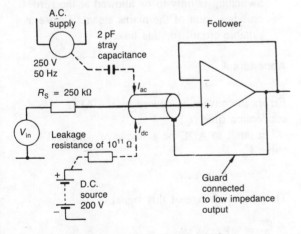

Fig. 6.57 Use of a guard or shield

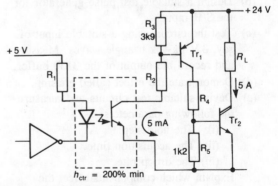

Fig. 6.58 Interface circuit

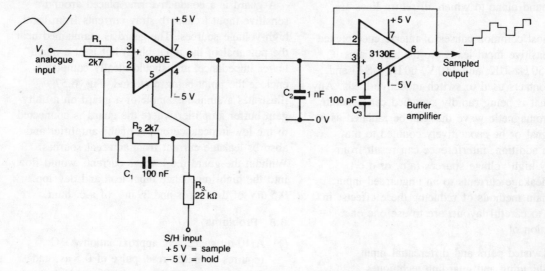

Frequency ≃ 150 Hz Sample time ≃ 50 μs

Fig. 6.59 Sample-and-hold circuit

(5) Modify the circuit in Fig. 6.58 so that an *N*-channel powerFET is used as the main switching element. Assume that the FET has a G_{fs} of 1.5 S and a gate-to-source threshold of 4 V.

6.9 Suggested project and assignment work

(1) Research a method for providing bipolar input operation to an ADC.
(2) The circuit in Fig. 6.59 is for a sample-and-hold using an OTA as the input amplifier and switch.
   (a) Describe the operation.
   (b) Design a suitable test pulse generator for the S/H input.
   (c) Test the circuit using a suitable input of, say, 3 V pk−pk triangle waves. Measure and record the output of the 3130 buffer.
   (d) Demonstrate the effect called aliasing.
   (e) Devise suitable test circuits and measure the following parameters:
      (i) The hold step.
      (ii) The acquisition time.
      (iii) The droop rate.
   Explain which components affect the above parameters.

(3) An 8-bit DAC with output resistance of 10 kΩ and V_{FS} equal to 2.500 V is to be interfaced via a power op-amp type 165, so that ±15 V pk−pk signals are provided to an 8 Ω load.

   Design the power amplifier portion of the circuit so that bipolar output is obtained; you may assume that the reference voltage of 2.500 V is available from a pin of the DAC.

(4) An isolated interface is required from a computer port to enable the logic output, which is TTL compatible, to switch a resistive load of 100 W in a 240 V 50 Hz mains supply. Switching is only to be allowed at the zero crossing point of the mains signal. Devise a suitable circuit for this task.

Appendix A

Errors in conversion caused by the ADC conversion time (t_c)

Let input to ADC be a sinewave with peak value V_p

$$\therefore v = V_p \sin \omega t$$

The rate of change of this signal is

$$\frac{dv}{dt} = \omega V_p \cos \omega t$$

This has a maximum value, at $t=0$, of

$$r = \omega V_p$$

If the sinewave peak-to-peak input to the ADC is assumed to occupy the whole of the ADC span, then:

$$1 \text{ LSB} = \frac{2V_p}{2^n}$$

where n = number of bits

$$\therefore 0.5 \text{ LSB} = V_p/2^n$$

Thus to avoid errors of greater than 0.5 LSB

$$rt_c \leq V_p/2^n$$

Since $r = \omega V_p = 2\pi f_m V_p$ (where f_m is maximum frequency allowed in V_{in})

$$\therefore 2\pi f_m V_p t_c \leq V_p/2^n$$

$$\therefore f_m = \frac{1}{2\pi t_c 2^n}$$

7 Answers and Solutions

7.1 Answers to problems in Chapter 1

(1) 104.3 Ω and about 7 Ω

(2) $h_{fe} = 324$ and $I_b = 0.2$ mA

(3) Use $A_v = g_m R_L$ where $g_m = 40 I_C$ mS
Therefore $g_m \approx 168$ mS
$$A_v \approx 300$$
$$h_{ie}(\text{min}) \approx 446 \, \Omega$$
$$h_{ie}(\text{max}) \approx 2200 \, \Omega$$

(4) High-frequency cut-off ≈ 1.8 MHz
Frequency where the magnitude of h_{fe} is 50 is 15 MHz

(5) $y_{os} = 42 \, \mu S$

(6) (a) See Fig. 7.1

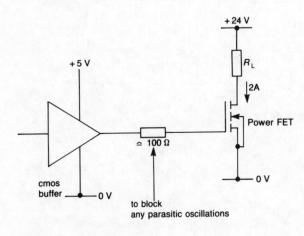

+24 V

R_L

2A

Power FET

+5 V

$\simeq 100 \, \Omega$

0 V

cmos buffer ——— 0 V

to block any parasitic oscillations

Fig. 7.1 Suggested circuit

(b) The drive is sufficient.
Required $V_{GS} = I_D/G_{fs} \approx 1.33$ V
Output from CMOS ≈ 4.5 V, leaving a drive voltage less the gate threshold of 2.1 V

(c) $V_{DS(on)} \approx I_D R_{DS(on)} \approx 0.5$ V

(d) $P_D \approx V_{DS(on)} I_D \approx 1$ W

7.2 Answers to problems in Chapter 2

(1) Since $f = {}^1/_{(2\pi CR)}$
$C = {}^1/_{(2\pi fR)} = 0.225 \, \mu F$
npv is 220 nF

(2) For a.c. equivalent see Fig. 7.2
(a) Since I_C is 10 mA $g_m \approx 400$ mS
Ignore both $r_{b'c}$ and r_{ce} since these are large compared with other associated resistor values. C_{ce} can also be ignored.
$$A_{vmb} = 202 \text{ or } 46.1 \text{ dB}$$
(b) $C_{in} = 579.3$ pF
$R_{in} = 156 \, \Omega$
Therefore upper cut-off frequency is 1.76 MHz

(3) (a) At 1 kHz $A_v = g_{fs} R_L // r_{ds}$
$$A_v = 17.4$$
(b) $f_h = 1/(2\pi C_{in} R_{in})$
$C_{in} = 71.2$ pF
$f_h = 186$ kHz
(c) $C_3 = 53$ nF

(4) 64 dB = 1585 as a ratio
(a) 12.4 as a ratio or 21.8 dB
(b) 4.089 MHz

(5) (a) 46.7 kΩ use 47 kΩ as npv
(b) Error is 22.5 μV, which is 0.45 per cent of input.

7.3 Answers to problems in Chapter 3

(1) 53.2%

(2) 18.1 W

(3) 2 °C/W, 87 °C

(4) 18 W, 62.8%

(5) 0.18%
Values for the TDA2030:
R_1: 22 k R_3: 22 k R_2: 1 k C_1: 7.2 μF (use

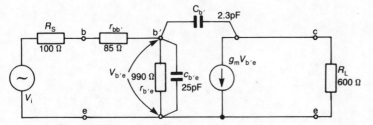

Fig. 7.2 Equivalent circuit

$10\,\mu\text{F}$) C_2: $16\,\mu\text{F}$ (use $22\,\mu\text{F}$) Power supply: at least $\pm 10.5\,\text{V}$ and $R_{th}(h-a)$: $6.8\,°\text{C/W}$.

buffer to input A, B and D.

(5) $F = A.B(1) + A.\bar{B}.(C) + \bar{A}.B.(0) + A.B.(C)$

(6) Lattice
Pal 16h8
pin 2 = a
pin 3 = b
pin 4 = c
pin 5 = d
Equations
f_1 = a.b.c+a.c.d+b.c.d+a.b.d ;
f_2 = a.d+/a./d ;
f_3 = /b./c./d+/a./b./d+/a./b./c+/a./c./d ;
end

7.4 Answers to problems in Chapter 4

(1) (a) 68.2%
   (b) $11\,\text{W}$
   (c) $12.4\,\text{mV}$
(2) $R_s = 1.77\,\text{k}\Omega$ (1k8 is npv)
   Change in V_{ref} is $12\,\text{mV}$
(3) (a) 6k8
   (b) $820\,\Omega$
   (c) $P_c = 12\,\text{W}$
      $R_{th}(h-a) = 3.33\,°\text{C/W}$
   (d) Regulation = 0.02%

(7) $J_A = \bar{C}$ $K_A = 1$
    $J_B = A$ $K_B = A$
    $J_C = A.B$ $K_C = 1$
(8) $J_C = \bar{C}$ $K_A = \bar{C}$
    $J_B = A.\bar{C}$ $K_B = A$
    $J_C = A.B$ $K_C = 1$
(9) $J_A = K_A = B$
    $J_B = K_B = 1$
(10) $A_n = A.\bar{D}$
    $B_n = A.\bar{B}.\bar{D} + \bar{A}.B.\bar{D}$
    $C_n = A.B.\bar{C}.\bar{D} + \bar{B}.C.\bar{D} + \bar{A}.C.\bar{D}$
    $D_n = A.B.C.\bar{D}$

7.5 Answers to problems in Chapter 5

(1) (A) $F_1 = \overline{\overline{A.\bar{B}}.\overline{C.A}}$

   (b) $F_2 = \overline{\overline{A.B}.\,\overline{C.D}}$

   (c) $F_3 = \overline{\bar{R}.S.T}$
(2) $F = A.\bar{B} + C.\bar{B} + C.\bar{A}$
(3) $F_1 = A.\bar{B} + C.\bar{B}$
   $F_2 = A.D + A.\bar{C}$
Both circuits require two ICs.

(4) $F = \overline{A.B}.\overline{\bar{B}.\bar{C}}.D$
   $\therefore F = A.B + \bar{B}.\bar{C}.D$
Expanding gives $F = A.B.(C+\bar{C}).(D+\bar{D})$
   $\qquad\qquad +\bar{B}.\bar{C}.D.(A.B)$
   $\therefore F = A.B.C.D + A.B.C.\bar{D} + A.B.\bar{C}.D$
   $\qquad\quad +A.B.\bar{C}.\bar{D} + A.\bar{B}.\bar{C}.D$
   $\qquad\quad +\bar{A}.\bar{B}.\bar{C}.D$
Missing couple in original circuit is $A.\bar{C}.D$
But a safer solution is to add an non-inverting

7.6 Answers to problems in Chapter 6

(1) Conversion time = $8\,\mu\text{s}$
   Maximum frequency component = $19.5\,\text{Hz}$
(2) Total noise = $7.82\,\text{mV rms}$
(3) Resistors are $R_1 = 33\,\text{k}\Omega$
   $\qquad\qquad\qquad R_2 = 50\,\text{k}\Omega$
(4) $R_1 = 1\text{k}2\,\Omega$
   $R_2 = 4\text{k}7\,\Omega$
   $R_4 = 470\,\Omega$

Index